DEVELOPING THE WHOLE CHILD
THE IMPORTANCE OF THE EMOTIONAL, SOCIAL, MORAL, AND SPIRITUAL IN EARLY YEARS EDUCATION AND CARE

Developing the Whole Child
The Importance of the Emotional, Social, Moral, and Spiritual in Early Years Education and Care

Mary Catherine Daly

Mellen Studies in Education
Volume 102

The Edwin Mellen Press
Lewiston•Queenston•Lampeter

Library of Congress Cataloging-in-Publication Data

Daly, Mary [Catherine], 1969-
   Developing the whole child ; the importance of the emotional, social, moral, and spiritual in early years education and care / Mary [Catherine] Daly.
     p. cm. -- (Mellen studies in education ; 102)
   [Includes bibliographical references and index.]
   ISBN 0-7734-6166-3
   1. Holistic education. 2. Early childhood education--Moral and ethical aspects. 3. Educational psychology. 4. Child development. I. Title. II. Series.

LC990.D35 2005
305.031--dc22

2004061784

This is volume 102 in the continuing series
Mellen Studies in Education
Volume 102 ISBN 0-7734-6166-3
MSE Series ISBN 0-88946-935-0

A CIP catalog record for this book is available from the British Library

The Edwin Mellen Press
Box 450
Lewiston, New York
USA 14092-0450

The Edwin Mellen Press
Box 67
Queenston, Ontario
CANADA L0S 1L0

The Edwin Mellen Press, Ltd.
Lampeter, Ceredigion, Wales
UNITED KINGDOM SA48 8LT

Printed in the United States of America

For my children – Conor, Orla and Aoife – who are a constant reminder that we must make the world a better place to live and grow up in.

TABLE OF CONTENTS

ACKNOWLEDGEMENTS   i

PREFACE by Professor Tricia David   iii

CLARIFICATIONS/EXPLANATIONS   v

CHAPTER ONE: **The Introduction**   1

Why we need to prioritise emotional, social, moral and
spiritual development   1
Education and holistic child development   7
Holistic child development and self-actualisation - a concept
for the early years   13
Emotional development   22
Social development   23
Moral development   24
Spiritual development   26
On becoming a reflective practitioner   28
The questions asked and an outline of what is included in this book   32

CHAPTER TWO: Historical Review of the Main Educational Theorists   37

Overview of main theorists   37
Plato   39
Aristotle   41
Luther   42
Comenius   43
Locke   47
Rousseau   48
The Edgeworths   51
Pestalozzi   51

Owen 54
Wilderspin 54
Froebel 55
The McMillan sisters 63
Steiner 65
Montessori 66
Dewey 76
Isaacs 80
Conclusion 82

CHAPTER THREE: Emotional Development 83

Introduction 83
Importance of the early years for emotional development 84
Implications of emotional development 85
Psychopathologies 87
Nature *versus* nurture 90
Interaction of different developmental areas 92
Emotions 93
Emotional development 97
Self-regulation of emotions 100
Gender differences in emotional development 104
Attachment 106
Self-concept, self-esteem and self-confidence 110
Discipline 115
Conclusion 116
Suggestions/guidelines for enhancing emotional
development 117

CHAPTER FOUR: Social Development 133

Introduction 133
Importance of the early years for social development 134
Ecological approach to child development 135
Socialisation 136
Social development 137
Attachment 139
Interaction of different developmental areas 140
Sex or gender role identification 141
  (i) Psychoanalytic theory 143
  (ii) Social learning theory 144
  (iii) Cognitive developmental theory 144
Racism and prejudice 146

Bullying and aggression 148
Friendships 151
Early years education and care 155
The media's impact on social development 157
Conclusion 158
Suggestions/guidelines for enhancing social development 159

CHAPTER FIVE: Moral Development 173

Introduction 173
The importance of the early years for moral
development 174
Morality 174
Morality and religion 177
Character development and character education 177
Moral development 179
Some views on morality 182
     (i) Morality as emotion 184
     (ii) Morality as concern and responsibility for others 185
     (iii) Morality as conformity to rules/authority 187
     (iv) Morality as conformity to one's own sense of belief 191
     (v) Morality as self-development 193
     (vi) Multiple perspectives 195
Children as philosophers 196
Conclusion 198
Suggestions/guidelines for enhancing moral
development 201

CHAPTER SIX: Spiritual Development 215

Introduction 215
The importance of the early years for
spiritual development 217
Spirituality 217
Spiritual quotient 221
Spirituality and religion 221
Spiritual development 223
Awe, wonder, myths and creativity 231
Meditation 235
A spiritual curriculum? 237
Research on spiritual development 238
Conclusion 240
Suggestions/guidelines for enhancing spiritual development 242

CHAPTER SEVEN: Holistic Child Development 253

    Introduction 253
    Physiological needs 253
    Safety needs 255
    Belongingness and love needs 257
    Esteem needs 261
    Cognitive needs 263
    Aesthetic needs 269
    Self-actualisation needs 272

CHAPTER EIGHT: A Vision for the Future 277

    Summary of the book 277
    So what now? 280
    Lost opportunities 284
    Hope for the future 286
    You the reader 287

BIBLIOGRAPHY 289

INDEX 339

ACKNOWLEDGEMENTS

I would like to acknowledge, my mentor, Dr Francis Douglas, Director of the B.A. in Early Childhood Studies at University College, Cork for his quiet persistence, patience and unfailing belief in the value of this book. He gave of up a great deal of his time to read and reread the many drafts of the work and his support, suggestions and steadfastness have been invaluable.

Without the co-operation and support of my husband, Pat Cashman, I could never have undertaken nor completed this book. His love and encouragement have been limitless and I remain deeply indebted to him.

My thanks to Professor Tricia David of Canterbury Christ Church University College, Canterbury for kindly agreeing to write the Preface.

I am grateful to Danah Zohar and Ian Marshall, authors of *Spiritual Intelligence: The Ultimate Intelligence* (2000) published by Bloomsbury for kindly agreeing to allow me publish the poem *Caring* by Marcial Losada, an abridged and translated version of Maturana's *The Student's Prayer*.

I also wish to acknowledge the input of many others: Geraldine O'Flaherty and Jenny Boyd who read early drafts and gave feedback and suggestions; Mary Horgan, Assistant Director of the B.A. in Early Childhood Studies, University College, Cork who provided some valuable insights; those who assisted with the layout and proof reading; and anyone else who helped in any way – I acknowledge and thank all of you.

PREFACE

This work is a powerful reminder to parents, policy makers and practitioners that attention to young children's emotional, social, moral and spiritual development is absolutely essential. Mary Daly provides a moving account of her own reasons for seeing these elements of a holistic view of human development as fundamental. In a world where economics and speed seem to take precedence over all other aspects of life, many people are recognising that this simply is not a basis for bringing up and educating our children.

We know from research on early brain development that being loved and participating in sensitive, responsive, playful interactions with familiar adults and older children help the human infant grow emotionally strong and resilient. What we also know is that it is these interactions and emotional strength which form the foundations for cognitive, or intellectual, growth. Further, it is in these encounters that children gain their moral understandings and codes, and their skills in socialising. Again, research on parental styles has demonstrated that babies who have experienced positive relationships will go on to be pupils who engage most positively with their peers and their teachers. However children need to practise these skills in order to become skilful and they cannot do that in silent classrooms, with teacher-led, desk-based regimes. Young children need opportunities to share ideas through play and talk in order to become interdependent.

Mary Daly's exploration of spiritual development is much needed by the field of early childhood. This is a relatively under-researched topic but one dear to my heart. I have come to believe more and more strongly over the years that matters of life, death and the here-after are of central importance to young children in their first six years, as they become increasingly aware of death, nature and the supernatural. Mary's analysis includes evidence about meditation, which is not only a key spiritual process, helping children find oases of peace in a troubled, noisy world, it also has benefits for physical as well as mental health.

This is a book to be read and re-read, and pondered over. Above all, it is a book to inform staff training, to evaluate existing practice and to stimulate action for the development of truly appropriate provision in early childhood education and care settings.

Tricia David BSc, MA, PhD, FRSA
Professor Emeritus
Canterbury Christ Church University College
CANTERBURY
England
May 2004

CLARIFICATIONS/EXPLANATIONS

A note about gender:

Throughout this work, in discussing the child, I use the pronoun 'he' to refer to either a male or female child. I do not like using he/she as I think it is confusing for the reader, hence my use of 'he'. However, the meaning is always 'he' or 'she'.

For the Early Years Practitioner I use the pronoun 'she'. However, here again, 'she' is meant to cover both male and female.

A note about terms:

While the term 'early years practitioner' is used in the book, this is a generic term used to cover all those who work with, educate and care for young children. It includes early years practitioners in sessional services, daycare workers, those in social care practice, social workers, play specialists, play therapists, parents, teachers in the formal education system. Also the suggestions at the end of each chapter can be used in any type of setting which involves children. The information contained in this book is relevant to anyone who cares about children, from parents, to practitioners to policy makers, to society in general.

CHAPTER ONE

The Introduction

Why we need to prioritise emotional, social, moral and spiritual development

I was born into a family where the three boys who were born before me had died (two at ten months and one at five years old). At 43 my mother had me. Unfortunately I was a girl but at least I lived. My childhood was full of fear - fear of my own death, fear of my parents dying, fear of the outside world, fear of not having any friends, fear of not being liked and fear of being worthless. During my first term in primary school my worst nightmare came true, as my father died, so then that just left my mother and me. He was buried before anyone decided to tell me he was dead. I was sent to my aunt's for three days and when I came home he was gone from my life forever without ever having the chance to say goodbye. After his departure I became afraid to leave my mother for any length of time in case something happened to her while I was not there and she was afraid to leave me in case something happened to me. My home life was full of sadness, loneliness and overprotection. The one break my mother and myself had from each other was when she reluctantly left me at the school gate every morning. On reading this, one might hope that I am going to tell you that the experiences I had at school helped make up for all the sadness and heartbreak at home. Living in a small village the teachers were very aware of my home circumstances and one might assume they would try to compensate in some way for my home life. Unfortunately this didn't happen and my first experiences in primary school (having never attended any sort of early years setting) were not positive. Negative early educational experiences, compounded by my 'only/sole surviving child' status helped to give another devastating blow to my already low self-esteem and self-confidence. These factors also contributed to my lack of social competence and confidence. I found it difficult to make or retain friends. My social interaction with other children was negligible and when I did interact with them I had no idea how to relate to them. The above probably explains why this book emphasises the areas of emotional and social development, but what about the other two: moral and spiritual? Morality comes into it quite easily. Morality is about living together and caring for one another. Who cared about me? Who asked me how it felt to have my father die? Who offered the hand of friendship to me? Why didn't the education system input supports and services to help vulnerable children like me? Was it moral that teachers ignored the needs of children in similar and often worse circumstances than mine? Thus, I had to include moral development in the book.

Spiritual development: what am I doing that for? Is there not only one true God and are children not educated in the religion of their parents? Isn't spiritual just another name for religious and why would you want to include it in a book on the early years? Again I suppose it goes back to my school days. I was educated in a Roman Catholic school in rural Ireland. As I grew up, I saw that the Roman Catholic Church and the education provided by religious congregations did not always do what was best for children. Many children suffered far worse consequences at the hands of the religious than I did. My experiences, and my knowledge of the experiences of others, caused me to question everything and I suppose I began to realise that religion was one thing, but true spirituality was another and that one did not have to be religious to be spiritual. Life with spirituality was so much better than life without it. So I had to include spiritual development because it is so important for children, especially young children. Spirituality has to do with love and wonder and contentment and is inextricably connected to emotional, social and moral development, so it has to form part of this book.

The early years of a child's life are vital, as early learning and experience remain crucial to all later development. We cannot argue that it is impossible to compensate later on for deprivation during the early years, but such compensation is difficult and uncertain. For most children, opportunities withheld or poorly presented during the early years can lead to escalating problems throughout childhood and indeed into and throughout adult life (Fontana 1984). I write this book on the emotional, social, moral and spiritual development of the young child in the hope that no child will ever be subjected to the type of early years experiences that I was exposed to at school. Nobody cared what happened to me emotionally, socially, morally or spiritually and it did lead to escalating problems throughout childhood and into adulthood. My mother wasn't able to cope, she had lost three children and a husband in the space of eight years and never received any support or counselling. How could she be expected to enhance the well-being of her sole surviving child when she could barely function herself?

On the other hand the education system was ideally placed to try to ameliorate my home circumstances by giving me positive experiences and by helping to put my shattered life back together. However, that is not what education was about in the 1970s. My education did plenty to develop my cognitive abilities but it did little to enhance my emotional, social, moral or spiritual development. I have had to live with the consequences of this and have worked very hard at compensating for those early deprivations. It would have been so much better if I had been loved, valued and supported in those vital early years and if the significant adults with whom I came in contact had scaffolded and supported my full development. As a result of my experiences my self-esteem and self-confidence were almost non-existent and though academically I was a high achiever, it didn't mean anything to me. I am not alone. Over the years I have met many people who struggle to cope with life and who believe their lives are worthless despite excelling at school. The high suicide rates and the high levels of children suffering depression show much hasn't changed since my school days. Educational experiences are in no way helping children to prepare to cope with the ups and downs of life. My personal experiences made me realise that a sense of well-being and a high level of emotional development are so important to us humans. Indeed they are of paramount importance to our survival. As a parent I work very hard on trying to ensure that my three children have a high level of self-esteem and that they feel a strong sense of well-being. I'm not so sure I can say the same about the education system in the western world. In 2004 I still don't believe it prioritises the areas of emotional, social, moral and spiritual development. In fact I believe the present education system devalues them with its emphasis on the individual, on competitiveness and achievement. The education system we expose children to is not helping them grow up to have a sense of well-being and daily they feel the negative consequences of this. Providing children with a holistic education which prioritises all the areas of development but which emphasises in particular emotional, social, moral and spiritual development will help children develop optimally. What children need is to have better memories of their childhood than I have of mine - what are your early memories like?

This book comes about as a consequence of my early experiences. A large part of it is taken from a Ph.D. I completed at University College, Cork on 'The Emotional, Social, Moral and Spiritual Development – Aiming Towards Self-Actualisation' (Daly 2002). The areas under review here are inextricably tied, with emotional development being the core area that acts as a linchpin for the other three. They are vital to every child's development and must be prioritised by parents and early years practitioners alike. The optimal emotional, social, moral and spiritual development of each and every young child is of paramount importance for the survival of the human species. Yet, these aspects of development are seldom highlighted or given the recognition and acknowledgement that they deserve. I hope to help redress this situation by focusing on these four areas in this book. To date few seem to care about them and certainly few highlight the fact that they are inextricably linked and that each on their own is important in its own right. Thus far the education system has not prioritised them; research on child development tends to sideline or ignore them. And for what? Just look at the kind of world we have created for our children.

We are living through a period of great change in what might be called 'post-modern' conditions (Dahlberg, Moss and Pence 1999). In the past, in more stable societies, children's lives and knowledge were all but predetermined, but in a society of rapid change such as exists today, it is difficult to anticipate the demands and requirements that the future will hold for them. Yet, children are expected to cope with this high degree of complexity, change and diversity. As well as this, the past no longer provides guarantees for the future. In particular, traditional reference points such as the church and politics have been weakened considerably with revelations of child abuse scandals and the discovery of high-profile cases of political corruption (Kirby 2002). Bonds of trust created in the past have been severed as never before. People who had previously seemed to have moral integrity are being found to have behaved with ruthlessness and self-interest. Hypocrisy in high places, increased crime, murder, neglect, abuse, national and international crisis after crisis, are taken for granted as part of modern life - what do these types of experiences do to our children? Does anyone care what it does to them?

We are not quite sure in which direction to turn any more. Modern society, with its lack of values and respect, has led us to a stage of alienation. There is a rupture within man himself (emotional), between man and man (sociological) between man and the environment (ecological) and between man and the divine (theological) (Hammés 1998). Nothing shocks or disgusts us any more. The development of technologies and prosperities which offered greater possibilities for a new humanism have in fact opened up new roads to unprecedented forms of inhumanity. New affiliations have been created but these are not based on basic human values. They are based instead on love of money and a naked desire for self-preservation, with little thought for the less well-off in our society (Fagan 1988).

The world's population has doubled since 1960 to 6.1 billion, with most growth in poorer countries. These countries are among the most severely challenged by soil and water degradation and are the most severely affected by food shortages.

Nearly two thirds of the 4.4 billion people in developing countries lack basic sanitation, about one third have no access to clean water, one quarter lack adequate housing while one fifth of the children there do not attend school. There is also a high rate of child mortality due to malnutrition with more than half of children's deaths there being attributed to it (World Health Organisation 1997). In contrast, in the last 20 years obesity has become a problem which is reaching crisis proportions in developed countries with 61 per cent of the adult population in the United States (U.S.) and over a quarter of the children there being obese. In the European Union (E.U.) Britain has the worst obesity problem with Ireland not that far behind. This is contributing to an increase in heart disease and diabetes and the World Health Organisation (W.H.O.) expects diabetes rates to continue to rise in the developed world, due to the rise in obesity, unhealthy diets, sedentary lifestyles and an ageing population (Schlosser 2002; W.H.O. 1997). What does this say about people?

Consumption expenditures have doubled between 1960 and the present. However, the increase in consumption has been mostly in richer countries. During this period we have created wealth of unimaginable scales yet half the world exists on less than $2 a day. Australia, the European Union and the United States have large surpluses of food for export and are capable of expanding production. However, most of the developing countries do not produce enough food to feed their people and cannot afford to import sufficient amounts to meet the shortage. A huge consumption gap exists between developing and industrialised countries. The wealthiest 20 per cent of the world's population accounts for 86 per cent of consumption while the poorest 20 per cent accounts for just 1.3 per cent (www.unfpa.org/sup/eng/choi.html). Why is it not within us to share and redistribute our resources?

Consumerism is generally what life is all about today and this has adopted a wasteful and destructive attitude to creation and to the environment. As a result of our wastefulness and our abuse of the environment, we now have a contaminated environment which is jeopardising our children's health. The link between environmental degradation and poor health is clearly established and the spread of disorders associated with environmental factors (asthma, injuries, neuro-developmental disorders, cancer, food and water-borne diseases) is reaching unacceptably high levels. Also, the rise in the earth's surface temperature and in damage to the ozone layer which has been caused by human activities is resulting in regional climate changes, and is damaging human, animal and ecological systems (Jimenez-Beltraum 2002; W.H.O. 2002a). We have desecrated the world's natural resources and if not careful, we will either exhaust or destroy our habitat. High growth economies such as Ireland's are contributing to this with an acceleration of pressures on the environment. Here in Ireland there is a growth in the emissions of greenhouse gases, our rivers and lakes are being polluted, and our waste management policy is almost non-existent. There is little or no attempt at either public or private level to reduce the amount of waste generated, we have relatively low levels of materials recycling and landfill continues to be relied on as the main disposal method (Stapleton, Lehane and Toner 2000). World-wide we cannot continue as we are - if we do, we do so at our peril.

Education and holistic child development

Today's experience of childhood can include violence, child abuse, stress, pressure, fear, anger, shame, poverty, family breakdown, homelessness, parental drug and alcohol abuse, and conflict over religious beliefs. How do we help children to cope with such experiences? What sort of coping strategies do we try to develop in them so that they can survive? A holistic education system (unlike the one I experienced) can help children deal with and overcome these issues. Offering peaceful early years settings, equity in learning opportunities, care and compassion in a safe environment, a sense of belonging to a classroom community, time to explore and think, acceptance, respect and adults who listen, means that education can provide a respite for children living in difficult circumstances (Branscombe, Castle, Dorsey, Surbeck and Taylor 2000). Society has a responsibility to create an educational system which addresses the inequalities and destructive elements in our world. The stewardship of the planet and the well-being of its people are a collective responsibility.

Education has the potential to promote principles of social justice, solidarity and equity but does not always fulfil its potential. Academic prowess in skills such as reading and writing are important, but my contention is that there are many paths towards productive and worthwhile participation in society. Intelligence Quotient (I.Q.) tests attempt to calculate a child's mental versus chronological age and over the years I.Q. tests have come to be regarded as an all-purpose gauge of a child's worth and potential. Yet, they focus on a narrow band of linguistic and logical-mathematical skills. Many traits that children use for solving problems and getting on with their lives - determination, imagination, leadership, creativity, social understanding, emotional competence and moral integrity, for example, cannot be assessed by such intelligence tests, yet are vital attributes for children. Children have a far wider range of abilities than are generally valued or prioritised in education. In particular, as already outlined, I advocate that we prioritise the areas of emotional, social, moral and spiritual development.

By overlooking the broad range of developmental areas such as those looked at in this book, to concentrate on the few that show up on paper and pencil and I.Q. tests, we doom children to years of frustration and disappointment as well as allowing inequalities and negative power systems to persist. As Brown (1998 p.2) says:

> We are under pressure to provide a more 'academic' environment for young children but the focus on subject divisions, formal learning and desirable outcomes interferes with and runs counter to the holistic and experiential way in which they learn.

Mills and Mills (1998) cited in Haynes (2002) claim that currently there is widespread concern about the formal instruction that very young children experience. Practitioners in countries where formal education starts much later, contend that it is cruel to teach and directly instruct four and five year olds in the way it is done in some western world countries such as the Britain and Ireland.

They contend that there is evidence to suggest that such a system is counter-productive and not beneficial to children's development, particularly in the long-term. The idea that education be a personally fulfilling and worthwhile pursuit has been sidelined and children are expected to derive satisfaction and a sense of worth directly from achievements that are primarily focused on ensuring they develop skills that make them employable. This "fundamental shift to education as *product* has cost us the arts in education and has led to a philistine curriculum couched in business language of *delivery, levels and standards*" (Haynes 2002 p.114). Thankfully this is beginning to be rejected as lacking in humanity and in quality, but how long will it take to turn it around fully?

Children do not begin school with equal chances of benefiting from it and for several reasons some children are disadvantaged on entering school. In particular, a proportion of children, particularly those living in poverty, are failing to gain from the educational system and there is widespread agreement that children from poorer backgrounds do not derive the same benefit from their schooling as do children from more comfortable backgrounds. Failure in school can have life-long implications, increasing the risk of experiencing unemployment or employment in low-paying or insecure jobs. It can also curtail personal development, the development of independence and self-confidence. These problems can become more pronounced over time, reinforcing an intergenerational cycle of poverty (Boldt, Devine, MacDevitt and Morgan 1998). Today, schools are not relevant to many children and thus they continue to experience 'school failure' or in reality schools fail them. Success in education and training is defined in terms of fairly limited forms of academic achievement, which the educational system, training agencies and those responsible for recruitment are generally agreed on (Kellaghan 1985).

Raftery (in Crooks and Stokes (eds.) 1987) says that education in Ireland, as in other western world countries, is hierarchical, competitive and authoritarian. On the other hand, Breen (1990) believes that many education systems have supported a policy of equality of educational opportunity which is not only misguided but which also maintains inequalities. He says that:

> Equality of opportunity, as an educational ideal, is inadequate because it proposes equality of treatment ... irrespective of differences in pupils' background. Yet, we know that pupils' home circumstances are of crucial importance (ibid. p.44).

Raftery (op. cit.) says that if education were to take seriously the goal of equalisation of basic attainments, then major changes would be necessary, not only in the curriculum but also in the organisation and ethos of schools. According to Boldt et al. (1998) the present education system with its intrinsically competitive and individually goal-oriented philosophy alienates and disadvantages those who do not fill the pre-cast mould. Unfortunately, the education system has been reduced to what Readings (1996) calls a 'logic of accounting'. It has become increasingly concerned with ever-faster progress up a ladder which entails the acquisition as rapidly and cost-effectively as possible of a predetermined body of knowledge. Boldt et al. (1998) ask are these the only legitimate ways of coming to knowledge and awareness? Are they the only ways of assessing human capacity? I believe not.

Hyland (2002) believes many children do not flourish in school because their abilities do not fit in with the traditional idea of 'intelligence'. Students who do not excel at academic subjects are immediately disadvantaged if not alienated from the whole formal education process from its earliest days, since reading and writing continue to be the cornerstones of the educational programme. Fawcett (2000) criticises the National Curriculum in Britain and says it stresses adult work opportunities and the need to train children for participation in competitive work environments rather than focusing on children's rights and the need for all-round development. Fawcett goes on to say that the 'Early Learning Goals' which replaced the Department of Education and Employment's 'Desirable Outcomes' are over-prescriptive and over-emphasise language and literacy. Fawcett also claims that the system disregards research findings in psychology, sociology and education which advocate the development of the whole child. According to Hazareesingh,

Simms and Anderson (1989 p.18), "this represents a specifically western, 'rationalist' approach to both childhood and learning, which by separating the mind from the heart, effectively denies the essential unity of the child". Fawcett (2000) says that the emphasis is mostly on preparation for the next stages and that sufficient status is not given to the pre-school years as a valid and vital stage of life. She goes on to say that this limited view of this stage is not uncommon and that children are often treated as empty vessels into which certain facts must be poured to fit prevailing social norms, similar to John Locke's *Tabula Rasa* in the 17th century. Just how far have we come in these few hundred years?

The current emphasis on academic goals for very young children is worrying. The need to use a sedentary, talk-based teacher-directed style of direct instruction rather than active programmes that encourage children's autonomy and sense of mastery to facilitate such a curriculum, raises huge concerns for many practitioners and theorists in the field (Nutbrown 1997). In the United States, Schweinhart and Weikart (1997) argue against such an approach and highlight the risks attached to such methods. Their much-quoted longitudinal research indicates that early educational experiences should encourage children to be active and to take responsibility for their actions. An emphasis on I.Q. and academic skills such as that outlined above, can have widespread negative impacts. It can result in children merely seeking to get high scores rather than trying to develop deeper understandings and insights and can critically damage self-esteem and self-worth. The emphasis on academic instruction of pre-school children can result in the neglect of equally, if not more important, areas of development such as those under review in this book. Severe damage can result from an undue emphasis on results while the prevalence of a narrow academic curriculum in many early years settings and classrooms gives children little reason to be interested or involved (Chen, Krechevsky, Viens, Isberg, Gardner and Feldman 1998). Purcell (2001) cites research from Japan where there has been an increase in the incidence of elementary school age children committing suicide, due to the fear that their grades were not satisfactory. Is this what we want for our children?

The mistaken emphasis on academia has resulted in the belief that there is nowhere better than the early years setting to inculcate the academic attitudes and skills that can carry a student towards greater and greater heights of academic achievement. Many, including parents, believe that starting as early as possible to teach academic material is the correct thing to do. Elkind (1992) says that today's parents and practitioners want 'superkids', they want them to excel, to achieve and to bypass the earlier stages of development and go straight to academic competence, despite the fact that childhood is a vital stage of life not just an anteroom to adulthood. Elkind warns of the dangers of concentrating on academic performance and competitiveness and calls it 'miseducation'. The Mental Health Foundation in Britain (1999 p.31) stresses that;

> the potentially negative impact of a narrowly focused academic definition of 'raising standards' can be seen in recent research showing evidence of increasing pupil distress in primary school...We believe that there is a pressing need to increase the emphasis of schools towards children's emotional well-being.

As well as this, one of the most prestigious professional organisations dealing with early childhood education, the National Association for the Education of Young Children (N.A.E.Y.C.) in the U.S. has produced explicit policy statements against academically oriented pre-school curricula and instruction. They say that instead, children should experience a broad-based education which covers all areas of development (Bredekamp 1987). Chen et al. (1998 p.20) suggest that:

> By shining a wider and brighter light on children and their activities and products, we hope to illuminate more of the potential of children's minds and to increase the likelihood that they will realise their potential both in and outside of school.

In order to shine this brighter light I intend to use Maslow's hierarchy of needs (1968) as the conceptual framework on which to hang my beliefs regarding the emotional, social, moral and spiritual development. I do this because I believe that from an operational and holistic point this provides the best fit for my vision for all round child development.

Holistic child development and 'self-actualisation' - a concept for the early years

There have been a number of psychological views proposed — the behavioural, cognitive, psychoanalytic and humanistic. Maslow forms part of the humanistic school. Before going on to describe this I would first like to take a brief look at the other schools of thought. Behavioural theorists rely on stimulus-response to explain child development and view learning as the most important aspect of the child. Behaviourists objectively measure behaviour and the ways in which stimulus-response relationships are formed. The view stresses observable environmental stimuli and the observable behaviours that occur in response to those stimuli (Watson 1931; Thorndike 1905; Skinner 1953). Behaviourism provides one very important insight into child development, that is the need for positive reinforcement from parents and significant adults to enhance children's self-esteem. It is also owed a debt of gratitude for emphasising the need to define terms carefully, to conduct controlled experiments and to make psychology more of a science. However, by ignoring the mind and stressing reactions to stimuli, the approach ignores the unobservable aspects of human behaviour such as emotion, thought and unconscious processes (Dworetzky 1994). Thus, it does not provide a comprehensive framework for holistic child development. On the other hand cognitive behavioural theorists focus not on what children and adults do, but on how they view themselves in the world. Their theory emphasises attention, pattern recognition, memory, language, literacy, reasoning and problem solving (Best 1989). They believe that humans are active information processors. This is the keystone of cognitive psychology and the theory concentrates on thoughts, beliefs, attitudes and opinions. However, again it does not provide a comprehensive framework for child development. Interestingly, psychoanalysis is probably one of the most widely publicised psychological systems among non-psychologists (Dworetzky 1994). It was originally developed by Viennese physician, Sigmund Freud (1859-1939). The theory has its roots in neurology and medicine and its goal was to understand human behaviour. It proposed that human behaviour was controlled primarily by drives and urges hidden deep within the subconscious. Freud believed all abnormal behaviours and in fact all aspects of personality, could be explained by analysing the motives and drives of the unconscious. The view has been severely criticised for its lack of scientific control and careful experimentation (Rosenzweig 1985). However, it has made a great contribution to psychology because of the interest it stimulated in many previously neglected areas such as the workings of the unconscious mind, sexuality, and very importantly, emotionality and childhood. Yet, the theory focuses on loss, internalisation of anger and gives an over-dependent role to external approval in the development of self-esteem. As an approach to overall child development its role is limited.

Several of Freud's contemporaries, many of whom had been students and colleagues of his, such as Jung, Adler, Erikson and Maslow, broke their links with him and went on to develop their own theories of personality (Grosskurth 1991). Included in these is the creation of the humanistic model or approach. This perspective takes a broader view of the developing personality. The focus of all humanistic theories of personality is the concept of 'self' and this refers to the individual's personal internal experiences and subjective evaluations. Humanists assess personality by examining people's subjective experiences, trying to elicit more about the individual, uncovering the forces that have created and maintained particular characteristics. Humanists believe that behaviourists are overly concerned with the scientific study and analysis of the actions of man, to the neglect of the basic conception of the individual as a thinking, feeling being. They also take issue with the deterministic orientation of psychoanalysis which postulates that the individual's early experiences and drives cause his behaviour. On the other hand, humanists tend to believe that the individual is responsible for his own attitudes and behaviour through intention and desire (Douglas 2002).

Prior to the development of humanism, all western psychology tended to ignore the great cultural, social and individual achievements of humanity (such as love, altruism, morality, mysticism and spirituality) whereas humanists were very keen on exploring these issues and potentialities. One of the founders of humanistic and transpersonal psychology, Abraham Maslow (1908-1970), in particular, wanted to broaden psychology to include what is best in humans as well as acknowledging the pathological. Maslow's psychology overlaps with that of Carl Rogers in many ways and he was also influenced by behaviourism and psychoanalysis. However, he went on to develop his own theory and his work is more a collection of thoughts, opinions and hypotheses than it is a fully developed theoretical system. He rarely came up with definitive answers but instead tended to formulate highly significant questions and suppositions. Specifically, he proposed that humans have a hierarchy of needs (Maslow 1968) ascending from basic biological needs to more complex psychological needs that become important only as basic needs have been at least partially satisfied. I suggest that looking at this hierarchy allows us to see what children really need in order to reach their potential - self-actualisation or becoming the best that one can become. This book aims for the self-acutalisation of every child – the summit of Maslow's hierarchy. As a result Chapter Seven of this book uses the levels of Maslow's hierarchy to show just what is involved in realising holistic child development. The following section outlines the levels on Maslow's hierarchy and shows where emotional, social, moral and spiritual development fit into this comprehensive framework of child development.

Maslow's hierarchy of needs is one with personal/basic needs on the bottom and growth needs, such as self-actualisation and realisation of personal potential, at the top. Maslow contended that the child can only properly attend to the higher reaches of the hierarchy if the needs lower down needs are at least partially satisfied. If a child has his physiological needs satisfied as well as having his safety needs met, he will become concerned with being socially accepted. Once accepted he will concern himself with his own self-esteem. Having satisfied these needs, the

16

Figure 1

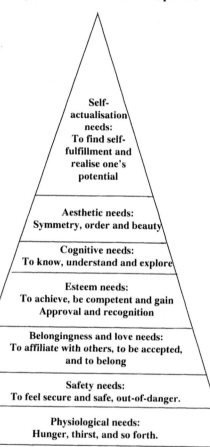

**Maslow's Hierarchy of Needs
(adapted from Fontana, 1995, p. 218)**

Self-
actualisation
needs:
To find self-
fulfillment and
realise one's
potential

Aesthetic needs:
Symmetry, order and beauty

Cognitive needs:
To know, understand and explore

Esteem needs:
To achieve, be competent and gain
Approval and recognition

Belongingness and love needs:
To affiliate with others, to be accepted,
and to belong

Safety needs:
To feel secure and safe, out-of-danger.

Physiological needs:
Hunger, thirst, and so forth.

child will go on to cognitive and aesthetic needs, arriving finally at a stage of self-actualisation, if all the needs lower down have been at least partially met. However, according to Maslow (1964) early frustration of a need can fixate the child at that level of functioning and a destructive environment or rigid authoritarian education can lead to unproductive habit patterns, which can inhibit growth and may mean the child never reaches his full potential – self-actualisation. Do our young children have unproductive habit patterns which are inhibiting their growth?

All the areas of child development are represented on Maslow's hierarchy and in particular the four areas that I wish to stress are well represented there. Physiological and safety needs are related to physical and emotional development. The child needs food in order to grow and he needs to feel safe and secure. Belongingness and love are tied to emotional, social and spiritual development. To be happy, the child needs to feel loved and to see himself as part of a family and community. He also needs to know he is part of a bigger scheme of things. Self-esteem is related to emotional and social development also. The child needs to like himself and to know that others like him too. He needs to have friends and people who care about him. Knowing and understanding are related to linguistic, moral and cognitive development. The child needs language, needs to know how to get along with others, how to be a contributing citizen as well as exploring and discovering things for himself. Aesthetic needs are correlated with creative, spiritual and emotional development. The child needs to experience and create beauty in life. Self-actualisation is related to all areas of child development, but is particularly related to spiritual development - the child needs to strive towards meeting his potentialities as well as needing to know that there is something greater than himself in the world. He also needs to respect and be in awe of the life given to him.

The work of psychologists such as Maslow helps to give us a fairly clear picture of how a child develops, what his needs are, and it also indicates what mature well-balanced humans are like. Such individuals have a range of qualities which make them effective, well-adjusted human beings who are aware of their own worth and that of others. They can empathise with others and relate warmly and openly with the people in their lives, instead of using them for selfish reasons or as instruments for satisfying their own personal inadequacies. This description might lead one to believe that maturity is something only achieved in adulthood and that it has little relevance in the early years of a child's life. However, it is possible for children to show maturity. Mature children are not individuals old before their time, but are beings commensurate with their years and experience who can show empathy, respect, friendliness and courage. "Many children have these qualities, just as many adults, however high their social or professional status, lack them" (Fontana 1995 p.273). However, children can only develop as mature, self-actualising, responsible beings if given the correct kinds of opportunities and experiences. Maslow highlighted the areas of social, emotional, moral and spiritual development as important steps on the path to the realisation of human potential and to self-actualisation. Self-actualisers are children who are developed holistically. They try to be of benefit to society and develop a symbiotic relationship with society, paying back what they have received from family, community and education by being contributing members of that society. On the other hand, children who are not self-actualised and who do not receive the respect, education and love that they are due, may pay back society in a different way. The symbiotic relationship is negative rather than positive, as seen by the increase in anti-social behaviour all over the world. Sister Stanislaus Kennedy of *Focus Ireland*, a leading organisation involved with the homeless and socially excluded in Ireland (quoted in Kirby 2002 p.169) said:

> We live in a time of a booming economy, where some people are doomed to poverty. We live in a time where the gap between the well-off and the poor has not only got wider but it has got deeper, as the poor are relatively poorer today than they were ten years ago ... We have always had poor in our society, eking out their living, but they were always part of society; for the first time in our history we have a large pool of people who are not wanted in our society, who are surplus to our society and they know that. The disturbing levels

of crime, violence and drug abuse are witness to their sense of hopelessness and helplessness and powerlessness – and in some cases their sense of revenge.

Walker (1969 p.236) agreed with this idea when she said: "Keep in mind always the present you are constructing. It should be the future you want". What is the present like for our young citizens today and what does it tell us about the future? If all children were developed holistically, would the world be a very different place from the one it is today? Would it be more inclusive and caring, less self-seeking and alienated? Education in the past and in the present is not aiding children's holistic development and every day we experience the repercussions of this. Issues such as those raised above show that it is becoming more and more imperative that we focus effort on the interventions that address the social, emotional, moral and spiritual development of the child, from as early as possible. These areas of development are difficult to determine and cannot be easily assessed or even verified. Yet, they are vital aspects in the overall development of the young child and are necessary for the smooth, equitable, safe and peaceful running of society.

Self-actualisation means children developing characteristics peculiar to mature and well-adjusted human beings. Maslow loosely defined self-actualisation as, "the full use and exploitation of talents, capabilities, potentialities, etc." (1970a p.150). It is not a static state but an ongoing process of using one's capacities fully, creatively and happily. Self-actualising children and people tend to see life clearly, are often committed to something greater than themselves and try to do well at their chosen task (however big or small). Creativity, spontaneity, courage and hard work are all characteristics of self-actualising children. Self-actualisation is "not an absence of problems but a moving from transitional or unreal problems to real problems" (Maslow 1968 p.115). Self-actualising individuals, despite pain, sorrow and disappointment, enjoy and appreciate the life given them. They tend to have a strong value system and though they may not be orthodox religious believers they all tend to believe in a meaningful universe and in a life that could be called spiritual.

Maslow found that some self-actualising individuals tended to have lots of peak experiences (this is a general term for the best moments in life, experiences of pure happiness, ecstasy, rapture, bliss or great joy). They were often more aware of the sacredness of all things and tended to think more holistically, being better able to transcend the categories of past, present and future, perceiving unity behind the apparent complexities and contradictions of life. They were more likely to be innovative and original thinkers and as their knowledge developed, so did their sense of humility, regarding the universe with increasing awe:

> At the highest levels of development of humanness, knowledge is positively rather than negatively correlated with a sense of mysticism, awe, humility, ultimate ignorance, reverence and a sense of oblation (Maslow 1971 p.291).

Many self-actualisers are said to be meta-motivated. This refers to behaviour inspired by growth needs and values and often takes the form of devotion to ideals, goals and things outside one's self. These higher level growth motivation needs are in contrast to the deficit motivation lower down needs, growing and feeling stronger rather than decreasing as they are fed. Maslow states that meta-motivation/meta needs are on a continuum with basic needs and that frustrations in these will lead to meta-pathologies. These refer to a lack of values, meaninglessness and a lack of fulfillment and isolation in life. Much like what many children's experiences of life are today and according to journalist Conor Lally, even some 'Irish toddlers are suicidal!' (1999 p.3). He claims children as young as four and five want to kill themselves, while others are indifferent as to whether they live or die. Louise Connolly (1999), Senior Registrar in Child and Adolescent Psychiatry in St Anne's Children's Centre at Taylor's Hill, Galway, Ireland, also says that suicidal tendencies can and do exist in pre-school aged children. This contention may seem rather extreme, yet it may be a fact, as more and more children are growing up with a lack of values and fulfillment. Many older children and adults in countries around the world certainly have such feelings and more than 500 people take their own lives in Ireland every year. There has been a four-fold increase in the suicide rate of males aged 15 to 24 between 1976 and 1998 and we have the fourth highest rate of attempted suicide in the European Union (W.H.O. 2002b). Something is very wrong when so many people feel like this.

Transpersonal psychology acknowledges the importance of the spiritual aspects of human experience. Prior to Maslow, spiritual experiences had been described primarily in religious literature, in unscientific and theologically biased language. Maslow tried to rectify this as he believed that: "The human being needs a framework of values, a philosophy of life ... to live by and stand by in about the same sense that he needs sunlight, calcium or love" (1968 p.206). Without it, "we get sick, violent and nihilistic, or else hopeless and apathetic" (ibid. p.iv). Yet, the spiritual aspect of life is almost completely neglected, but at what price?

The higher levels of Maslow's hierarchy represent a long-term commitment to growth and to the development of capabilities to their fullest. These echelons involve the choice of worthwhile, creative problems and have, as concomitants, children who are willing to cope with uncertainty and ambiguity, children who prefer challenge to easy solutions. The pursuit of higher needs is in itself an indicator of psychological health, and fulfillment of these higher needs is intrinsically satisfying since, "as the person becomes integrated, so does his world. As he feels good, so does the world look good" (Maslow 1968 p.204). Though, in principle, self-actualisation may seem fairly easy and achievable, in practice it rarely happens and according to Maslow less than one per cent of the population is self-actualised (ibid.). One wonders why this is so.

Along with personal childhood experiences, one of the real spurs that convinced me to write this book comes from the results unearthed in a nationwide questionnaire survey conducted in Ireland in 2002. The survey was carried out to elicit the views of early years practitioners regarding the areas of emotional, social, moral and spiritual development as part of a Ph.D. Thesis (Daly 2002). The questionnaire was sent to 662 practitioners (204 voluntary sector and 442 state sector) and returned a final response rate of 64 per cent. The findings revealed that in theory both sets of respondents seemed to be aware that the areas under discussion were important. In fact the vast majority agreed that emotional, social and moral development were as important as cognitive development, while about two thirds of them said that spiritual development was as important as cognitive development. However, on being asked about their practice, significant disparities were revealed. Only half said they prioritised emotional development, while three-quarters said they prioritised social development. Just two-thirds said they prioritised moral development while only one-third said they believed spiritual development should be prioritised in the early years setting. The results of the survey indicate that the areas of emotional, social, moral and spiritual development are not being prioritised in early years settings and the negative repercussions of this are reverberating throughout Irish society. These findings are backed by the literature and unfortunately are universal realities - neglecting these areas of development in a child in Ireland, in Romania, in Britain or in the United States has negative repercussions, regardless of nationality or social background. We have to start prioritising these areas today.

Emotional development

Emotions are at the very heart of children's lives, they impact on the child's well-being, on his sense of self and on his understanding of the world. Emotional development is about the development of the emotions and the ability to express them. To understand and regulate emotions is a very crucial element in children's functioning and is vital to their overall development (Dworetzky 1994). Optimum emotional development can aid children on their journey to self-actualisation. On the other hand, immature emotional development can lead to a diversity of problems and thus it is imperative that children are taught to deal with their emotions in constructive and creative ways. Many children's and adults' emotions are out of control today and increasing numbers of people, including young children, are suffering from depression and aggression. Goleman (1996 p.xiii) said:

There is a world-wide trend for the present generation of children to be more troubled emotionally than the last, more lonely and depressed, more angry and unruly, more nervous and prone to worry, more impulsive and aggressive.

Doing the best for a child comes down to building and nurturing self-esteem, self-confidence and self-reliance. Lack of self-esteem is given increasingly as a reason why so many people get themselves into trouble with the law, why so many young people commit suicide and why there is such an increase in mental and stress-related illnesses. Low self-esteem can cause great anguish, heartache, under-achievement, bad behaviour and depression in children. Having good self-esteem means that children will have confidence in themselves, will know who they are, will like who they are and will be content to face the world as they are. A confident, trusting child, secure in his belief in his own particular abilities and what it is that makes him unique, will play, concentrate, love, give and communicate better. Childhood is by far the best time to develop the emotions, as they are much more difficult to develop, regulate and recondition in later years (Hartley-Brewer 1998). However, it is debatable whether children's emotions are developed optimally in the early years. Research data from Ireland (Daly 2002) indicates that while those who responded to a nationwide questionnaire believed that some mental health problems could be prevented by prioritising emotional development, they admitted they did not, on the whole, make emotional development a priority. They continue to prioritise other areas of development (particularly academic skills) while allowing emotional development to be the 'Cinderella' of cognitive development, but at what price?

Social development

The process of social development involves the development of an awareness of oneself as well as an awareness of others. Humans are social beings and need the company of others from birth in order to survive. Attachments to others are sought very early in life and it appears that such attachments can lay the foundations for later social relationships. Friendship is a very important part of social development as it allows children to be democratic, affectionate and tolerant. It also enhances self-esteem and develops an awareness of others' needs. If social development is considered a vital component of all activities in which children are engaged, then development in all areas of children's lives can be enhanced. The relationships and connections we form with others throughout our lives are the network of our social world and to a large extent measure the success we have in life, in that they tend to determine how happy our life will be (Wood 1981). Yet, a sizeable proportion of the world's population, including young children, do not feel a sense of belonging or connection, but instead feel marginalised and excluded. So what has gone wrong in the area of social development, if so many people feel like this? On being questioned early years practitioners in Ireland, (Daly 2002), said that they considered social development to be as important as cognitive development. Many admitted that some children in their settings experienced rejection and lack of friends and about two thirds acknowledged that some pre-school aged children could show prejudicial/racist tendencies. The vast majority of respondents agreed with the statement that 'social experiences in the early years setting are a good way of helping children to develop socially' and the vast majority said that social development through interaction in small groups should be a priority. However, many of these same respondents did not allow children to take part in small group activities frequently, nor did they frequently use drama, make-believe play or circle time. Yet, these are the very activities and settings which could encourage positive social development, so why aren't they using them and what impact is their lack of use having on young children's social development?

Moral development

Children develop their sense of morality (their ability to live co-operatively and safely together) through their relationships with others. The material side of life is stressed so much nowadays that we have ended up believing that materialism alone is what is real, significant and worthwhile. This elevation has done little to raise our sense of decency. We do not take better care of the weaker members of our society as a result of it, nor is there greater solidarity, happiness or fulfillment in the world. Instead, it has opened up greater forms of cruelty and distress. Is this moral and just?

Humans, and in particular children, have an impressive capacity for developing morally, given the appropriate circumstances. Moral development depends on cognitive development, on the structure of the problem the child is encountering, on adult example/instruction/identification and on peer group influences. To be profoundly moral is to show concern for others and to be altruistic, which many of us are failing to be. Moral development is often seen as a movement towards the possession of sound, universalistic moral principles and living by them with greater consistency. It incorporates a sense of respect, fairness, honesty and promise-keeping.

From about three, many children can speak clearly about their awareness of moral issues such as lying, violence and stealing. At six some children have a desire to be tactful, courteous, generous in their willingness to see the world through the eyes of others and to act on that knowledge with kindness. However, many children and adults do not have this ability. This moral development (or lack of it) is not acquired by memorisation of rules and regulations, it occurs as a consequence of learning how to be with others; how to behave towards them and why. Children hunger and thirst and seek hard, on their own, to develop this ability, but they also need the help of adults in this. The aim of adults must be to get the child to stick to certain behavioural and moral principles, not just because of fear of punishment, but because the child thinks and believes that it is the right and decent thing to do (Duska and Whelan 1975; Kitwood 1990; Siegal 1982a). Thus in the early years, given favourable circumstances, the child becomes an intensely moral creature, quite interested in figuring out the reasons why he should behave in various ways. This is the stage in the young child's life during which the conscience and character can be built on and consolidated and if a child is to develop morally he must come to understand the mechanics of moral and character education. With methods that are appropriate to each stage of his psychological development, the child should be helped to see what factors need to be considered in any given situation, how they are to be balanced one against the other and how he is to decide what is morally the best thing to do and why (Coles 1997). Yet, at present, many adults and children are not developed morally and are not prepared to act for the common good and do not show care and concern for their fellow man. In Ireland a recent survey (Daly 2002) regarding moral development in the early years, revealed that the great majority of respondents considered moral development to be as important as cognitive development. The vast majority agreed that early years settings should try to promote respect for all and that early education could have an influence on the formation of a child's morals. However, using class instruction, with the adult addressing the class as a whole, does not enable children to be active learners. It minimises their ability to become good, productive, contributing citizens and it does not ensure that practitioners promote respect and responsibility to the same degree that they try to promote reading, writing and arithmetic. Yet these are the settings that the respondents continue to use. Many respondents admit that they do not use small group settings or circle time (time for informal chats and stories with a moral) frequently. Yet, the vast majority of them considered social interaction to be necessary for the formation of moral judgements, so just when are children supposed to get this social and moral interaction? In reality, exactly how many respondents actually believe that moral development is as important as cognitive development?

Spiritual development

Spirituality is needed by people today, probably more than ever before, as modern man is depicted as hollow, devoid of a personal centre of strengths and values (Hammés 1998). The heart of spirituality is about being able to look inward in search of meaning. It is about purposely seeking an understanding of what truly matters and why it matters. Today, few cultural or religious symbols are given the care and respect they once enjoyed, and consequently they have lost their power to thrill, inspire and motivate. Maslow (1971) terms this refusal to treat anything with deep seriousness and concern as 'desacralising'. Spirituality tends to give adults and children alike a sense of purpose and direction in life and allows people to treat things and life with love, respect and concern. Children need a sense of the spiritual. Even pre-school children are constantly trying to comprehend how they should think about the gift of life given to them as they ponder about what they should do with it and about who gave it to them. Without spirituality, something vital is missing from a child's life.

Yet, the issue of children's spiritual development is rarely mentioned. There is little published in developmental terms about how children develop spiritually. Many books on child development do not even mention it. Lindon (1999) is one of the few authors who tackles the subject and defines spirituality as, "an awareness of and connectedness to that part of human existence that does not have to answer to rational analysis" (p.89). It incorporates, according to Lindon, an inner life of feelings (awe, appreciation, respect and delight) and encompasses a sense of the infinite and of powers and forces beyond human experience or control and gives life a meaning and purpose. Such a sense is vital for young children, yet only 65 per cent of those who responded to a nationwide survey in Ireland (Daly 2002) considered spiritual development to be as important as cognitive development. Many of them (70 per cent) believed that spiritual well-being and development impacted on physical well-being while 76 per cent of them believed that spiritual development impacted on psychological well-being. Yet, only 30 per cent of voluntary and 42 per cent of state sector respondents thought spiritual development should be a priority in the early years curriculum. Is this because practitioners feel that the physical and psychological well-being of children does not really matter? The results of the questionnaire reflect the literature which shows that spiritual development is not an area of development that people want to get involved in and is certainly not an area that is seen as being a priority. In 2001, the head of the Irish government, Mr. Bertie Ahern, himself admitted that 'spirituality presents government with the problem of knowing how to respond to it' (Ahern cited in Carroll 2002 p.67). It also presents many others, including practitioners, with the problem of knowing how to respond to it and in many ways rather than responding to it, we ignore it. Yet, its neglect has all sorts of negative repercussions for children. Can we really go on ignoring this vital area of development?

The results of the nationwide survey show that the areas of emotional, social, moral and spiritual development are not priorities in the early years curriculum. The peripheral status of each of these areas is evidenced when practitioners were asked what they actually do or would do in their curricula and the results are alarming to say the least, and spurred me on to do something about it – hence the publication of this book.

On becoming a reflective practitioner

On reading this book you need to reflect on what it is saying. You need to ask your self what point is the book trying to make? Where is the writer going with this? What is the evidence for the book? In the end does it matter any way? What difference does it make? Having thought about it, one needs to relate theory to practice. Learning to become an early years practitioner is a deeply personal and difficult process. Each individual brings their own unique past experiences, current understanding, learning styles, expectations and personality to the setting and individual experiences and knowledge will differ profoundly from those of others. In the process of becoming a practitioner one begins to make explicit the beliefs and values which guide one's actions and decision making. Reflecting on one's own experiences and deriving personal meaning from them will provide strategies and decisions on how to do the best for the children. Decisions will be made in the light of analysis of events, using specialised knowledge and consideration of possible consequences of alternative strategies, such as reading this book and reflecting on what it says, and then doing something different or better with the children in the early years setting as a result of it. It is vital that knowledge and actions be reflected on in ways that lead to deeper understandings and insights. Challenging or extending knowledge requires looking for new understandings and meanings and then considering them in the light of existing knowledge and then if necessary changing and enhancing practice. The practitioner must be an active participant in her own learning, critically examining and reflecting upon experiences and then constructing 'new' knowledge and understandings in order to progress. In order to make decisions, the practitioner must be able to observe, to describe events, to reflect on and analyse situations, to consider alternative strategies, to decide on and carry through a course of action and then to evaluate the effectiveness of decisions and actions (Perry 1997). How often do practitioners do this?

Facilitating the holistic development of the young child is complex and the practitioners privileged enough to be given this vital task need expertise in a wide variety of areas. The most effective practitioners are the ones who acknowledge just how important their role is and who are willing to evaluate their work. They are aware of the demands they encounter and are conscious that they will never be able to do the job as well as they would like, but are willing to give it their best shot. They are critical of themselves and strive to improve their practice. They are committed to offering the young children they encounter the best possible experiences that they can. The early years practitioner needs to reflect on, evaluate and adapt her practice in response to her own observations and to the wealth of research evidence that is available. By placing the needs of the child at the centre of the curriculum, practitioners must regularly confront their own assumptions and prejudices. Initial training should help students to begin the often painful self-evaluation process. They must be helped to see that they have formed a set of values and attitudes based on their own life experiences and that these are not necessarily shared by others. They must also recognise that attitudes and values are not fixed – they must be prepared to question themselves in the light of new experiences and through being challenged by altering points of view. Unless practitioners are aware of their own beliefs and values and how they were acquired (consciously and unconsciously from birth) practitioners run the risk of communicating "values and attitudes which may not only be unfamiliar to many children but may also seem to reject their own experiences" (Hazareesingh, Simms and Anderson 1989 p.24).

Early years practitioners will be confronted by a range of different views – those held by colleagues, parents, children, members of the community as well as writers and theorists in the field. Consequently their own attitudes will be questioned. This requires an openness to looking deeply within one's self and to responding in a positive, not defensive, way. Practitioners have to be able to answer the 'why' questions which will be asked of them and they must review and sometimes change their attitudes in a thoughtful way that shows respect for the concerns and beliefs of others. This ability to respect others depends a great deal on one's own self-awareness and is vital for both adult and child. The more the self is confronted the less likely the adult is to be afraid of the questions of others. If they allow themselves to learn form a variety of sources they will have ample opportunities to reflect on their own assumptions and may be offered different but often equally valid ways of looking at the world (Lally 1991).

Initial and in-service training which emphasises the questioning and analysis of attitudes, situations and problems is vital. The 'old tips for teachers' transmission model of training where the trainer offered ideas and gave strict guidance on how and what to do in practice is no longer appropriate. However, many practitioners still want to be told what to do, for these the process of thinking issues through for themselves is a difficult and frightening prospect. They find it stressful to accept personal responsibility for their teaching and they often have not realised or may not want to acknowledge that they carry a large burden of responsibility for what goes on in their settings. They are reluctant to make choices, preferring to be directed rather than actively being involved and try to avoid responsibility and the confrontation of issues. This is why I emphasise that the suggestions given at the end of Chapters Three, Four, Five and Six are merely that – suggestions to be tried, tested and altered – they are not the old prescriptive tips. The effective practitioner welcomes that opportunity to analyse and regarding the suggestions at the end of the chapters in this book would question and analyse them before adapting them to meet the needs of the children in her individual setting. The reflective practitioner does not accept easy answers but delves deeply looking for deeper insights and better understandings, enhancing professional learning, promoting observation, self-evaluation and critical thinking skills as well as raising the awareness of the complexity of being a practitioner.

Dewey (1933 p.9) stressed the value of reflection as a means of carefully and persistently considering a belief or form of knowledge "in the light of the grounds that support it and the further conclusions which it tends". Schon (1983, 1987) built on this notion and talked about 'knowledge-in-action' and 'reflection-in-action'. Schon's 'knowledge-in-action' concept describes scenarios where the practitioner uses a tacit type of knowledge. On the other hand, 'reflection-in-action' is where the practitioner consciously interacts with a problematic situation and thinks about the problem by drawing on various knowledge sources in order to develop strategies and to test out possible solutions. Reflection brings an added dimension to one's understanding. It challenges thinking and contributes detailed descriptions of situations to link actions and responses and helps clarify things. Reflection is helped by undertaking readings and research, by seeking views from experienced others, by analysing situational influences, by testing out strategies in practice and observing and assessing effects, responses and action in the light of knowledge and beliefs. Reflecting helps to clarify and give reasons for actions, it gives a better understanding of decisions and actions and raises questions and issues that challenge current thinking (Perry 1997). The process of reflection, of thinking about a problem and analysing different solutions to reach a hypothesis to test, is a critical element of the early years practitioner. Contemplating events, whether on one's own or with another, leads to further thinking.

Reflection includes the process of looking back and projecting into the future. Reflection allows a sharper perspective of the situation and gives an opportunity to see the parts of the whole and the connections between the parts of the whole. Reflection allows for the construction of theories and the ability to test and evaluate them. When reflecting, you ask yourself questions linking previous ideas, experiences and observations to present ones. You examine, clarify, organise, analyse, hypothesise, predict, assess. Reflecting can help create new ideas, alternative strategies and involves asking 'why' and 'how' questions (Branscombe et al. 2000). Ongoing reflection and its careful documentation can lead to more complex and expanded views of learning and teaching and must be undertaken if the holistic development of the child is to be realised. Through identifying, questioning and relating theory to practice, the quality of services will be enhanced. This book is to be read as a stimulus and the suggestions given at the end of the four main chapters are not intended to be prescriptive. They are included to relate theory to practice and to encourage readers to try out new ideas and to adapt the suggestions to suit individual settings and individual children. They are to act as a catalyst and to show that with a little thought and not that much money, great strides can be made in enhancing the emotional, social, moral and spiritual development of the young child.

The questions asked and an outline of what is included in this book

This book is an attempt to redress the lack of understanding of the importance of the areas of social, emotional, moral and spiritual development. It is intended to provide information and to answer questions raised regarding young children's development in the areas of emotional, social, moral and spiritual development. The development of children's emotions provokes many questions that need to be looked at with regard to early childhood education and care. Is emotional development really important in the early years of development? Which is more important in emotional development, nature or nurture? Have there been any recent developments/findings regarding emotional development? Could some mental health problems be prevented by teaching young children to deal positively with the emotions they experience? Does emotional development impact on other areas of development? Should children be encouraged to talk freely about their feelings? Are the early years an important time for identifying children who are not developing emotionally? Should early years settings encourage the reward of achievement or effort? Is it important to allow children to make mistakes or should emphasis be put on getting things right? Should education try to compensate for children's lack of emotional development or experience at home? How can the practitioner relate her knowledge of emotional development into practical ways to help the child develop emotionally?

What about social development - is it important in the early years? How can early years practitioners help to enhance children's social development? What kind of setting/grouping best promotes social development? Are friendships important in the early years or is it only later that friendship becomes important? Can pre-school children be described as showing pro-social behaviour? Are social skills important for young children? Should early years settings try to compensate for children's lack of social interaction/experience at home? Does gender stereotyping impact on social development in the early years? Should integration of children who are 'different' be encouraged or discouraged? Who should be 'included' or 'excluded' for that matter? Can young children show racist behaviour? What strategies can early years practitioners use to deal with the incidence of bullying? Does the experience of bullying have long-term repercussions? What sort of experiences can enhance social development?

What is moral development? Can young children ever be described as moral? Is adult example an important factor in children's moral development? Who says what is moral and what isn't? What values, if any, should be promoted in the early years setting? What sort of factors influence moral development? Is morality connected to religion? Is moral development as important as cognitive development? Can moral development be enhanced in the early years setting? There is very little research done on any aspect of spiritual development, so this book will go some way towards redressing this and raises the issue of spiritual development even though it is an area that is seen as highly sensitive by many.

The book will attempt to raise the profile of the area and to answer questions such as what actually constitutes spiritual development. Have there been any new research findings regarding spiritual development? Does spiritual development impact on a child's overall feeling of well-being and health? Should early years practitioners try to develop children's spiritual dimension or should this be delayed until the child is older? Must the spiritual be religious or is a fully secular spirituality conceivable? If the conventional early years curriculum lacks a spiritual dimension, can it then be really educational at all? Is it important to encourage a sense of balance between the inner and outer world of the child? Is a sense of awe and wonder important for children's development? In education, should other, different, views be acknowledged and respected (other religious or philosophical commitments) by children or should they be ignored in case they confuse the young child? How can early years settings contribute to spiritual development? Spiritual development is such a huge, though largely unresearched area that the questions to be answered are innumerable. This book names the issue but accepts there is a long and difficult road ahead while reiterating that this is too important an area to be omitted from children's lives.

This book focuses on four specific areas of child development - the emotional, social, moral and spiritual development of the young child within the framework of developing the whole child, using Maslow's hierarchy of needs as its conceptual framework. Chapter One, The Introduction, lays the background for the book. It outlines why we need to prioritise the areas of emotional, social, moral and spiritual development and puts forward the concept of holistic child development, based on Maslow's hierarchy of needs and on his self-actualisation theory (Maslow 1968). Chapter Two sets down the historical evolution of our beliefs regarding emotional, social, moral and spiritual development, within the development of the whole child. This long and important history can be traced from the time of Plato (427-347 B.C.). Indeed, the work of philosophers, practitioners and educators such as those reviewed in this chapter, which has been formulated from pre-Christian times to the recent past, is of great significance, since it helped to develop a heuristic child-centred approach to the education and care of young children. Looking at the work of Plato, Comenius, Froebel, Montessori and Isaacs, to name but a few, highlights the fact that for more than two thousand years there has been a recognition that optimally developing the emotional, social, moral and spiritual aspects is vital for the overall development of the child. Thus, development of these areas must be the foundation for children's holistic and optimal development, but is it? Chapters Three, Four, Five and Six respectively contain a critical analysis of modern and current literature regarding the emotional, social, moral and spiritual development of the young child. Each of these chapters is followed by a series of practical suggestions on how to enhance the pre-school aged child's development within the early years setting. Chapter Three on emotional development is longer than the following three chapters as I contend that this is the most important area of development and it is this which acts as the linchpin for the other three areas, indeed for all areas of development. Chapter Seven provides an outline of holistic child development based on Maslow's hierarchy of needs. Chapter Eight ends on a philosophical note stressing the need to change if we want to do the best for our children.

The period before eight years old is foundational and early experiences and deprivations can have cumulative if not multiplying effects. In particular, deficiencies in the areas of emotional, social, moral and spiritual development can have devastating consequences. My contention is that many children today are experiencing deprivation in these developmental areas and this is having an adverse effect on their lives and on the life of society. This situation has to be redressed and this book is intended only as a start, I hope that others will follow and take up the gauntlet. It is up to you...

CHAPTER TWO

Historical Review of the Main Educational Theorists

Overview of main theorists

This chapter examines the theories and ideas of philosophers and educators over the past 2000 years, who have contributed to our knowledge of the social, emotional, moral and spiritual development of the young child within the framework of the whole child. The work of all the philosophers and educators has been examined in terms of their contribution to the body of knowledge which has resulted in our present day understanding of the nature and importance of the social, emotional, moral and spiritual attributes in the overall development of the young child. These theorists have paved the way for our work today. Their efforts developed and refined the roles and responsibilities of contemporary early years practitioners. This backward journey details significant events that have changed the field. It is not exhaustive; it is intended to provide some insight into how certain individuals challenged traditional ways of looking at education and care and how this led to change. Many of today's ideas and trends are co-ordinations and transformations of past experiences. Acknowledging this empowers our present, allows us to identify issues, perturbations and trends in the field and can help predict our future. We can investigate how events, programmes and theories have enabled or hindered children in becoming all that they are capable of. Many fearless men and women pioneered the field of early childhood care and education and their ideas still influence us today. Many of the issues that they were confronted by still continue to confront early years practitioners today (Branscombe et al. 2000).

The examination begins in pre-Christian times, by looking at the beliefs of Plato (428-347 B.C.) and Aristotle (384-322 B.C.). It then moves on to examine Luther (1483-1546), who saw education as being necessary to Christian life and details his interest in the cognitive, moral and spiritual development of the child. Comenius (1592-1670), theologian, philosopher and pedagogue, stressed that only through education could man achieve his full potential and go on to lead a truly harmonious life. Locke (1632-1704) was one of the most influential philosophers of the 18th century and an examination of his work highlights his belief in the *Tabula Rasa* (1659) theory of mind. Rousseau (1712-1778), romantic, naturalist and sentimentalist, saw children as innately good. Looking at his work highlights his belief that education could not begin too early. His work also claims that education should conform to the laws of nature, this being of particular importance for the child's emotional development.

In Ireland the Edgeworths, Richard (1744-1817) and his daughter Maria (1767-1849), intended to offer advice on how to help children develop. They prioritised first hand experiences and outlined the educational value of certain toys, advocating toys that appealed to children's senses, imagination and initiative. Pestalozzi (1746-1827), was concerned with educating all children, including the poor. The main purpose of his life and work was to impact on the social regeneration of humanity through the education system. Owen (1771-1858), was influenced by Pestalozzi and was concerned about the education of children, particularly working class children, and his ideas for education were social in nature. Wilderspin (1792-1866), stressed physical and co-operative play as being vital and he envisaged providing playgrounds with gardens, swings and climbing frames, advocating that over half of children's time in school should be spent on these activities. Froebel (1782-1852), one of the pioneers of early educational reform, stressed that every child possessed within himself at birth his own full developmental potential and that an appropriate educational environment was necessary to help that child develop holistically.

In Italy Montessori (1870-1952), introduced a philosophy of education based upon her own personal observations of children and her work highlights, in particular, the moral and spiritual life of the child. Looking at the work of the McMillan sisters, Rachel (1859-1917) and Margaret (1860-1931), shows their emphasis on relationships, on feelings and ideas, as well as their belief in promoting the physical aspects of development and learning. A brief look at the work of Steiner (1861-1925) shows that he based his pedagogy and didactics on his belief that the child is trichotomous; comprising body, soul and spirit. The educational philosophy of Dewey (1859-1952) appears to have grown out of his experiments in the establishment of an ideal school in connection with his pedagogic work in the University of Chicago. Dewey considered every social experience to be educative and he believed education could transform society. In particular, he stressed the social and moral development of the child. Isaacs (1885-1948) made detailed observations of children and put forward a five-phased theory of development, with the child passing imperceptibly from one phase to the next. Isaacs valued play, believing it gave children the freedom to feel, think and relate and she was particularly concerned with children's emotional and social growth. In essence, all of the aforementioned philosophers and educators recognised and acknowledged the critical importance of developing the child emotionally, socially, morally and spiritually.

Plato

Plato (428-347 B.C.) was one of the first recorded philosophers to show an interest in the education of young children. To read Plato for its historical and literary value is instructive. However, many of his ideas for both education and politics, though conservative by modern standards, were far ahead of those of his contemporaries. The theories he put forward were often borrowed from others but the way he set them down was original and groundbreaking. He put most of his ideas into written dialogues and these have been preserved by his followers (Smith 1984). *The Republic* (1803) outlined Plato's educational ideas and in it he inquired into the nature of justice, morality, righteousness and moral education. He saw justice as essentially a social virtue and in his writings he constructed an ideal state where co-operative effort and justice were the underlying principles. He proposed a good and simple educational environment for children and he highlighted good example and imitation as important factors in moral development and character formation (Curtis and Boultwood 1970).

In *The Laws* (cited in Rusk 1918) Plato emphasised the positive significance of play and he also highlighted the importance of early education. According to Rusk (1918), the treatment of education in *The Laws* supplements that of *The Republic* as in it Plato emphasised the practical aspects of education. Plato claimed that education can help develop the perfect citizen and he said those who are rightly educated usually become good men. He stressed that education is for the good of the individual and for the safety of the state and in both *The Republic* and *The Laws* Plato called for the education of both sexes. However, his call did not have much of a practical impact on furthering the education of women.

Education had a twofold purpose in Plato's era - education for citizenship and for leadership. This meant that it was vital that children learned such virtues as docility, obedience and manliness. However, Plato believed early education should be different from this slavish training for mere professional purposes and he advocated a more humane education which developed children socially, morally, emotionally and cognitively. He did not believe in corporal punishment, but he did believe that many materials should be censored, as children should only be exposed to things of high moral value. He acknowledged the importance of educating the three to six year old children and he set down a curriculum for them which included community play in small groups, lots of movement and music, fostering co-operation, self-control, confidence-building and respect. His work gave rise to ideas such as the state control of schools, the education of the masses, early learning though the use of concrete objects, play and active experiences (Lodge 1950; Branscombe et al. 2000).

Aristotle

Aristotle (384-322 B.C.) was one of Plato's most dedicated followers. However, he was more scientific and empirical than Plato and he incorporated empirical observation into his Platonic views. Aristotle made some useful conclusions regarding the moral and social nature of humans. He said humans were social beings and he concluded that the supreme good was happiness. However, he conceded that people disagreed over what constituted happiness. For Aristotle, happiness was to be achieved by enhancing uniqueness and individuality and he believed education should set about doing this. Aristotle's philosophy inquired into virtue, character and the good life. He called on people to manage their emotional and moral lives with intelligence and he said the problem was not with emotionality but with the appropriateness of emotions and their expression (Goleman 1996).

Aristotle stressed that children needed to be morally and intellectually developed, contending that education should develop habits which would in turn develop moral and rational virtues. This ethical and intellectual training or character building was to be achieved by a liberal education, through daily practices which promoted moral virtues. He stressed the importance of taking a child's nature and all the influences of his environment (nurture) into account. He believed if this was done, all humans could live co-operatively and productively together in the *polis* (small cities). He differed from Plato in that he trusted his natural observations and he welcomed human difference. He also supported the education of children under the age of six but wanted this to happen in the home with a personal tutor to bring out specific talents and abilities of the individual child. His writings and the academy he set up have effected western educational traditions and are unrivalled in influence and fame, particularly in the areas of ethics, moral development, politics and social science (Smith 1984).

Luther

Interest in early years education waned and was not rekindled until many centuries later, with the work of Martin Luther (1483-1546). For Luther, education was necessary to Christian life, as a person's eternal salvation depended on his ability to read and understand scripture. He saw life as being divided into three interrelated spheres: the family; the state; and the church. Each was important, since it contributed to salvation and each was seen as being dependent on education for potentialisation. His major educational work *Letter to the Mayors and Aldermen of Germany on Behalf of Christian Schools* (1524 in Painter 1980) developed his educational ideas and in it he argued that education had deteriorated as a result of political unrest. He also said that some parents neglected their children's education, in particular the moral and spiritual aspects of their development. Luther proposed that the state should redress this by setting up schools which would help children develop according to their natures, using their natural curiosity and activity to further their education (Painter 1980 quoting Luther). In *The Sermon on the Duty of Sending Children to School* (1530 in Painter 1980) Luther argues for schools to provide ministers to aid in children's spiritual and moral development. In his *Large Catechism* Luther spoke out against corporal punishment and he said education for the young should incorporate play and should illustrate and enforce abstract truths with concrete examples and that force should not be used as a means of punishing or controlling children.

Luther's involvement in the practical side of education was extensive. He translated the Bible into German, he composed more than thirty popular hymns and he was involved in the foundation of a Latin school. Smith (1984) contends that it was as a teacher and preacher that he made the greatest educational contribution, as he was deeply concerned about young children and their intellectual, moral and spiritual development. His contributions to education come mainly from his theological underpinnings and he stressed that each person was directly responsible for his own salvation. He also insisted that the state had an obligation to support education and this led to the development of public support of education and for compulsory attendance laws. His unhappiness with bookish and scholastic learning also moved education in the direction of practical learning.

Comenius

One century after Luther and a century before the Enlightenment, John Amos Comenius (1592-1670), born in what is today the Czech Republic, was a theologian, philosopher and pedagogue who believed that only through education could man achieve his full potential and lead a truly harmonious life. All of Comenius' life was devoted to the cause of education, both as a teacher and educational theorist. Many of his motivating theories originated in his own experiences as a teacher. Piaget (1967) cites Comenius as being influenced by Aristotle and also says he often sounds a neo-Platonic note. Comenius, like his successor Froebel, also inherited an idealist tradition and in trying to work out his logical thought, he was very impressed by the methods of Decartes (Bowen 1974).

In Comenius' day, education and schools were the subject of general dissatisfaction and in *Prodromus* (from *A Reformation of Schools* 1642 p.8 cited in Murphy 1995) Comenius said: "Learning, as it is commonly taught, is not enough accommodated to the uses of life". Education was seen as giving only bookish knowledge and was unsystematic and cruel, owing to the chaotic state of school organisation and due to the lack of trained and skilled teachers and also because of the belief in the corrective powers of corporal punishment. Comenius called these schools, "the slaughterhouses of minds and the terrors of children" (ibid.). He realised that this situation should not be allowed to continue and he set about developing a theory of education which would redress this. He saw education as a right for all and he firmly believed that social and intellectual class should not be the chief factors in determining educational opportunity (Boyd 1921; Dupuis 1966).

Although Comenius' efforts for educational reform were inspired by religious motives, the great interest of his life, apart from religion, lay in a scheme of universal knowledge - 'pansophism'. According to Comenius in *The Way of Light* (1668 in Murphy 1995) the purpose of pansophism was not so much to make men learned as to make them wise. When Comenius was almost 60, he was invited by a Protestant prince to organise a school along 'pansophic' lines in Hungary. This opportunity seemed to offer Comenius the chance to make a breakthrough for his 'pansophic' theories. However, for many reasons the venture was not the success he had hoped for, partly because the educational standards of the children were very poor and the pupils were not able to use the textbooks available to them. To rectify this, Comenius set about producing a picture book which would introduce children to Latin through the study of things around them. Unfortunately, the book was not completed until after Comenius left the school but his *Orbus Pictus* (1658 in Curtis and Boultwood 1970) became one of the most popular schoolbooks in Europe for several centuries after.

Comenius' main work, *The Great Didactic* (1632 in Rusk 1918), opens with an analysis of man's place in the universe. He believed everything grew in nature, and man likewise should grow and improve, following nature's laws and through the right education, ideas later built upon by Rousseau, Pestalozzi and Froebel. Comenius said education should begin early and that it should be continuous and should not be coercive. He offered a curriculum of education for the home and primary school and according to Piaget (1967) *The Great Didactic* (1632) is looked on as one of the classic works on which all types of systematic teaching are based. In it Comenius highlighted the right of the child to dignity and respect, promoting emotional and moral development, a view not held by many of his contemporaries. Comenius conceived of the relationship between the teacher and pupil as being collaborative, requiring respect on the part of both for each other and this conception was deeply in contrast with the authoritarian model of teaching of his era and has only recently been taken on board by many practitioners.

Comenius, with greater insistence than any of his predecessors, restated that the child should be instructed in things before being taught to express them in language and he believed particularly that in the early years, everything should be first learned through the senses. In *The Great Didactic* (1632 p.38 ibid.) he said children "must learn to know and investigate the things themselves, and not the observations that other people have made about the things". His psychology was of the most primitive variety but he anticipated the psychological principle of Pestalozzi when he affirmed that nothing should be taught to the young child until he is ready for it. Comenius recognised that expecting too much of the child could and would impede emotional development. Like Montessori, he believed in exposing the child to real things and real experiences and he said, "those things that are placed before the young must be real things and not the shadows of things" (Comenius 1632 p.xx ibid). Yet, unlike Montessori, Comenius argued for the use of visual aids and for dramatic play and he regarded free play activities as having considerable educative value, particularly for the social and emotional development of the young child. In the *School of Infancy* (1631a in Rusk 1933) he advocated that all adults have a reverence for childhood and he advised parents to educate their children spiritually, emotionally, morally and intellectually. He clearly enunciated the principles of infant education and he indicated how the neglect of infant education in theory and practice could impact negatively on children.

Comenius was in favour of a school education, since parents had neither the time nor the expertise to teach their children at home. However, he did also stress the importance of parents and in particular he highlighted the important role of mothers in their children's development. He foreshadowed Froebel's kindergarten with his vision of a school for children under six. Comenius advocated changes in instruction and he also believed that all schools should be made more agreeable to children. His early education involved developing the native language, social behaviours, religion, music and art. He suggested schools be situated in quiet, pleasant places, that classrooms should be bright and clean with pictures on the walls. Access should be available to a garden with plants and flowers and play and walks should take place regularly (Dupuis 1966). These thoughts are very similar to those put forward later by Froebel and also by modern day researchers such as Denham (1998) who pinpoint the fact that environmental experiences affect children's emotional development.

Comenius saw the promotion of individual freedom as central to the whole educational process, but highlighted it as being particularly important in the realms of social, emotional and moral development. Like his successors, Froebel and Montessori, Comenius saw freedom not as the end process but as a means to a higher objective - the fostering of the universal human potential for love, the development of social cohesion and the realisation of individual and universal rights. The curriculum that he envisaged was a liberal one, with its cultivation of the full range of human potentialities - spiritual, religious, moral, emotional, aesthetic, cognitive, social and physical. He realised the importance of providing a broad-balanced, substantive and largely undifferentiated curriculum and three hundred years before the modern ecumenical movement developed, Comenius recognised the dangers of sectarianism and advocated religious tolerance. He also recognised the ever-present threat to peace and freedom which comes from social injustice and inequity. He said the way to overcome these was not in political revolution but in personal revolution; in individual self-reform; and in the assumption of personal responsibility in accordance with the dictates of faith. This, he believed, could be achieved through a right education which began in infancy through the fostering of conscience, by promoting spirituality and by a way of life focused on the practical expression of the law of love (Murphy 1995).

Comenius can be seen as part of a line of progressive educators, the most recent of whom is American, John Dewey. The similarities between Comenius and Dewey are fairly obvious. Both stand for a learner-centred and heuristic pedagogy, both stressed the importance of learning through individual enquiry and discovery. Both men also condemned coercive methods of enforcing classroom discipline and both stressed the need to make knowledge meaningful, by relating it to the individual experience of the learner. However, there are fundamental differences between them, particularly in regard to religion. Comenius prioritised spiritual experience with religious underpinnings, while the spiritual philosophy proposed by Dewey is predominantly secular and humanist in character. Also, Comenius and

Dewey differ in their views on the role of the teacher and on the design, structure and content of the curriculum (Murphy 1995).

Comenius strove for the holistic development of the child and believed in the need for world unity if education was to be truly successful. According to Ulich (1956) Comenius saw education as the instrument to lead a suffering and divided world out of war and division towards peace and international understanding. Kokoschka (1942 p.65) says that:

> Three centuries later the world still suffers misery and chaos because Comenius, the man with the message of universal brotherhood in knowledge and love, failed ... Today we need more than ever the faith of Comenius in the talents latent in man.

Locke

The seventeenth century also produced a most influential English philosopher, John Locke (1632-1704). Locke did not look favourably on the schools of his time, disagreeing with their heavy reliance on physical punishment. He was one of the first to point out that teaching should vary according to the nature of the person and that it should not have to be forced, as a lesson learned under pressure has only superficial effect and is quickly forgotten. Locke advised educators and practitioners to acknowledge the importance of understanding the child's needs and of trying to meet these needs. He fought against rote learning and advocated the development of understanding and thought. Locke also emphasised moral development and he wrote in detail about the need for a proper balance between freedom and authority and claimed this balance was the secret of a true education (Lubienski Wentworth 1999).

Some Thoughts Concerning Education (1693 in Curtis and Boultwood 1970) details many of Locke's ideas. This was written to advise a friend on how to bring up his eight-year-old son. Locke stresses the holistic development of the child and he cites four aspects of development as being of particular importance - virtuousness, wisdom, breeding and learning. The aim of education was to optimally develop these. He stressed the need to appeal to the child's curiosity and he highlighted the importance of classroom atmosphere on emotional and social development. He also advocated the use of educational aids. Like many other early scholars Locke placed emphasis on natural education and play. He also advocated the use of experience rather than textbooks and the integration of physical and intellectual development. Locke's most influential educational ideas deal with his theory of knowledge. His main work *An Essay Concerning Knowledge* (in Axtell 1968) deals with the nature, origin and validity of knowledge and from there he formulated his *Tabula Rasa* theory of mind. In book II of *An Essay Concerning Human Understanding* (1659 in Axtell 1968) he contends that children are born with blank minds and he says that 90 per cent of knowledge is developed from experience and nurturance with only 10 per cent being innate. This belief, that the child was in essence like a piece of wax to be moulded and fashioned, resulted in the belief that the child was in fact a miniature adult and led to adult-centred rather than child-centred approaches to early childhood education (Rusk 1918).

Rousseau

Jean Jacques Rousseau (1712-1778) was one of the most influential educational thinkers of the 18th century and he was a romantic, naturalist and sentimentalist (Wise 1964). Rousseau stressed that humans needed a good education in order to develop fully and this good education should reconcile man with nature and should enable him to adhere to the demands of civic society. In *The Project for the Education of Madame de Sainte Marie* (1740 in Rusk 1918) Rousseau stressed that the aim of education is to form heart, judgement and mind in the order that he named them. Also, many of Rousseau's writings such as *Emile* (1762 ibid.) and *Nouvelle Heloise* (1764 ibid.) explore the consequences, for man, of the tensions between nature, civilisation, society and education. The book *Emile* (1762, 1979) is an experiment in restoring harmony to the world by redressing man's imbalances and by potentialising his abilities. Books I-III of *Emile* are devoted to the rearing of a child and books IV and V attempt to incorporate the young man into society. Rousseau saw children as innately good and *Emile* outlines this belief. He also assumed an equality among children and he said inequalities were the result of the effect of a perverted society. He stressed that education was necessary to develop the best possible disposition and to deal with the inequalities of society and, like Plato, Rousseau believed education could not begin too early. He said that the most important stage of education was the first part but he conceded that this was the part that the world neglected (Rousseau in Rusk 1918).

Rousseau was influenced by Locke and like him he stressed the predominance of environmental influences over hereditary ones. Yet, he differed from him in that Locke's search for a better educational system grew mainly out of his religious beliefs, whereas Rousseau's were secular in nature. Rousseau advocated educating children according to the laws of nature and he believed that society should conform to nature and that under these conditions, an ideal education could take place. He stressed that childhood was different to every other phase of life and in *Emile* (1782, 1979 p.54) he said: "Childhood has its own ways of seeing, thinking and feeling". He highlighted the negative impact on emotional development that pushing or hurrying the child could have and he said, "nothing is useful and good to him which is unbefitting his age" (Rousseau 1782, 1979 p.212). He put forward a stage theory and he also proposed that each stage must be fully lived through before progressing to the next, principles later taken up by others such as Froebel, Montessori and Dewey. Rousseau also advocated firsthand experiences and his attempt to shift the emphasis from the curriculum to the child can be regarded as a revolution in education (Boyd 1921).

Like Locke, Rousseau wanted education to be free, but he acknowledged that liberty and constraint were compatible and that both were necessary, in their own way, for the child's emotional and moral well-being. He cited the best educators as the family, as it was the family which stood between nature and society. This position allowed the child to develop his individual powers with the minimum of restraint, while preparing him for his place in the world. Rousseau saw moral and emotional development as being very important. Kindness and understanding were to be what the child experienced, thus allowing for positive emotional experiences. Similarly, moral development would not occur through preaching but was to be imbibed by children through their experiences of good example, respect and compassion (Rusk 1933).

Though Rousseau had a romanticised view of education, his work had a great impact on other educational thinkers, from Pestalozzi to Dewey. Many cite *Emile* and the idealistic bohemian education advocated by Rousseau as being limited in practicality. However, *Emile* was not just about taking the child away and living with nature, it also proposed a philosophy of life. Rousseau intended it to show that only by understanding nature and history could man develop. Rousseau presented an alternative education, one that envisaged developing the whole child. In particular it advocated sensory experiences, physical activity and stressed the value of appealing to the child's natural instincts, curiosity and emotions. Boyd (1921) claims that *Emile* was by far the most important book written on education in the 18th century and maybe ever written. It aroused a deep interest in the subject of childhood and it turned the attention of politicians, society and educators towards children and their education. It also planted the idea that education could reform society.

Rusk (1933) claims that Rousseau stands in the history of infant education as the champion of the rights of childhood and he says: "To Rousseau almost all the positive developments in educational theory and practice can be attributed" (p.19). Rousseau emphasised nature and the natural ways of doing things. He saw children as innately good yet acknowledged that they could become corrupted by the institutions of civilised society and he set about redressing this. Rousseau saw childhood as a unique life stage and he said education should be child-centred. He repudiated the use of force and corporal punishment in education and he advocated that education should be informal, growing out of everyday experiences. He believed experiences and emotions were the true teachers and he stressed that what a child feels is what really matters. He argued that good individuals make a good society and he advocated that education develop good individuals. He encouraged parents to be involved in their children's education and acknowledged their vital role in their children's development. He encouraged the development of curiosity and interest as a motivating factor and he advised teachers to act as guides and facilitators. According to Wise (1964) Rousseau always put the child first and this is one of the best and strongest points in his psychology of education.

The Edgeworths

Many people including the Edgeworths, Richard (1744-1817) and his daughter Maria (1767-1849), were influenced by Rousseau. In 1798 their book *Practical Education* was published and this was intended to offer advice on how to help children develop in an 'Emile-like' fashion. In Ireland, the Edgeworths prioritised first hand experiences and outlined the educational value of certain toys, advocating toys that appealed to children's senses, imagination and initiative. Emotionally they were against hurrying children and believed that learning should never be forced. They advocated that the pace of learning and teaching be adjusted to the age and ability of the individual child. Morally, the Edgeworths agreed with Locke that the cultivation of good habits and the development of character were to be the primary aims of education. Socially, they pointed out the advantages of a good home but recognised the benefits of schools for young children's social development. Curtis and Boultwood (1970) claim that they kept spiritual education in the background and that they downplayed aesthetic development by ignoring the study of music, art and poetry. However, they were ahead of their time in advocating the education of girls and in highlighting the importance of having a well-trained teacher, yet their endeavours did not have a wide following and were aimed, in any case, at interested middle-class parents.

Pestalozzi

Johann Heinrich Pestalozzi (1746-1827) was also a disciple of Rousseau's. Pestalozzi lived at a time when education was the privilege of the higher classes but he was concerned with the education of children of all classes, including the poor, and the main purpose of his life was to effect the social regeneration of all people through education. Pestalozzi advocated educating the whole child, body, mind and soul and he opposed rote learning and corporal punishment. He believed that education began at birth and that learning should be centred around objects more than books. Pestalozzi tried to establish schools which were in accord with children's nature. His educational theory grew out of his educational practice and he, more than any other, acknowledged the importance of the mother in the early education of her children. He believed in character development and was particularly concerned about moral development (Rusk 1933).

Morally, he wanted teachers and pupils to respect each other and to engage in dialogue. His basic principles say that education is primarily concerned with the individual child and he believed that the basis of education is general knowledge. He saw the role of the teacher as directing the natural growth of the child, preparing him for his place in society. He believed that it was the family that lays the basis for the ideal school and he used the object lesson to get children actively involved in their own development. He said the classroom atmosphere should be one of love and affection, optimising emotional development and he stressed that education was the harmonious development of all the child's powers, not just the intellect. He further emphasised the importance of social development and realised that the child depended on society for the stimulus to grow in mind and body. He observed children and developed his teaching methods accordingly and advised others to do the same. His curriculum included music, drama, group work, field trips and play (Smith 1984). He advocated sensory development and *anschauung* was the basis of his philosophy. This concept meant sense perception/awareness and apprehension and was, according to Pestalozzi (1781), the basis of all experience and knowledge. He advocated learning by doing and he urged teachers to introduce simple and concrete things to children before giving them complex or abstract materials. He also advocated relating new information to what the child already knew, a view also carried by Piaget (Boyd 1921).

Pestalozzi took up many of Rousseau's ideas and developed and implemented them. He developed Rousseau's idea of a natural education, believing that nature was a better teacher than man. He tried to base instruction on psychological principles and to produce a general methodology on this. His writings and work have contributed to psychology, sociology and to the philosophy of education. Pestalozzi wrote a series of stories including a short story expanded into a novel called *Leonard and Gertrude* (1781 in Rusk 1918). This established him as a writer with promise. In this, Pestalozzi described how, by means of education which develops fitness for life, the regeneration of a small community is effected by the noble efforts of a moral and pious woman. Several years after this, Pestalozzi published his most important treatise on educational method, *How Gertrude Teaches her Children* (1801 ibid.). In this, Pestalozzi laid down the aim of education as the development of human nature with the harmonious cultivation of all its powers and talents. He broke the educational process down into three parts - the physical, the intellectual and the moral-religious and he stressed the need for well-balanced instruction which, in particular, developed the child morally and spiritually. In *Letters to Greaves* (1827 in Smith 1984) he stressed the spiritual virtue of the child and his ability to develop a conscience. He also stressed that moral virtues originate in the relationship between the child and mother and he stressed his belief in the innate goodness of children, but stressed that relationships and education could impact on this for good or evil.

According to Pestalozzi, the goal of education was social reform and through education man could become a responsible citizen. Pestalozzi's efforts in education were tentative and experimental yet his experiences and beliefs possess a reliability that has endured. He advocated the education of the whole child with a balance between the head, hand and heart. These had to be integrated for a child to develop harmoniously. His insistence that teaching should follow an orderly sequence, his formulation of a teaching method based on psychological principles and his recognition of the practical, emotional, moral and spiritual aspects of personality, have been accepted by many of his successors. He also helped lay the basis for elementary school education and reinforced the democratic tradition in education (Rusk 1918; Branscombe et al. 2000).

Owen

Robert Owen (1771-1858), Quaker and Welsh capitalist turned utopian socialist, was concerned about the education of children and was influenced by the doctrine of his contemporary, Pestalozzi. Like Rousseau, Owen believed children were born with an innate goodness and he stressed that the evils which humanity encountered were attributable to social conditions and influences. Owen believed these social ills could be redressed by education. He abhorred corporal punishment and he disapproved of the over-use of bookish learning. He advocated educating the poor and he provided schools, including nursery schools and teachers, in order to improve the plight of working class children (Rusk 1933). Owen saw education as a total process of character formation and he believed education could create a new, fairer society based on the equality of people inhabiting a community of common property. He was dedicated to creating such a society and he advocated early childhood and infant education as the first step in this process. His educational plan called for conditioning children on the correct dispositions and developing men and women who could live co-operatively in a communal society. His theory was a comprehensive one for restructuring society, branching out into economic, political, social and educational arenas. He wanted to reorder society and to restore integrity and morality to personal and social life. Unfortunately for Owen, his plan did not succeed. Yet, he was a visionary who believed it was possible to create a better world. He is credited with establishing the first infant school in England in 1816. His curriculum provided for the care of children and stressed play, music and physical activity. As a social and educational critic he pinpointed much needed reform and his social and educational proposals revealed the sociological basis which underlies education (Smith 1984).

Wilderspin

Samuel Wilderspin (1792-1866), a highly esteemed teacher in England, founded the Infant School Society around 1822 with the aim of educating children aged two to six. Wilderspin was particularly interested in developing children morally and socially and he contended that if children were placed with peers, under a kind and just teacher, the child would develop optimally. Wilderspin set down his ideas in *Early Discipline* (1832 in Curtis and Boultwood 1966) stressing physical and co-operative play as being vital and he envisaged providing playgrounds with gardens, swings and climbing frames, advocating that over half of children's time in school should be spent on these activities. His curriculum involved the training of the body and senses through physical education, object lessons and music. However, in practice, there were large amounts of rote learning, question and answer sessions and memory work in his school. Yet, Wilderspin did highlight the importance of educating young children. In particular he stressed children's need for movement as well as emphasising moral and social development (Curtis and Boultwood 1966).

Froebel

Friedrich Froebel (1782-1852) was one of the pioneers of early educational reform. He believed that childhood was an important period of human growth and development in its own right and he stressed that adults should refrain from imposing their views and ways upon children. Historically, many early childhood educators had supported the idea that children should be trained as soon as possible to become productive members of society, so that the cultural heritage of each society could be preserved from one generation to the next. This cultivation imposition theory has been prevalent throughout the educational history of the world. However, Froebel disagreed with this and instead advocated that young children should encounter what they are ready for, not what is expected or advocated by society (Rusk 1918).

Froebel believed every child possessed within himself at birth his own full educational potential and that an appropriate educational environment was necessary to help that child develop optimally. This was in sharp contrast to the views of John Locke and his *Tabula Rasa* (1659). To Locke, the child's whole development depended on the environment. Froebel emphasised both heredity and the environment, a view taken by most modern researchers. Nash (1997) says that experts now agree that a child does not come into the world as a genetically pre-programmed machine nor is a child a blank slate at the mercy of the environment. For this reason, the debate that engaged countless generations of philosophers as to whether nature or nurture is the dominant influence, no longer interests most scientists. Nature and nurture are now both recognised as being of more or less equal importance and Greenspan (1997 p.54), a psychiatrist at George Washington University in the United States says: "It's not a competition, it's a dance".

Froebel had an overwhelming love of humanity and like his predecessors he was deeply upset by the arbitrary way in which children were looked upon and cared for. According to Marenholtz Bulow (1887) he was seldom moved by anything which concerned him personally, but was only interested in things which concerned his cause - education. Throughout his life, he sacrificed himself and his personal interests for the development and propagation of his ideas. Froebel himself maintained there was nothing new in his philosophy and that he had just brought together the ideas of his predecessors. Liebschner (1988) discusses the fact that though much of his philosophy is not original and can be found in the writings and actions of others, this does not in any way detract from his achievements. Froebel's original contribution may be in the way he forged together and developed many original ideas.

The philosophy that Froebel inherited was one of idealism (a belief that the ultimate principle of explanation of the universe is a spiritual one). Through his attendance at the University of Jena he read and studied a certain amount of Kant, Fiche, Schelling and Hegel. In particular, he was influenced by Schelling, whose concept of art as the unity of the natural and spiritual world was a bridge between German idealism and romanticism. Froebel was also clearly a product of the pre-Darwinian thinking of his time and he was influenced by the work of Ernst Moritz Arndt (1769-1860). Arndt's writings drew a picture of contemporary man as being a shell without a core and like Rousseau he advised man to return to nature. Arndt stressed the innate goodness of man and talked about the stages of development. He also highlighted the years from birth to six as being of great importance. Many of these principles Froebel developed in his own philosophy (Liebschner 1988).

Comenius also affected Froebel's thinking. Comenius believed that man was innately good and also stressed the fact that nature provided everything in the right measure and at the right time for children's development. Froebel in his book *Mother Songs and Plays* (1844 in Rusk 1918) encouraged parents to surround their children with nature and he developed this belief in the importance of nature, in his kindergarten. Comenius had previously acknowledged the critical importance of the early years and had expressed concern about the fact that education was not provided for children under six. Froebel also held all of these beliefs. However, a comparison of Froebel's and Comenius' ideas show both differences and similarities in their thinking. Both believed in common that education should start at birth, that subject matter should be broken down into easily understandable components and that the principles of education could be gleaned from the laws of nature (Woodham, Smith, Slight, Priestman, Hamilton and Issacs 1952). However, Comenius lived at a time when children were still seen and treated like little adults and it was only after he had died that childhood began to be looked on as a separate and very special period in life. Froebel lived at a time when this development was beginning. The French philosopher, Aries detailed the development of childhood as a separate life stage in his book *Centuries of Childhood* (1962) and he stated that in medieval society the idea of childhood did not exist and the theory of childhood only emerged in Europe between the 15th and 18th centuries. Thus, Froebel had the advantage of the concept of childhood whereas Comenius did not.

Froebel developed many of the theories that came before him, including that of Rousseau. Rousseau in *Emile* had put forward the theory that man comes from God and that everything in the world is connected to God. He also outlined his belief that education should not be directive and interfering but that it should bring to the child a clear understanding of himself, leading to peace with nature and to union with God. These ideas Froebel also took on board. However, it was probably

Pestalozzi who had the greatest influence of all on Froebel. Froebel studied with him in his school at Yverdon from 1808-1810 and ever after valued his experiences there, as they helped him to formulate his own principles and thoughts. He left there accepting many of Pestalozzi's basic ideas, but set about giving them a sounder philosophical base and organised and systematised them into a more comprehensive and extended form. Although he was critical of some of Pestalozzi's practices, Froebel considered Pestalozzi to be his spiritual father in educational terms (Rusk 1933).

Bruce, Findlay, Read and Scarborough (1995) highlight Froebel's most basic principle as being his belief in connection and unity. He stressed that there should be a connection between everything in the child's life and he imparted to his pupils a thorough knowledge of the inner connections and oneness of all things. Inner connection was in fact for Froebel a law of development, his principle of evolution. He wanted children to live harmoniously with the natural and spiritual world, saying that the child was a child of nature, a child of God and a human child. All children have a need for unity, children long to find a connecting principle or bond to give their lives security and significance. Lack of unity hinders emotional development and Froebel recognised this fact. This recognition enabled him to see, better than other educators, the need and the means of educating and developing the emotions and feelings of the young child. Lilley (1967) says Froebel's work shows a remarkable comprehension of emotional and social development and highlights the fact that in many ways he was very much ahead of his time.

Froebel's philosophy of education encompassed some basic components and these included free self-activity, creativity, social participation, motor expression, spirituality and a loving and pleasant environment. Morally and emotionally Froebel saw the early years as being very important and he believed the child should only encounter good things, as bad early experiences could have long-term negative repercussions. Froebel (1887 p.24) said:

> It is momentous for the present and the future life of anyone that he should assimilate nothing unwholesome, mean or vulgar, nothing questionable or bad. The glances and gestures of all those in the

child's vicinity should be innocent and steadfast, awakening and fostering trust. The environment itself should so far as this is possible be pure and bright, with fresh air, well lit and favourably situated for locality. For unfortunately the impressions assimilated in infancy are scarcely ever eradicated since the child's whole nature like a sensitive plate is exposed to every influence from without. The hardest conflicts encountered by a person and the most adverse and depressing vicissitudes of later life have often their source in this early stage of development.

Froebel, in his writings, declared that the child developed progressively and he insisted that each stage should be fully gone through before progressing to the next, progressing only when the child was ready. Aristotle was one of the first to initiate the idea that we must watch the nature of the child in order to encourage and nurture his various faculties in the proper sequence of their development. Froebel, along with Rousseau, Montessori and others, developed this idea. Rushing or skipping a stage was not a good idea and Froebel was a strong advocate of the view that earlier was not necessarily better. Froebel (1887 p.8) said:

We grant space and time to young plants and animals because we know that in accordance with the laws that live in them, they will develop properly and grow well; young animals and plants are given rest and arbitrary interference with their growth is avoided, because it is known that the opposite practice would disturb their pure unfolding and sound development but the young human being is looked upon as a piece of wax, a lump of clay which man could mould into what he pleases.

Froebel knew that rushing or pushing the child could have a negative impact on his emotional development and he urged educators to let the child be the guide. Elkind (2001) reinforces this idea in *The Hurried Child*.

The Education of Man, originally published in 1826, had a profound effect on the approach to early childhood education, as it changed the way in which children were viewed. In it, Froebel set down his beliefs about cognitive and moral development and he advocated play and self-activity as the main means of achieving development. Froebel, like Comenius, Pestalozzi and later Montessori, was of the opinion that self-activity must be a priority of education and Froebel stressed the fact that experience is the key to development. He said that if words ran ahead of a child's experiences, then all was lost and that education would be hollow, dead and mechanical. Structured play would give the experiences needed to help the child develop holistically. Froebel (1887 p.55) said:

> Play is the purest, most spiritual activity of man at this stage, and at the same time, typical of life as a whole, of the inner hidden natural life in man and all things. It gives therefore, joy, freedom, contentment, inner and outer rest, peace with the world. It holds the sources of all that is good. A child that plays thoroughly with self-active determination, perseveringly until physical fatigue forbids, will surely be a thorough determined man, typical of self-sacrifice for the promotion of the welfare of himself and others.

To assist in the child's growth and development Froebel provided children with many stimulating activities to enhance their creative powers and abilities. He designed a series of instructional materials that he called gifts, occupations and mother songs to help children develop. Froebel's principles and instructional materials have at times been misinterpreted, misunderstood and misused by those who came in contact with them. In particular many have been quick to adapt the practical devices of the gifts and occupations and have misused them, not reflecting on their true significance. According to Liebschner (1988) the true greatness of Froebel's philosophy has at times been dulled by copyists and misguided followers who have missed out on the spirit and true philosophy which he promoted and instead focused on literally interpreting his written word in a prescriptive manner.

Froebel believed that providing a setting similar to the family home within the school environment would provide children with opportunities for interacting socially in a non-threatening manner and thus the idea for the kindergarten came about. In his *Letters on the Kindergarten* (1891 in Rusk 1918) he outlined his hope that the kindergarten would be a place where children's faculties would be developed through self-activity and play, leading to an integrated development of the whole person, ensuring optimal development. All the elements of a society of equals were to be experienced by the child here, establishing an atmosphere of universal goodwill, developing and fostering the habits of sympathy, gratitude and helpfulness, encouraging social, moral and spiritual development. There was also to be an emphasis on the need to develop a stable and trusting relationship between the teacher and the child, creating a genuine bond and a mutual respect. The kindergarten was to provide the ideal world for the child; it was to be an institution where future adults could learn the art of co-ordination, co-operation and leadership, as well as developing the spiritual aspects of their beings. Froebel demanded a happy and harmonious environment for children in the kindergarten and it is now acknowledged that a child's environment has a distinct impact on his personality traits and emotional development. A nurturing and caring environment can build neural pathways that encourage emotional stability, while repeated exposure to stress can create connections that trigger fear and apprehension (Bocchino 1999). Greenman (1988 p.5) claims that:

> An environment is a living, changing system. More than the physical space, it includes the way time is structured and the roles we are expected to play. It conditions how we feel, think, and behave; and it dramatically affects the quality of our lives. The environment either works for us or against us as we conduct our lives.

Lilley (1967), in discussing a selection of Froebel's writings, stresses that Froebel's philosophy had a huge spiritual dimension to it and that he was keenly interested in the spiritual development of the young child. Like Montessori, Froebel did not propose teaching a certain creed, religion or formula. Instead, he advocated having children's lives encompassed with a spiritual awareness - admiration awakened by observation of nature, desire for knowledge stirred among the mysteries and wonders of the universe and the knowledge and experience of love and protection. These would all develop a feeling of spirituality in the child. Later there would be time for words and explanations. Froebel (in Marenholtz Bulow 1887 p.67-68) said:

We must open the eyes of our children that they may learn to know the creator through his creation. Only then, when they have found God the creator through the help of visible things or seen him foreshadowed in them, will they be able to apprehend the meaning of the term God in spirit and in truth, and learn to be Christians. First comes the visible world, and then the invisible truth, the idea. These opposites, visible and invisible must for the young child be united by concrete images, not by word, which at most gives him only a vague impression.

Froebel's theory and practice illustrated that learning succeeds best when undertaken by a self-active and searching mind. Bruce et al. (1995) say that Froebel showed that freedom from rote learning can open the door to real understanding and that freedom for children to explore their environment can result in responsible actions and is not in opposition to harmony and order. Froebel allowed children to experience freedom. His freedom, like Montessori's, did not mean no limits or boundaries. He wanted children to be allowed to do things freely but he realised that there is no such thing as absolute freedom. Everything has limits and boundaries and this allows for social cohesion and security. Froebel (1887) said that true freedom is obedience to a law which is in conformity with man's highest nature and as such is self-imposed and that such obedience will help the child to develop emotionally and morally.

Kilpatrick (1916) severely criticised Froebel's philosophical position and present-day writers also criticise his philosophy, saying it produces a theory of education which takes its model from non-organic life and from plants. This growth theory of education is found lacking by many, yet many such, as Brubacher (1969) support it. Froebel's wealth of writings develop and elaborate his ideas, but many of them were published on a piecemeal basis and come in the form of letters, articles and pamphlets and have suffered from lack of serious analysis. The difficulty of his writing style can be seen in his most famous work *The Education of Man* (1887) and in all his writings there are formidable problems with respect to presentation and meaning, with his language often being vague and philosophical. Yet, there is a remarkable continuity in his work as his basic assumptions and beliefs, once established, never altered. Bruce et al. (1995) state that Froebel's teachings have caused major changes for the better in the education of young children and few theorists have had so clearly marked and so beneficial an influence as he. Liebschner (1988) sets down his greatest contributions to educational thinking as being found in his ideas and observations of how children learn. He was one of the first educationalists to emphasise the importance of a child-centred approach to education and he stressed the fact that children's education should involve parents, specially trained teachers and an appropriately adapted environment. His views on the role of adults as guides, facilitators and learners have contributed significantly to the education of young children. He was called an old fool by many of his contemporaries because of the way he played with children. Yet, Baroness von Marenholtz Bulow (1887) said that he was one to whom future generations would erect monuments because of the way he engaged children and she compared him to the Pied Piper of Hamlin in the way he could get children to interact and engage with him.

The McMillan sisters

In Britain the McMillan sisters, Rachel (1859-1917) and Margaret (1860-1931) held staunch socialist beliefs and their early work centred around working women. However, by the 1890s they had turned their attention to children and in particular they tried to improve the position of poorer children. They were influenced by the work of Seguin (1812-1880), whose work also strongly influenced Montessori, and they were also influenced by Froebel's ideas. Margaret McMillan sat on the Council of the Froebel Society in 1907. The McMillans emphasised relationships, feelings and ideas as well as promoting the physical aspects of learning and moving. They advocated the use of play, believing that children became whole through play and also that play helped children to apply what they were learning and what they already knew (Bruce and Meggitt 1999). In particular, Rachel emphasised free play and in her book, *The Nursery School* (1930 p.80) she said, "most of the best opportunities for achievement lie in the domain of free play". Margaret wrote profusely about the care and education of young children, in her book *Early Childhood* (1900) and in pamphlets such as *Education through the Imagination* (1904), *The Child and the State* (1907) and in *Citizens of Tomorrow* (1906) (in Stewart 1972). Margaret McMillan pioneered the development of nursery schools, seeing them as an extension of the home. She believed in working closely with parents and she also advocated adult learning and training. She proposed feeding children while at school and providing school medical services, believing that children could not learn when they are undernourished, cold or sick. These beliefs were reiterated by Maslow (1970a) in his hierarchy of needs, as he also believed that the child's primary motivation was to meet his physiological needs and that until these were at least partially met he could not concentrate on anything else. Margaret McMillan also placed enormous importance on the level of training of adults working with children and she stressed that they needed to be imaginative and inventive in the way they worked, a belief that underlies education today (Humphreys 1993; National Research Council 2000; Lally 1991).

Rachel, meanwhile, devoted much of her time to teaching children and their parents about hygiene and its impact on health and development, in her position as a sanitary inspector for Kent Education Committee. In 1908, both sisters opened their first school/clinic. Their programme was primarily social in character, with their main focus of attention being cleanliness and health. Despite their efforts, the school was not a success and two years afterwards they moved and set up another school. Again, the school was mainly social in ethos but this time it was a success and in 1911 the school expanded to include an open air camp school for children six to fourteen years of age and a day nursery for the under fives. The curriculum of the nursery school was based on an experiential philosophy with lots of sense training. Care of animals and plants, drama, elocution, singing, art and crafts, water and sand play were also introduced and this development laid the basis for later nursery education in the United Kingdom and they are credited with being the first to use the term 'nursery school'. The life long struggle of the McMillans was for the creation of a more just society. They believed that through education, a new and better society could be achieved. Their interest in the total development of the child and their emphasis on exposure to sunshine, play and attention to children's medical needs are to be highly commended. Though they were primarily political reformers, with their campaign centring mostly on fighting poverty and squalor, they also achieved success in their educational exploits, particularly in the physical and social domains (Bradburn 1989; Bruce and Meggitt 1999; Branscombe et al. 2000).

Steiner

Rudolf Steiner (1861-1925) based his pedagogy and didactics on his belief that the child is trichotomous - comprising body, soul and spirit. He outlined his beliefs in *The Essentials of Education* (1926) and thought of childhood as evolving in three phases:

1. The will, 0-7 when the spirit fuses with the body;
2. The heart, 7-14 years the rhythmic system of the beating heart, the chest and the respiratory system means that feelings are particularly important;
3. The head, from 14 on is the period of thinking.

Steiner believed in reincarnation and he saw the years zero to seven as a time when the child was finding his way, with the reincarnated soul needing protection. He stressed the need for a carefully prepared environment during this period so that the child could develop holistically. Steiner considered the child's emotional development and temperament to be very important and he believed that adults should never go against the child's temperament, but should always go with it. He also stressed the importance of social development, believing that relationships with others were very important and he believed children should have the same teacher for a number of years, in order to build up a relationship (Bruce and Meggitt 1999). Steiner contended that the education of the young child should focus on his will and feelings and he based his curriculum on bodily movement which served the will, and on artistic activity which served emotion. The intellect was allowed to absorb what was appropriate for each individual child and 'real' cognitive education only began in adolescence. Baking, gardening, modelling, painting, singing, dressing up, stories, were all activities in a carefully designed community in the child-centred Waldorf School. However, like Montessori, Steiner has had less influence on the public sector than on the private and his philosophy only ever had a very limited following (Steward 1972).

Montessori

Maria Montessori (1870-1952) introduced a philosophy of education based upon her own personal observations of children and her ideology also followed on the work of past educators and philosophers. After qualifying as a medical doctor in 1896 she joined the staff of Rome University's psychiatric clinic. As part of her duties she was involved with children with special needs and she became convinced that these children would benefit from special education. In order to develop such an education system, Montessori went abroad to study the work of earlier pioneers in the area and for two years after this, she worked with special needs children and was amazed at how much they could learn and develop. Their success led her to the belief that such an education system would be of even greater benefit to children without special needs and for the rest of her life Montessori was devoted to the education of children in general. Prior to her, educators had set about developing an educational system for a particular section of the population. Rousseau, even though his conception of education was very similar to Montessori's, evaded all the difficulties of educational work by expounding his method with reference to the exceptional case of one particular child (Emile). Montessori lived in an age when education was no longer just for the rich and she had to tackle the task of educating all children (Boyd 1914).

Standing (1957) says her genealogical tree could be said to come from Plato, Comenius, Locke, Rousseau, Pestalozzi and Froebel and like these she was intensely dissatisfied with traditional forms of education. As well as being influenced by these she was also inspired by Jean Itard (1775-1838) and Edouard

Seguin (1812-1880), pioneers in the development of special needs education. She developed Seguin's idea of emphasising development through the senses. In his work, he had set about detailing the child's muscular, neural and motor mechanisms and believed that redirecting basic impulses would bring about an improvement in sensory and intellectual development. Following on this, Montessori developed didactic apparatus based on Seguin's principles to help the child develop (Lillard 1972).

Many look on the philosophies of Froebel and Montessori as being profoundly different and incompatible, but according to Rusk (1933 p.31), "were Froebel alive today he would doubtless be the first to acknowledge that the Montessori system, both philosophically and pedagogically, is a natural development of his own". This does not mean that the two are in agreement on all aspects, there are certain differences, yet in spirit they are akin to one another in their attitude to love and reverence for the child as a spiritual being. Differences lie in the details of their systems, but it could be said that Froebel prepared the soil in which Montessori's ideas were later to take root. Although some of Montessori's doctrine is unacceptable to Froebelians, they would concede that it was she who put the child back in the centre of the educational picture, making them realise just how far they were straying from Froebel in imposing a ready-made unity on children, instead of fostering the child's own growth towards unity (Standing 1957). As well as being influenced by those of the past, Montessori herself had a direct and positive influence on many others including Freud, Erikson and Piaget, and Montessorian education is still very much in vogue today.

To prepare for her role as an educator, Montessori returned to university and studied philosophy, psychology and anthropology. Her active life as an educator really began in 1907 when she was asked to direct a day-care centre in a housing project in one of the slum areas of San Lorenzo in Italy. Montessori set up as natural an environment as possible to help the children develop. After that she relied on her own observations of what happened there in order to develop her method. The children in the Montessori classroom began to exhibit extraordinary characteristics, such as a newly developed self-possession, being dignified, working and concentrating for long periods. They also started to show a sense of community and discipline as well as displaying a deep concern and respect for each other and in *The Discovery of the Child* (1967a) Montessori describes these changes in detail. She believed she had identified hitherto unknown and significant facts about children's behaviour. She also realised that in order to consider these observations and developments as universal, she would have to study children in different places and under different conditions. This she did and no matter where she went the results were the same. Word of Montessori's work quickly spread and visitors from all over the world arrived to verify her observations and results. Montessori spent the remainder of her life developing her method, writing, lecturing, travelling, developing schools and teacher training colleges. Through her observations, Montessori became convinced that the child possesses an intense motivation toward his own self-construction and self-realisation and she published her initial findings in 1909 in *The Montessori Method*. She believed the full development of himself is the child's unique and ultimate goal in life. Her main aim was to assist the child's natural development by aiding his growth to full independence and self-sufficiency (Gettman 1987). Montessori stated that the child's whole being and health (mental and physical) literally depended on his constant striving to develop and become himself. She believed that her method enabled children to fulfil their instinctual and personal developmental needs and to go on to create satisfied and well-balanced adults whose innate goodness could shine forth.

Unlike many educational philosophers, Montessori developed an educational method to implement her philosophy. This method was comprised of a prepared environment and also involved an indirect teaching method. The Montessori classroom was to have six basic components: freedom; structure and order; reality and nature; beauty and atmosphere; the Montessori materials; and the development of community life. Her emphasis on the environment is still very much in tune with current beliefs and there are significant correlations between the beliefs of Montessori and the *Reggio Emilia* system which is developing in Italy at present, particularly regarding the environment. The *Reggio* system is a collection of schools for young children where their intellectual, emotional, social, moral and spiritual potential are carefully cultivated and guided. Today in *Reggio* classrooms in Italy two co-equal teachers work as colleagues and the environment is seen as a third teacher. The design and use of spaces is very important and there is an underlying order and beauty in the design and organisation of all the space in the school and of the equipment and materials within it (Chen et al.1998).

As part of developing the whole child Montessori was extremely interested in developing the spiritual dimensions of the young child and this development is detailed in *The Formation of Man* (1989). She felt that, "man, as a spiritual being, has been left to the mercy of outer circumstances and is on the way to becoming a destroyer of his own circumstances" (Montessori 1989 p.10). The real danger that was threatening humanity was the emptiness in men's souls, all the rest was a mere consequence of this. Life, according to Montessori, was extremely complex and was fraught with contradictions. It was a time of gloom and of spiritual darkness. Men were basking in the light of their outer achievements but were enveloped in darkness spiritually. Humans were in desperate need of spiritual tranquillity and peace. They needed to get to know themselves and Montessori believed it was the child who could reveal to others the secrets of the spiritual life of man, as from the spiritual point of view, the child was the most powerful being in the world. If one wanted to see a pure being who had neither political nor philosophical theologies, this neutral being was to be found in the child, according to both Froebel and Montessori. The child was the exhibitor of the mystery of humanity and others could discover in him a fundamental goodness that adult lives belied. A new humanity could be achieved through the child.

Montessori felt that in a future civilisation, spiritual values would take precedence over purely physical ones and that humanity had an opportunity of becoming regenerated through a new way of educating its children (Lubienski Wentworth 1999). However, to achieve this, a different type of education would have to be available to children, one that prioritised spiritual development.

Spirituality was to be aimed at in education, it could not be taught directly. A reverence for truth, inner as well as outer, would allow children to grow, leading to a better understanding of human purposes. Education was to inspire in children an admiration for all those who had gone before, who possessed the flame which had lighted the path of humanity. This would, according to Montessori, uplift the soul and conscience.

Up to six, Montessori says the child absorbs most from his environment and it is at this stage that it is vital to nourish the child spiritually. Children could be immersed in a spiritual atmosphere and the whole spiritual world could be opened up to them (Montessori 1967a). Education should recognise and observe this. Educators should admire, know, love and serve the inner forces of the child and should set about co-operating with the child so that his personality, with its inner presence, was potentialised. Montessori (1979 p.99) said, "We must set ourselves to see the marvels hidden in the child and help him to unfold them". To date, Montessori said the child's soul and his spiritual development have been neglected because the child who holds within him the possibility of progress in the soul, has always been regarded as the son of man rather than the father of man.

Education, according to Montessori, had caused the child's soul to dry up and had made his spiritual value wither away. She said society must prepare a world and an education capable of ensuring the optimum spiritual development of the child. Such a task was no small undertaking, but it was worth doing because it was about saving humanity. It would involve full spiritual development of the child as well as enhancing the child's value as an individual:

> The child is both a hope and a promise for mankind. If we therefore
> mind this embryo as our most precious treasure, we will be working
> for the greatness of humanity (Montessori 1992 p.31).

If, however, adults continued to misunderstand and mistreat children, the child's spirit would sicken, he would become impoverished and all the potential wealth that he possessed would come to nothing. Montessori's recognition of the importance of spirituality formed an ever-present background to her philosophy. Although a devout Catholic herself, she did not push any one religious stance, but saw in all children and in all school subjects, opportunities for developing the human spirit and therefore treated both with a corresponding dignity and respect.

Montessori recognised that children are social beings and in *What You Should Know About Your Child* (1961) she said that if the child is to adapt himself to the environment he has to take part in public life and to be a witness to the customs which characterise his race. If the child is not given this exposure, he will become repressed, underdeveloped and deformed, eventually becoming incapable of adaptation because he has been deprived of the means necessary to develop socially. Montessori said that there was an ever-increasing number of children who were backward, who lacked character and initiative, who hesitated and who grew up to be unbalanced adults, suffering from psychic abnormalities, because of a lack of social development in their early years. Throughout history, small children always took part in adult social life, since they were seldom separated from their mothers. However, modern society, according to Montessori, condemned the child to a lonely and unstimulating childhood by leaving children in the care of nannies in lonely nurseries, depriving them of contact with parents and others. As well as that, the education they received further compounded this isolation and lack of social development, according to Montessori. She stressed; "The need for social life, the need to go out and see people and converse with them, is a great need of the child" (1961 p.27).

Montessori claimed the desire to associate with other people is something so strong that it is possible "that some of the errors of adult society are due only to the fact that education of young children has aimed so much at frustrating this desire" (Montessori 1989 p.104). She said that young children must experience social life through living and through experiences. If children do not get a chance to engage in a true social life, they will not develop a sense of discipline, morality or respect for themselves or for others. Montessori (1989 p.109) believed schools were not adequately preparing children for social life and were replacing "true social life with a degrading caricature of it". Yet the contribution of the Montessori classroom to the development of a social life sometimes goes unnoticed, because of the emphasis on the inner growth of the child. However, in *The Absorbent Mind* (1967a) Montessori detailed the child's social development and she stressed that the child needed to deal with himself before and as well as relating to others. She said social development was more than mutual contact, as a long period of inner growth and indirect preparation was also vital for the child, to enable him to relate well to others. Denial of the importance of inner development denies the child the help he needs to become what he is intended to be, that is, a social being.

Montessori has been severely criticised for her views on social development. Boyd (1914) criticises her for overrating individual factors and individual development in education and says she underrates real social development. He says she does not emphasise the importance of group work or group play. Separate tables and mats are provided so that the child can be isolated and have independence and this does tend to de-emphasise social development as we know it. Kilpatrick (1914 p.15-16) in *The Montessori System Examined* also criticises her because, "she does not provide situations for more adequate social co-operation". He also criticises the Montessori materials as not being sufficiently social and the one area that he looked on favourably was the practical life exercises as they were useful and met real and immediate social needs. Education and life demand continual adjustment and readjustment to our environment and to others. Froebel's philosophy tends to take greater cognisance of this and he advocates the social grouping more, as well as encouraging each individual child to express his own thoughts and his own interests. Froebel also emphasises and encourages co-operative work and play, developing interdependence, independence, dependence and co-operative spirit.

Montessori stressed the fact that all was not well with people's emotions. She said there was a lack of balance between progress in the environment and in human progress. In *The Child, Society and The World* (1979) she said that despite all the discoveries and achievements of man, he still wasn't happy. Society, according to her, needed to awaken from its deep-rooted errors regarding young children and should instead set about preparing an environment adapted to their supreme psychological needs. Montessori believed that growth and development through self-activity was one of nature's greatest miracles. The problem for education was to give the child the necessary help (excluding any unnecessary help) so that he could develop independence. Independence would then help the child's self-esteem, self-confidence and self-reliance to develop. It was only by leading the child to the fullest development of his powers that he could develop emotionally.

Montessori and Freud have both contributed greatly to our understanding of human emotions. Freud studied unconscious drives and their manifestations in emotionally disturbed adults within a special therapeutic situation. Conversely, Montessori studied the behaviour of 'normalised' children in a specially prepared pedagogic situation. Both sought to explain the phenomena they observed and both found general patterns in the development of the human being, thus confirming and complementing each other. Montessori endeavoured to provide an environment where children could develop emotionally, giving them freedom so that they could act according to their inner needs, rhythms and tempo. As a result of which, these children showed characteristics not generally attributed to young children, such as prolonged concentration and repetition of exercises for their own sake. They also showed a sense of maturity, character and self-control not generally seen in children of similar ages. Children who showed maladaptive behaviour on entering Montessori classrooms also changed. Such behaviour disappeared once the child began to concentrate and they started to develop self-control and self-acceptance through the discovery of themselves and their capabilities (Montessori Junior 1992).

Moral development is a very important aspect in the overall holistic development of children, according to Montessori, and she envisaged that in the Montessori classroom a society by cohesion would develop. She wanted the child to learn to live within society and to be able to adapt himself to it. Children were to be taught to respect and to follow the demands of an ordered environment, as well as respecting the people in it. According to Lubesnki Wentworth (1999) a salient characteristic of the Montessori method is that character building goes hand in hand with cognitive development. Also, the attributes of empathy, respect for others and the ability to know right from wrong were expected to develop more or less spontaneously, without much help from the teacher. *The Child, Society and the World* (1979 p.26) outlines Montessori's conviction that "character formation cannot be taught as it comes from experience and not from explanation". In *To Educate the Human Potential* (1948) Montessori highlighted her belief that the question of moral education was a very difficult one to deal with. She said moral development was not just about correcting and preaching, nor was it possible to deal with it through direct teaching, it was correlated to the psychological life of the child and to society as a whole. The teaching of morality had to be indirect - the adult, the child and the environment being a trinity.

Montessori saw a great need for change and she wanted to build an environment where the child's individual consciousness could develop. She believed that moral development was not just an internalised penal code impressed on the child by an outsider. "Moral education is about the development of character and neither threat nor promises are needed but conditions of life" (Montessori 1963b p.46). She said the great motivator of moral behaviour and development should be love and an inner desire to do right and that exposure to the right type of environment helped this develop. Lillard (1972) believes that through the freedom given to the child in the Montessori environment, the child has a unique opportunity to reflect on his own behaviour and actions. He can determine the consequences of his behaviour both for himself and for others. This freedom also allows him to develop his own will, it gives him permission to test himself against the limits of reality and to develop a sense of what is fair and what is not. It also allows him to develop respect for others, for himself and for his environment, thus helping him to become a truly moral being. Freedom, in the Montessori philosophy, is not freedom in any absolute sense. What Montessori wanted, was for the child to have freedom from undue influence by others, particularly the teacher, as well as having the liberty to make his own choices within the structured possibilities offered. Montessori believed that it was only by choosing to adhere to the discipline of learning from this responsive environment that personal autonomy was achievable.

Lubienski Wentworth (1999 p.12) quotes Montessori as saying: "Liberty is not being free to do anything one likes. It is being able to act without help".

Many criticisms have been made about Montessori and her method. She has been criticised for the harshness of her structured apparatus and for her set and formal, inflexible use of them. She has been accused of wanting all activities and concepts spelt out in prescriptive detail. Froebel provided materials such as his gifts and occupations but he did not set down so rigidly how they were to be used. Montessori intended developing each sense separately and the apparatus was to be observed and graded systematically. Froebel set about training the senses incidentally and simultaneously with the children being in reach of an abundant variety of materials to be mixed and matched as they saw fit. Also, Montessori apparatus is not designed to help the child show his feelings or to express himself, the apparatus is designed almost entirely for sense training and the use of informal free play and imagination is not emphasised or encouraged (Lillard 1972). Dewey (1916) criticises the Montessori material as limiting the child. He says the child is, "free to choose which apparatus he will use, but never to choose his own ends, never to bend a material to his own plans" (ibid. 1916 p.157-158). The materials must be used in a particular and prescribed way. If the child uses it in a way not prescribed he is seen as misusing the materials and is to be stopped. Like every educational method created by one mind, the Montessori system reflects the limitations of its author's personality and in Montessori's case this method is underlined by her medical and scientific concerns and has an element of austerity in it. Many of Montessori's practical suggestions are of great value in themselves, but are insufficient as a basis for the reconstruction of education that Montessori herself aspired to. Her methods and philosophy were an aggregation of methods and her own education, knowledge and experiments became for her the measure of truth (Boyd 1914).

Yet, Montessori education has special significance in our contemporary world, since mankind has disrespected the laws of nature and may in fact have endangered the life of the whole planet we inhabit. Montessori regarded man's interdependence with nature as both spiritual and physical. Botany and zoology (now called ecology) are an integral part of the Montessori curriculum, as are respect for self, others, nature and the environment, and are very pertinent in today's society. The child, like all living creatures, has his own natural laws and Montessori, unlike many in today's world, took cognisance of these. Contemporary society, with its emphasis on consumerism and materialism, needs to refer to Montessori's underlying philosophy. Also the critical importance of first hand experiences, of being in tune with children, of social and moral development, of liberty and of child-centredness had previously been mentioned by Plato, Comenius, Rousseau, Pestalozzi and by Froebel in different ways. However, it was Montessori who attempted to relate theory to practice in a real and meaningful way (Lillard 1972). Also Montessori herself gave us the best advice to follow in her concluding remarks at the Ninth International Montessori Congress in London in May 1951. This is where she said: "The highest honour and the deepest gratitude you can pay me is to turn your attention from me in the direction in which I am pointing - the child" (Montessori in Standing 1957 p.59).

Dewey

John Dewey (1859-1952) was deeply influenced by Darwin's theory of evolution and by the strides that were occurring in science and psychology in his day. His educational philosophy grew out of his experiments in the establishment of an ideal school in connection with his pedagogical work in the University of Chicago. He never had any formal teacher training, but he observed closely the goings on in the laboratory and ideal school and concentrated on the theoretical aspects of education (Boyd 1921; Moorish 1967). Dewey considered that every social experience was essentially educative and he advocated a problem-solving method to be used in teaching young children with the need to know coming from the child himself. Like Locke, he stressed that children learn by doing and he believed that school does not prepare us for life but rather *is* life. In *Democracy and Education* (1916) he put forward the view that society could only transform or reproduce itself by sharing its experiences with the young. Dewey argued that education is the process of forming fundamental intelligence and emotional dispositions and that philosophy is the general theory of forming such dispositions. Thus, philosophy could be defined as the general theory of education - education was philosophy in action.

Rusk (1918) says that Dewey was a great educationalist because he was also a great philosopher and he claims that no one since the Sophists (the great ancient Greek philosophy teachers) had so intimately identified philosophy and education as Dewey had done. In his *Pedagogic Creed* (1897) Dewey stressed the psychological and sociological side of the educational process. Schools were to be special places which concentrated on the best way of using all children's powers for social ends and of developing them as social beings. He also said that traditional education separated the social classes through academic elitism - separating leisure and labour, people and nature, mind and body, thought and action. Education itself was isolated from society and all this isolation meant that an understanding of the whole of knowledge was impossible, life lacked connections and was fragmented, schools tried to fit the child to the school instead of *vice versa*. Traditional education was, according to Dewey, a one way channel of communication with direct and didactic methods which involved rote learning and memorisation (Smith 1984).

Dewey believed education needed to change and one of the areas that he encouraged was moral development. He believed it was developed by participation in the common aims and needs of society and he stressed that there was little done in schools to organise pupils as a social unit and this neglected children's social and moral development. He wanted to see a change in how social and moral problems were dealt with, as the old ways were incapable of dealing effectively with the changing requirements of human events. *The Reconstruction in Philosophy* (1920) and *The Quest for Certainty* (1929) outline his approach to moral development and character formation through scientific psychology, using reflective intelligence as a means of modifying behaviour. In *School and Society and the Child and the Curriculum* (1900 p.28) Dewey said:

> In the schoolroom, the motive and cement of social organisation are alike wanting. Upon the ethical side, the tragic weakness of the present school is that it endeavours to prepare future members of the social order in a medium in which the conditions of the social spirit are eminently wanting.

In *Democracy and Education* (1916) he stressed that the development of democratic habits and character must begin in the earliest years of a child's educational experience. The school was to be viewed as an extension of civil society and the young child encouraged to participate as a member of a community actively pursuing interests in co-operation with others - a process of self-directed learning guided by the cultural resources provided by teachers. Dewey thought this was the best way to prepare the child to be a responsible member of a democratic society. He advocated helping children develop for complete living in their social world and his experimental school aimed at realising this ideal. Like Pestalozzi, Dewey found the model for his ideal school in the ideal home and the school was to be an extended family (Boyd 1921).

Dewey drew on Rousseau's work and advocated linguistic development, construction, artistic expression and he highlighted the value of discovery and enquiry. He also prioritised social and emotional development. He wanted schools to be places of activity, occupation and social interaction, not just places for formal study. The aim of life, according to Dewey, was growth. School was to be a place of natural growth and adjustment, with children being taught how to negotiate continuously with the changing world of experience about them. Education, as Dewey found it, was a dead experience. He advocated that educators make use of children's experiences and he stressed that the primary unit of life was the relative experience of each person in transaction with the environment, with each individual thinking his own way through problems by intelligent reconstruction of the situation as he saw it. The method of discovery was to be a basic teaching method, allowing children to think and reason for themselves.

Dewey made philosophical thoughts relevant to the needs of children, his was a live philosophy and he wanted it to be judged by its consequences. He advocated self-realisation of the child and children all over the world are educated differently today because of him. Dewey allowed children to experience more satisfaction from ordinary everyday life experiences. He prioritised social development and interaction; he stressed the widespread benefits of leisure, culture and participation, the importance of the process not the product, the need to experience challenge, joy and contentment for each individual child and for children as a group. He saw beauty in industry, in science, in democracy and in people. However, he rejected all things religious and though brought up a Christian, he later became an atheist. His early work (1879-1892) had an explicitly Christian orientation, underpinned by Hegelian idealistic metaphysics. However, in his middle years, from 1892-1924, he gave up his Christian beliefs and emphasised scientific method and rationality. In the later period of his life (1925-1952) Dewey wrote of the common faith found in experience, emphasising social action, participation and naturalistic metaphysics. Although he had long left organised religion behind, Dewey's funeral service was held in the New York City Community Church. This had as its purpose a faith in life and the realisation on earth of community life, ideals which Dewey approved of. There was a time when the name of John Dewey was rejected in religious education circles as he (Dewey) rejected institutional religion, claiming that such groups clung to outmoded beliefs and practices which retarded the growth of the distinctly human in persons. Though rejecting institutional religion of every kind, he stressed the importance of what many call the spiritual. Since the 1970s Dewey has made something of a comeback with Christian thinkers and these have increasingly abandoned negative pre-judgements about him and have begun to let his ideas speak on their own merits (Ratcliff 1992).

Dewey made some very positive contributions to the education of children; in particular he tried to change the focus of school work, seeing the need for self-activity and play. He prioritised social development and he stressed the social responsibility of schools and wanted schools to form society and not *vice versa*. His life and philosophy were a constant struggle and search for an integration of all thought (Roth 1962). Dewey promoted progressive education and he was a part of the progressive tendencies of his age and country. According to Wise (1964) he is the most important American philosopher to date. Dewey's philosophy underwent constant revision. He stated everything was temporary, nothing ultimate and he stressed that knowledge was an instrument, not an end in itself, hence the title of his philosophy - *instrumentalism*. He believed that practice inspired theory and that educational practices and direct experience in the field originate and determine educational ends and theories. Yet, at times his teachings have been cited as being anti-intellectual, anti-religious, radical and even subversive. However, Rusk (1918) says that Dewey's ideas brought education into line with contemporary life and that his philosophy and application of it called for both philosophy and education to reflect modern thought and to develop an education system where social development and learning by experience occurred. He also systematised the philosophies of his predecessors - in particular those of Comenius, Pestalozzi and Froebel - resulting in a child-centred, integrated, environmentally orientated curriculum and a heuristic approach to education under the guidance of a trained teacher. One of the outcomes of his ideas is the project approach to education – an approach which integrates all subject matter around children's real life experiences and encourages them to engage in projects of their choosing. He remains one of the best known North American educational theorists and his writings on the interrelations and connections between philosophy, education, experience and politics are acknowledged and respected throughout the world (Smith 1984; Branscombe et al. 2000).

Isaacs

Susan Isaacs (1885-1948), like many others, felt the influence of Friedrich Froebel. She was also influenced by psychoanalysts such as Freud and Klein and she ran her school along Deweyian lines. Isaacs made detailed observations of children in her Malting House School in Cambridge during the 1930s. She put forward a theory of child development in her book *Intellectual Growth in Young Children* (1931). In this she outlines five phases of development, with the child passing imperceptibly from one phase to the next. She conceded that individual children differ widely in their progress and she firmly disagreed with Piaget's stage theory (Moorish 1967).

Isaacs valued play, believing it gave children freedom to feel, think and relate. She was intensely interested in children's emotional and social development and she advocated in particular the use of dramatic play in aiding children's development in these areas. In her books *Social Development in Young Children* (1933) and *The Psychological Aspects of Child Development* (1935) she described children's relationships, feelings and fears. She stressed that through play children can move in and out of reality and can begin to balance their feelings, relationships and ideas. In the *Nursery Years* (1968) and in *The Children we Teach* (1932) Isaacs cited children, not schools and teaching, as being important. She favoured teachers and educators having a wide knowledge of child development and believed that they should observe children in their daily lives.

Isaacs repudiated the sudden contrast between pre-school and primary education and she said it impacted negatively on the child, emotionally and psychologically. She said that the period from two to five years was the most difficult period of a young child's life and she believed formal education should not begin until the age of seven, stressing the importance of the attachment of the young child to his home and family. She valued parents as the primary educators in their child's life and she asked educators to acknowledge the child's feelings towards his family in order to facilitate a healthy transition from home to school. She believed that social and intellectual development were connected at every stage and that both should be optimised. She advocated the need for smaller classes, for group games and social interaction highlighting their social, emotional and moral value. She also stressed the need for children to take turns, to learn to cope with failure as well as success and the need to play with others. She also said children needed the opportunity to be both followers and leaders as all these, "offer rich food for social growth" (Isaacs 1932 p.99).

Isaacs emphasised that children are practical people, concerned with doing and experiencing things. The child's active social experiences, his own doing, thinking and talking, should be the chief means of his education (Isaacs 1932). She advocated looking at children's inner feelings and she encouraged children to express all their feelings. Like Froebel and the McMillans, she saw the nursery school as an extension of, not a substitute for, the home and thus, like many of her predecessors, Isaacs hoped to help optimise young children's holistic development (Gardner 1969).

Conclusion

This chapter examined the evolution of our beliefs regarding the holistic development of the young child; as well as concentrating on those who stressed the importance of social, emotional, moral and spiritual development from the time of Plato to the mid-twentieth century. It took the form of a review and critical analysis and highlights the fact that since the time of Plato there has been a recognition that optimally developing the social, emotional, moral and spiritual aspects of the child is vital for overall development and that development of these areas must be the foundations of all early years settings. These ideas have remained constant throughout the history of early childhood education and care, as have the contentions that active experience and play are vital to the learning process and that learning is most effective when it builds on the interests of the learner. This begs the question, 'have we taken on board what past philosophers and educators tried to tell us?' The following four chapters will reinforce the fact that our predecessors were correct in stressing these areas within the holistic development of the child. However, the chapters will also show that much work needs to be done if today's children are to reach their potential in these areas.

CHAPTER THREE

Emotional Development

Introduction

In our contemporary world there seems to be a creeping sense of emotions out of control. An emotional sickness is occurring with increasing numbers of people, including young children, showing aggressive tendencies and also suffering from depression and desperation. Emotional problems are seeping into and poisoning children's early experiences and unfortunately emotional maladaptation seems to be a universal price of modern life for children (Goleman 1996). The National Children's Strategy in Ireland (2000) acknowledges that there is a growing debate about the well-being of the general population of children and the effect on them of the modern world. The Strategy (2000 p.45) says:

> There is disquiet at what appears to be growing levels of substance abuse and violence, the number of children with mental health problems, teenage suicides and the number of children in crisis appearing before the courts".

Depression, a problem not much associated with young children in the past, is being increasingly recognised as a growing problem in the lives of our young citizens. It can manifest itself in behaviour which is withdrawn, disruptive and anxious (Fawcett 2000). At present, many children are not happy emotionally and Dr Pat McKoen (1999), Chairperson of the Irish Depression Support Group AWARE, states that children of all ages can suffer feelings of depression and some have feelings of self-worth so low that they may want to harm themselves. Is this how we want our children to feel?

More and more people are coming to the end of their emotional and personal resources and are suffering from burn-out, anxiety, desperation and a plethora of stress-related illnesses. As Purcell (2001) says, this is the age of anxiety. Greater output is demanded of everyone, including children, while less and less support mechanisms are available. Today's children have to cope with pressures far more subtle and complicated than those experienced in the past. Over the last four centuries science and technology have become powerful cultural influences and the material and consumerist sides of life are stressed with a de-emphasis on what people feel. Yet feelings and emotions are the threads that hold life, and in particular mental life, together (Hannan 1995).

Importance of the early years for emotional development

Brazelton (1992) claims there is a growing body of evidence that shows that success in school and in later life depends, to a surprising extent, on the emotional characteristics formed in the first four to five years of a child's life. That is, in the years before children enter formal education. Thus, it appears that the best opportunity for shaping and encouraging children's emotional development is in the earliest years, as although these capacities do continue to grow throughout the later school years, the emotional abilities that children acquire and develop in later life build on those of the earliest years.

Dyer (1998) backs Brazelton, claiming that emotions and feelings are one of the most important aspects of a child's life. Yet Dyer goes on to say that the emotional aspect of child development is almost completely ignored because of the over-emphasis on cognitive development, even though emotion takes precedence in almost all of life's important decisions and situations. The first three or four years of life are a period when a child's brain grows to about two thirds of its full size and evolves in complexity at a faster rate than it ever will again. During this stage, vital kinds of learning are occurring, emotional learning and development being foremost amongst them. Severe stress or neglect at this vital time can damage a child's learning centres and though this can be remedied to some degree, the impact of early experiences and learning is profound:

> A young child who cannot focus his attention, who is suspicious rather than trusting, sad or angry rather than optimistic, destructive rather than respectful and one who is overcome with anxiety, preoccupied with frightening fantasy and feels generally unhappy about himself - such a child has little opportunity at all, let alone equal opportunity to claim the possibilities of the world as his own (National Center for Clinical Infant Programs 1992 p.13).

Thus, it appears that the key skills of emotional intelligence and development have critical periods in childhood, with each representing a window for helping children instill beneficial emotional habits or conversely, if missed, making it much more difficult to offer corrective lessons later. The human brain is by no means fully developed at birth and it continues to be shaped throughout life. However, children are born with many more neurons than their mature brain will retain, so through a process called pruning, the brain loses some neural connections that are used infrequently. Thus, experiences in childhood sculpt the brain and this massive pruning and sculpting of neural networks in childhood may be an underlying reason why early emotional traumas and hardships have such pervasive and enduring effects later (Goleman 1996).

Implications of emotional development

Prioritising human emotions is vital for many reasons. Denham (1998) highlights the repercussions for children who are not developed emotionally, claiming they are at long-term risk for depression, aggressiveness, violent crime, problems in relationships and parenting as well as being at risk for poor physical and mental health, including being more prone to addictions and self-destruction. Borysenko (1987) claims that a clear link between emotional well-being and physical health has been established. She says the connection between the ability to manage emotions and the functioning of the immune system are clearly documented. The dangers of helplessness and the feeling of a loss of control contribute to illness. Conversely, a willingness to be fully aware, to break the anxiety cycle and to manage emotional responses contributes to health. These facts help to indicate just how important emotional development really is.

As well as this, our inner world is very different from our outer world and part of that inner world involves the development of the emotions. Inner development is different for every child and the development of one's inner world as a self-accepting human being involves taking full responsibility for that inner development. No one else is capable of controlling what goes on inside them. Failure to accept this will result in children who blame, complain, whine, seek approval, who believe they do not have the capacity to make decisions or to cope with the inevitable ups and downs of life. Children who learn to handle their emotions in an appropriate manner are more effective at soothing themselves when upset and get upset less often. They also become more biologically relaxed, having lower levels of stress hormones and lower physiological indicators of emotional arousal. Such children are also more popular with and better liked by peers. They are better able to focus on the task at hand and can harness the emotions they experience more productively. They are also seen by other adults and teachers as more socially skilled, are rated as having fewer behavioural problems and can pay attention better, so are more effective learners. Thus, they are better prepared both for life and for learning (Humphreys 1996).

Schweinhart and Weikart (1993, 1997) through their longitudinal study, show the positive long-term implications that a quality early years setting can have on holistic development. In particular, it resulted in improved social and emotional development. Also, the work of Siraj-Blatchford (1996), Donaldson (1978) and Vygotsky (1978) have all highlighted the importance of becoming emotionally capable. In essence, optimum emotional development is a vital element in our increasingly pluralist society as emotional competence enhances human survival (Lappe and Dubois 1994).

Psychopathologies

Not prioritising children's emotional development can lead to the development of mental health disorders and psychopathologies, since many if not most of these are emotionally based. Mental health is optimised by emotional order and what mental health problems and psychopathologies often reflect is a breakdown or ceasing of emotional development. The child experiences severe and distressing psychological symptoms which means that normal functioning is seriously impaired and in severe cases the child experiencing the symptoms can no longer cope, resulting in complete mental breakdown (Mental Health Association of Ireland 2002).

Researchers claim that childhood emotional disorders/mental health problems occur in two broad categories: a) externalising disorders characterised by anger and aggression; and b) internalising disorders characterised by sadness, anxiety, fear and depression (Oatley and Jenkins 1996). The Department of Health (2002) in Britain claims that between 10 and 20 per cent of children have psychological problems (such as those listed above) that are severe enough to require help. They also say that two in every one hundred children under age twelve are so depressed that they would benefit from professional help. Offend, Boyle and Racine (1989) say that while most children fall within the category of normal, typical research has shown that up to 10 per cent of school children have a mental disorder. They go on to say that a substantial proportion of these children have more than one mental disorder, being co-morbid. For example, children with depression also show signs of anxiety disorders while children with conduct disorders often have symptoms of hyperactivity. These figures are consistent with mental health surveys from other countries such as Garralda and Bailey (1986); Rutter, Tizard and Yule (1976); Velez, Johnson and Cohen (1989). Research on pre-schoolers in the last ten years also identified similar if not higher percentages of children as having psychological difficulties varying from excessive aggression and non-compliance to withdrawal and anxiety (Campbell 1995; Landy, Peters, Arnold, Allen, Brookes and Jewell 1998). These researchers suggest that half of pre-schoolers with such problems will continue to have difficulties unless they receive costly and intense interventions and even then they may never recover fully. Yet, many researchers claim that this incidence could be decreased by prioritising emotional development and by teaching children how to deal positively with the emotions they experience. Brian Mooney (2001), President of the Guidance Counsellors of Ireland, backs this contention. He says he is at a loss to understand why we continue to neglect emotional development. He cites being at a conference listening to men and women who had spent years dealing with the consequences of mental illness. Listening to them he felt an overwhelming sense of the sheer waste of human life involved. Most of them attributed their eventual illness to feelings of anxiety, inadequacy and lack of self-esteem dating from childhood. He suggests that if these people had received the proper guidance and help when they were young, their lives might have been different. He goes on to say that even today there is indifference to the emotional and personal problems of young children and their families. He asks why are we not providing our children with the necessary support structures to build self-confidence and self-esteem. I also wonder why we neglect children's emotional development.

Research highlights six principal stresses or risks for childhood psychopathology - conflict between parents; parental depression or other psychiatric problems; neglect, abuse and other such features in the parent-child relationship; poor socio-economic status; large family size; and parental criminality (Oatley and Jenkins 1996). One of the most consistent findings for longitudinal studies of development is that one or even two risk factors, unless they are extreme, rarely have a negative impact on development. However, as the number of risk factors increases the negative effect is not just additive but multiplicative. The existence of four or more risk factors can lead not just to four times the risk in development but rather to a sixteen- fold increase in difficulties. On the reverse, in the same way, the number of protective factors (for example personal characteristics within the child such as good social skills; a positive temperament; high intelligence; a secure relationship with a warm, empathic adult; or a social environment or community that reinforces and supports positive efforts made by the child) can also act as what is called a 'cumulative protection index' (Bradley, Whiteside, Mundform and Casey 1994); Sansor, Oberklaid, Pedlow and Prior (1991). Thus, by prioritising children's emotional development through high quality early years experiences, the effects of home/personal stresses/risk factors can be lessened and the prevalence of psychopathologies reduced. Early years settings and society in general can do much to protect children from the harmful effects of stressful home environments if they ensure that optimum emotional development is high on the agenda.

Early emotional stresses can affect neuron development and can lead to depression even decades later. However, teaching children more productive and positive ways of looking at their lives and difficulties lowers their risk of depression, as emotional competence plays a role over and above familial and economic factors in a child's life. Long-term studies of children brought up in the most difficult of circumstances show that those who were resilient to the most grinding hardships tended to share key emotional skills and competencies. These included a winning sociability that drew people to them, a feeling of self-confidence, the ability to recover quickly from upsets, an optimistic persistence in the face of frustration and failure and an easy-going nature (Garmezy 1987). It is within the brief of early years practitioners and settings to enhance the development of these key emotional skills if the will is there. So are we doing this?

The Department of Health (2002) in Britain gives a list of strategies to stave off and/or cope with emotional and psychological problems if and when they arise. Being creative - scribbling, drawing, painting, making a collage - these are all seen as being good ways of converting a negative feeling into something more positive. They advise people to let out their emotions - to cry, be angry, scream - and they warn against bottling up emotions as this only causes more problems. They also suggest listening to music, seeing a film, going for a walk, connecting with nature, giving one's self the time and space to think. See friends, they say, it's good for mental well-being. Exercising regularly is a good way of converting anxiety and negative feelings into positive energy, they claim. Talking about one's feelings and finding someone to tell your worries to is also strongly advocated. All these strategies could easily be adapted and developed for use with young children. They would enhance emotional development as well as helping children who are already showing emotional problems. The Irish National Children's Strategy (2000) also stresses that children need opportunities to relax, have fun, exercise their imaginations and cultivate a sense of the aesthetic if they are to enjoy optimal mental and emotional well-being. This clearly has implications for public policy and key service areas such as education and health, as children have to be supported to reach optimal emotional maturity. Do we provide such supports?

Recognising the critical importance of emotional development and finding strategies to cultivate it are essential. Realising when and how children are at risk for developmental delays and learning to recognise disturbance in expected milestones are also important. When milestones of emotional development are not negotiated successfully, young children are at risk of psychopathology, both at that time and later in life. Knowing the risk factors, identifying delays in the development of emotions and finding ways to intervene are vital if the centrality of emotional development is to be taken seriously (Knitzner 1993; Oatley and Jenkins 1996).

Nature *versus* nurture

From the first hours of life, children show marked individual differences in their behaviour and emotions, and such differences are called temperament. Temperament is defined as the stable, early-appearing collection of individual personality attributes which are believed to have a hereditary base. However, stability and change in an infant's emotionality are affected over time by the emotional tones of the caring environment (Goldsmith 1993). Thus, a huge debate has grown as to whether nature or nurture is the determining factor in emotions. Goleman (1996) says a child's genetic heritage endows him with a series of emotional structures that help to determine his temperament. However, he goes on to state that the brain's circuitry is highly malleable so temperament is not destiny.

To some degree every child has a favoured emotional range. Temperament is part of one's genetic lottery that has a role in the child's development but experience can modify it. Experiences can have a profound impact on temperament, either accentuating or muting an innate predisposition. Our emotional and social lives are governed by a layer of neural structures known as the limbic system and each child is born with his own unique emotional makeup. This is then impacted upon by the unique environment in which the child is brought up - his family and social world; his experiences of tenderness or abuse; cuddling or criticism; attention or neglect; discipline or disorder; by the forms of emotional display and social interaction he sees modelled by those around him. Nature and nurture combine and the child's limbic system becomes wired to produce a singular human personality (Eliot 1999).

The huge plasticity of a child's brain means that experiences during those vital early years can have a lasting impact on the sculpturing of neural pathways. Kagan's work (1981) is a prime example of this, showing clearly that the emotional lessons and responses children learn as they grow are vital. The habits of emotional management that are repeated over and over again during childhood help mould the brain's circuitry. This means that childhood provides a crucial window of opportunity for shaping lifelong emotional responses. Habits acquired in childhood become ingrained in the basic synaptic wiring of the neural architecture and the older a child becomes the harder they are to change. Thus, both nature and nurture contribute to a child's emotional development. Genes give children the raw materials out of which to build their emotions. They specify the kind of nervous system the child will have, the kinds of neural process in which it can engage and the kinds of bodily functions it can control. Yet the exact way each child acts, thinks and feels in a particular situation is determined by many other factors not predestined by genes. Eliot (1999) agrees that nature and nurture are both important. However, she contends that although we can do little to change a child's genes, a great deal can be done about the kind of environment we provide for our children, so it is this on which we should concentrate our attention.

Interaction of different developmental areas

Emotional development impacts on and is impacted upon by all the other areas of development, in particular social, cognitive, moral and spiritual. The link between children's emotions and other aspects of their development has only recently been emphasised, as in the past little attention was paid to the affective aspects of development. There is increasing evidence and recognition that emotional abilities have been under-rated in the role they play in helping to ensure a successful and fulfilling life. Both rational and affective abilities are now seen as being equally influential in determining what people achieve and how they enjoy life. Yet, the ability to tune into the feelings of others, to read body language, to listen actively and to express emotions and feelings have all been neglected and are in danger of becoming unused and redundant, due to the over-emphasis on academic learning (O'Donnchadha 2000).

Meadows (1994) describes emotions as the 'Cinderella' of cognitive development and claims that the over-emphasis on cognitive development has led to the under development of other areas of vital importance to children. Goleman (1996 p.36) says, "academic intelligence offers virtually no preparation for the turmoil - or opportunity - life's vicissitudes bring". He goes on to say that I.Q. is important but childhood abilities such as controlling emotions, handling frustration and getting on with other people make the greater difference for success in life. Early years practitioners are beginning to realise that there is an alarming deficiency in emotional development and they acknowledge that, at present, we leave the emotional education of our children to chance. However, acknowledging this is not enough, as this troubling deficiency is not being addressed.

Since the time of the ancient Greeks there has been a compulsion to separate thinking from feeling and this separation has had serious consequences for aspects of education (Downey and Kelly 1978). Current research seems to suggest that emotion and cognition usually work together in the creation of most experiences, with neither taking precedence over the other, although at times one or the other may take the lead (Bower 1981; Maccoby and Martin 1983). However, in the past, emotions came to be regarded by many as unfortunate areas of humanity, which stood in the way of proper reason and were seen as aspects of life which should be repressed and ignored. This led to an emphasis on the cognitive development of children at the expense of other aspects of their development. This divorce of feeling and intellect led to a devaluing of any activity which did not have a full intellectual content. Yet, emotions and cognition are interconnected and interdependent.

Emotional development also impacts heavily on social development as expression and regulation of certain emotions contribute to success in the young child's social world. Different social contexts elicit very different viewpoints from children on what is going on emotionally. Children who are fairly positively expressive and who know how to cope with negative emotions when they occur, who can understand their own and others' emotions, are better liked by peers. They are also considered more co-operative, friendly, pro-social, assertive and non-aggressive by their teachers and by other adults. Emotions are an important part of a child's everyday experience and, thus, emotional understanding contributes to knowledge about others and about oneself. Moral development is about our ability to live successfully together and thus emotional development, how we feel about ourselves and others, impacts heavily on this. Spiritual development is about having a sense of purpose and meaning in life. Optimum emotional development allows children to feel positive about themselves, the world and about all aspects of life including the spiritual. It helps them to feel a true sense of purpose and wonder, as well as allowing them to acknowledge that there is something greater than themselves at work in the world. Thus, emotional development does not occur in isolation, it impacts on and is impacted on by all the other areas of development.

Emotions

Emotions are an important part of affective development and consist of feelings which are accompanied by inner body reactions in the brain, nervous system and internal organs. During intense emotional reactions, the nervous system becomes more active and several physical changes can occur - pupils may dilate, mouth may become dry, heartbeat can increase, tears can be produced, adrenaline may flow and sweating can increase (Dworetzky 1994). Emotion is characterised by feelings - for example, feelings of fear, anxiety, hate, anger, love, joy, despair, hope or affection. Emotions stimulate a total human response or reaction and involve the whole being - the conscious, unconscious, psychic and physical. Emotions are impacted upon by several factors such as temperament, age, sex, developmental status and particular events or situations. A vast array of emotions are said to exist but the idea of an emotion is an abstract one, in that one cannot see one's own or another's emotion directly (Bukatto and Daehler 1995).

There are many different approaches to understanding emotions and modern research on emotion is represented in many domains including psychology, psychiatry, biology, anthropology, sociology, education, literature and philosophy. Thus, understanding emotions entails a multidisciplinary approach. In the main the psychoanalytic, cognitive developmental and the traditional learning theory approaches have had the most direct influences on beliefs regarding children's emotional development. Of all the major developmental theories, psychoanalytic theory has placed the greatest emphasis on emotion as a contributor to development and has pinpointed the ways in which emotions influence children's lives. Particularly in his early work, Freud viewed emotion as the root cause of all behaviour. As a follower of Freud, Erikson (1963) shared many of his mentor's views, including the belief that affect and emotion were the basis for human activity and the primary impetus for growth. Like Freud, he also emphasised that conscious feelings could be expressed indirectly and symbolically and his theory stressed the harmful psychological consequences of denial or repression of impulses. However, Erikson was more specific than Freud in describing how children in all cultures reach their deepest feelings through play and other symbolic activities. Also, Erikson placed more emphasis on positive emotions and emotion-related tendencies than Freud did.

Erikson set out development as a consequence of encountering conflicts at different stages in the life span. In his theory, healthy emotional development results from a resolution of each conflict: infancy - trust versus mistrust; early childhood - autonomy versus shame and doubt; play age - initiative versus guilt; school age - industry versus inferiority; adolescence - identity versus identity confusion; young adulthood - intimacy versus isolation; adulthood - generativity versus stagnation; and old age - integrity versus despair. From Erikson's viewpoint, development can be said to centre around opposing emotional tendencies and as the child emerges from each crisis, hopefully more positive emotions predominate. More recently, Greenspan and Greenspan (1985) developed a framework of six overlapping stages and milestones which occur in the first four years of children's emotional development - interest in the world; falling in love; developing intentional communication; emergence of an organised sense of self; creating emotional ideas and emotional thinking; and self-regulation. They also stress the importance of adult support of children's age-appropriate experiences for building an emotional and social climate conducive to children's well-being. Their theory is underlined by a neo-Freudian view and they claim that at every developmental stage, children are active constructors of their own emotional development, with two basic tendencies guiding children's development – regulation and harmony; and exploration of new experiences and practices.

Cognitive theories also have an emotional element but theorists such as Piaget, unlike Freud and Erikson, downplay the role of emotions in children's development and behaviour. However, others such as Cowan (1978) claim that Piaget highlighted the emotional aspect of development more than he is given credit for and draws attention to Piaget's often repeated claim that although cognition supplies essential structure for development, emotion provides the motivational energy. However, without question emotion plays a much less significant role in Piaget's theory (Plutchik and Kellerman 1983). Learning theories have also been criticised for neglecting the emotional development of children. They have not ignored emotions entirely as Watson (1919, 1931) claimed children possessed innate emotions such as fear, rage and love. However, later versions of learning theory place less emphasis on these, stressing the outward manifestation of emotions, rather than unconscious or unobservable feelings. None of the theories put forward so far has given a comprehensive view of emotional development. Each has its own narrow, incomplete view of the functions of emotions and all lack a strong research basis (Hyson 1994). Yet emotional development is vital in all societies as emotions have a central role in the human psyche.

Emotion offers a distinctive readiness to act and each emotion points us in a direction that has worked well in the past to handle the recurring challenges of human life. These recurring situations were repeated throughout evolutionary history, and the survival of the emotional repertoire can be attested to by its becoming imprinted in our nerves as innate automatic tendencies. Our appraisal of every personal encounter and our emotional response to it are shaped by our rational judgement, by our personal history and by our distant ancestral past. Emotions are adaptive responses that have motivating and organising functions which help individuals in the pursuit of their goals. Furthermore, emotion is experienced as a feeling that motivates, organises and guides perception, thought and action (Campos, Campos and Barrett 1989; Ekman 1992). Our emotions are part of what makes us human and the range of emotions experienced is very wide and also very deep. Emotions occur in situations that are meaningful to the individual and are usually aroused by changes in conditions. Experience of an emotion is very subjective and no two children will feel an emotion in exactly the same way, as each child has his own emotional repertoire. Clearly emotions have many functions, but if uncontrolled they can overwhelm us, so children must be able to cope with and manage the emotions they experience.

Emotional development

Emotional development is about the awareness, recognition and regulation of emotions. Perhaps, because it is so much a part of our own daily lives, we tend to take it for granted. We seldom think about the ways in which children's emotional abilities evolve, despite the fact that this aspect of development is in many ways one of the most important, since it establishes the critical foundation on which every other mental skill can flourish. All the brainpower in the world will not guarantee success if a child lacks the emotional skills and maturity to put it to use (Eliot 1999). Psychologists and psychiatrists recognise that emotions are one of the most complex and intricate parts of development. They have their own timing and rhythm and cannot be hurried; growing up emotionally is complicated and difficult. Emotional development is one of the most fundamental areas of human development. Yet it is also one of the most elusive, as much emotional growth and change occurs at a level which is not readily observable. However, the past decade has seen an unparalleled burst of scientific studies on emotion. New brain imaging techniques have made dramatic glimpses of the brain possible and this flood of neuro-biological information aids us in understanding more clearly how the brain centres for emotions move humans (Le Doux 1998).

A person's emotional competency or development is a key factor in determining and predicting future success in all aspects of life. The ability to understand and manage emotions resourcefully, to communicate effectively and to self-coach are essential to every child and are what emotional development is all about. An education that fosters emotional competency will be much richer, not only for the individuals within but for the whole community, and there is a persistent call for the development of emotional competency in children (Bocchino 1999). Researchers and theorists such as Gardner (1983), Slavin (1995) and Langer (1989) have redefined what it means to be intelligent and their work supports the call for prioritising emotional competence. Out of research such as theirs, a much more powerful predictor of future success than I.Q. has emerged; that is emotional literacy. This term is a purposeful distinction from emotional intelligence (E.I.) as this (E.I.) is the characteristic, the personality dynamic or the emotional potential that can be nurtured and developed in the child to gain emotional literacy or competency. Emotional literacy or competency is the constellation of understandings, strategies, tools and skills that are learned in order to become emotionally developed. Like any innate human predisposition or potential, just as in music, sports or language, emotional competency needs to be nurtured and developed (Steiner 1997).

Emotional development is characterised by the ability to monitor feelings. An emotionally developed child may be conscious of the physiological responses that accompany certain emotions. He may purposely take time to record these emotions or he may carefully track which emotions are present at different times and circumstances in his daily life. This self-awareness is the vital step towards managing emotions in a useful and healthy way. The child in the setting who can identify his feelings of frustration, who can weigh up a range of choices in dealing with it and who can manage through self-talk, to proceed in a useful way, is seen as being emotionally developed (Bocchino 1999). Since emotional competency is 'developable' it is a vital area for education.

The work of Radke-Yarrow, Zahn-Waxler and Chapman (1983) helps to indicate something of children's sensitivity to the emotional states of others in the pre-school years. They are beginning to comprehend social rules, adult standards and the nature of power relationships and are quite capable of understanding that others have different feelings and intentions. Also, during these years the child is sensitive to the response of others - approval, disapproval, support, interest and so on. Sensitivity to others is an important aspect of the child's developing self-awareness, as they begin to recognise others' feelings and to understand social rules. Questions about the feelings, perceptions and mental states of others increase in proportion and in frequency during the third year. During this time they also become increasingly curious about and try to understand the causes of pain, distress, anger, pleasure, displeasure, comfort and fear in others as well as in themselves. Their responsiveness to the feeling states of others shows that the foundations of caring, consolation and kindness are well laid by age three (Blum 1987). The work of Radke-Yarrow et al. (1983) also makes it clear that exposure to adult aggression makes children become upset and may result in the children themselves reacting aggressively, so cognisance must be taken of this.

Self-recognition and the realisation of self and other differences throughout the second year of life, lay the foundation for the expression of certain emotions, in particular self-conscious and social emotions - embarrassment, empathy, envy, pride, shame, guilt (Lewis 1993; Zahn-Waxler and Kochanska 1990). Shame and guilt in particular, are related to the development of self-conscious and self-evaluating internal attribution along with moral overtones. Feelings of guilt often arise from doing a particular behaviour or transgression. The same goes for feelings of shame, but the ramifications of a sense of shame go well beyond those of guilt for the young child. The main concern when feeling shame is with one's worth as a person and feeling shame is a lot more painful and destructive for the child. Shamed children frequently become angry with maladaptive anger management strategies, for example, kicking and biting. Shame-prone children also often lack empathy for others and blame others for the shame-inducing event. Thus, shame motivates behaviours that interfere with social relations and the tendency to feel shame has been consistently linked to a range of psychological symptoms (Tangney, Wagner Barlow, Marschall, Sanftner, Mohr and Gramzow 1996). In contrast, guilt motivates corrective action rather than motivating avoidance and is more likely to keep the child constructively engaged in social situations. The regret and tension of guilt is likely to lead the child to confess, apologise and/or amend. Guilt focuses on the offending behaviour and its harmful consequences whilst shame focuses on devaluing the child. Pre-school children do experience shame, guilt and pride. These emotions require self-awareness, rule following behaviour and a definite standard for one's own particular behaviour. It is important to remedy the negative social relationships that inspire shame in pre-schoolers and to foster the positive experiences that engender pride and on occasion, if necessary, a sense of guilt.

A lot of change occurs in emotional expressiveness during the pre-school era. Personal styles of emotional expressiveness become established and children gain flexibility in using expressions of basic emotions, for example, using facial expressions and vocalisation differently. The voluntary management of emotions also increases. Children entering early years settings are often adept in expressing emotions as goal-directed behaviours and as social signals. As children enter formal school settings their emotions become more difficult to ascertain as they can be masked, dissembled and/or blended as the child learns to manage emotional expression voluntarily, showing expressiveness according to cultural display rules, hiding and faking certain expressions. Their emotional lives are also more complex as they experience more guilt, shame, pride and embarrassment than their younger counterparts. These all indicate the development of a complex and rich emotional life and each individual child has a distinguishable emotional style which shows stability over time. Thus, pre-school aged children can be quite adept at several components of emotional competence, provided their experiences and education promote it (Saarni 1990).

Self-regulation of emotions

All children need help in becoming emotionally developed. Whether children's emotions become a rich, life enhancing source of experience or whether they become a frightening, incomprehensible array of feelings is influenced by how parents and schools help the child to develop his emotions. Thus, the nature of the early childhood curriculum, its developmental appropriateness and the emotional tone its practice creates are vital. Emotions dominate children's early lives more than they ever will again and while children gradually develop longer and longer stretches of self-control, the pre-school years are really one extended roller coaster (Eliot 1999). Emotions can be and are stressful and can sometimes flood a child's conscious awareness. When this happens the child's behaviour and/or thought process can become disorganised. Thus, the child needs to learn to regulate his own emotions as soon as possible (Barrett and Campos 1991; Eisenberg and Fabes 1992).

Our brains are primarily designed to ensure our survival and that function of the brain overrides all other functions such as problem solving, logic and higher order thinking. Though this survival function is a very valuable role of the brain, children also need to develop strategies and skills to manage the tendency of their brains to revert to high-alert survival states and to the limited choices of 'fight or flight'. There are mechanisms that can be learned and through practice every child can manage his own emotional responses. When emotions are on high alert, for example when a child is stressed or afraid, significant neural energy is concentrated on 'fight or flight' responses. The child's emotions are hijacked and he cannot concentrate on anything else. This is not always what is best for the child, so the child must develop positive coping strategies (Bocchino 1999).

Childhood stress is a growing problem, although its impact is only beginning to be recognised. Even pre-school aged children are susceptible. In many cases behaviour that appears to be regressive, disruptive or attention seeking may be signals of stress. Children can experience a cocktail of stressors in everyday life – exposure to high parental expectations, lack of routine, family breakdown, loss of a pet, exposure to violence, hunger, fatigue, over/under stimulation. All humans including young children have a 'stress threshold' which is a point after which they cannot adapt or cope. Each child's threshold is unique and is based on the child's developmental level, on his previous life experiences, on his coping/regulation of emotions in the past and indeed on his physiology (nature and nurture combine to set the threshold). The younger the child the greater the impact of new events and the more powerful and potentially dangerous stress becomes. Stress is a normal part of every child's life and is necessary for life. However, excess stress can have immediate and far-reaching repercussions. A child under stress may appear more fearful, tense, aggressive, irritable or have difficulty concentrating. Excessive worrying, obsessive interest in objects, food, routines and excessive clinging can also be indicators of a child under stress as can headaches, low energy, nail biting or regressive behaviour (soiling, wetting). It is likely to be a series of 'stressors' or problems that cause a stress reaction although it may be one individual stressor that tips a child over the edge. Adults need to be aware of the physical and emotional manifestations of stress. Although the early years practitioner is unlikely to be the source of stress, events within the setting can add to the child's load (especially if they are vulnerable or under pressure in other areas of their lives). Therefore adults need to watch out for children who are stressed and potential stresses in the environment should be reduced as much as possible, if undue stress is to be avoided (Sullivan 2002).

Regulation of emotion and being able to deal with stress is of paramount importance for children and has many benefits. It allows them to reach their goals and makes them feel better, preventing them from being overwhelmed. It gives them a sense of mastery and allows them to become more socially competent as well as allowing them to become integrated into their culture. Children are expected to self-regulate their behaviours and emotions quite early on and one of the first steps in managing emotional response states involves developing greater consciousness. It is the ability to discern what emotional response state is appropriate and useful in a given circumstance, as well as the possession of a wide range of alternative strategies, that leads to conscious choices and a rich emotional repertoire. Emotional control has to be exercised under difficult conditions and is enormously complicated. For this reason, society must be quite tolerant of the expression of emotion by children, as much learning has to be done and it takes a long time and unfortunately some children never learn to master it (Oatley and Jenkins 1996).

Emotion regulation means being able to alter, adjust, manage and control one's emotional state, either maintaining or changing it. It is a developmental process which is influenced by individual differences among children and is also influenced by the environmental context within which the child is developing. Self-regulation is the process by which children are expected to control their own behaviour and emotions in accordance with the standards and desires of caregivers and communities and thus is an important aspect of emotional development. Movement along a continuum of autonomy towards more active, flexible strategies for regulating emotion is a natural phenomenon which is fuelled by children's innate propensities to master their environment and to take on or internalise regulatory structures provided by caregivers. Emotion regulation provides important links with later peer relations, coping strategies and, if unregulated, emotions can put children at risk for psychopathologies (Koplow 1996).

Many children are able to regulate their emotional behaviour before they are aware of what they are doing and can do it long before they can talk about it. Children's ability to talk is an important factor affecting how they regulate their emotions and behaviour. Being able to use language to explain emotional issues has an impact on children's relationships as they begin to "argue rather than resort to physical violence, to wait rather than wail, to contain their impatience rather than explode in tantrums" (Dunn and Brown 1991 p.89). Children become increasingly less reliant on caregivers and adults to regulate emotions as they approach the pre-school age. However, to think of emotion regulation as an entirely internal event does not tell the whole story. One of the most important factors in helping humans, both children and adults, to maintain emotional equilibrium is the presence of caring and supportive people in their lives. Maintaining emotional equilibrium is not a task for the child alone.

Emotional arousal is inevitable and emotions register at all times. Managing one's emotions is a full-time job and keeping distressing ideas and thoughts in check is one of the keys to emotional well-being. Emotion regulation usually refers to down-regulating emotion but up-regulating it is also sometimes necessary. Emotional regulation is needed when either the presence or absence of emotional expression and experience interferes with a child's goals. It consists of the extrinsic and intrinsic processes responsible for monitoring, evaluating and modifying emotional reactions (Thompson 1994). Young children can decrease, increase or sustain emotional experiences by emotion-related, cognitive and behavioural means. Emotion regulation represents the useful end of emotional expressiveness, understanding and socialisation from all the significant people in a child's life. It is a very important aspect of their emotional development and affects their success in the social world. Today, emotion and its regulation is the centre of investigation in work on attachment, social competence, moral development, psychopathology, socialisation and many other topics (Saarni, Mumme and Campos 1998).

Gender differences in emotional development

Emotional development appears to be impacted on by the sex of the child as different messages about emotions are given to boys and girls. The work of Dunn, Bretherton and Munn (1987) clearly shows this. Other studies offer further evidence to reinforce this finding (Brody and Hall 1993; Kraemer 2000). Gender differences have been noted in pre-schoolers' expression of emotions and these usually parallel differences in problematic emotions reported for boys and girls at later ages; with pre-school boys expressing more anger than girls, and girls expressing more sadness. These early gender-related experiences and consequent emotional differences often continue into adulthood (Malatesta-Magai, Leak, Tesman, Shephard, Culver and Smaggia 1994).

Boys and girls experience separate emotional worlds while growing up. Each is taught very different lessons about handling emotions. In general, parents discuss emotions more with their daughters than with their sons, with the exception of discussing angry emotions more with boys. Girls are exposed to more information about emotions and from an early age boys are discouraged from showing their feelings. How often have you heard two and three year olds being told that 'big boys don't cry'? Girls grow up tending to be more aware of and explicit about their feelings, while boys tend not to be able to express their emotions and often feel uncomfortable without knowing why. Brody and Hall (1993) surmise that because girls develop language more quickly than boys, this leads girls to be more experienced at articulating their feelings and more skilled than boys at using words to explore and substitute for emotional reactions. In contrast, they claim that, "boys, for whom the verbalisation of affects is de-emphasised, may become largely unconscious of their emotional states, both in themselves and in others" (p.456). This may partly explain why girls become adept at reading both verbal and non-verbal emotional signals, at expressing and communicating their feelings, and results in boys becoming adept at minimising emotions. This is not such a good idea for the male species and can have negative repercussions. Kraemer (2000 p.1612) says that such research has implications for the upbringing of boys and he suggests that: "If parents were more aware of male sensitivity, they might change the way they treat their sons". Perhaps, if early years practitioners were more aware of it they might also change the way they treat the boys in their care.

In 2002 Kraemer went on to say that in the early years, boys are physically and emotionally less mature than girls. This is in line with Rutter and Rutter (1993) who state that boys are more vulnerable than girls to stresses of many kinds, including psychological and physical ones, with their responses being more overt and extreme. Three to four times as many boys as girls also have reading and language delays, clumsiness, stammering, autism and asperger syndrome, hyperactivity and attention deficits. Boys are also more likely than girls to suffer seizures, asthma, bed-wetting, and conduct/behavioural/operational disorders. Kraemer says there is also evidence to show that boys suffer more than girls where there is emotional and social stress. However, Kraemer warns that although adversity appears to affect boys more obviously than girls in the early years, it is the other way around in adolescence and adulthood. Girls suffer more than boys do from depression, eating disorders and suicide attempts and Kraemer believes childhood problems may be stored up by girls until they are older. Rutter and Rutter (1993) also back this contention, saying that girls' responses to psychological stresses may be different but may be just as damaging with girls showing more depression and self-harm as they get older. However, though teenage girls are more likely than teenage boys to engage in self-harming behaviour, they are less likely to engage in lethal acts and the rate of suicide is far greater for males than for females.

Thus, many emotional problems exist for both boys and girls and while gender differences have some impact on emotional development, in reality all children differ emotionally, regardless of their sex. Yet we still know very little about the neural basis for interpersonal difference - why are some children sad, others happy, some shy, others outgoing (Eliot 1999). Though we still do not know why, what we do know is that ensuring the development of some aspects of emotional competence (such as attachment, self-esteem and self-confidence) can help children, both boys and girls, cope better with problems, thus leading them to live happier lives, so maybe this should be our focus.

Attachment

The importance of stable, caring relationships in children's lives is seen by many as central to emotional development and research has confirmed the importance of secure attachment as a protective factor as well as a positive influence on later development (Landy 2002). There is evidence to show that infants who are securely attached to significant adults in their lives are more confident, can cope better with new situations, make friends more easily, have better information processing and problem solving skills (Osofsky 2002; Smith and Cowie 1991). The attachment relationship has been a focus for many years and is seen as providing a prototype that shapes the remainder of the developing child's life, especially influencing his capacity for love and his ability to motivate himself. However, the actual effect of this relationship is questioned by many, and authors including Rutter (1981) suggest that while it is important for a child to form an attachment, this need not be with the mother or mother figure. Children can develop attachments to more than one caregiver provided that person provides security, care and protection. Furthermore he says the experience of separation may not be as damaging as proposed in the past. It is the type, length and cause of separation that seems to influence the outcome. Thus, it appears that Bowlby (1953) may have overstated the importance of the attachment role. However, attachment is still acknowledged as being important and: "The presence of a close, confiding relationship protects adults of all ages as well as children against stress" (Landy 2002 p.189).

Bowlby broke ranks with the Freudian psychoanalytic view and developed the prevailing theory of attachment, which guides most development research on the topic today. Attachment theory as proposed by Bowlby (1953) provides us with one of the most developed and influential views about the relationship between main caregiver and infant. Attachment is seen as the emotional tie that develops between baby and primary caregiver and is believed to play a crucial part in the social and emotional growth of the child. Ainsworth's research (1989) built on that of Bowlby. She made attachment theory a subject for experimentation and highlighted individual differences. She developed the 'strange situation test' to assess separation anxiety and attachment in children and her work showed three basic patterns of attachment – secure; anxious/ambivalent; and anxious/avoidant. Oatley and Jenkins (1996) claim that being without a primary attachment figure in early childhood puts children at risk emotionally, as does misattunement in an attachment relationship. However, unlike in the past it is now accepted that a number of factors interact with each other to influence attachment and attunement. For example, parental/caregiver history and experience; parental/caregiver and child characteristics; the environment; and also family and social supports all impact heavily on the adult/child relationship (Belsky, Steinberg and Walker 1982; Belsky 1997). Parents or other caregivers who are numbed, frightened, anxious or depressed make it difficult for children's healthy socio-emotional development to take place, since young children's development of trust and security comes from adults who are emotionally available. Exposure to trauma and violence can lead children to withdraw, show disorganised behaviours and show aggressive behaviour (Landy 2002). Thus contextual stresses, or on the other hand supports, affect the sensitivity of care given to the child. This in turn affects emotional and temperamental development which in turn affects whether or not the child develops a secure attachment. One of the most urgent needs of a young child is to have a strong relationship with a competent, positive, caring adult. Whether or not the child develops such an attachment/relationship seems to affect how he functions, particularly emotionally and socially. Thus, attachment is a vital area of a child's life and can influence his general view of life. Every child needs to relate/attach in an emotional way to another person. This attachment impacts on his personality traits related to trust and autonomy, on his patterns of peer interaction, on his responses to others' feelings and on general cognitive functioning (Schickendanz, Schickendanz, Hansen and Forsyth 1990).

Kelmer Pringle's work (1975, 1996) emphasises the need for children to have secure and loving relationships with others in order to strengthen their emotional lives. Rogers and Kutnick (1990) also stress that if children are to thrive emotionally they need to feel love and security. Thus, the adult is seen as the key in helping children to experience and develop sound qualities and attitudes. Hochschild (1979) states that very young children learn the 'feeling rules' of their communities from their own personal experiences and from the socialisation of adults. Family life is the first school for emotional learning and it fulfils the irreplaceable function of laying the basis for the adjustment of the individual within society. The capacity for co-operation, integration and creativity has its roots in family life. However, Hooven, Katz and Gottman (1994 p.190) claim that, "some parents are gifted emotional teachers, others atrocious". In order for caregivers and teachers to be effective, they must themselves have a good grasp of the rudiments of emotional intelligence/competence and sadly this is not always the case. Also, the adult's own level of self-esteem can impact for better or for worse on children's emotional development. Parents and teachers with high self-esteem seem to effect high self-esteem in the children with whom they come in contact. Sadly the reverse is also true. Parents and teachers who reason, encourage, reward, praise and who provide a warm home and early years environment seem to produce children who show low aggression, high self-esteem, greater feelings of responsibility, high levels of conscience, low undesirable dependency and high sociability. On the other hand, parents and teachers who scold, derogate, threaten and punish, who are unloving or only moderately loving and who show little interest in the children they come in contact with, appear to develop children who show negative behaviour traits (Lewis 1993; Humphreys 1996). How adults behave towards children in the early years continues to effect self-esteem for many years afterwards. An increasing number of children are growing up in poverty and in communities characterised by violence, crime and substance abuse. These factors place increased strain on families, especially vulnerable families, who have little support from their extended families or communities. There are a growing number of parents saying that they are feeling physically and psychologically burdened by their parenting responsibilities. Societal and family pressures are causing stress and this is adversely affecting neurological development in children, actually destroying synapses. Since so many children do not have the opportunity to live and develop in positive, nurturing home environments, a focus on what is important for the healthy emotional development of children is vital in out-of-home settings. The development of support systems to help parents cope better is also critical (Osofsky 2002; Sapolsky 1994).

According to Fogel (1980) no matter what emotions arise, the extent to which they are understood, fully experienced, and used for the benefit of the child is dependent almost fully on the behaviour and attitudes of the adult, including the early years practitioner. A child who has known little affection will seldom grow into a person capable of independence, and love and human life withers away and is destroyed without love. Children do not mature, cannot learn, cannot communicate or even grow properly (non-organic failure to thrive) if they are not loved. If a child does not receive warmth and love throughout childhood, anxiety, depression and general emotional impoverishment can ensue. Love must be unconditional on the part of parents and practitioners. Conditional love breeds multiple fears, dependence and self-esteem difficulties. It means that behaviour becomes more important than the child. The child and his behaviour are separate entities and must always be seen as such (Hartley-Brewer 1998). Receiving unconditional love through well-attuned attachment relationships will help the child develop high levels of self-esteem and self-confidence.

Self-concept, self-esteem and self-confidence

Young children develop a sense of self and an awareness of others quite quickly and one of the most basic steps a child must take is to realise that he is distinct from everyone else. One of the early landmarks of this is referred to as 'person permanence' and this has been assessed in terms of infants' recognition of others and their search for them when that person disappears from view. At around the same time as this ability is occurring, self-recognition is also developing as is self-concept or self-image. This is the child's awareness of his own mental and physical characteristics. Early impressions are of body image. With cognitive development, more refined physical and mental impressions occur. Self-concept plays an important role in emotional development and is the general term for how someone thinks about themselves. It can refer to all aspects of the self - appearance, personality, ability, as well as gender, nationality or ethnic group. Some aspects of self-concept are evaluative and self-concept can be the starting point for understanding self-esteem (Lawrence 1996; Smith and Cowie 1991).

Having good self-esteem means a child can weather almost all the storms and earthquakes that life throws at him. Life is not easy and there are many emotional ups and downs which the child must be able to deal with. Good self-esteem is self-sustaining and can help a child cope when things go against him (Hartley-Brewer 1998). If children are helped to understand themselves better and come to feel more confident about themselves, then they will be in a stronger position to cope with the inevitable stresses of life, as well as being more moral citizens. The well-being of all human systems is largely determined by the level of self-esteem of the child and his experiences, good and bad, help determine his level of self-esteem, which in turn helps determine his level of emotional, social, moral and educational progress (Humphreys 1996). As Briggs (1975 p.3) says, self-esteem "is a quiet sense of self-respect, a feeling of self-worth. When you have it deep inside you're glad you're you."

Self-esteem is a vital aspect of emotional development. It consists of the negative or positive feelings a child has about himself and children prone to positive emotionality are relatively resilient, more socially competent, have later life satisfaction and happiness (Eisenberg and Fabes 1992). Young children's views about themselves develop as a reflection of the views transmitted to them in social interaction. Much evidence exists to suggest that children who develop positive self-images and positive feelings of self-worth have been surrounded, in the vital years, by unconditional love and emotional warmth. The adults in their worlds have transmitted to them powerfully that they are valued by others and so they come to value themselves as a consequence of this (Whitebread 1996). Thus, developing self-esteem needs both a supportive social milieu and the formation and acceptance of realistic personal goals.

Self-esteem is not fixed and can change according to the people we are with and the situations we experience. In the early years, it is the people who are closest to the child and who have an emotional link to him who have the most profound effect on his self-esteem. They are often described as 'significant others' and include family, friends, carers and early years practitioners. Self-esteem can be enhanced by treating the child as an individual, by realising that a child is not his actions, by providing opportunities for the child to be responsible and for making decisions. Teaching enjoyment of life every day and, most importantly, providing the child with love and affection also help. In addition, self-esteem is aided by respecting the child and encouraging him to respect others and by providing encouragement and praise rather than criticism. Getting the child to think and talk about his feelings is also of tremendous benefit, as children tend to become what they think, as thinking determines self-image, which in turn determines feeling and behaviour (Gura 1996). It seems clear that from a research and theoretical perspective, having optimal self-esteem is important and can influence development in a positive way. On the other hand, low self-esteem has been consistently linked with depression, since it contributes to a sense of helplessness and a lack of internal control (Landy 2002).

Self-confidence is close to but different from self-esteem. It relates to a belief not in one's intrinsic worth but involves a view of one's self as seen from the outside. It is about trusting one's own ability to form and sustain relationships, to complete tasks well, to know that others value one's abilities, to trust one's own judgements and common sense. Children who do not have a measure of consistency and predictability in their lives find it difficult to acquire trust in others and in themselves and so often do not become self-confident. Self-confidence helps children to be open and outgoing and allows them to be both trusting and trust-worthy. It also helps them to be determined and perseverant and involves having firm expectations of others and of not being afraid of failure (Lawrence 1996).

Confidence is a characteristic that is valued by all and is one that parents really want for their children. Confident children are well equipped to deal with life, they are comfortable with themselves and have insights into their own strengths and weaknesses. Conversely, under-confident children find it difficult to cope with all aspects of life. In a world that demands so much of them, children need to become confident from as early an age as possible. Children's levels of confidence are influenced by their early experiences, by the thoughts they have about themselves and by other people's reactions to them, as well as by the personality they inherit. Children's confidence is linked closely to becoming aware of themselves (self-concept), by developing a view of themselves, either positive or negative (self-esteem) and by getting to know about their strengths and weaknesses (self-knowledge) (Dowling 2000).

Confidence is also impacted on by new situations, new experiences and new people, as these can result in self-doubt. As the young child develops, he starts to learn about himself and about what he can do. He begins to recognise things that he finds easy and things that are more difficult. Early on, the child has limited self-insight and looks to others to provide information, in particular regarding his behaviour. The small child who is confident of being loved and who learns to adopt behaviour which is approved of, will receive further recognition and will grow to value himself. To develop positive emotional feelings, children need to experience feeling in control. This feeling of empowerment is vital to children developing positive attitudes to themselves and is of particular importance to their view of themselves as learners. The reverse is also true. When children become unsure of themselves and become anxious, they feel sorry for themselves, demand attention and feel they are helpless and useless. Since the young child cannot separate himself from his behaviour, he comes to believe he is not liked and does not matter. Thus, initially children are dependent on the adults around them to help them become aware of their strengths and weaknesses. This means that it is vital that adults endeavour to help children gain a sense of control over their own lives and to build up their own aspirations, problem solving skills and decision making processes as soon as possible (Dyer 1998).

If children are to experience the exhilaration of success, they must also learn how to cope with failure. Failing at a task does not mean we fail as a person. Failure and mistakes are not the problems; it is the reactions of others that are. Normal emotional development is a process of coping with the experience of failure. In order to accept this, our attitudes towards winning and towards achievement must change. The freedom to make mistakes, to cope with frustration and to deal with failure, are important aspects of emotional development, as when children are given the freedom to make mistakes they are given the freedom to grow. Being able to take risks and to accept both the possibility and the responsibility for making mistakes is a prerequisite for healthy development (Scott Peck 1990). For optimum emotional development, children must be willing to take risks and to experience failure. Failing is an inevitable part of growing up and is the first part of the process of becoming competent. Children must be taught to cope constructively with frustration, failure and disappointment. Effort should be praised and promoted, attainment and competition should be de-emphasised where possible, as the pursuit of external symbols of success is not particularly good for emotional development. Aronson (1995) says competition is inherently destructive, believing that it destroys self-esteem, poisons relationships and causes anxiety. She says there is no such thing as healthy competition as competition makes a person dependent on the social construct of winning and undermines intrinsic motivation. Without such motivation children may be afraid to try.

O'Donnchadha (2000) claims that children show either helpless or mastery patterns of behaviour when confronted with obstacles in learning. Within developmental psychology there has been a significant amount of research into this aspect of emotional development and its relation to children's motivation. It is concerned in particular with what is called 'attribution theory', that is the cause to which children attribute their success and failure. Research shows that when children feel that their performance is determined by factors within their control, for example, how much effort they put into a particular task, they respond positively to failure and are willing to try harder the next time, believing it is in their own ability to be successful. However, where they feel that their performance is determined by factors outside their control, factors such as their ability or luck, they respond negatively to failure and are unwilling to try again. They believe that they will not succeed, no matter how hard they try and such 'learned helplessness' is extremely damaging. This model of attribution explains how poor self-esteem can result in a lack of motivation, which in turn leads to a lack of effort and consequent poor performance, thus reinforcing the child's negative view of himself. It appears that one of the crucial things in developing a willingness to try and to risk failure is the attitude of adults to the child's mistakes and failures. If the response is one of negative criticism and judgement, the child will be afraid to try again because of fear of failure. The child must have the confidence to try with the knowledge that it will be alright even if he fails. If the child is afraid to try or if he feels others do not have confidence in him, he will become unable and unwilling to try again. Yet, children have to be able to survive knocks and to bounce back, as life is full of difficulties and disappointments (Lewis 1995; Whitebread 1996).

Thus components of self-confidence include: the willingness to become a risk taker; the ability to challenge one's self; the ability to accept the possibility of failure; and the capacity for courage and assertiveness. Self-confidence is built by action and by doing, not by worrying, dithering or by being fearful. However, self-confidence is a relative term, as every person is more confident in some areas and not in others. Yet, children must feel confident enough in all areas in order to be willing to learn and to be open to new people and new experiences.

Discipline

Discipline is also part of emotional development and discipline, in its best sense, can and should be seen as a positive and constructive force. Although most children become amenable to discipline by age three to four, a small but none-the-less significant number develop severe behavioural difficulties that become chronic, leading to serious consequences. The term, discipline, has in many cases become synonymous with punishment. The word in fact derives from the word 'disciple' which means to teach and lead (Landy 2002). Discipline demonstrates that actions have consequences and aids the smooth running of society. Real discipline is about helping children to gain self-control, to care for and respect the rights and feelings of others and to know right from wrong. It is not about controlling a child and is the help which adults give to children initially, so that they can learn to control and manage their own behaviour. It makes clear how we expect children to behave in different situations. It helps keep them safe, teaches them to think of others and provides a predictable and secure environment for them. It also helps them to develop a constructive independence, makes clear the difference between acceptable and unacceptable behaviour and is intertwined with emotion regulation as described earlier. Adults use a variety of strategies to discipline young children including time-outs, natural consequences, ignoring, positive reinforcement, distractions and variations of these. A considerable proportion of mistaken adults continue to physically punish children for misdemeanours. Overall with regard to discipline some adults are too lax, some too strict, others fluctuate between the two. A fortunate few can establish a co-operative environment within which conflicts are kept to a minimum and where the child learns to internalise values and to control his impulses. There is a real need to focus on children's understanding, as the goal of discipline as compliance just for its own sake is not productive. The child's long-term internalisation of values must be the aim and the child must feel he wants to behave responsibly. Discipline should not be based on dictatorship but should be based on fairness and mutual respect if children are to develop emotionally. Research seems to indicate that the most effective method of disciplining children is to use induction. This is reasoning with the child about how his behaviour affects others and then working together on how to change the negative behaviour in positive ways (Schickendanz et al. 1990; Lewis 1995).

Conclusion

Emotional development must be respected and nurtured. Children have the right to both witness and experience different feelings and their true emotions must not and should not be repressed. Adults must acknowledge what the child is feeling with empathy and so long as love and care are prevalent, children will flourish and grow. The key to living and learning successfully lies within the child himself. It has to do with his views and attitudes and what he makes of what he is given and in this way, he can achieve optimum emotional development. Unfortunately, at present this does not always occur (Nutbrown 1996).

For a child, of all the judgements and beliefs he has, none is more important than the ones he has about himself. His belief in himself, which develops as a result of how much he feels he is loved and respected, is the single most telling factor in determining his success and happiness in life. Children who believe that the world is a positive and miraculous place and that they are special and loved have a huge advantage over children who are doubting and negative (Denham 1998). There are five key factors which must be taken into account in the emotional development of children: 1) biological and physical characteristics; 2) individual differences in temperament; 3) skills and limitations in other developmental areas including the cognitive, linguistic, moral, spiritual and social domains; 4) family environment and relationships (including love); 5) cultural influences (Hyson 1994). Emotional development has a huge impact on a child's overall development and it must receive the attention it is due if young children are to optimally develop their emotions. Doing this means children become better able to fulfil their roles and potential in life. It is not just children with emotional problems who will benefit from prioritising emotional development. All children will benefit from being emotionally developed. It is an 'inoculation for life' (Goleman 1996) which helps enhance overall development and happiness as well as preventing the development of emotional problems and psychopathologies. The following section outlines a number of suggestions that can enhance the emotional development of the young child.

Suggestions/guidelines for enhancing emotional development

There is a myriad of things that can be done to enhance emotional development in the early years setting. The following are a list of suggestions which have been selected from various sources including: *Emotional Literacy* (Bocchino 1999); *Someone to talk to: a handbook on childhood bereavement* (Donnelly 2001); *Project E.Y.E. An Irish Curriculum for the three to four year old child – Volume One: Spiritual, Emotional and Moral Development* and *Volume Four: Creative Development* (Douglas, Horgan and O'Brien 2000); *Young Children's Personal, Social and Emotional Development* (Dowling 2000); *Supporting Quality: Guidelines for Best Practice in Early Childhood Services* (French 2003); *Educating Young Children* (Hohmann and Weikart 2002); *The Excellence of Play* (Moyles ed.1994); and *Just Playing* (Moyles 1989).

- Provide a psychologically supportive environment for children. This will make them feel safe and secure, will encourage them to talk about their feelings and will help their self-esteem and self-confidence.

- There should be a regular yet flexible routine in the setting. A wall mounted daily routine poster (in a linear pictorial/ photographic form) should be posted on the wall which clarifies for children what happens during each session. This allows children to anticipate what happens next and gives them a sense of control over what is happening during each part of the day.

- The setting needs to be divided into clearly defined areas (for example - messy, quiet, construction, pretend, computer and outdoor areas). Having defined areas promotes greater investment in play and gives children a greater feeling of security as they know what goes on in each area and where exactly to find what they need, increasing their confidence and independence (and the complexity of their play). Within each area materials should be ordered logically and easily accessible at the child's level.

- Early years settings must provide time for attachment, to allow children to form secure relationships with at least one practitioner who becomes their key worker. Parents should be informed who this person is and can then talk to them about any concerns they may have. As far as is practically possible there must be a responsiveness from staff to ensure that each individual child's needs are met; no two children have the same needs and the setting must try to adapt to meet each child's needs.

- Each child's family experience should be valued. This can be enhanced by building strong ties with parents/guardians. Open relationships between children's families and the early years setting should be created and the setting should deepen and extend the child's sense of home values.

- The setting should have lots of familiar items and should be 'homely' with rugs, cushions, beanbags, plants, photographs and so on.

- Have a good range of toy telephones and old (adult) mobile telephones available so that children can express what they are feeling.

- Children must feel comfortable and secure as they move between home and the early years setting. Where possible undertake a home visit. This is one of the best ways to learn about children and their families. If a home visit can't occur, meet the child and family at the setting, show them around, let them sit in on a session, talk to them about their child and about their expectation of the setting.

- Children must feel welcome in the setting and posters/displays must reflect their homes and communities. Particularly in the first term, let them bring in comfort items from home and have a photograph of each family that the child can look at or hold if they are feeling lonely or upset.

- Children and their families must feel a sense of belonging and settings must connect with families and the wider world. To involve parents/families, have family gatherings at the setting, chat with parents at drop off/pick up and encourage them to confide in you if there are any problems/areas of concern. Encourage parents to join outings and offer regular staff/parent meetings. Provide parents with a Parent Handbook which includes information on the setting, policies, procedures and so on.

- Allow children to be active learners. They must be allowed to experience objects, ideas, events and people. In the early years setting they must be allowed to move, listen, search, discover, feel and manipulate. It must be ensured that there is access to a wide variety of materials and that children are given the freedom to manipulate, transform and use them in their own way at their own pace.

- Children need to be encouraged to initiate activities that grow from personal interests and intentions. Discover children's interests and abilities and allow them to make choices and decisions. Be responsive and supportive of children's interests. This allows children to learn that their behaviour is accepted and valued and results in feelings of confidence and high self-esteem in the child.

- Support the child in his development and collaborate with him in the development of a self that is valued and true. Find out his likes and dislikes, his strengths and the areas he finds more difficult, encourage him to take risks and to try out new activities and experiences.

- Talk to children about the fact that one won't always succeed but that it is important to try, always encourage effort and stress this rather than the end result – the process rather than the product.

- Provide children with a supportive interpersonal climate; ensure that children and adults interact positively with each other free from fear, aggression, worry, neglect and boredom. Adults must share control, focus on children's strengths, develop real relationships, support children's play and adopt a problem-solving approach to all conflicts. Adult support of children's experiences is essential for building a social and emotional climate that is conducive to enhancing children's well-being. In such a setting, children will feel a sense of full emotional engagement, mastery and control.

- Allow children to solve problems for themselves – to find out where the piece of jigsaw goes, to find the correct lid for the saucepan. Doing this stimulates learning and development and gives children a sense of control and mastery.

- Observe children closely and note changes in behaviour and in their progress. Look out for children in need of comfort and contact. Offering simple acknowledgement or a lap to curl up on can make all the difference. Discuss changes with parents.

- Encourage children to talk about themselves and about their feelings; circle time can be useful for this or sometimes working in a small group or with an individual child is better. A secure, non-threatening environment needs to be provided to enable children to discuss emotional insecurities. Children should be helped to see the benefits of social skills, taking turns, being kind and offering to play with a new child. Such times are also a good opportunity to talk about different aspects of life: death, birth, sickness, going to the hospital. Tell little stories, ask children to tell stories as this is another way of getting children to express their feelings or ask children what makes them feel sad/happy or how would they feel if…. Children need to be supported to express their fears, anticipation, sadness. Be tactful here and tread carefully, don't ask probing questions but follow the child's lead.

- Sit down and work regularly with small groups of children using puppets and miniature dolls to enact scenarios and provoke discussion.

- Have lots of small group discussions. These are of value in satisfying all of children's needs but are particularly of benefit in giving children who normally command little attention an attentive audience and greater personal esteem. Having a pretend microphone that is passed from one person to the other when it is his turn to speak is of benefit as this helps ensure everyone, not just confident and talkative children, get a chance to speak. Don't pressure any child into speaking, if they don't want to. Allow them to pass on this occasion but always give them the opportunity. An alternative to the microphone is to have a special teddy who is passed from child to child and who does the talking 'Teddy says he is sad today because....'

- Encourage children to learn to recognise when they have hurt someone else or have done something wrong. Help them to take responsibility, to ask for forgiveness and to make amends. Get them to verbalise what they are feeling 'I get mad when...' or 'I feel so upset when...'.

- Encourage children to identify feelings of frustration and anger. Support them to weigh up the range of choices in dealing with these feelings; to ask rather than to hit for instance. Encourage them to talk about the things that led to such feelings.

- Educate the children to take responsibility for themselves. Frequently remind children of their responsibilities within the setting, at home and in the larger community. Being respectful of own and other's property; carrying out requests; tidying up; hanging up bag/coat; communicating with others in a respectful way and at an acceptable volume; sharing toys; picking up papers; recycling; playing with others in a safe way; these all encourage emotional development.

- Organise a broad range of activities that will enable children to express their feelings in different ways. For example, have a punch bag to vent anger on; a set of worry beads for children who are anxious or worried; some soothing classical music for children who are stressed; allow a child who is frustrated to squeeze water, using a sponge, from one bowl into another.

- Provide individual children with areas of responsibility - keeping the book area tidy; checking that all the jigsaw bits are together; giving out the juice. Have rotas so that every child is allowed to have responsibility.

- Children must be encouraged to think positively and a positive atmosphere must be promoted in the setting – get them to look on the bright side and to notice the good things that are going on around them.

- Talk to a child who is upset/angry. Give him the language to describe what is happening to him, make him aware of the physiological changes that are occurring (e.g. heart pounding, palms sweaty, mouth dry and so on). Being conscious of the arousal can help the child deal positively with the emotion. Give children strategies to deal with emotions, particularly negative ones – for example, if a child is angry get him to move away, to verbalise what he is feeling.

- Encourage children to recognise, accept and talk about feelings. Teach children to self-coach – to identify emotions and feelings, to weigh the choices and to manage (through self-talk) to proceed in a positive way. Show them how to read body language and to notice changes in other people's emotions, encourage them to tune into the feelings of others.

- Encourage children to discern what emotional response state is appropriate and useful in a particular circumstance and teach them to keep distressing ideas and thoughts in check.

- Play lots of listening games and ensure that children develop the skill of listening actively.

- In conflict situations approach calmly, get down to the child's level, make eye contact, acknowledge feelings, ask what happened, restate the problem and ask for solutions. Choose one together and be prepared to give follow-up support.

- Have posters of people showing different emotions around the setting and ask the children to describe the feelings of the people on the posters, encourage children to discuss how they know the person is sad, angry etc.

- Frequently use the language of feelings; sad, happy, angry, excited, gloomy, worried, fed up, bubbly. Encourage children to use a wide vocabulary in relation to their own and others' feelings.

- On different occasions the adult should talk to the children about things that make her happy or sad, worried, frightened or excited.

- Play a mime game with a small group of children. Get the children to mime different facial expressions – happy, sad, angry or worried faces. Ask the children to guess what the expression is and to discuss what people are feeling when they make such faces. Ask children to make a face which reflects how they feel.

- Allow children to experience a wide range of art materials, these will help children to work through emotions in a non-verbal manner. Allow children to make a mess and to get dirty. They should be allowed to experience finger painting, foot painting, painting on different material – paper of different colours, cardboard, wood and so on. Have a variety of pencils, crayons, felt tip pens, chalk, paints and paper freely available during the session.

- Set limits and boundaries for children and be consistent – no should mean no and yes should mean yes. Children need adults to set clear and reasonable limits so that the setting is safe and enjoyable. Have a few rules which are consistently adhered to and explain them clearly to the children. Ensure children know what is expected of them. Have a clear behaviour management policy and make sure parents are aware of it and also ensure they are aware of the rules and limits of the setting.

- If there is a recurring problem with a child's behaviour, ask to meet with the child's parents and if necessary, in collaboration with parents, seek additional support and advice from other professionals. Do not let the problem escalate or get out of hand. Take note of challenging behaviour and describe what happened clearly. This may help identify any triggers or patterns.

- Support families in their parenting role. Provide training and development courses for parents on play, on caring for the young child, on behaviour management and on personal development. Welcome parents into the setting and ensure parents know you are willing to listen to them. Reassure them of your confidentiality policy. However, do not promise to keep a secret if you cannot, for example if a child protection issue is disclosed.

- Know the signs of child abuse and neglect and if in doubt take action.

- Ensure that children have eaten when they arrive in the morning, if necessary provide a healthy breakfast – children who are hungry will be unable to concentrate and will be cranky and argumentative.

- Be careful not to label a child no matter what type of behaviour he exhibits - no bullies, no stars, no troublemakers, no best, no worst, no winners, no losers. Labelling a child can result in a self-fulfilling prophecy and the tag can follow the child from one setting to the next.

- Have a quiet corner where a child who is upset, tired or fed up can go and lie down on a comfortable sofa or beanbag. Provide a large stuffed toy there and introduce it as a special friend for anyone who is lonely or upset.

- The adult must consider how her demeanour impacts on the children in her care. A frown and a cross tone of voice communicate stress and irritability while a genuine smile, good eye contact and a warm voice communicate approachability and friendliness. The adult needs to think about how she appears to the children and needs to leave personal problems outside the setting.

- There will be days when the adult feels stressed, sad, unwell or irritable. She needs to be aware of how she feels and to talk to the children about it. 'I'm a bit sad/cross/worried today' and reassure them that it is not anything they are doing to make her feel like this (and if it is something they are doing then tell them also).

- Time must be made for every child. It is important to get down to the child's level when talking to and listening to him. Don't interrupt, contradict or ask him to hurry up, be interested in what he is saying, ask for opinions and allow children to be part of the decision-making process.

- Make up a collage of each child's life. Ask children to bring in photos of their families, pets and of themselves on their own. Get them to do a hand/foot print with paint. Ask them about their likes and dislikes, the food they eat, the clothes they wear, their favourite activities at home and at school. Get them to cut pictures out of old magazines and toy catalogues of the toys they like. Stick all their 'bits about me' on a large page. Hang it on the wall in the setting under a heading, 'All about ...' or make it into individual books for the children to keep.

- Encourage children's capacity to sympathise and empathise with others. Get them to think about how the other child is feeling after he has had a toy removed from him or when his dog dies or when he gets a new baby brother.

- Encourage and support children to do things for themselves, to take care of their own physical needs, to tidy up, to put on and take off their coats and to hang them up. Ensure the hanger is at child's level and have the child's photograph and name pasted above each one.

- Clay, dough, woodwork, sand, water, large blocks should be available daily. All children, in particular those with aggressive or disruptive behaviours, will get satisfaction from being legitimately constructive and destructive.

- Teddy bears, dolls, and all soft toys are particularly good for children who are lonely, upset or distressed. They give comfort, companionship and security. They can help the child work through a problem at second hand in the same way as books and stories.

- Yoga should be introduced to help combat stress and to enable children to relax. Get the children to form a circle and to sit with legs crossed, ensure each child has enough space to stretch out on his own mat. Lower the lights or pull the curtains and light a small lamp or candle. Then with some quiet soothing music playing in the background children can do neck rolls, back stretches, balancing, breathing (in through nose and out through mouth). Visualisation could be introduced, like asking children to close their eyes and to imagine they are getting rid of all their worries and fears and telling them that they are in their favourite place.

- Children should be allowed to run around to work off excess energy for a specific amount of time every day. Physical activity releases positive hormones which are vital for children and their emotional development. Where possible children should be allowed access to the outdoors every day, regardless of the weather.

- Large indoor and outdoor toys, tractors, trampolines, climbing frames, bikes are a necessity for emotional expression. These can give excited, tired or over-active children a chance to gain some feelings of physical and mental well-being.

- Role and pretend play is vital for all areas of development, but is a necessity for emotional development. Shops, home corner, hospital corner, dressing up - these are good for everything but especially for co-operation, for differentiating self from others, for building up tolerance and patience, role taking perspective, seeing and accepting difference. A wide range of props, dress up clothes and equipment should be available in the pretend area so that a wide variety of scenarios can be enacted. Adults should be on hand to participate in this play but it is the children, not the adult, who should have control. However, the adult can help to extend and develop the play and can contribute in very positive ways when the children take the lead and invite the adults to join in these very complex and vital scenarios.

- Death is a natural part of life and we cannot protect children from the reality of it happening in their lives. Talk about the life cycle, have stories that deal with death and dying. If a child in the group is bereaved, accompany them on their journey through grief with informed support, information and encouragement. Despite the pain and sadness of a bereavement, most children can manage to cope with their loss and continue to grow and develop creatively, but it is vital that children are given the help and support they need. If left to cope alone, they may never fully recover from the trauma.

- At the end of the day ask children to reflect on what they have done, ask them what they liked best, least, what they would like to do the following day and so on.

- Every setting should have a book area, preferably a quiet corner or an area that can be cut off with a low partition. The area should be cosy and comfortable with child-sized sofas, beanbags, cushions and a low-level table. Books should be displayed on wall mounts with the front of the book facing the child.

- Books and stories are a brilliant way of enhancing emotional development. Reading either to an individual child, a small or large group of children enhances emotional development. If reading to a large group keep the story short, ensure that every child can see the book you are reading, ask questions to help children concentrate and encourage children to talk about the pictures. Big picture books (large size) are useful for reading to a large group of children. Many publishers do large and small versions and a group of children can easily see the big version.

- Reading stories can open up wonderful conversations and can introduce new concepts as well as clarifying many things for children. Books should be chosen to reflect the interests and needs of children. Books should be available that deal with life's issues - death, divorce, going to hospital, going to formal school, self-esteem, sibling rivalry, feeling sad, worried and so on.

- There are many, many books available which can aid in the development of the child's emotions so use them regularly and in an interactive way to develop children's thinking and their awareness and experience of emotions.

- Go to the website www.aaabooksearch.com and use the ISBN number of each of the books to read a synopsis of the contents. On the site you can also get reviews of the book and find links to similar books. This is useful in helping you decide on which are the most useful books for your setting.

- A large variety of books should be available and these need to be changed and updated regularly. Joining the local library is an inexpensive way of doing this. Also suggest to parents to join the library and give them ideas on the kind of books to look out for. Encourage them to buy their children books for Christmas, birthdays and special occasions.

Children's books which are useful for emotional development

Starting School (ISBN 014050737X) by Janet and Allan Ahlberg.
What Makes Me Happy? (ISBN 1564028283) by Catherine and Laurence Anholt.
Granpa (ISBN 0099434083) by John Burningham.
The Red Woolen Blanket (ISBN 1564028488) by Jethro Byrde.
Double Dip Feelings – stories to help children understand emotions (ISBN 1557988129) by Barbara Cain.
The Bad Tempered Ladybird (ISBN 0140503986) by Eric Carle.
I Like Me (ISBN 0140508198) by Nancy Carlson.

Going to School (ISBN 0794501052), *Going to the Dentist* (ISBN 0746041195), *Going to the Doctor* (ISBN 0746041179), *Moving House* (ISBN 0746049277) and *The New Puppy* (ISBN 0746049315) - the Usborne 'First Experiences' series by Anne Civardi.

Lost in the Museum (ISBN 0440410959) by Miriam Cohen.

So Much (ISBN 0763602965) by Trish Cooke.

Big Brother, Little Brother (ISBN 0763601462) by Penny Dale.

First Day Jitters (ISBN 158089061X) by Julie Danneberg.

Jim's Lion (ISBN 0763611751) by Russell Hoban.

The Huge Bag of Worries (ISBN 0750021241) by Virginia Ironside.

A Quilt for Baby (ISBN 0763619256) by Kim Lewis.

I am Happy (ISBN 0763617539) by Steve Light.

How Do You Feel Big Book (ISBN 0237518880) by Gillian Liu.

Who's Going to Take Care of Me (ISBN 0060241063) by Michelle Magorian.

The New Baby (ISBN 0307119424) by Mercer Mayer.

Glad Monster, Sad Monster (ISBN 0316573957) by Anne Miranda.

Sad isn't Bad: A good-grief guidebook for kids dealing with loss (ISBN 0870293214) by Michaelene Mundy.

I Like it When (ISBN 0749731192) by Mary Murphy.

Jealous (ISBN 156766671X) by Slyvia Root Tester.

We're Going on a Bear Hunt (ISBN 0689815816) by Michael Rosen.

Sometimes Mama and Papa Fight (ISBN 0060256125) by Marjorie Sharmat.

Mom and Dad Don't Live Together Anymore (ISBN 0920236871) by Kathy Stinson.

Katie Goes to the Hospital (ISBN 1858549264) by Barbara Taylor Cork

Badger's Parting Gift (ISBN 0688115187) by Susan Varley.

The Owl Babies (ISBN 1564029654), *Can't You Sleep Little Bear* (ISBN 0763619299) and *You and Me Little Bear* (ISBN 0763605743) by Martin Waddell.

Edward's First Night Away (ISBN 0744544874) by Rosemary Wells.

CHAPTER FOUR

Social Development

Introduction

One of the most disturbing failures of modern society is the sense of isolation and loneliness expressed by so many children and young people. Moreover, there is an epidemic of feelings of isolation, loneliness and extreme shyness and anxiety in all age groups in many countries all over the world. The more technological communication has developed, the more isolated people, and in particular children, feel (O'Donnchadha 2000). Elkind (2001 p.5) says: "It is indeed no small irony that at the very time the stress of social life and change is threatening the existence of childhood, we know far more about childhood than we have ever known in the past". Today's society is experiencing higher rates of crime, cruelty and violence than in the past and these rates have led to an increasing interest, in the academic community, in combating these trends by discovering how to develop social competence and caring behaviour in children. Schweinhart and Weikart (1997) claim that the priority of academic over social objectives in the early years setting is a contributor to these social problems and leads to longitudinal disadvantages, as highlighted by their long-term research. Lack of personal contact and social development is cited as aiding the breakdown of community life and many believe that the social fabric is falling apart.

Social development is about developing the social aspects of humanity. One of the main reasons that children need to develop socially is so that society can continue to exist. Societies are founded on their social structure, that is, the relatively stable patterns of social behaviour which underlie them. Each element of social structure such as the family, religion, childhood, politics and economic system has specific social functions or roles to fulfil in order for civilisation to continue. Babies are born into a highly complex social world with its intricate underlying social structures and functions. From birth, they are active participants in a world of other people and quite early on they must begin to understand the intentions, feelings and actions of others as well as understanding the social rules of the world, if they are to develop socially (Macionis 1989). The whole basis for living and working together is founded on good relationships and on social development. Thus, one would imagine that achieving optimum social development would be a priority, but is it?

Importance of early years for social development

No one can become fully human without social experiences. The cases of children such as Genie (Pines 1981) clearly show the crucial importance of social competence for the development of human personality. Genie was a 13-year-old girl who was kept in isolation in a small room from age two. Prior to discovery she had been deprived in every way and though subsequently exposed to intensive treatment she never fully caught up. Judging by cases such as that of Genie, it seems there may be a point at which social isolation in human infancy results in developmental damage that cannot be fully repaired later on. Exactly at what point this occurs is not clear and for obvious ethical reasons researchers cannot conduct experiments which involve the isolation of human beings. Thus, much of what we know about the effects of social isolation comes from the rare cases of children placed in isolation, such as those of Genie and also children living in Romanian orphanages (Gunnar 1998). The research of Rutter and the ERA team (1998) which follows the adjustment of children adopted into British families from Romanian orphanages shows that although these children make great strides in catching up in height, weight and cognitive domains, they continue to have difficulties in social areas such as in play and in attachment behaviours. Research on animals and primates, for example, Harlow and Harlow (1962) is also significant. Their work on rhesus monkeys also showed that there may be a point at which social isolation results in irreparable damage. Thus, the importance of social experience is clearly evident in the lack of human development characteristics of socially isolated children and primates and evidence suggests that if early childhood is devoid of social experience some permanent limitation in development may occur. Eliot (1999 p.324) says: "In humans, the critical period for social nurturing probably extends until about three years of age, with deprivation during the first year being the most devastating". This clearly shows that the early years are vital for social development.

Ecological approach to child development

Children's lives and social development are profoundly influenced by events that happen in the world outside their homes, as recognised by Bronfenbrenner's ecological approach to child development (1979). Bronfenbrenner claimed that in order to understand both the subtle and the obvious ways in which children interact with others and with their environment, their lives should be thought of as a "nested arrangement of concentric structures, each contained within the next" (ibid. p.22). Bronfenbrenner's four-nested system of the 'micro', 'meso', 'exo' and 'macrosystem' illustrates the complexity of child development and, in particular, social development. The 'microsystem' is what a child experiences in a given setting, for example his home. The 'mesosystem' refers to links amongst settings in which the child directly participates. For example, the quality of his childminder's environment might affect his behaviour in the early years setting. The 'exosystem' refers to links to settings in which the child does not participate directly, but which do affect him, such as his mother's work environment may affect her behaviour at home and hence the quality of her childcare. Finally, the 'macrosystem' refers to the general pattern of ideology and organisation of social institutions in the society or subculture the child is in. Thus, for example, the experience of a Traveller child in an early years setting is influenced by views of society in general towards ethnic minorities, Travellers in particular.

In psychology, ecology is understood as the range of situations in which adults and children engage, the roles they play, the situations they encounter and the consequences of these encounters. Ecological descriptions provide an overall picture of people's niches in the world. With respect to children, ecology gives us a sense of the whole child and the many influences that impact on that child's learning and development and it helps show the many social expectations small children encounter. Each relationship in Bronfenbrenner's model is reciprocal - the child is influenced by the parent and *vice versa*. This reciprocal relationship reverberates onto wider society which both shapes and is shaped by its individual members. In advocating this model of human development, Bronfenbrenner is warning of the dangers of focusing on the individual without taking into account the context within which he lives: individual; family; community; society; and larger world factors, impact on a child's development. Early on, the environment which has the most direct influence is the home and family and as the child grows he gets greater exposure to the wider world. Children do not develop in a vacuum – each child is born into an ecological, familial, cultural, geographical and historical context. As Isenberg and Jalongo (1997 p.11) say:

> Early childhood education can never be decontextualised or occur in isolation. Rather, our work on behalf of young children is deeply woven into the social, political and historical fabric of our lives, children's lives, and their families' lives both in and out of school.

Introducing children to the complex world outside the family exposes children to serious challenges and involves great strides in a child's social development. All encounters, good and bad, impact on his development. Such encounters are called the socialisation process (Cole and Cole 1989).

Socialisation

Socialisation is a vital aspect of social development, is based on all social experiences and occurs everywhere. It is not a simple process of learning, but is a complex balancing act in which children encounter a huge range of ideas in the process of forming their own distinctive personality. Socialisation shapes how we think, feel and act and children learn a myriad of social skills through interacting with others. Through socialisation they also learn the values and behaviours accepted in their society. Children's social contact with others assists their learning and such social experiences hopefully provide the child with qualities and capacities that are associated with being a fully integrated, socially competent human being (Dowling 2000).

Social development

Social development is a double-sided process in which children become integrated into the larger social community, while at the same time becoming differentiated as distinctive individuals. Being accepted into the community comes about through a process of socialisation. Through socialisation, children come to know the standards and values of their society. Through personality formation, the individual child gets a sense of himself and develops a distinctive way of thinking and feeling, and personality development is closely aligned and intertwined with socialisation (Damon 1983).

Through social development, children come to adopt as reasonable, and even necessary, the rules prescribed by their social groups. By the age of six, many children will have learned a great deal about the roles they are expected to play and how to behave in accordance with them. Some enter school being used to warm loving relationships within the family and will have had many and varied chances to meet a wide variety of different adults and children. Other children will have had few opportunities to develop socially. They will have experienced few social contacts and will not fully understand the social categories, rules, roles and expectations that are needed in order to take part in the social world. Studies suggest that the first six to seven years of development are critical for the development of social skills, so it is vital that children are helped to develop socially in the early years, both at home and at school (Parker and Asher 1987).

From birth, children are social beings preferring to interact with people rather than things. From 18 months on they talk with increasing frequency about others and from about two they increasingly talk about feeling states, the reasons that underlie them and about how social rules apply to others. From around three on, they connect to the mental states of others (thinking, knowing, believing, remembering). Their understanding and use of social rules becomes rapidly more elaborate and more explicitly anticipated during the third year. They also show a practical knowledge of the ideas of responsibility, of excuses, of intent and incapacity, of how rules apply differently to different family members, how rules can be questioned and how transgressions can be justified. They are beginning to understand something of the authority relations within the family structure and can comment on the behaviour of others. Children of two and three have a far greater and deeper understanding of their social world than was thought in the past. With development, their understanding becomes increasingly explicit and they can use their capacities in an even wider range of situations. As children's ideas about others and their social world become clearer, their theories about other people become more elaborate. These developments in the ability to conceive of others' minds in the second half of the third year have profound consequences for children's understanding of their social world and lead to a new state in their social development (Dunn 1988).

Socialisation during these early years is vital, as this is when children construct their first understanding of community. These early interpretations of adult expectations and roles form the foundations for future social development. Thus, socialisation needs the active participation of adults and children. Through socialisation, children learn how to act in social situations, how to share and how to be fair, how to express themselves and how to solve problems without hurting or depriving others. It also allows them to enjoy, trust and care for others. Between three and six, children make great strides in controlling their aggressive impulses, in caring for others and in resisting what they know they should not do in order to be accepted socially: "A child experiences and makes sense out of society, only by gaining knowledge of such social relations as authority, attachment and friendships, and through such social transactions as punishment, sharing, kindness and hostility" (Damon 1977 p.2). A child's social development is impacted upon by the socialisation process, his attachment history, his level of cognitive development and his temperament. No single factor explains how a child develops socially. Thus, both nature and nurture influence social development and both are so intertwined that is it difficult to separate the effects of each (Dodge 1990).

Dunn (1988) and Radke-Yarrow, Zahn-Waxler and Chapman (1983) agree regarding children's sensitivity to others in their social world. They claim that children monitor, with intent, the relations between others as well as commenting on and intervening in their interactions. They co-operate with others in conflicts against another and are able to use one family member against another. The entry to early years settings and formal school expose children to unfamiliar people and experiences and introduce several new elements into children's socialisation experiences. Children who attend day-care widen their socialisation process very early on. However, most children develop early social knowledge as a family member and part of this usually includes developing an attachment to a parent or main caregiver.

Attachment

The attachment relationship (also discussed in Chapter Three) impacts on the child's orientation and feelings towards others in his social world. The quality of the attachment relationship is closely correlated with the child's ability to become independent, socially competent, confident, positive, and flexible on the one hand or on the other hand may result in the child becoming rigid, withdrawn, negative and easily frustrated, if the relationship is not attuned. Thus, the child's social style with others is strongly influenced by his attachment history. Also, children with problems in their attachment history seem to evoke reactions from others that keep them in negative relationships and that prevent them from developing more positive social behaviours (Schickendanz et al. 1990).

Children's attachment history has a strong influence on their social and emotional development and by the time they reach formal school some are popular and preferred as playmates while others are disliked and rejected. The ones who are popular are often children who have positive, friendly personalities. They do not engage in much aggressive, hostile or harassing behaviour and their social style seems to be related to their attachment history. There also seems to be a connection between attachment history and the tendency to be a bully or victim. Studies show that most victims (children who are passive in the face of aggression) had anxious/ambivalent attachments. Victimisers or bullies on the other hand seem to have experienced anxious/avoidant attachments while children with secure attachments tend not to be either victims or victimisers (Troy and Sroute 1987). Thus, the effects of attachment and social development can reverberate through all aspects of the child's life including all the different areas of child development, long after infancy and toddlerhood are over, since all areas of his life and development influence each other and are deeply intertwined.

Interaction of different developmental areas

Social development impacts on each and every other area of development and social development is impacted on by all other areas also. Moral development, values taught and socialisation processes used by parents and other adults influence whether children develop in pro- or anti- social ways. Emotional development also impacts on social development, and how a child feels about himself and others has huge repercussions for his social growth. Spirituality allows the child to transcend the gap between self and others, giving him an understanding of who he is and what things and people mean to him. Cognitive development also impacts on social development and *vice versa*. Theorists such as Vygotsky (1896-1934) explore the idea of the child as someone who negotiates meaning and understanding in a social context, emphasising the intricate and reciprocal relationships between the individual child and the social context. Vygotsky (1978) argued that it is as a result of the social interactions between the growing child and other members of that child's community that he acquires the tools of learning and thinking. Vygotsky (ibid.) claims that it is in fact out of this co-operative process of engaging in mutual activities with more expert others that the child becomes more knowledgeable.

A central concept of Vygotsky's is the zone of proximal development, (Z.P.D.). Z.P.D. is the distance between the child's actual developmental level and his potential level of development under the guidance of a more expert adult or peer, his argument being that children learn from other people who are more knowledgeable than themselves. This expert intervention should be at a level just beyond the child's existing developmental level, so that it provides some challenge, but should not be too far ahead to make the child feel unduly stressed. The point being that within the Z.P.D. the child can accomplish something he cannot do alone, learning from the experience and support of others (Vygotsky 1978; Smith and Cowie 1991). Thus, social and cognitive development are interconnected and interdependent. Also, as children grow, their level of social cognition, their ability to understand other people's problems and feelings grows. With greater understanding it becomes easier for children to respond in socially appropriate ways. However, a higher level of social cognition does not automatically result in better behaviour, as many other things also impact on this ability, in particular emotional and moral development. Thus, it seems that developmental areas such as cognitive, moral, social, spiritual and emotional development are all deeply intertwined and equally important.

Sex or gender role identification

As children grow and mature in all areas of development, they encounter greater social diversity and they become more aware of their own social categories - race, colour, language and so on, and they also become acutely aware of their own particular gender (Finkelstein and Haskins 1983). Sex refers to the division of humanity into biological categories of male and female, while gender is said to refer to the human traits linked by culture to each sex. The full significance of being feminine and masculine is not fully evident among infants and manifests as children grow in their social environment. Within society, males are schooled to be masculine and females are taught to be feminine. Gender guides how children think of themselves and how they interact with others, so gender development is a fundamental element of the socialisation process. From birth human feelings, thoughts and actions reflect cultural definitions of gender. As children interact, they quickly learn that boys and girls are defined as different kinds of human beings and by three to four they can apply the distinction to themselves (Bem 1981).

Actual gender roles are the attitudes and activities that a culture links to each sex and throughout life children experience pressure to conform to gender roles with gender becoming a blueprint imposed on children by all agents of socialisation. The importance of gender is emphasised by the way that children are dressed and groomed in appropriate masculine or feminine ways. Also, play is a serious means of teaching children how their culture defines the role of each sex and the ways they are asked to help at home and at school often serve to reinforce the distinct gender-based racial worlds of the male and female. The toys presented are also likely to reflect cultural expectations for each sex - wheeled toys and building equipment for boys and dolls, dolls' houses and miniature kitchens for girls. Best (1983) claims this 'second' curriculum encourages children to adopt the identity and role considered appropriate to their sex. The books provided to children in the not too distant past also presented the lives of males and females in stereotypical ways, with males engaging in diverse and interesting activities while females helped at home or played with dolls. However, the growing realisation that what is learned in childhood affects people's lives as adults has led to some changes in publishing and today's books for children tend to portray males and females in a more balanced way.

During the pre-school years, children gradually develop well-articulated concepts of what it means to be a girl or a boy and this shapes their behaviour. Between two and six they are piecing together their conceptual structures and both biological and social factors play important roles in promoting sex-appropriate behaviours and the development of basic sex role categories. From around three, conceptual thinking is more in evidence, but as yet children are still struggling to reconcile a great deal of information. Not until they reach six or seven do they have a stable concept of their own identity as male or female (Perry and Bussey 1984). By age five, children begin to associate certain personality traits with females and males. Williams and Best (1990) in their cross cultural study of twenty four countries, state that the most clearly stereotyped (a stereotype is an over-simplified generalisation not based on evidence and usually carrying negative implications) traits for females were gentleness, weakness, soft-heartedness and appreciativeness. Aggression, strength, cruelty and coarseness were the traits identified for males. Very early on, children begin to take on the role of male or female and to associate particular traits and behaviours with that role and to maintain those beliefs over time. Exactly how this occurs it not entirely clear. It appears that socialisation needs identification (the child must have a sense of who he is and who he wants to be) and identification follows a different pattern for boys and girls, with the developmental path that brings boys and girls to their respective identity being different. Three proposed mechanisms have featured prominently in discussions on identification: differentiation and affiliation; observation and imitation; and cognition.

(i)   Psychoanalytical theory
(Differentiation and affiliation)

Sigmund Freud's work is one of the best known accounts of identity formation. His theory gives primacy to the manner in which children satisfy their basic drives as the necessary condition for their survival. He claimed all biological drives have as their aim the survival and propagation of the species. He believed the sexual nature of all gratification remained constant throughout life, although the forms of that gratification changed. He claimed sexual gratification passed through an orderly sequence of stages, defined in term of the parts of the body that people used to satisfy their drives, with human beings striving at each stage to satisfy the drives that dominated that stage. His theory of identification, as part of his overall theory, assumes that the process occurs indirectly. The child is caught in hidden conflict between his fears and his desires and resolves these conflicts through identification. It is believed that male identification requires differentiation from the mother, while female identification needs continued affiliation with the mother (Freud 1933). Freud's work can be criticised on both methodological and theoretical grounds, but it remains influential in contemporary developmental research.

(ii)   Social learning theory
(Observation and imitation)

Unlike Freud, social learning theorists assume that the process of identification is not driven by inner conflicts, they claim it is simply a matter of observation and imitation. Bandura and Walters (1969) and Mischel (1977) claim that behaviour is shaped by the environment; children observe that males and females behave differently. Thus, children develop different hypotheses about appropriate female and male behaviours and roles. Also, children are rewarded differently by adults for different kinds of behaviour and so learn and choose to engage in sex-appropriate behaviours that will lead to rewards. Social learning theorists assume that these appropriate behaviours are shaped by the distribution of rewards and punishments in the environment. However, this theory's explanation is limited and cannot be looked on as a comprehensive explanation (Cole and Cole 1989).

(iii)   Cognitive developmental theory

The cognitive developmental theorists such as Piaget (1932) and Kohlberg (1966) believe that a child's concepts are central to socialisation and to sex role acquisition. They stress the child's active structuring of his own experiences and claim children are not passive products of social training. According to Kohlberg, the crucial factor in sex role identification is children's developing ability to categorise themselves as either boys or girls. Once formed, this concept is difficult to reverse and is maintained regardless of the social environment. Well before children manifest knowledge of sexual stereotypes, girls and boys often (from about one and a half to two) act very differently from each other and are already developing somewhat distinctive styles of play. They also often prefer to play with different things, playing more with sex identified toys even when non-sex typed toys are simultaneously available. This suggests that even at this stage, children have developed sex-typed preferences. However, children make such sex-typed choices without expressing conscious awareness of sexual identity and show little evidence that their behaviour is, as yet, guided by conceptual understanding (Maccoby 1980).

Freudian and cognitive developmentalists believe that a child's sexual identification and later sex role behaviour cannot be affected by anything but the most drastic changes in environmental circumstances. On the other hand, social learning theorists disagree and place emphasis on the environment and on the adult's power to shape the child. It is not yet clear whose beliefs are the more correct but by whatever means, children entering formal education have acquired the belief that they are members of one sex or the other and usually act in accordance with this belief. Such a belief serves as an important basis for acquiring and shaping other roles that contribute to a child's personality, such as that of son/daughter, brother/sister, nephew/niece, grandson/daughter, friend, pupil and so on. Precisely how the development of gender/sex identification occurs remains a matter for discussion and according to Elkind (2001) each of the theories contains a certain amount of truth. However, it does appear that the socialisation process links personal identity to gender (gender identity) and teaches males and females to engage in distinctive activities (gender roles). The social world of the child and all the major socialisation agents - the family, peer group, school, the mass media and society in general, reinforce cultural definitions of what it means to be either masculine or feminine. Thus, the macro-system plays a large role in a child's gender identification. The macro-system also influences how children who are different are treated in the early years setting.

Racism and prejudice

Some young children experience rejection and lack of friends because they differ in some way from the majority of their peer group. Such differences may include having different religious, racial or ethnic backgrounds, skin colour or being differently-abled. Historically, Ireland has seen itself essentially as a homogenous society and as a country of emigration not immigration. Our deep conservatism in relation to culture and our isolated situation has 'protected' us to a large degree from having to make decisions about multiculturalism and diversity. However, the reality is that there has been a variety of individuals and groups, all along, who experienced racism and prejudice in Ireland. (For example, the general lack of respect and recognition of the travelling community or the status of people who have a disability). Cultural diversity and racism existed in Ireland long before the recent increase in the numbers of people coming to live here, so racism is not new, but only of late has it become more visible because of the changes that have occurred in our society (Murray 2001). The increase in the immigration of non-European Union minority communities has shaken Irish society and has shown up uncomfortable tensions in relation to racism, prejudice, social values, diversity and identity issues. These changes are challenging and have implications for every sector of society, including early years education and care. Racism in Ireland affects everyone. The belief that it is only a problem for ethnic minorities reflects a public denial of racism as an issue and has to be challenged and changed.

Institutional racism also occurs everywhere and this type of racism is not the sort of racism that is overt, such as name calling or violent acts against minority groups. It is more subtle and pervasive and could be defined as the policies and practices in institutions such as schools and organisations. Such racism has the effect of perpetuating racial inequality without actually acknowledging that unfair practices or procedures are occurring. Racism and discrimination need to be addressed immediately. In particular, people working with young children need to address these issues personally and professionally and they need to be trained to understand and redirect their behaviour and the behaviour of the children with whom they are working. Research on the impact of racism on child development exposes the damage it inflicts on all children involved. By the age of four, children can have already internalised stereotypical gender roles, racial bias and negative feelings about peers and so children are receptive to both negative and positive attitudes and behaviours, including stereotyping and misinformation about certain groups (Murray 1999). This forcefully points to the need for an anti-bias education for young children. Active intervention is necessary if children are to develop positive attitudes about people of different ethnic backgrounds, physical and mental ability and so on.

Every country has its own unique history, cultures and conditions, that shape its work with young children, including the area of anti-discrimination. However, certain dynamics appear to cut across national boundaries. At the beginning of the 21st century the challenge of ending discrimination of all kinds is vital to our survival (Derman-Sparks 1998). The early years are of extreme importance in this regard, as young children are at the very beginning of their development of attitudes about themselves and others. We need an anti-bias approach in both training and practice. Early years practitioners typically have no previous experience of working with immigrant groups or differently-abled children, so they need training. The realisation and recognition that all cultures have different values, languages, religious beliefs, family structures and customs must inform practice. Practice then has to change to meet the needs of children from minority groups rather than expecting them to give up their own culture to survive in the dominant culture system. We also need an anti-bias education, the underlying intention of which is to foster the development of children and adults who have the emotional strength, critical thinking ability and activist skills to work with others to build caring, just, diverse communities and societies for all (Derman-Sparks 1989). Adults should also be aware that multi-cultural, anti-bias education is not a just set of activities added on to the existing curriculum. Instead it embodies a perspective rather than a curriculum. Every decision the adult makes about material, the organisation of the setting, the role of parents and the approach to the curriculum reflects attitudes towards cultures. According to Murray (2001) what is needed is a mainstream education system which does not treat all children as the 'same' but which acknowledges the particularity of each individual child. If this is not done, children may continue to develop in ways which do not contribute positively to their social development. A culturally appropriate curriculum would ensure that all children and their families feel included, motivated and empowered and by countering misinformation and stereotypical thinking that children have already learned, a contribution can be made to their all round development. Remedial steps must be taken to limit aggressive tendencies, bullying, prejudice and discrimination. There is a need not just to tolerate but to recognise, understand and accept that cultural diversity is positive and to appreciate what we can gain from this diversity in our society. We have serious choices to make, we can guide children to develop a strong identity and teach them to value all people or we can allow them to build an unstable self-identity which is based on ignorance and fear of people who are different from themselves. In many cases to date, the latter rather than the former has occurred and as a result racism and negative prejudice have manifested themselves as bullying or aggressive behaviour.

Bullying and aggression

Bullying is a deliberate, aggressive act which is intended to cause distress, harm or damage. The act may be verbal, physical or psychological. The problem is so great in Ireland, according to Murray and Keane (1998), that 20 per cent of children are afraid to go to school because of it. Bullying can result in the destruction of confidence and self-esteem. Victims encounter feelings of shame and guilt, worthlessness, helplessness, loss of sleep/appetite, panic, nightmares, behaviour problems, depression and even suicide. Many factors conspire to allow bullying: genetic and biological make up combine with social structures, power structures and hierarchies. Thus, psychological, biological and social factors combine to bring bullying about. A survey carried out by the North Eastern Health Board in Ireland in early 2002 revealed frightening results regarding bullying, as it exposed the fact that one in five teenagers (12-16) who suffer or suffered bullying think or thought about taking their own lives (Irish Examiner Newspaper 2nd May 2002). Thus, bullying can be a dreadfully serious problem for children of all ages.

Childhood aggression impacts on social development. For most children, while a certain amount of assertive and aggressive behaviour is normal, it is kept within reasonable bounds so that it does not become disruptive of peer group activities and thus children avoid rejection by peers. However, some children show high levels of aggression which can be stable over time. If not dealt with, such children show persistent high aggressiveness and are at greatly increased risks for antisocial and violent behaviour and may even become delinquent. Also, high aggression with low social skills leads to unpopularity and rejection in peer relationships (Farrington 1990). Parenting seems to have an important role here and children who experience irritable and ineffective discipline at home, together with a lack of parental warmth, are very likely to become aggressive in peer groups and at school (Cole and Cole 1989).

Bullying or harassment emerged as one of three types of aggressive behaviour highlighted by Manning, Heron and Marshall (1978) as occurring in the early years setting. The developmental task of growing up ensures that some conflict between children is inevitable. In the early years setting children of different shapes, sizes, colours, intellectual ability, language capacity, financial background, social skills and common sense are brought together. This is where bullying begins and later educational establishments become a breeding ground for this type of behaviour (Murray and Keane 1998). Landy (2002) says that research now indicates that pre-school aged children are particularly at risk for being victimised and bullied, compared with older children. Bullying can be carried out by a group or by one individual child and is usually a repeated action against a particular victim. The child/children doing the bullying are generally thought of or perceived as being stronger and the victim usually does not feel himself to be in a position to retaliate effectively. Bullying can take the form of hitting, pushing, and taking food, toys or money. It can also involve name calling, teasing and social exclusion. In the early years, the playground is the most likely place for bullying to occur and research such as that of O'Moore, Kirkham and Smith (1997) shows that bullying is quite widespread in schools and probably goes on to a much greater degree than parents, practitioners or teachers realise.

O'Moore et al. (1997) carried out a nationwide study on bullying in Irish schools. They found that 27 per cent of primary schools did not recognise bullying as a problem, yet the study found that 43 per cent of children in primary school were involved in bullying either as victims, bullies, or bully-victims. Also, alarmingly, only 38 per cent of pupils reported that their teacher almost always tried to put a stop to bullying. O'Moore et al. (1997) also found that 22 per cent of primary schools had not developed a bullying policy one year after they had received a copy of the Department of Education's National Guidelines on Countering Bullying in Schools. This is disappointing since research shows that vigorous, concerted, sustained and co-operative implementation of policies to combat bullying in schools is effective in significantly reducing school bullying (Murray and Keane 1998). O'Moore (1997) says all adults need to be targeted to dispel the myths about bullying which still exist and she stresses the need to identify bullying among children. O'Moore says there needs to be a strong emphasis on the prevention of bullying and that a lot of bullying could be avoided if adults were more sensitive to children. As well as this, the survey found that children who bully have significantly lower global self-esteem than children who are not involved in bullying. 'Bullies' see themselves as being more unhappy and dissatisfied, as having lower intellectual and school status and as being troublesome. They also see themselves as being anxious, unattractive physically and unpopular. Thus, again the argument is raised for preventing low self-esteem and enhancing poor self-esteem. If adults can be sensitised to the ill effects of bullying, much can be done to reduce bullying/victimisation problems. Any training provided for adults should include what is meant by bullying and victimisation, the extent, the signs, the effects, the causes, preventative measures, how to deal with bully/victim problems and how to develop a policy to counter bullying behaviour. Also, the formation of friendships can do much to counteract bullying so the development of friendships must be part of all early years curricula.

Friendships

Friendship is one of life's most essential and rewarding forms of interaction and is a feature of every culture in the world (Bukowski, Newcomb and Hartup 1996). From as early as 12-18 months on, peers seem to be especially interesting to young children and friendships can be identified among infants and toddlers, although the cognitive and linguistic associates of these relationships are not yet apparent. There is a low level of actual interaction at this stage, probably because infants have not yet learnt the skills of social interaction such as the appropriate behaviours for particular situations, the behaviours to expect returned and so on. However, adults can 'scaffold' (support) early infant social interactions but it does take another two to three years before children become really competent at interacting socially with peers. However, interactions increase when small children are brought together regularly and such children often become involved in play and social game activities that involve taking turns, repetition, imitation, laughing and smiling. Parten (1932) observed the play and social behaviour of pre-school children in the 1920s. She outlined the types of play that young children engaged in and labelled them as being unoccupied, onlooker on other's activities, being involved in solitary or parallel play and later associative or co-operative activity with others. Parallel play is when children play near each other with the same material but do not interact very much, associative play is when children interact together at an activity, doing similar things and co-operative play is when children interact together in complementary ways. She found that the first types of play declined with age whereas associative and co-operative activities, the ones which involved peer interaction, increased with age. Later researchers used Parten's categories but fine-tuned them to 1) solitary (including unoccupied and onlooker), 2) parallel and 3) group (associative and co-operative). Research shows that pre-school aged children engaged in free play divide their time among these three categories but shift towards group play as they reach the later stages of the pre-school era, showing their need to form relationships and friendships (Smith 1978). Also, one of the most striking features of children's ability to co-operate at this early stage is in their ability to engage in make-believe play. Such pretend play leads to the shared exploration of social rules and roles and helps children understand how and why people behave as they do. By three to four children show a remarkable breadth of interest in their social world and have a coherent grasp of the basis of human action in terms of beliefs, intentions and desires (Miller and Garver 1984; Tizard and Hughes 1984).

It is becoming more and more commonplace for younger children to form friendships as more infants and toddlers experience out-of-home childcare arrangements (Fein and Rivkin 1986). Family relationships also affect children's friendships and children's friendships reflect, and are likely to be influenced by, qualities of their parents' interpersonal relationships. The parent-child relationship, including the quality of parent-child attachment, general parenting style, the parental relationship and the family's wider social contexts (extended family, friends and so on) influence children's ability to make and retain friends. Lytton, Watts and Dunn (1986) stress that the absence of parental warmth has been associated with social maladjustment and delinquency and affects a child's ability to form attachments and friendships. Conversely, Jacobson and Frye (1991) show that securely attached children show greater social competence with peers at all ages and have been found to engage in more reciprocal and less hostile or negative interaction with peers as well as receiving more positive interaction bids from peers.

Sullivan (1965) claims that children from three to four on have a uniquely important need for playmates and friends, as these relationships enhance their self-esteem and self-worth. Friendship is a very important aspect of social development. Friends are emotionally important to a child, even at three and four, as illustrated by the work of Field (1984) who showed the upset caused when one group of children were leaving another group in kindergarten to go on to primary school. Field observed increased upset even after the other children had gone, with the children left behind showing a grief response for the friends they had lost.   Landy (2002) backs this contention by stating that children who lose friends when they move away can show a decline in social competence for a significant period showing just how vital these friendships can be. By age four, friendship means more than just playing together - it becomes subtler and is based on shared experience over a period of time. Slowly, children come to understand what is involved in being a friend, how to maintain that friendship and they may experience rejection and acceptance in that process. Similarities in sex, race, age and activity preferences seem to be important in friendships at all ages and are particularly important for young children's friendships (Rubin 1993). Thus, a young child may not have friends and can quickly become rejected or isolated because he differs in some respect from the majority of his class, as highlighted earlier.

The relationships pre-school aged children form with peers provides substantial benefits, such as emotional support in unfamiliar settings, the opportunity to play with a partner, opportunities to lead, follow, make suggestions, try out new ideas and to negotiate and compromise (Hohmann and Weikart 2002). Friendships impact on children's social and emotional growth and the social relations of young children are centred on their friends as well as their families. In other words, friendships serve an important social role that is different from that of kin relationships. Friendship is closely tied to liking and to taking pleasure in another person's company. It can be defined as a relationship that satisfies specified social needs such as companionship, intimacy, support and affection. Peers and friends can be as strong an influence on children's behaviour as parents, and friends provide different experiences with more reciprocity and co-operation between equals. Friendships are specific attachments which carry expectations and Rubin (1993) claims there are complex social skills involved in making friends. These include the ability to gain entry to group activities, to be approving and supportive of one's peers, being able to manage conflicts appropriately and to exercise tact and sensitivity. Children must also learn to assess other children's play, as the key to success in entering a new group seems to lie in comprehending what is going on in the group and then using that knowledge to go with the flow as if one were already a member of the group. Gaining access to group activities, learning to become desirable companions and dealing with rejection are all beneficial to social development. Also in today's world, it is vital that we find connections to others and that we feel we are members of many groups. These connections promote emotional and moral as well as social development and encourage children to care. There is a clear sense of self-worth, well-being and pride when children show the ethic of friendship and caring. To create a sense of community, to teach caring and to develop friendships is an ongoing challenge. In early years settings friendships and communities can be built by ensuring that children know each other's names and interests, by taking turns, by sharing, by making room in the circle for new children or for late comers, by being friendly and polite, by co-operating and collaborating and by solving conflicts (Charney 1998). Once children form friendships with peers, the qualities of generosity and a desire to share and help others are evoked, as friendships give opportunities for children to be democratic, affectionate and tolerant.

Small group sizes are particularly important to the quality of early years settings and have been found to be the best formation for optimising children's development. The small group seems to be the most favourable type of organisation for an education which is based on relationships and which hopes to foster both cognitive and social development. Such groupings promote children's development and provide opportunities for negotiation and communication and thus must be the main type of format used in all early years settings (Cole and Cole 1989).

The skills that children acquire for building enduring social relations are essential to their effectiveness and happiness as adults. Also, friendships are believed to be vital to the acquisition of skills and competencies essential to a child's social, cognitive, emotional and moral development. They also provide a unique context for development as what is gained in a friendship relation cannot be as effectively achieved in any other relationship. Correctional studies show that children who have friends are more socially competent than children who do not. They show many desirable characteristics including friendliness, co-operativeness, altruism, good perspective-taking, lower aggressive tendencies, higher sociability, better emotional adjustment, lower anxiety/depression and higher self-esteem (Bukowski et al. 1996). Hartup and Moore (1990 p.2) claim that:

> Considerable evidence suggests that peer relations contribute positively to mental health, both in childhood and later on. The elements in child-child relations believed to be responsible for these contributions are the developmental equivalence of children and their companions and the egalitarian nature of their interaction.

According to Parker and Asher (1987), participation in and quality of friendships impacts on psychological well-being as having friends seems to have a positive effect on mental health. Longitudinal research by Cowen, Pederson, Babigian, Izzo and Trost (1973) showed that adults who needed psychiatric help were two and a half times more likely to have had negative peer ratings in the early school years. So, it seems that friendship exerts a positive force on development; and the quality of children's friendships as well as their popularity or status in the peer group may be important determinants of social development and adjustment (Furman and Robbins 1985).

Clearly children's desire and need for companionship is well worth our support. Early years settings should nurture children's connections with one another and should build their capacity to live, work and play in a group, if their social development is to be optimised. The socio-emotional goals for the early years should include friendship-building, the development of co-operation and consideration, it should teach children to listen well, to keep promises, to be responsible, independent and to think of others, but do they?

Early years education and care

As stated earlier the primary force of socialisation in the child's early life is the home. However, once the child starts to spend more time outside the home the nature of the child's exposure changes and the parents' direct control is changed in a decisive way. Early years settings are the first out-of-home setting for many children, where they are expected to stay on their own without a primary attachment figure, such as parent or childminder. Attending such a setting means children must learn to share equipment, to make choices and compromises, to take turns, to take responsibility for their own actions and to get along with adults who, unlike parents, do not know their special likes and dislikes. They must also learn to interact successfully with a variety of other children, to learn to take their needs into account and to share the time of the adults who are present. Such experiences can provide more opportunity for companionship, for sharing, turn taking, affection, amusement, play, for creating a sense of identity and belonging, depending on the quality of the setting. Experiences with peer groups can also help children to learn about their strengths and weaknesses. According to Rubin (1980 p.17) by the time children are age three:

> They are able to manage interactions with one another that contain,
> in fledgling form, all the basic features of social interactions among
> older children or adults - sustained attention, turn-taking, and mutual
> responsiveness.

Thus out-of-home experiences can impact very positively on social development. The most clear-cut influence of out-of-home care is believed to be in the realm of social development. Children exposed to early years settings are seen as being more self-sufficient and more independent of parents, practitioners and teachers, more helpful and co-operative with peers and others, more knowledgeable about the social world and more comfortable in new situations. However, these effects can vary with the quality of provision, the practitioner's or teacher's attitude and the level of parental involvement (Howes and Olenick 1986). Not all early years settings and out-of-home care experiences prioritise social development. In Ireland, Douglas (1993) looked at the experiences of children in four types of early years settings in the Cork area. In relation to social play and social groups, his study revealed that children played alone (during free play sessions) without interacting for 45% of the total time and where social interactions did occur he found they tended to last less than two minutes. In Dublin, Hayes, O'Flaherty and Kernan (1997) in their research support Douglas' (1993) findings as they observed few interactions between adults and children and between children themselves. They also saw little nurturing behaviour or expressions of emotions in any of the settings observed so these issues might suggest that settings are not optimising social development. Therefore, this issue needs to be addressed. As well as this, many children's social development can be impacted on due to modern day exposure to mass media such as television, or can it?

The media's impact on social development

The sheer magnitude of children's exposure to modern media such as television, video, computers, written materials and so on makes it an important aspect of socialisation. Television is one of the most influential mass media and is a powerful force in the socialisation process, as it can impact on a child's attitudes and beliefs as well as reinforcing gender stereotypes. Both the content (cartoon, fairy tale, adventure story, news programme) and the form (brief images, longer exposure) are widely claimed to exert long-term effects on the development of children's interests, emotions, cognitive skills and social behaviour (Greenfield 1984).

Also, research seems to indicate that watching violence on television can increase the risk of violent behaviours among many child viewers (Phillips 1982; Potts, Huston and Wright 1986). Such violence is learned through observation and Singer and Singer (1980) demonstrated a significant relationship between frequent television viewing at home and the level of overt aggression experienced in the early years setting. However, the evidence that television watching affects children's behaviour negatively is complemented by equally strong evidence that the family can effect the way that it influences children by supervising what their children view and by watching and explaining programmes to them (Macionis 1989).

All in all, research shows that the influence of a particular form of mediated experience is neither good nor bad. How one assesses the value of a book or a television programme depends on how one sees the social values of the home, school, community and future life for which the child is being prepared. The parent and early years practitioner can play a key role in this, exposing children to the medium that will best suit the individual child's optimum development. From the beginning, research has indicated that children are most influenced by portrayals/models which are not counteracted or put into perspective by things in their immediate environment. Thus, besides encouraging things like responsible viewing, parents and practitioners can talk about programmes with children and can discuss attitudes and information which are being transmitted. Thus, adults can have an appreciable influence on how such programmes impact on children's social behaviour and attitudes. Despite the emphasis given to the possible social ills of television, in reality a more balanced view of the medium's impact on children's development is probably warranted (Greenfield 1984; Gunter and McAleer 1997).

Conclusion

Humans are social beings and need contact with others in order to survive. Social exchange is essential to learning and to life. Through shared activities, communication, co-operation and even conflict, children co-construct their knowledge of the world (Edwards, Gandini and Forman 1998). As children grow, they also become aware of differences and similarities. They come to know if they are boys or girls and to notice that all children are not the same. Social development is a two-edged sword - one side being the child's individual growth and development, his becoming differentiated as an individual - the other side his integration into a community, being accepted and getting along with others. Being developed as an individual and being part of a group are important to children. They want to be independent and self-sufficient while at the same time they want to have friends and to be accepted as part of the bigger group or community.

The adults in the child's world play a crucial role in providing an environment which is supportive and responsive to all children and difference and diversity must be welcomed and celebrated in our pluralist society. Many forces outside the child, in the 'micro', 'meso', 'exo' and 'macrosystem' impact on his development. The early years are particularly important and all areas of the child's life influence his social development. Every effort must be made to optimise young children's social development. The present over-emphasis on cognition, on didactic skills, on focused intellectual learning in the early years is in part responsible for the increase in children's aggressive and selfish tendencies. This concentration compromises children's ability to take the needs of others into account and can increase their anti-social behaviour for many years afterwards (Lewis 1995). Also, many children carry horrific baggage to school, baggage that can seriously impair and compromise their social development and their capacity to be with others. Child abuse, parental disputes, poverty, neglect, drug/alcohol addicted parents all impact negatively on children. Therefore, cognisance must be taken by practitioners of the multifaceted factors which could be inhibiting the child's overall development, if early years settings and schools are to try to compensate for lack of social development/social experience in the home (Hartley-Brewer 1998). Social development is of paramount importance, not only to the individual person but also to the smooth running of society. Children's development as social beings is central to their progress as autonomous human beings and is every bit as important as their intellectual growth. In essence, children must learn to live, work and play collaboratively if society is to function.

Suggestions/guidelines for enhancing social development

There are numerous things that can be done to prioritise social development in the early years setting. The following is a list of suggestions which have been selected from various sources including: *Unlearning Discrimination in the Early Years* (Brown 1998); *A Curriculum for the Pre-school Child* (Curtis 1986); *The Emotional, Social, Moral and Spiritual Development of the Pre-school Child* (Daly 2002); *Project E.Y.E. Irish Curriculum for the three to four year old child – Volume Six: Social Development* and *Volume Seven: Cultural Development*, (Douglas, Horgan and O'Brien 2000); *Young Children's Personal, Social and Emotional Development*, (Dowling 2000); and *Educating Young Children* (Hohmann and Weikart 2002).

- Greet children warmly and positively when they arrive at the setting. Respect them and invest a genuine part of your self in your interactions with children. Be kind and patient, support and care for the children. When this is done children learn to appreciate these qualities and in dealing with others will hopefully exhibit similar qualities themselves.

- Spend time on developing social skills. Teach children how to be friends, how to care, share, co-operate and collaborate with others. Ensure there are opportunities for taking turns, sharing, caring, including others in the group, helping, saying sorry and learning to forgive. Encourage children to say please, excuse me and thank you. Teach children how to shake hands and how to introduce themselves.

- Introduce the theme of friendship at circle time, ask children to say why they like to have friends and extend this to what they like to do with their friends. The adult should bring in a picture of her friend and discuss with the children why she is her friend. Talk about why it is important to have friends and to be a friend. Get them to try to imagine what it would be like not to have any friends.

- Get all children to mix by having group games, by changing seating arrangements and small work groups regularly and actively encourage different children to play together.

- Get all children to say their names in turn and to talk about their favourite food/toys/television programme. This is particularly helpful at the beginning of the academic year to help children to get to know a bit about each other.

- Foster a sense of togetherness and a sense of belonging by making lunch time a wonderful social occasion where children chat and share, it should have rituals and be a pleasant and convivial occasion.

- Have round tables in the setting as these facilitate social interaction.

- Encourage children to work in pairs when tidying up, if one child is having difficulties doing up buttons or closing or undoing a zip ask others to give a 'helping hand'.

- Encourage an inclusive atmosphere and scaffold friendships. Allow lots of free play, observe children and watch out for those who are not invited to partake in games with others. See who are the most popular and those who have difficulties in making friends. Never underestimate how overwhelming feelings of isolation, alienation, anger, bewilderment and rejection can be for young children who are excluded from play. Encourage and scaffold these children to have at least one special friend. The adult should take action if a child is persistently refused admission to play with others.

- Encourage parents to have children's friends visit each other at home or to meet outside of the setting at the local playground or park.

- Give new children who start mid-term a ready-made friend/buddy on arrival. Emphasise the importance of the role of the 'buddy' and encourage him to take real responsibility for the new child.

- Encourage children to play supermarket, bus stop etc – ask children to form a queue, to take turn. If someone breaks the queue stress the importance of waiting your turn.

- Use project work and collaborative play in the early years setting. Encourage children to work together in small groups to paint pictures, to make models, collages, to find out how something works. Project work refers to in-depth studies of particular topics, by groups of children and emphasises the need to co-operate and collaborate. Working and playing collaboratively together allows children to recognise and respect the skills and knowledge of each of them individually and as a group. Such tasks require the skills, ideas and contributions of a number of children. It also turns the emphasis away from individual competitive learning to active co-operative learning and problem solving. Collaborative play has its ups and downs as children try to rise to the challenge of conflicting view points, desires and experiences. However, despite the conflicts that arise, or maybe because of them, such play stretches and enhances development. It helps children understand that others have different thoughts, feelings and perspectives and gives them the opportunity to assert themselves and to argue and put their point across.

- Provide materials that encourage collaborative play – musical instruments to make a band, work benches and a variety of tools and pieces of timber, doctors' sets and uniforms. Provide large materials that require or invite more than one child, items such as climbers, parachutes, large cardboard boxes, building blocks.

- Have plenty of large floor jigsaws available as three or four children can co-operate and do them together.

- Be sensitive about children's behaviour. The social skills and behaviour accepted at home may be very different from what is acceptable in a formal setting. Take time to explain to children and be patient.

- There should be plenty of opportunities for children to play together free from adult interference. These situations where no one is in charge help children to learn to co-operate, to make concessions, to learn to assert themselves, to argue, to resolve conflicts and to come to appreciate the dynamics of group interaction. Peer group experiences provide valuable learning experiences. Children have to learn that even friends have their differences and that the resolution of these differences involves co-operation and adjustment to each other's point of view.

- Although children need help occasionally in resolving conflicts, where possible children should sort things out for themselves.

- An environment should be provided which emphasises co-operation, caring and sharing. Opportunities must also be provided for 'rough and tumble' play. The opportunity to display strength and to experience the strength of others is positive and can build mutual respect. Depriving children of the opportunity to display aggressive behaviour can actually contribute to aggressive problems in children, particularly boys.

- Try the game 'Let's all pull together'. Tell the children you all have to move a big thing (something large enough that only the group as a whole can move). Get a long rope and tie it around the object and shout encouragement to the children as they move it. The adult can also pull. When the task is completed thank them and discuss the team effort and the concept that none of them on their own could have done the job. Read *The Enormous Turnip* by Nicola Baxter (ISBN 0721416950) to extend this to show that the smallest person can make a great difference, as in that story it was the contribution of the mouse that finally got the turnip out of the ground.

- Do a three-legged tour. Have a brief discussion on the value of co-operation and invite the children to go into pairs. Tie their adjacent legs together with a scarf and, emphasising co-operation not competition, get them to walk around the setting or outside.

- Play pass the parcel – tie up an object with several layers of wrapping and get children to pass it around and to take off one layer of paper when the music stops. Continue this until all the wrapping is undone. This game involves a number of social and motor skills. Children must learn to listen, to unwrap the parcel, they must not snatch it from another child and they have to learn to accept that some children will have more then one chance to unwrap and also that only one person will ultimately discover what the object is.

- Co-operative musical chairs – This game is played like musical chairs but when the music stops everyone must be seated on a chair or on someone's lap. The idea is to develop the co-operational rather than the competitive element.

- Kindness and care – Discuss the meaning of the words kindness, warmth, affection, gentleness. Tell the children how important it is to be gentle. Bring a tame pet such as a rabbit into the class and allow the children to handle the pet and praise any particularly gentle behaviour. Suggest alternative strategies to those who are a bit over zealous. To extend read 'Baa Bear's' story about the frightened kitten and discuss how Baa upset and scared poor pussy – *Bartholomew Bear* by Virginia Miller (ISBN 0744575788).

- Play 'Leading the blind game'. A selection of items is placed around the room. One child then leads another child who is blindfolded around the room telling him where the objects are and leading him safely around them. They then change roles.

- Play 'Make me laugh games'. Children work in pairs and take turns to make each other laugh by pulling funny faces, telling jokes, making up nonsense words.

- Be aware of how boys and girls are treated, what is expected of them, the toys, books, activities and games they are exposed to. Choose toys, books and other learning materials which challenge stereotypes and present positive images of and for all children.

- Encourage children to play in a wide variety of imaginative scenarios such as hospitals, factories, space ships, garages and homes. Provide tool chests, hard hats, overalls, hats, jewellery and other dressing up clothes to help children change stereotyped attitudes they may already hold. Make sure both boys and girls have access to all toys and equipment and ensure no child is made fun of if they are partaking in an activity which is usually played by a particular sex.

- Each child comes from his own family but often does not have any conception of the differences between households and family life-styles. Talk about different family settings to inform children and to enable them to accept the cultural/social differences which exist in our society.

- Provide books and resources which represent a number of different family dynamics, single mothers and fathers, mothers in jobs outside the home, fathers that work full-time in the home, families with differently-abled members as well as different ethnic and cultural groups.

- Provide examples of men and women doing different jobs. Use stories, jigsaws and photographic displays to show adults in different roles. Invite adults to speak to children whose roles help to counter stereotypes (e.g. a post woman, a male childcare worker and so on).

- Have a Behaviour Management and Bullying Policy and ensure it is adhered to. Have discussions on bullying and how it makes the people involved feel and ask children to make a contract to keep their own room free of bullies. Read stories which show the incident of bullying and its repercussions. Use videos, role-play, drama, puppets and circle-time to raise awareness of bullying behaviour.

- Invite people from the community into the group - to help out, to talk to children about themselves. Give children opportunities to make contact with the community at large, visit the old folks home, the library, the police and fire station. Also encourage children to call on elderly neighbours and to make friends where ever possible.

- Set appropriate expectations for every child and have a sensitive awareness of each child's rights, abilities and needs.

- Listen to children as they play with each other or as they are looking at books. Note any derogatory names that they use towards each other or towards pictures of other children. Use such comments to develop discussions.

- Take full details of children's names on filling in application forms. Ask children and their parents how they would like to be addressed and ensure that each child's name is pronounced correctly by everyone in the setting. For children whose home language is not English learn a few key phrases in the child's home language.

- Have discussions at circle time on why skin colour, language, illness, disability is a fact and is normal and valuable – ask children why people are different colours, why boys and girls are different, why some people have to use wheelchairs, why people use different languages.

- Show interest in each child's background and ask them to bring in something special from home. Ask them to share these precious memorabilia with a small group of other children. Talk about their backgrounds and about how everyone's background is different and special.

- Use photographs/pictures/postcards to show children in their own homes as well as displaying children from other parts of the world. Use these to interest children in other people and places in order to develop balanced views.

- Make sure to respect any special/cultural dietary/eating requirements that parents may have.

- The home corner should have a variety of cooking utensils, furniture and food packets.

- Use the home corner to depict different types of homes (trailer/caravan, house, tent). Help children to appreciate the different circumstances of living in these homes (cooking, washing, collecting water, not having electricity, television) so that their play can develop their understanding.

- Show children pictures of different dwellings – apartments, igloos, bungalows, two-storey houses, barges, trailers/caravans and so on. Discuss similarities and differences between where they live and the dwellings in the pictures. Indicate the reasons for the different kinds of materials being used (climate, natural resources etc.) Get the children to make models of the ones they like.

- Suitable play materials and books which depict different ways of life should be available, for example trailers and other features of the Traveller way of life should be provided. A trailer home corner could be set up and themes such as transport and animals could help others to appreciate the history, experiences, culture, beliefs and values of Travellers.

- Posters of children of different backgrounds and colours should be displayed on the walls.

- Children living in rural areas should be informed and exposed to information and experiences of living in urban areas and *vice versa*. Visits to other environments will help children build up concepts about different ways of life and living.

- Adults need to look deep inside themselves and to review their own attitudes towards other people and other races – ask yourself how do you really feel about these issues. Some aspects of your own beliefs may have to be confronted if you are to develop positive dispositions in the children in your care. Be aware of how our attitudes, assumptions and expectations of children and their parents affect the way we relate to them.

- Children should be encouraged to discuss how their lives are similar yet different. This allows them to identify with their own culture as well as other cultures. Such discussion may help overcome the development of negative stereotypes about minority groups. Children need to be helped to understand why they should not hurt and tease others about differences and they should be supported instead to value and appreciate them.

- It is important to include discussion and activities related to different types of clothing, language, music, food, and celebration on a regular basis in the setting.

- Children should be encouraged to appreciate that others have their own points of view and feelings that are different from their own.

- A map or globe of the world should be on display and discussions regarding the concept of different countries and continents should take place.

- 'Welcome' in a number of different languages should be displayed either on the door of the setting or somewhere near the entrance.

- An Equal Opportunities Admissions Policy should be developed and services should be committed to offering access to the facilities to all children regardless of race, religion, gender, national origin, culture or ability.

- Premises should be wheelchair accessible and children with special/additional needs should be fully integrated.

- Ensure that the individuality of children with developmental or physical needs is respected and valued through having an open and flexible curriculum. For children who come to the setting, build on what they can do, focus on their abilities and strengths, not their disabilities. Allow them to develop at their own pace and be aware that no one is perfect, everyone has some impairment.

- Children who are learning English as an additional language should be encouraged to take part in a wide variety of activities which stimulate communication in an environment that reflects their own cultural and linguistic background. They also need to be exposed to language which is appropriate to their level of development and it must be meaningful and based on concrete and visual experiences.

- Ensure that the dressing up area is fully equipped (uniforms, national dress, lengths of fabric, hats) to allow children to take on different roles. Ensure that the clothes do not reinforce stereotypical roles, for example have male nurse's uniforms.

- Have pictures of national costumes available (kilts, saris, kimonos, turbans and so on) or better still get others to bring in the real thing. Talk about the clothes and the climate and context in which they are worn.

- Listen to music from a variety of countries and cultures – Irish jigs, Eastern music. Introduce children to different musical instruments from different countries – for example harps, bagpipes, didgeridoos.

- Review and revise the management, organisation and ethos of the settings. Be aware of how material is presented and how we relate to children and how they are encouraged to learn – is power shared and is co-operation encouraged?

- Take photographs of the local community – shops, places of worship, schools, post office, houses, fire station etc., get them enlarged and display on the wall as a poster of 'Our Community'.

- Understand children's home cultures. This includes food, dress, music, dance, art, lifestyle, medicine, history, holiday, language, religious beliefs, rules, education, child-rearing practices and attitudes towards others.

- Implement culturally appropriate curricula that include the past and present contributions and experiences to human progress of Women, Black, Working Class and Disabled people. Make equality issues and anti-racist and anti-discriminatory practice a part of the daily curriculum.

- Ensure there is a variety of multicultural toys and equipment available, female and male dolls should be available and should reflect different skin colours, hair styles, facial features and special/additional needs.

- Display photographs of each child on the wall. Print the child's name underneath it. Work with small groups to talk about the picture, who is it?, how do we know it is…?, why don't we all look the same?

- Discuss differences and similarities in the home lives of children – meal times, going to bed, holidays, what happens at the weekend, celebrations and birthdays.

- Invite parents to bring in prepared traditional dishes from their own culture to share with the children or get them to come in and allow children to help them cook something (Scottish shortbread/Greek salad).

- Celebrate festivals – Christmas, Easter, Holloween, the Chinese New Year, Diwali, the Passover. Adults must be fully aware of the significance of all such festivals so that they can be made meaningful for children.

- Role-play and experiential learning should be used to help children see another's view - being blindfolded, trying to reach things from a wheelchair, having ears covered so that they can't hear. These experiences can paint a clear picture for 'normal' children to see the challenges that some children have to face.

Children's books which are useful for social development

Topsy and Tim Make a New Friend (ISBN 0721428436) by Jean and Gareth Adamson.

Hug (ISBN 0763615765) and *Watch Out Big Bro's Coming* (ISBN 0763605840) by Jez Alborough.

Big Book of Little Children (ISBN 0763622109) by Catherine and Laurence Anholt.

Knee High (ISBN 0744578388) by Lawrence Anholt.

Why Do Some People Use Wheelchairs? (ISBN 0789420570) and *Why Are All Families Different?* (ISBN 0789420554) by Mary Atkinson.

Piggybook (ISBN 067980837X), *Willy the Wimp* (ISBN 0763618437) and *Voices in The Park* (ISBN 078948191X) by Anthony Browne.

Handa's Surprise (ISBN 0763608637) and *Handa's Hen* (ISBN 0744575028) by Eileen Browne.

Do You Want to Be My Friend? (ISBN 0399215980) by Eric Carle.

One Day at Wood Green Animal Shelter (ISBN 0763612103) by Patricia Casey.

Will I Have a Friend (ISBN 0689713339) by Miriam Cohen.

Big Brother, Little Brother (ISBN 0803728700) by Marci Curtis.

Whoever You Are (ISBN 0152164065) by Mem Fox.

Rose Meets Mr. Wintergarten (ISBN 1564023958) by Bob Graham.

Baby Duck and the New Eyeglasses (ISBN 0744552206) by Amy Hest and Jill Barton.

Wake Up, World A Day in the Life of Children Around the World (ISBN 0711214840) by Beatrice Hollyer.

Leon and Bob (ISBN 1564029913) by Simon James.

My Hippie Grandmother (ISBN 0763606715) by Reeve Lindbergh.

Where The Big Fish Are (ISBN 0763609226) by Jonathan London.

Let's Build a House (ISBN 0749638621) by Mick Manning and Brita Granstrom.

Two Homes (ISBN 0763619841) by Clare Masurel and Kady MacDonald Denton.

The Visitors Who Came to Stay (ISBN 0670747149) by Annalena McAfee and Anthony Browne.

Little Beaver and The Echo (ISBN 0698116283) by Amy McDonald.

Have You Seen Who's Just Moved in Next Door to Us (ISBN 0744530431) by Colin McNaughton.

This is My Hair (ISBN 0316692360) by Todd Parr.

That's What Friends Are For (ISBN 0763613975) by Florence Parry Heide and Sylvia Van Clief.

Making Friends (ISBN 0698114094) by Fred Rogers.

This is Our House (ISBN 0763602906) by Michael Rosen.

Moving (ISBN 0140548955) by Michael Rosen and Sophy Williams.

Good Job, Little Bear (ISBN 0763617091) by Martin Waddell.

Doing things for himself leads to a sense of independence and autonomy for the child enhancing emotional development.

**Friendship and play are vital aspects of social develop-
ment.**

Co-operating and helping others enhances moral development.

Connecting with nature allows the child to develop spiritually.

CHAPTER FIVE

Moral Development

Introduction

Modern society is by no means certain as to what it means to be moral and, consequently, we are under stress today about questions of right and wrong, about how to keep ourselves on a straight path and how to guide our children. Family structures are fluid and continually change, while our sense of community and tradition has broken down. There is huge confusion in the world - confusion about values, about what and how to teach. The moral goal posts seem to have moved and we do not know what game we are playing, never mind what the rules are. We live in a period of instability and change. As a result, many people feel lost, disorientated, even terrified. Previous generations were much more certain about what it meant to be moral and about how to produce moral individuals. As well as this, the vast cultural changes in the last few decades have impacted on moral life and we have ended up not knowing what is real, significant and worthwhile. The threat to personal values is greater today than ever before, as the modern mindset has a world-view which centres on things versus relationships. However, the death of the old ethics and morality, and the decline of the whole frame of mind on which it was based, gives us an opportunity to forge a new, better morality, if we so choose (Wood 1981; Hannan 1995; Neville 1989).

The importance of the early years for moral development

Morally, the early years are vital, since what one comes to believe about what is right, good and just as a child is central to how one lives one's life from then on. In a world filled with global violence, threats of nuclear and environmental devastation, where drugs and alcohol are freely available, learning to be more decent and building caring communities is not a waste of time. We must see early years settings and schools as centres dedicated to social growth and ethical behaviour. To help children to become good, productive, contributing citizens we must teach them to think rationally and to behave responsibly. Children must love learning and love living in a society that is fair, and where responsibilities are equally as important as rights and freedoms (Deroche and Williams 1998). Education can have a powerful influence on the formation of morals, ethics, values and standards, but conversely it can contribute negatively if enough care and attention is not paid to optimising children's moral development, particularly in the early years. As Gert (1998 p.385) says, teaching children to be moral and virtuous should be done in the early years since, "if children do not learn to care for others while they are young, it may be impossible to teach them when they are older". We must ask whether we are teaching children that to be fulfilled and happy they will also need to be moral and refrain from acts of destruction towards self, others and the environment or are we teaching children that money and self-centredness can buy everything including happiness?

Morality

In the past, morality was largely a precise list of do's and don'ts and for every moral question there was a clear solution, or at least fixed principles to be applied in the case of doubt, often a case of do as I say, not as I do. Teaching was handed down from one generation to the next and children and adults were conditioned to accept and agree, not to question or contradict. Also it is only in the last twenty or so years that the concept of holism has been brought to the fore. In the past things were deeply compartmentalised: in education children learned literacy, history and geography. Subject separation prevailed and in terms of values, what came into the classroom were not profound moral questions. Instead a set of rules existed which children were expected to follow, for example children were required to show respect while very often not being given it. Children acquiesced not because they thought it was the correct thing to do but because of fear (Hawkes 2000). As a result of this, today's adults are often at a loss when it comes to explaining and handing on the moral principles on which they themselves were reared. They feel helpless in trying to form the consciences of children, since they themselves were seldom encouraged to explore the full meaning of conscience or to use it in a really personal way. As Fagan (1988) says they did not reach the potential heights of moral development. Large numbers of adults are imprisoned by immature consciences, living in constant fear of divine retribution and punishment. Traditional society tended to remove the burden of choice from the individual and this led morality to be seen as a force antagonistic to life. For many, morality is restricted to legality (right and wrong are understood in terms of what is allowed and what is forbidden) and in many people's minds the word 'moral' indicates 'ought' and is seen as negative, destructive and life denying. It is envisioned as part of a system of explicit or hidden blackmail in which a person's own life is stifled. This kind of morality, that of the authoritarian, obsessional, hypocritical moralist, has not been advantageous to children's moral development (Kitwood 1990).

Today, there is much more onus on the individual to make moral decisions. In addition to this, human knowledge is increasingly organised and disseminated in new ways - the Internet, experts of various kinds, the media. Children today are bombarded with powerful and seductive messages. These permeate everyday life and young children and adults have to attempt to make sense of their individual lives and the situations in which they find themselves. Despite this, many adults have abdicated the responsibility for teaching values to children and have left a vacuum to be filled by television and by negative, materialistic messages from several sources (Farrer 2000). There is an increasing range of competing theories and choices available, with wider horizons and possibilities, which were unthinkable for previous generations. This has led to an intensification of individualism, with each child unavoidably faced with choices - choices which affect not only his own but others' lives as well. Yet, while greater choice is available, children are very unclear as to what morality and moral development are, and education must help redress this situation. Children have the right to be stimulated to make sound moral judgements based on informed conscience and education must help fulfil this right (Beck 1998).

Morality, as discussed in this work, is based on the belief that morality is about the ability of humans to live together. Morality is important for the organisation of society and epitomises how people come to grips with the inevitable conflicts that arise between their own needs and their social obligations, how and why they come to see some things as good and others as evil. Morality deals with human experience, it is about the ordinary cares and concerns of everyday life and a living morality must be truly human, emphasising the importance of people and their relationships to one another. A person's definition of being moral has as much, if not more, to do with belonging as it does with defining what is right and wrong. Morality is really the tendency to think in terms of relationships, and questions of care and the quality of the relationships are what is crucial. Morality is about living together in love and it takes a long time to develop morally and to learn about being a truly moral human being (Hoffman 1988 cited in Bornstein and Lamb (eds.). Coles (1997 p.20) claims that: "Moral intelligence and strong values are the basis for a balanced and happy life". He goes on to say that morality incorporates a sense of fairness, a respect for others and a commitment of mind, heart and soul to one's family, neighbourhood, nation and world. He asserts that moral knowledge is intimately bound up with the ability to make judgements about the nature of behaviour and its ethical basis and appropriateness. Being moral and having values are the foundation of education and of healthy development and morality is in many respects a social phenomenon. Durkheim (1933 p.399) said that it is not a simple juxtaposition of individuals who bring an intrinsic morality with them, but rather:

> Man is a moral being only because he lives in society, since morality consists in being with a group and varying with this solidarity. Let all social life disappear, and moral life will disappear with it, since it would no longer be objective.

Awareness of morality is a fact of life and has been an abiding reality in history, in all cultures. As man developed from pre-historic times, arbitrary standards of behaviour based on what was right and fair were set down. In order to survive and for a better quality of hunting, sharing and living, rules were established with punishments for those who failed to obey. These rules became part of the culture and were imbibed by individuals as they grew up. While this was a primitive form of morality, it shows that organisation and rules are necessary in order for humans to live together (Shelton 1990; Gardner 1993).

Morality and religion

Common morality is a complex and subtle public system and so applies only to those to whom it is known. Those who hold that morality is universal must hold that all rational persons know what morality requires, prohibits, encourages and allows. Thus, unless they deny either that morality is a public system or is universal they cannot hold that morality is based on religion, for no religion is known to all rational persons (Gert 1998). Morality can and does exist independently of religion yet: "Some Christians collapse the whole of morality into religion" (MacNamara 1988 p.14). However, there are many who are firmly convinced of the validity of morality and who are deeply conscious and willing to abide by it but who do not believe in God. Some of the most important movements for moral progress have been initiated and inspired by those who were not Christian and some of whom were anti-Christian (McNamara 1988; Thompson 1999). Thus, morality is a phenomenon that in itself is independent of religion.

Character development and character education

Character development is the acceptable modern-day term for what in the past was called moral development. Character development emphasises in particular one important aspect of moral development – socialisation: the need to help children to learn how to live co-operatively, caringly and civilly (Ryan 1986). Moral/character development is about the making of sound, autonomous moral decisions and is a slow, gradual process. It is not about indoctrination and the blind and uncritical acceptance of certain beliefs and values; it is about being able to co-exist with others.

Thus, one of the most important tasks of education is to help children to develop their characters and to grow up to be rational and responsible persons in fellowship with others and to have positive values. Yet, this task has become more and more difficult over the years. Character education is a moral enterprise which involves continuous and conscious effort to guide children to know and pursue what is good and worthwhile and should be at the heart of all school activities and must be a priority in every early years setting. Parents and caregivers are the primary moral educators and practitioners must build partnerships with these to foster in children personal and civic virtues such as integrity, courage, responsibility, diligence, service and respect. Character education is about developing virtues and is not about acquiring the right views. It also involves the discussion of abstract and complex concepts such as justice, freedom, morality, power. These are not things that are usually associated with very young children. However, young children are able to consider quite complicated hypothetical situations when given the opportunity to do so (Farrer 2000). All adults in society must be educated about, reflect on and embody morality and moral development if they are to assist children's moral journeys. Also character education, with all that it entails, must become an integral part of schools and early years settings if they are to become communities of virtue.

The early years setting is a microcosm of the world. What is created there today can provide a glimpse of how our world can be tomorrow. Therefore, having developed characters means children can judge and evaluate events and phenomena for themselves. It means they will have a commitment to values and have the ability to use such values in determining choices. The values which need to be modelled and fostered are those that promote life and people's ability to live together. Character development also encompasses having moral integrity, understanding the need for moral conduct and desiring to strengthen the moral fabric of society (Goodlad 1984). Developing morally is the recognition by everyone that each individual has ethical responsibilities. The kind of moral development that children need is to allow them to see what it means to be a real person, to know and love self and others. Children need guidance and have to be given the tools with which to make decisions. Decisions and their consequences then need to be considered in a safe and supportive way. During the early formative years, children are learning the building blocks for life so that later on, when they find themselves in difficult situations, they will be able to cope. To be profoundly moral is to show concern for human relationships and for others. Morality is important from the very start of life and it is not a phenomenon that can be added on in adulthood (Kitwood 1990). Character education is a concerted effort by early years settings, schools and communities to educate children about an agreed set of values. It begins in a family setting and occurs as children witness and imitate others modelling the consensus values. It occurs in settings and communities when children come to know values through the ethos, environment, curriculum (open and hidden) and through extra-curricular activities. It happens when children have opportunities to study, clarify, reflect, reason, debate, decide and act on values and is enhanced when children are provided with guidance and given opportunities to engage in and practise values. It is verified and modified as children grow and develop.

Moral development

Wynne (1986 p.31) says:

We can assume that renewed attention to character development will be good for pupils, their families, educators and the nation. For, in the end, the welfare and the very existence of our society does not so much depend on the I.Q.'s of its inhabitants, as on their character.

The quality of the social environment has a large impact on the rate of moral/character development, as morality exists in a complex network of relationships between persons as individuals in communities and between communities (Downey and Kelly 1978). In this context, morally good actions are those that foster good relations and relationships, morally bad actions are those that damage relationships and block growth. Each encounter with another is a point of growth and it is the presence and needs of others that give rise to morality and moral obligations, so a child is what his relationships enable him to be.

Brown (1965) says that the reason why people behave in particular ways in specific circumstances does not depend on some straightforward, universally applicable guides. Moral behaviour, to a greater or lessor extent, involves a decision-making process and is influenced by age and developmental status, by the culture in which a child lives, by the specific situation and by his personality. In addition, his moral knowledge will influence how he makes his judgements about what is wrong or right. For an action to be considered moral it must involve, directly or indirectly, one or more humans and it must involve a situation in which rational thought can be applied and there must be a sufficient degree of freedom involved to permit the possibility of alternative courses of action. Circumstances make a huge difference to what is considered right or wrong and it can be argued that observing different social customs and values in different societies leads to moral relativism, since what is right in one society could be viewed as wrong in another. Thus, ethical and moral theories are produced from within a cultural and historical period and are influenced by the prevailing modes of thought of the time (Thompson 1999).

In a strongly symbolic way the child represents the good in society. Children are seen as needing protection against evil, against abusers, molesters and exploiters. They also need to be protected against the materialistic consumer-driven society that adults have created, with its inherent dangers, pollutants, injustices and inequalities. The relief of suffering, the banishment of evil, the restoration of good are set down as being morality's aims and we want all children to be allowed to grow and develop, to strive for the good and to live successfully and co-operatively together (King 1997). Young children can be and are moral beings. In the second and third years of life they begin to understand the ideas of responsibility. Explicit discussions of responsibility for breaches of rules and the occasional use of moral terms to correct behaviour begin to appear by the end of the second year. Children between two and three are beginning to understand the principles of harm to others, of responsibility for such behaviour and of excuses from responsibility on the basis of involuntariness, lack of intention or incapacity. They understand that rules should apply to all but that infringement can sometimes be justified and during the third year they become quite sophisticated in their own defence.

During this stage children also begin to exhibit pro-social and caring behaviour. However, the motivation behind young children's acts of sharing and helping is difficult to decipher and asking children their reasons leads to even more ambiguity. Eisenberg and Neal (1979) carried out a series of studies on the pro-social behaviour and moral reasoning of young children, exploring the relations between the spontaneous sharing, comforting and helping behaviour of nursery school children. They examined children's explanations for why they behaved as they did and also assessed their moral reasoning about hypothetical dilemmas presented to them in stories. Eisenberg and Neal (ibid.) found that children explained their own behaviour primarily in terms of the needs of others and that sharing was correlated with moral reasoning in terms of others' needs in the hypothetical tasks. Thus, Eisenberg and Neal (ibid. p.229) suggest that:

> It is logical to suggest that pre-schoolers' references to others' needs when justifying pro-social acts represents a primitive empathic orientation ... In brief, empathic concerns appear to frequently motivate the child's pro-social behaviour.

Young children can behave in pro-social ways and can co-operate and show empathy. Mussen and Eisenberg (1977) define pro-social behaviour as behaviour which refers to actions that are intended to aid or benefit another person or group of people without the actor's anticipation of external rewards. It involves caring, sharing and helping and psychologists now agree that very young children are developing morally and can exhibit pro-social and altruistic behaviour. They can also show intense emotional reactions to what adults regard as moral violations, but when asked to articulate their concern or to make judgements on rightness or wrongness they cannot verbalise their feelings. At this early stage they do not have a 'theoretical morality' and they have no clear intellectual conception of people as moral agents, but this does not mean that their moral development should be neglected or ignored (Kitwood 1990).

Stayton, Hogan and Ainsworth (1971) put forward the idea that the child is genetically endowed with a predisposition to conform to group norms and to show concern for others, because such activities further the survival of the species. However, Grusec and Mills (in Worrell 1982) state that recent research on moral development stresses that children must be actively taught to engage in moral behaviour and moral thinking. This view states that children must know what the values and beliefs of their society are and that they must want to behave in accordance with them. Thus, developing morally is not an easy task and involves a complex interplay of nature and nurture as well as incorporating some of the most basic and profound issues of human existence.

Some views on morality

According to Coles (1997), character is higher than intellect, and character is ultimately who we are as expressed in action - in how we live, in what we do or do not do. Home, early years settings and school must try to develop characteristics in children such as patience, thoughtfulness, sensitivity, responsiveness to others, conscientiousness, kind-heartedness and generosity, as moral intelligence and strong values and beliefs are the basis for a decent and fulfilling life. Zillman, Bryant and Huston (1994 p.186) say that: "Moral development is critical for healthy overall human development". Yet at present most school curricula do not optimise moral development and the greater part of mainstream education is geared to the training of the intellect, while forcing moral education into a marginal place on the sidelines - that is if it is incorporated into the curriculum at all (Kitwood 1990). Full-fledged membership of a human community requires a very long apprenticeship and therefore a huge amount of formal and informal knowledge has to be transmitted to children before the rights and responsibilities of independent life and morality can be bestowed on them (Grusec and Mills in Worrell, 1982).

A rounded and comprehensive perspective on morality can be attained by appreciating the various ways in which children think about the nature of morality itself. In the context of daily decisions and life experiences, we all reflect on morality almost unconsciously and we all have our own ideas on how to go about living well. Harrington (1996 p.10) contends that there are a number of ways of looking at morality and he says, "it is like looking into a room through its different windows, each view is real and true and it is still only one view". He puts forward five views of morality: morality as law; as inner conviction; as personal growth; as love; and as social transformation. Fagan (1997) sets down a similar series of different models of morality: the legal model; the love model; the discipleship model; the inner conviction model; the liberation model; and the personal growth model.

From a review of the literature, including the above, a variety of models emerge: morality as emotion; as concern and responsibility for others; as conformity to authority and rules; as conformity to one's own sense of belief; and as self-development. Morality as emotion is the first model of morality discussed in this work, as from his very early days a child empathises with others (for example, in the first year of life he will often cry when he hears another crying). Soon afterwards, he will show concern and responsibility for others and will often offer his favourite teddy bear to a child who has been hurt. Thus, this is the model that is next outlined. Later again he will show conformity to rules and this is the third model that is reviewed. As he grows, the child will develop his own sense of belief and will do something because he thinks it is the right thing to do. This is discussed in the fourth model. The fifth and final model of morality cites morality as self-development and here the child has developed his own sense of values and displays personal qualities that are the outcome of behaving consistently in specific ways.

(i)   Morality as emotion

This view of morality stresses the essential importance of the emotions in morality. It places emphasis on feelings, not on logic, and on care versus hurt and is concerned with love and empathy. It focuses on a child's own feelings and on the feelings of those around him - on his intra- and interpersonal relationships. It could be said to relate closely to the empathic or emotional morality theory or as Shelton (1990) calls it 'morality of the heart'. Shelton says there is a growing discontent with earlier theories; in particular, the cognitive developmental approach to interpreting morality. He claims it is difficult to reconcile this latter view with children's everyday experiences. Kagan (1984 p.xiv) reiterates this view by stating that:

> Construction of a persuasive rational basis for behaving morally has been the problem on which most moral philosophers have stubbed their toes. I believe they will continue to do so until they recognise what Chinese philosophers have appreciated for a long time: namely, feeling, not logic, sustains the superego.

Hoff-Somers (1985 p.51) says that, "too little attention is paid to the personal aspects of morality - courage, compassion, generosity, honour and self-respect, or on the negative side, hypocrisy, self-deception, jealously and narcissism". He says that what is needed is an essential orientation to care and to reflect on values for societies' everyday functioning. Unlike Kohlberg's (1964) belief that moral thinking is related to life and death situations and rule orientated decisions, this view of morality involves the tendency to think in terms of others and is about the ability to respond with concern and empathy. Compassion and love are the keys that unlock this capacity to care for and think about others and since empathy includes both emotional and intellectual components, pro-social behaviour engendered by empathic arousal provides a perfect forum for encompassing both self-awareness and positive social interactions. Given proper social reinforcement and environmental supports, empathic expressions could provide a useful antidote to the impoverished understanding of moral development as it stands at present, according to Shelton (1990). Duska and Whelan (1975) say that empathy is necessary for moral development and that it is through empathy that a child develops an understanding of what a community is and that this understanding allows him to begin to judge action as right or wrong on the basis of mutual respect. However, they stress that empathy on its own is not sufficient to develop a child morally.

Yet, emotions have been given far too little credit in discussions on morality and emotions serve as vital, if not central, ingredients in sculpturing moral identity and development. Awareness of our empathic yearning, reflection on emotional attachments, in particular love, awareness of the psychological processes of conscience and defence mechanisms are essential for fostering moral development (Shelton 1990). These resonate with human experience and human morality and provide a viable foundation for morality, rooted within human existence. Morality as emotion involves a deep personal concern for the welfare of others and should inspire moral behaviour. Take the case of James and Michael. James is crying in the corner in the early years setting, Michael goes over and asks him what is wrong. James says his toy tractor is broken, Michael acknowledges James' feelings and says that he himself also felt sad when his favourite racing car got broken. Michael offers to fix James' tractor and when he can't he calls the adult over to try to help alleviate the situation.

(ii)   Morality as concern and responsibility for others

Morality as concern and responsibility for others views morality in terms of community and sees the moral agent as fundamentally social. Being moral entails being faithful to the fact of our inter-relatedness and to the demands of relationships and can be expressed in terms of communion versus isolation and relates in many ways to Durkheim's theory. This view of morality goes beyond the small world of interpersonal relationships to the larger world that is society and the concept connected to this perspective is justice and, in particular, social justice. Being moral is about being personally affected by suffering and being motivated to question and respond. This view is based on justice and solidarity and on unity versus division.

French sociologist, Emile Durkheim (1858-1917) is regarded as the father of modern moral education. For Durkheim, morality was an inherently social phenomenon and was comprised of a body of social rules and activities created by and aimed at societies. He was concerned with children's freedom but he believed that morality and freedom were derived from the acceptance of the rationality of internalising social demands. Durkheim (1956 p.89) said, "to be free is not to do what one pleases ... it is to know how to act with reason, how to perform one's duty, how to take on self-responsibility". Durkheim (1961) highlighted three important aspects in the moral education of children - the teacher, the social context and the subject matter. Moral education for him was a process of creating autonomous French citizens by developing the moral attitudes of responsibility, respect, altruism, rationality and independence.

Education was the means of organising the child, individual and social, into a disciplined, stable, moral, meaningful unit and the internalisation of values and discipline represented for Durkheim the child's initiation into his society (Morrish 1967). Durkheim introduced the social dimension to discussions on moral development. He argued for schools to educate children morally as well as providing a framework within which to do it, identifying those qualities which moral education should develop in each and every child. In a very real way he saw the need for a new approach to morality by stressing the need for a re-evaluation of moral education. He set forth new ideals and provided a new set of standards to fully inform individuals with an awareness of what it means to be truly moral and why.

Morality as concern and responsibility for others recognises the social dimension and highlights the fact that the struggle for justice is an essential part of morality. Many have developed the social justice/concern for others aspect of morality and it is now viewed as a vital ingredient of moral development. Moral development impinges on every aspect of human life and this model of concern and responsibility is in sharp contrast to the over-individualistic traditional approach to morality. It is an inspiring model, challenging everyone to integrate it into their own model of morality. Take the case of the group of four year olds who raised money for charity or the three year old girl who gave her favourite Barbie doll away to another little girl whose house had burned down and who had lost all her own toys.

(iii) Morality as conformity to rules/authority

Seeing morality as conformity to rules and to authority is probably one of the most familiar views. This view of morality can be seen most clearly in the work of the cognitive developmentalists, in particular in the early stages of their theories of moral development. The social learning theorists also concentrate on this view of morality, emphasising reinforcement, reward and punishment. Morality as conformity to rules and to authority sees morality as something external, something imposed and is based on duty and obedience and on reward versus punishment. The two main contributors to the cognitive developmental school of moral development are Jean Piaget (1896-1980) and Lawrence Kohlberg (1927-1987). Piaget spent over forty years researching children's moral development. Most of his findings are documented in his book *The Moral Judgement of the Child* (1932). This book highlights Piaget's belief that children experience two types of morality, heteronomous and autonomous. He said that early on, children experience a morality of constraint and that they regard rules as absolute and unchangeable. Later, autonomy follows as a result of cognitive changes and because of social interaction as children come to see that rules are not absolute, but are to be adhered to by social consensus (Kay 1968). Piaget's belief in assimilation, accommodation and schemata and his stages of cognitive development (the sensory motor, pre-operational, operational and formal operational) are a good framework for characterising children's cognitive capacities and for analysing moral development (Duska and Whelan 1975). Piaget's theory sets children down as progressing from

188

moral realism to moral relativism as their cognitive capacities develop. He stressed that all morality consisted of a system of rules and that the essence of this was to be sought in the respect which the individual acquires for those rules (Piaget 1932).

On the other hand, Kohlberg's theory of moral development tended to focus on the older child and adult. Kohlberg was deeply influenced by Piaget and, in particular, by his ideas on moral realism and morality of co-operation (Alston 1971). The foundation stone of Kohlberg's theory was his belief in an innate sense of justice in all humans, in all cultures, and he looked on the child as a moral philosopher (1968). He believed morality developed as a product of a universal human concern for justice, for reciprocity and equality in the relation of one person to another. Kohlberg (1963) also stressed his belief that as children grow cognitively and socially in a linear pattern so did they progress morally and he outlined a definite series of stages that he believed humans go through on their way to developing morally. These are outlined below.

Level I	**Premoral/Preconventional morality (2-7 years approximately)**
Type 1	Heteronomous morality/Punishment and obedience orientation.
Type 2	Individualism, instrumental purpose and exchange/Personal reward orientations (satisfying own desires).
Level II	**Conventional level morality (7-11 years approximately)**
Type 3	Good boy/girl orientation (mutual interpersonal expectations, relations and conformity).
Type 4	Law and order orientation/Authority morality.
Level III	**Post conventional morality (12 years on)**
Type 5	Social contract of individual rights and of democratically accepted laws.
Type 6	Universal ethical principles of conscience.

(Adapted from Smith and Cowie 1991).

Piaget and Kohlberg have contributed greatly to our understanding of moral development. Kohlberg alerted educators and others to recognise that children are moral thinkers and that discussing moral issues helps children grow morally, while Piaget laid the foundations for later researchers to build on and the questions he raised stimulated further research. However, their work has also received much criticism. Siegal (1982a) says that despite a child's cognitive capacity he may not attain Piaget's morality of mutual respect and Kitwood (1990) says that Piaget greatly overestimated the potential of modern societies to foster autonomy and morality. He also says that the development of concern for others is not primarily cognitive and that it is as complex and convoluted as life. Chen et al. (1998) say that Piaget was mostly interested in the characteristics of the child's mind and that he was not particularly interested in interactions among children or in the place of the child in the wider community and society.

Kitwood (1990 p.7) also criticises Kohlberg and says that although his work told us a great deal about how one kind of theoretical morality develops, "its approach is not sufficient as a linchpin for holding the whole edifice of moral development together". Simpson (1974) claims that Kolhberg's theory is culturally biased, in that it is based on a style of thinking and a social organisation that is peculiar to western society. Siegal (1982a) claims that the greatest shortcoming of Kohlberg's theory is his under-valuation of socialisation pressures on children and he went on to say that another major shortcoming of his is that he (Kohlberg) incorporates no strong, direct, positive role for the adult. In fact, along with many developmental psychologists including Piaget, he sought to minimise the positive role of direct adult instruction and teaching on moral development. Eisenberg (1986) and Fontana (1995) say that Kohlberg was short-sighted in ignoring pro-social and good behaviour since he concentrated only on bad behaviour and wrongdoing (stealing, disobedience, punishment and so on) to assess moral development. Gilligan (1982) one of Kohlberg's former students, further criticises him as being biased against females while Kilpatrick (1992) also claims that his theory and research are gender biased, relativistic, situational and morally neutral.

Crossen (1996) and Helwig (1997) argue that Kohlberg did not sufficiently stress what children feel, emphasising that how children feel, think and act about good and bad also plays an important role in moral development. These criticisms appear to indicate that though moral development depends on cognitive development there is more to it than that. The cognitive developmental approach to morality, with its obedience to rules which, though enacted for the common good, leads to people thinking of morality as exclusively related to law. However, obedience to rules is not always right and moral. No community or society can survive without some generally accepted values and these should be reflected in the laws agreed on by the people for the common good, but morality is about much more than adherence to a certain set of rules. Children can show conformity to rules and authority in their early years. Take Claire aged three, for example, who knows she is not allowed to hit her baby brother and doesn't while her mother is in the room. However, when her Mum is out of the room she hits him. She conforms to the rules while someone is watching her but when she is on her own she does not conform. Conforming for the sake of a rule is not enough, moral development is deeper than this.

Learning theories such as those put forward by the work of Sears, Maccoby and Levine (1957), Eysenck (1964) and Bandura (1962, 1977) say that moral development and moral behaviour is the result of reinforcement - of rewards and punishments - and that a child's moral conduct is based on modelling himself on an admired adult. This theory also stresses the importance of conforming to rules and to authority and states that a child often adopts a parent's standards for rules of behaviour. The adult behaviour serves as a model for the child and the adult reinforces what the child says or does by praise or reward, directing the child on how to control their own behaviour. Accordingly, first adult and then peer group influences are the complementary contributors to the development of morality. These theorists believe that children are not congenitally moral and often do not think of the interests or feelings of others unless prompted to do so. They suggest it is adult instruction through imitation and reinforcement that conveys the necessity of acting fairly and morally (Bandura and Walters 1969).

Downey and Kelly (1978) argue that since conduct or behaviour is central to this assumption, the learning theory view of moral development is, in fact, only applicable to moral training, as such theorists do not deal with moral feelings, moral reasoning or judgement. Learning theorists' explanations look on children as passive learners, responding or reacting to the influence of others rather than acting and interpreting their world and learning to form their own moral principles according to the differing demands of prevailing circumstances. Downey and Kelly (ibid.) claim there is a danger in relying too heavily on habits or on what has been taught by others and that this is where the limitations of a learning theory approach to moral development lie. Learning that relies solely on reward and punishment can impede rather than promote moral development and for this reason the behaviouristic learning approach of the above is seen as an insufficient explanation of moral development. Because of this, some theorists decided to combine the cognitive and social learning theories and to develop the social-cognitive approach.

Theorists such as Vygotsky (1962a,b) and Siegal (1982b) accept the cognitive view but also assign importance to imitation and socialisation. They propose that both phenomena are important aspects of moral development. They contend that the more advanced the cognitive development, the more abstract and difficult are the problems which the child can solve fairly. They also stress the need for positive adult to peer interaction. However, this on its own is not a comprehensive enough view or explanation of moral development

(iv) Morality as conformity to one's own sense of belief

Another way of looking at morality is as conforming to one's own sense of belief and could be said to be found in the psychoanalytical theories. This view sees morality as coming from within, as internalisation, as coming later in life than obedience and as involving the ability to think for one's self, seeing why the law permits this and forbids that. Values become personal convictions and not arbitrary impositions and this view of morality is based on conscience and integrity and on inner peace versus disquiet.

The psychoanalytical approach to moral development, as put forward by psychologists such as Sigmund Freud (1933), sees morality as conforming to cultural standards through a process of internalisation. Freud raised awareness about the effects of the unconscious on human behaviour. Regarding moral development, he assumed an end-state of rationality, concentrating on explaining why some children and adults deviate from rational behaviour and show exaggerated or distorted modes of rule-following. For Freud, the development of the child's superego (the mechanism which issues moral imperatives derived from standards of adults close to the child which he himself has internalised) was how the child developed morally (Freud ibid.). Freud's model of the superego is a useful way of seeing what can happen as the child develops morally and is in sharp contrast to the theory put forward by Piaget and Kohlberg (Fontana 1995). Although Freud offered no positive theory of moral development, apart from the general notion of the importance of a good loving relationship with parents/caregivers in the early years, his work raises questions which are of fundamental importance for moral development (Peters 1975; Jones 1972).

Morality as conformity to one's own sense of belief means one becomes personally convinced that something is right or wrong and commits oneself to doing what is morally right for its own sake. For most of human history, group consciousness has taken precedence over personal choice but today, instead of conformity to predetermined rules, the emphasis is on personal responsibility. It is up to the person to do what his inner convictions tell him, values become internalised and conviction comes from within. Take Jake, who is three and a half years old, who sees Mark, his two-year-old brother, kicking Toby the dog. Jake tells Mark to stop as it is wrong to hurt the dog. Jake believes it is wrong to hurt another, he has moved beyond not hurting others because someone in authority says it is wrong to kick.

(v)   **Morality as self-development**

Morality as self-development focuses not so much on moral behaviour but on the person behaving in a certain manner. It moves attention from the action being done to the person doing it. This view is represented by the language of virtue and vice and emphasises personal qualities that are the outcome of behaving consistently in particular ways. This is a more dynamic view of morality and involves development versus regression and wholeness versus fragmentation. In particular, truthfulness, courage, humility, non-violence and compassion are emphasised.

The contemporary values clarification theory of morality could be said to relate to morality as self-development in that it emphasises the individual. Values Clarification (V.C) is among the most popular of the new approaches to moral development and education. It presents clear and convincing arguments for its validity, contending that children and young people today exist in a new and complicated world of competing and confusing value perspectives. These perspectives are reflected in the religious, political and moral codes and ideologies that society tries to impose on its young. The imposition of these has led to a crisis in moral development and has led to the development of V.C.. Louis Rath is credited with being the senior author and central figure in the original statement of V.C.. Values Clarification regards values as a matter of personal concern, reflection and choice and it contends that external forces should not be allowed to invade this personal arena. Values are, to a large extent, a matter of personal choice and the child is seen as developing his own values rather than accepting society's values. In V.C. there is an implicit assumption that the moral norms of society have largely broken down and as a result the moral pluralism of today's world enforces each individual to define his own value commitments (Scharf 1978). V.C., like Freud, tries to restore the locus of influence to the individual and it opposes any notion of morality as conformity to some external set of values. It views the teacher as a facilitator and therapist and sees her role as one of helping children to relate personally and emotionally to moral issues, stressing the inter- and intra-personal ability to stimulate reflection and expression. However, one of the problems with it is that it does not have a fully developed comprehensive philosophical theory that can be translated into practical terms. Instead it is an evolving set of assumptions about educational values that may or may not constitute an organic theory (Chazan 1985). Simon, Howe and Kirschenbaum (1995) reiterate this criticism, claiming that the major reason for the decline of the movement was the failure to deepen theory, expand the research, develop the curriculum and improve teacher training.

V.C. advocates student participation as a way of fostering the development of the child's personal value system and this approach encourages children through a method of value processing to choose, prize and act on values they deem appropriate for a given situation. Shelton (1990) quotes Kohlberg as saying that the inadequacy of the Values Clarification approach is in the relativity to which all values are reduced and as a consequence all values are options. The crux of Kohlberg's argument resides in his belief that V.C.'s method lacks a moral reference point, no criterion exists to judge values against, and this leads to a 'moral hodge podge' that lacks clarity. Yet, V.C. is perhaps the most paradigmatic of contemporary theories of moral education and development and challenges theory with the contention that the only true test of a values based approach to education is in the domain of practice. The greatest weakness of V.C. is the belief that on its own it could contribute positively to the moral behaviour and development of children (Deroche and Williams 1998). However, V.C. did legitimise value-laden and moral issues as appropriate for schools and other educational settings and in conjunction with other aspects of moral development it could contribute positively to children's moral development. As Hersh and Paolitto (1978 p.140) said: "Perhaps the most pervasive attempt to recognise the legitimacy of the study of values in schools is the Values Clarification approach".

Morality as self-development is about enhancing one's own self-identity and once this is done, acceptance and affirmation of others can occur. This model of morality focuses on the centrality and uniqueness of each individual human being and from there is about developing one's own set of values and responding to others with appropriate moral responses by reaching out and helping. This allows one to grow and develop into the higher self. For example, Maria, aged five, is attending primary school. She is very friendly with Jane, whose mum doesn't like Travellers. So Jane says to Maria that they mustn't play with Betty, the Traveller child in her class. However, despite this, Maria asks Jane to allow Betty to play also. She has developed a set of values which accepts all people.

(vi)   Multiple perspectives

All these perspectives on morality are correct in their own way, each offering some indispensable truth and insight into morality but each on its own is incomplete. Thus, a truly comprehensive view of morality can only be reached by appreciating and integrating the insights contained in all of the perspectives. Through children's decisions they create their own moral character and by their response to others they affect their own and others' growth, encouraging and developing it, or stunting and blocking it. There can be no static morality; the elements of process and growth are ever present. Adults and children must balance the various models of morality as each has its advantages and disadvantages. There are no definitive answers to all moral questions; false absolutes must be relativised and the lust for certainty must be controlled, as children learn to live with a degree of uncertainty; a vital element of moral maturity is the ability to live creatively with tension and change (Fagan 1997; Harrington 1996). The more questions we ask, both in relation to ourselves and to our world, the more subsequent questions we generate and the less certain we are that there are answers, let alone definitive ones. Children and adults must be willing to set out on a voyage of discovery and must be willing to ask questions, some of which may never be answered (Lally 1991). Circle time can sometimes be helpful in beginning this process. Most early years practitioners try to make sure that there is room to explore issues of interest to children and to such ends circle time has become an important part of early years education. Circle time can emphasise the building of effective communication and helps the development of good relationships as well as providing a forum where problems can be tackled constructively. In circle time children can be encouraged to listen to others, to explore feelings, to take turns speaking, to raise questions, to look at alternatives, to seek solutions (Mosley 2000). However, to develop morally, a more in-depth thinking capacity than that which is normally developed in circle time is required.

Children as philosophers

In order to help children to develop morally, they need to be encouraged to be philosophers who think reflectively. Philosophy is not just conversation – it is, "an emergent, multi-vocal and interactive story about the world, and about persons thinking in the world" (Kennedy 1999 cited in Haynes 2002 p.49). Central to the practice of philosophy with children is that all discussion comes from children's questions, questions usually raised in response to a particular stimulus such as a story, poem, incident in the setting or in the home. The process of choosing a question and of engaging in enquiry is a democratic one and the adult strives to enable children's discussion to follow its own course, not steering it in a pre-planned way. Children are encouraged to think creatively, logically and critically, to reason and reflect, deliberating with an open-minded disposition. The adult's role is to model the language of philosophical discourse and to attempt to introduce conceptual tools to extend or to record the development of ideas. Children are scaffolded to collaborate, not towards unanimity but towards shedding light on a particular question from different angles. Disagreement and divergence are normal. The practice of philosophy in the early years setting is a collaborative and collective endeavour as well as an individual one. Children, like adults, have individual strengths in different areas such as logical reasoning, imaginative ideas, the ability to see the whole, to spot patterns and connections and to see flaws or injustices in an argument. The freedom and benefit of such divergent and complementary strengths is immeasurable. Young children can philosophise on such subjects as friendship, bullying, differences, anger, punishment, death, fairness, justice, religion (Haynes 2002).

The appropriateness of philosophy with children has been challenged by some who argue that young children are not developmentally capable of the type of abstract and de-centred thinking that they believe is required in philosophy. It is also criticised by those who believe that young children should be provided with a solid diet of basic prescriptive education. Kennedy in Haynes (2002) claims that the historical devaluation of children's ability to reason is part and parcel of their assigned status as a politically inferior and dis-empowered group. Children do not have the same rights as adults. They are awarded some degree of protection but are very short of power. Their ability to make choices is curtailed, they are referred to as minor and do not enjoy the full rights of citizenship. Fawcett (2000 p.6) says that: "Adults still have enormous power over children's lives, and may feel threatened by changes in the status quo". Philosophical enquiry offers a method of teaching that undoes some of this damage by providing a vehicle for exploring many of the issues which effect children. It can help to promote and exercise children's rights as citizens and can help practitioners and children alike to find humane ways of assessing individual contributions and values as well as helping them to recognise personal development. Encouraging questions and critical thinking involves engagement in a practice that has been fundamental to the idea of a rounded values based education. Questions that promote thought include: What do you think about ...? Why do you think that? How do you know? How do you know what you know is true? What are your reasons for thinking that? How does your idea compare to [another child's idea]? What if you ...? What if you didn't? Would it make a difference if...? What might happen if.....? (Branscombe et al. 2000). Magee (1998) proposes that Ancient Greece was the first society in which students were taught to think for themselves – to discuss, debate, value, argue and criticise – not just to regurgitate the values, views and opinions of their elders. This reflection led to the most rapid expansion of understanding there had ever been and showed that knowledge can actually grow through criticism, and confirms that in a democratic society, moral principles must be freely chosen rather than externally imposed and must be self-accepted rather than uncritically imbibed. Such philosophical thought is necessary if young children are to become truly moral beings.

Conclusion

Morality and moral development are very broad concepts which in essence are about valuing self, relationships, the environment and society. Valuing these enables children to live together more co-operatively, peacefully and contentedly. Valuing the self and developing the self entails seeing each person, including the self, as a unique being of intrinsic worth with potential for development and change. It puts the onus on the child to try to understand his own character, strengths and weaknesses. It involves developing a sense of self-confidence and self-reliance and is about discovering meaning and purpose in life and deciding how life ought to be lived. It is about living up to a shared moral code, making responsible use of rights and privileges and striving for knowledge and wisdom. It also entails taking responsibility for one's own life within one's capacities. Valuing relationships involves respecting others not for what they have or what they can do for us. Children must value others, as relationships are vital to their development and for the good of the community. Children must earn loyalty, trust and confidence and they must work and play co-operatively with others and be mutually supportive. They must respect and acknowledge the beliefs, lives, privacy and property of others and they must try to resolve disputes peacefully. Valuing the environment means children must value the natural world as a source of wonder and inspiration. They must accept their responsibility and duty to maintain a sustainable environment for future generations. The onus is on us as humans to preserve areas of beauty and to understand the rightful place of human beings within the world. Valuing society means children value truth, human rights, the law, justice and collective endeavour for the common good of society. Thus, children must understand and accept their responsibilities as citizens. They must be ready to challenge values or actions which may be harmful to individuals or communities and they must accept diversity and respect others' rights to religious and cultural differences. Opportunities must be provided for all children to participate in democracy, since children must contribute to, as well as benefit from society (Beck 1998). Then and only then, can children learn to be moral beings. The development of a shared respect, a mutuality of regard, a capacity for the child and parents/practitioners to see the world through the eyes of others is what is desired by moral development today. Thus, the child becomes a good citizen carrying his own fair share of responsibility, caring and respect (Coles 1997).

Moral/character development is a slowly evolving process, but values are learned by children very early on and a long moral road is started in the first years of life. The early years matter a great deal morally. Moral development is best facilitated by giving children the opportunity to understand principles and reasons rather than teaching them specific actions which may be situation dependent. Moral values must underscore every action, rule and statement. Children develop morally from identifying with significant others who live by certain values, by internalising such values from others and by learning to love the good in themselves. Experiencing reinforcement of behaviour that demonstrates such values, experiencing logical consequences from adults for behaviours opposing values, developing perspective taking and acquiring higher levels of moral reasoning all contribute to moral development (Berger 1996).

Kay (1968) says that to understand moral development one must know:

- something about the quality of behaviour natural to each stage of child development;
- the characteristic sanctions which operate at each level of development;
- the nature of moral judgement exercised as children grow;
- the personality or psycho-social maturity of the child.

These must all be brought together before a comprehensive picture of moral development can take place. As well as these factors, the influence of the home, school, community and sub-cultural variations must also be considered. To date, no research has considered all of these. Dunn (1988) says that there are striking features of social and moral development, which have been neglected by all the theories of moral development put forward so far. Each researcher to date has simply selected one psychological element or dimension of moral development and dealt with it to the exclusion of all others. In future, explorations of moral development must be concerned with the total development of the child. This will take the researcher into a multidisciplinary area and it means only collaboration and co-operation between professionals in the different areas, such as sociology, psychology, education, theology, social studies and philosophy will lead to a true description and understanding of moral development.

However, going on what we do know, my contention is that if children are encouraged to combine the above five models of moral development: morality as emotion; as concern and responsibility for others; as conformity to rules/authority; as conformity to one's sense of belief; and as self development, then they will optimise their moral and character development. If we are open to seeing that there is a variety of aspects to moral development and if we try to develop all such aspects by prioritising self, others and the environment, then children's moral development will be enhanced. Also, children must be encouraged to act in moral ways. The more they can translate their own internal values into conscious and deliberate actions, the more they can make positive choices based on their beliefs (Charney 1998). Opportunities need to be found to develop children's understanding of civic values in society so that they can act as responsible citizens and can contribute fully to their family, school, community and society. To develop civic values, children need to learn the social and negotiating skills which are essential to effective participation in civic life, and this can be aided by experiencing practical opportunities to participate and become involved. Education must provide these opportunities. Philosophical enquiry must take place on a regular basis to allow children to become reflective thinkers who know what morality is and to know how to be moral citizens.

It is not possible to pinpoint exactly how children develop morally. Much debate today focuses on a combination of theories and this seems to be a positive step. However, in order to delve more deeply into this domain, a more inter-disciplinary approach to morality needs to occur. Different theories, on the surface, appear to offer contradictory and incompatible views. Yet, underlying each of them is the need for people to live moral lives in order to form relationships, to bond and to live co-operatively and collaboratively together. As Wilson, Williams and Sugarman (1967, p.168) said: "To try to impose values is immoral, but to fail to create frameworks within which people can choose their own values is just as bad". We must also always remember that, in order to survive, humans need to form relationships and as a result of such relationships, morality develops. No community and no child can function for long without it. Thus, moral development must be a core area in every early years setting and in all future curriculum development it is vital that as well as emphasising the three Rs - reading, writing and arithmetic, we must also prioritise the fourth and fifth Rs - respect and responsibility.

Suggestions/guidelines for enhancing moral development

Many things can be done to ensure that moral development is given a higher profile in the early years setting. The following are a list of suggestions which have been selected from various sources including: *A Curriculum for the Pre-school Child* (Curtis 1986); *The Emotional, Social, Moral and Spiritual Development of the Pre-school Child* (Daly 2002); *Project E.Y.E. An Irish Curriculum for the three to four year old child – Volume One: Spiritual, Emotional and Moral Development* (Douglas, Horgan and O'Brien 2000); *Young Children's Personal, Social and Emotional Development* (Dowling 2000); *BASIC Montessori* (Gettman 1987); *Positive Parenting* (Hartley-Brewer 1994); *Caring for the under-8s* (Lindon and Lindon 1993); *The Handbook of Environmental Education* (Palmer and Neal 1994); *Setting the What if Free: Some theoretical perspectives on talking and thinking in an infant classroom - an investigation into one teacher's practice* (Roche 2003); and *Educating the Whole Child: cross-curricular skills, themes and dimensions* (1995) Siraj-Blatchford and Siraj-Blatchford 1995).

- The example set by early years practitioners, carers, family members, friends, peers and the media all impact on children's moral development, so take note of this. They watch, listen, copy, do what others do, not what others say. What we are and how we behave is what matters, not what we say or believe we say, so be aware of this and act on it.

- Ensure the setting is non-judgemental and non-authoritarian.

- Write a mission statement for the setting with the help of the children – for example our mission is to care for ourselves, for others and for the earth. Refer to it on a regular basis and see that it is being adhered to.

- Allow children to be active in decision and rule making, agree three or four key rules and display them pictorially in the room. Help children understand the reasons for rules: for example, why there is a rule about not running in the setting or why only four children are allowed in the playhouse at the one time. Adults must adhere to rules also and rules need to be repeated often so that children are familiar with them.

- Discuss your Behaviour Management Policy with parents. Ask them to read it and get them to sign off after reading it. Continuity between home and school views on morality/discipline/rules and managing challenging behaviour is vital. Ensure that policies and procedures are implemented consistently and review and update them regularly.

- Be aware of adult expectations and beliefs. Are boys and girls treated differently - are boys who are physically fighting left to sort it out for themselves while the adult steps in quickly when girls are involved? Is it assumed that the boys have started it when both sexes are involved? Be honest because children will notice how you react and will note differences very quickly and will take their cue from the adult.

- Have routines and explain what it is you want children to do. Be clear and don't assume that because you know what is expected and acceptable that they know too. Have realistic expectations about children and their behaviour. Give simple instructions, ask children to repeat these after you in their own words to make sure they understand.

- If rules are broken, ensure that it is the behaviour and not the child that is disapproved of. Find out why the rule has been challenged and deal with it in an appropriate way. Be aware of what is going on for the child involved. Try not to reprimand the child in public, with an audience of children. Talk to the child on his own and never belittle him. Be straightforward and honest – Say 'I am upset that you hit out at x.' and so on.

- Observe children in their role-play to gain insights into their moral understandings and level of development – develop such insights through individual, small and large group work.

- With small groups have sessions on good manners – please, thank you, how to knock on a door, how to answer the telephone, how to ask for something, how to get someone's attention, how to shake hands. Do role-play in the groups and encourage children to give feedback.

- Show children what it is to be gentle; tone down the atmosphere by lowering the lights, by playing soft music, by speaking in a low voice.

- Help children to develop listening skills – scaffold them to respect another's right to speak, emphasise the importance of body language and eye contact. Ask them to be considerate of others' needs and request them not to interrupt when others are speaking.

- Explain and show the children that everything has a place and why it needs to be replaced there. Children may have no concept of having to tidy away. Show them (by example) how to hold and lift things, how to put things back in their box.

- Encourage children not to push, for example when trying to get a desired item or if going outside or on a bus. Show them how to form a queue and how to wait their turn, encourage them to let others go first.

- Scaffold children to include others, to invite them into the game, to sit beside them at lunch break, story time and so on.

- Encourage children to be tolerant and patient, explain that some children take longer than others to do things and that some tasks are easier for some than for others.

- Ensure that bullying behaviour of any kind is not tolerated in the setting. Ensure children are familiar with the term and know that it not acceptable.

- Don't allow children to make fun of others or to call them names. Talk about how it feels to be laughed at and to be hurt by such behaviour.

- Don't allow individuals to spoil games or to interrupt play. Observe when and who does this and support different behaviour.

- Encourage children to help others and to accept advice and help from others and create opportunities for children to be kind to each other.

- Ensure that each child understands what is involved in the concept of co-operation. Show them how it can be useful for two or more people to work together to complete a task or to solve a problem. Have lots of small groups and project work in the setting.

- Circle time is an ideal opportunity to trigger discussions. Events in the news or in the community can be used to highlight issues, to spark discussion and children's questions can present practitioners with 'teachable moments'.

- Have a rota system so that all children get a chance to help out, to partake in games and so on. Put two or three children together to form a team, make sure everyone gets their fair share.

- Explore the theme of fair and unfair play with children – discover what they understand by the words and ask them to share out fruit/treats fairly.

- Provide children with many tangible examples of moral behaviour, bring in newspaper cuttings of moral acts. Also show them immoral acts – stealing cars, robbing an old person, vandalising property – get them involved in discussions.

- Encourage children to give clothes and toys to local charity shops.

- Encourage children to talk about their own and other's kindnesses. Sit the children in a circle. Let them take turns to stand up, holding up photographs of their parent/sibling/any family member. Ask them to say one kind action that that person does for them and *vice versa*, e.g. Mummy makes my breakfast every day and I help her find her keys when she loses them. The adult could extend this discussion by saying isn't that kind and how important it is to be kind to others and for others to be kind to the child.

- Help children to express their needs and wants in words rather than physically. When the level of frustration appears overwhelming, the adult needs to step in and offer support to enable the children to sort things out. Listen to both sides and ask for alternative solutions. Encourage constructive conflict resolution by helping children work through problem solving by considering all viewpoints and deciding on what is best for everyone involved. Help children to identify the causes of conflicts, to describe the possible alternative actions and to consider their consequences. Discuss the values of compromise, negotiation, sharing, etc. and the negative value of using violence and aggression as a means of resolving conflicts. All children occasionally show hostile behaviour. The adult's role is to prevent this from becoming a pattern, by helping children learn alternative ways to handle situations that anger, frighten or upset them.

- Display pictures of people or animals that need help (a cat up a tree, a house on fire). Get the children to discuss what would be needed to help the situation.

- Have simple games in the setting which necessitate that the children adhere to rules. Explain the reasons for the rules. Do they think that rules can't be changed or do they believe rules can be changed?

- Play 'true or false games' – The adult makes statements and the children must decide if they are true or false, e.g. 'It is dark', 'Anne is a boy' and so on. Talk about the difference between truth and lies.

- Challenge children to take responsibility for actions and discuss the importance of saying sorry and really meaning it. Talk about times when we should say sorry – when we lose our temper, when we bump into someone, if we wrongly blame someone. Talk about extending the apology by shaking hands, hugging, sharing a treat. Stress the importance of genuinely feeling sorry, not just blurting it out without any real feeling behind it.

- Discuss how you should react when someone says sorry to you – i.e. forgiving the other person and not trying to get your own back.

- Introduce a puppet who does 'naughty' things into the setting, explain that he does not know how to behave and will need to be told about the agreed rules – get the children to explain the rules to him and to expand on why they are necessary.

- Use a variety of puppets or soft toys to play out scenarios involving different aspects of behaviour – e.g. rows about taking turns, sharing, tidying up and so on. Ask children for possible solutions.

- Greater emphasis needs to be placed on a 'values education' and there should be discussions on values and on the laws of natural justice - respect and responsibility, love, unity, peace, happiness, simplicity, compassion, loyalty, empathy, generosity, tact, courtesy, fairness, trust, freedom, understanding, thoughtfulness, honesty, patience, responsiveness to others and learning to act for the common good.

- Discuss issues as they come up in the setting - conflict, squabbling, name-calling – this will help children to realise the impact of their thoughts and actions on themselves and others. Look back over incidents to see how they could, should, did behave.

- Encourage children to learn to respect by whatever means - other people, nature, the environment, other people's possessions, public property.

- The setting should be set up so that justice prevails for everyone. Treat children as you would like to be treated and encourage children to do the same. All children will then see the benefits of moral behaviour for self and others. Teach them to act for the common good and to look at things from a more global perspective.

- Encourage children to be good citizens. Have discussions and workshops on the duties, responsibilities and rights of being a citizen in the early years setting and beyond.

- Foster in children the confidence and courage to say no when others are doing wrong.

- Help children to think ahead and to appreciate the wider consequences of different actions, talk about intent and how our actions impact on others, give examples.

- Tell stories with a moral dilemma and ask children to think about them and to decide the outcome; this will help them to use reason and foster their ability to reflect.

- Allow children to resolve moral dilemmas through role-play; occasionally set up scenarios for this to happen.

- Provide opportunities for philosophical enquiry. Make room for children to discuss issues and ideas. Early on provide a story, poem or newspaper report, as time goes on encourage children to raise questions directly from their own experience or draw questions from sources that the children have chosen.

- Show by example that everyone is special and that they all deserve to be treated with care and respect.

- Find one thing to praise about every child every day, praise the deed rather than the person and the process rather than the product. Appreciate children's efforts.

- If the adult does or says something wrong – admit the error, take responsibility, apologise and move on.

- Create situations where it is easy for children to share and take turns, ensure there are sufficient resources where possible (scissors, glue, cars, dolls) for all children. For resources which are in short supply, get children to ask for a turn, make up a list of children waiting (if necessary), use an egg timer to time children using equipment/toy and when time is up ask the child who is using the toy to hand it over.

- Have a caring and sharing week. Send a note home about it and say that each child may bring in a toy/game to share. Make sure the article is labelled with the child's name and during the week encourage sharing and caring.

- Consider having 'development education' as part of the curriculum. The objective of this is to enable people to participate in the development of their community, their nation and world as a whole and to understand development processes within and between all countries – rich and poor. Development education is concerned with issues of human rights, dignity, self-reliance and social justice. We need to do this to offer children an education system which will prepare them to behave appropriately and justly, particularly for when they grow up and are in positions of power, relative to those from poorer countries. The seeds of this can be sown in the early years setting.

- Introduce issue-based themes and topics such as regions of the world being overpopulated and not having enough food or water. Ask the children to imagine what it would be like to live there, ask them what could be done to help. Make children aware of why it is important not to waste water or food.

- Introduce local issues of poverty and unemployment – ask children to discuss how they feel about them.

- Show children the complex inter-relationships between man and his environment; for example explain to children the effects the waste we create has on the environment, the decline in rainforests and so on.

- Teach children about the environment and encourage them to develop an attitude of concern for environmental matters. Emphasise the development of environment-friendly values, attitudes and skills.

- Introduce the concept of 'global warming' to children during circle time. Stress the need to sustain our planet and its resources.

- Provide children with opportunities to acquire the knowledge, values, commitment and skills needed to protect and improve the environment – conserving energy, cutting down on waste, recycling, respecting animals and nature.

- Encourage children to keep the setting clear of litter, save energy by switching off unwanted lights and heaters.

- Talk about recycling and the kind of things that can be recycled – have displays of these things on the walls and encourage parents to recycle also. Recycle as much as possible from cans, bottles, tinfoil to stamps; and take a trip to the local recycling plant. Have a composter to take green/food waste.

- Address issues of environmental education through the study of the local area - pollution in the local river, dumping in the picnic area. This enables children to work from the concrete to the abstract.

- Get children to feed the birds with their left over lunch.

- Discuss taking care of ourselves – healthy eating, exercise, getting enough sleep, being careful crossing the road, wearing seat belts in cars and so on – encourage children to take responsibility for these and to take the message out of the settings to homes and communities.

- Allow plants/pets in the setting. These will allow children to respect and appreciate their environment through the care of living things and their habitats in and around the setting. Have rotas for feeding, cleaning up etc.

- Have a curriculum which embraces civics and develop the theme of social responsibility. For example ask children to help out even if they haven't contributed to the problem. If they refuse, talk about our social responsibilities and develop the theme wherever possible.

- Carry out an audit to see what opportunities are offered to children to exercise responsibility in the setting.

- Introduce children to the concept of consumerism. Tell them about the use of advertising to target markets and for example at Christmas when writing to Santa ask them to be conscious of what they are asking for – get them to reflect on why they like it and why they want it – do they really like it or is it because they saw it advertised on television? Also make them aware of the excess packaging used in such products (and highlight the benefits of recycling).

- Encourage children to develop a sense of responsibility towards home, early years setting and the community – ask them if they help out at home, suggest ways they could contribute to their homes and communities.

- Encourage children to talk about what the most important things in life are. Tell a story about a boy who was able to wish for the three most precious things to have forever in his life. Ask the children for suggestions or offer a limited number of choices and get children to choose – provide a tray with options – a photo of a mum/dad, a bike, a dog, a bar of chocolate, ice-cream. Ask the children in turn to make their choices and open up discussion about what sorts of things are important and why. This will give insights into children's developing values.

- Use stories to raise moral questions and conflicts – aspects of laws and rules, friendship issues, the fair treatment of property, authority and power, respect for others, the environment and community issues.

- Turn daily events into stories for circle time – making and breaking friendships, taking something that doesn't belong to you, hurting another, helping someone, being generous, calling someone names, not telling the truth, sharing and so on.

- Code of behaviour, values, curriculum, hidden curriculum, interactions between staff; staff and parents; staff and children; and between the children themselves all need to be monitored on a constant basis. If there are problems or disagreements, deal with them – don't let them simmer under the surface.

- Develop a peace curriculum. Peace education has been identified as an alternative curriculum for early years education. A peace curriculum includes subjects like teaching children about non-violence, conflict resolution through peaceful means, economics, politics and concern for the environment.

- Ask yourself do the children in the setting have the right to make autonomous judgments about what is right or what is true? Will doing this help them to understand what society holds to be true or right? Are children encouraged to think for themselves? Do you model respect and fairness? Do you provide opportunities for children to question and ponder and criticise? Do you encourage children to become reflective? Does the setting foster and encourage dialogue? Is there an atmosphere of mutual respect in the setting? Do you think the setting prioritises moral development?

Children's books which are useful for moral development

Topsy and Tim Green Activity Book (ISBN 0216940966) by Jean and Gareth Adamson.

The Little Piggy's Book of Manners (ISBN 0805067698) by Kathryn Allen.

The Story of Rosy Dock (ISBN 068814911) by Jeannie Baker.

Willie's Not The Hugging Kind (ISBN 0064432645) by Joyce Barrett.

The Berenstain Bears and The Truth (ISBN 0394856406) by Stan and Jan Berenstain.

Franklin is Bossy (ISBN 0590477579) by Paulette Bourgeois.

Francis the Scaredy Cat (ISBN 0763617679) by Edward Boxall.

Look at What I've Got (ISBN 0531041182) by Anthony Browne.

Mr. Grumpy's Outing (ISBN 0805066292) by John Burningham.

Let's Get a Pup (ISBN 0763621935) by Jethro Byrde.

I Want It (ISBN 1884734146) by Elisabeth Crary.

Clean Your Room, Harvey Moon (ISBN 0689717989) by Pat Cummings.

Weslandia (ISBN 0763610526) by Paul Fleischman.

Please Princess Primrose (ISBN 0744569419) by Vivian French.

I'll Take You to Mrs. Cole (ISBN 0916291391) by Nigel Gray.

Rabbit Food (ISBN 0763612936) by Susanna Gretz.

Mums Don't Get Sick (ISBN 0744547229) by Marylin Hafner.

Jig, Fig and Mrs. Pig (ISBN 1564028321) by Peter Hansard.

And the Good Brown Earth (ISBN 0763623016) by Kathy Henderson.

Dogger (ISBN 068811704X) by Shirley Hughes.

Winnie the Witch (ISBN 068811704X) by Paul Korky and Valerie Thomas.

Clever Tortoise (ISBN 0763605069) and *The Honey Hunters* (ISBN 156402086X) by Francesca Martin.

I'll Always be Your Friend (ISBN 006029485X) and *I'm Sorry* (ISBN 0006646298) by Sam McBratney.

One Smile (ISBN 0935699236) by Cindy McKinley.

Enemy Pie (ISBN 081182778X) by Derek Munson.

All For One (ISBN 0763607851) and *Five Minutes Peace* (ISBN 0698117875) by Jill Murphy.

How Kind (ISBN 0763623075) by Mary Murphy.
Do's and Don'ts (ISBN 0316520551) by Todd Parr.
Because David Hugged His Mother (ISBN 1883220890) by David Rice.
Aunt Nancy and Cousin Lazybones (ISBN 1564024253) by Phyllis Root.
No David! (ISBN 0590930028) by David Shannon.
The Giving Tree (ISBN 0060256656) by Shel Silverstein.
The Chocolate Covered Cookie Tantrum (ISBN 0395700280) by Harvey Stevenson and Deborah Blumenthal.
Pizza Kittens (ISBN 0763616222) and *Ginger* (ISBN 0763607886) by Charlotte Voake.
Farmer Duck (ISBN 1564025969), *Bertie was a Watchdog* (ISBN 0763613851) and *Amy Said* (ISBN 0316916366) by Martin Waddell.
Katje The Windmill Cat (ISBN 0763613479) by Gretchen Woelfle.

CHAPTER SIX

Spiritual Development

Introduction

> The more we succeed in transforming our hearts and minds through cultivating spiritual qualities, the better able we will be to cope with adversity and the greater the likelihood that our actions will be ethically wholesome (The Dalai Lama quoted in Farrer 2000, p.37).

The heart of spirituality is to look inward in search of meaning and purpose. It is to seek an understanding of what truly matters and why it matters. Spirituality can be described as those attitudes, beliefs, values and practices which emanate from a person's life. Being spiritually developed involves reaching the highest self and is about serving, not being served, and love is at its heart. It means having a proper balance between one's outer and inner world and is a search for quality and unity in life. Yet, today the world and its people are more fragmented than ever before. We live at surface level, not belonging to any group at any real depth. People are unable to be intimate with themselves or with others and a spiritual vacuum exists which needs to be filled.

The technological age has introduced the fragmentation of tasks, the shattering of community and the ascendancy of technological and materialistic values to the detriment of the spiritual. According to Randle (1989 p.61):

> Our civilisation has suppressed truths about the human being's inner life, denied the importance of the non-material, and peddled a perverted spirituality, in the form of conventional religion, as a major weapon against the growth of the free, spiritually-connected, whole citizen.

This has had drastic negative consequences for humans, particularly young children, and the experience of this vacuum gives rise to frustration, sadness, loneliness and to a sense of isolation and alienation. Pessimism is in the air as we begin the third millennium. All is not well with the world spiritually and as Aronson (1995 p.216) says: "Collectively as a society, we are starving for spirit; we whine from hunger pains; we are malnourished". Science, economics, technology and the consumer culture have so dominated and diminished the spiritual side of life that it has been repressed to almost non-existence.

The 21st century needs to reflect on a new level of spiritual wisdom and intuitive insight. There has been no golden age and every generation has struggled spiritually, just as we struggle today. Naivety about the nature of spiritual energy, pathological busyness, restlessness and distraction, and a problem with balance leading to a sense of isolation and breakdown of community, underlie our contemporary struggle for healthy spirituality. We live in a world that is clear in almost everything except spirituality (Rolheiser 1998). Two of the top ten causes of death in the western world today, suicide and alcoholism, are frequently related to a crisis of meaning. Russell (2003) looks at the spiritual dimension in addiction and recounts the link between addiction and our thirst for a deeper spiritual dimension. Russell claims that this search manifests itself in attachments to alcohol, drugs and other external sources, because of a lack of spiritual development. People, including children, ask who am I? What is my place in the world? What am I doing with my life? Is my life worth anything? Such questions cannot be answered by mere I.Q. The despair that drives a person to suicide is the deepest form of spiritual stuntedness. If the spirit is not developed we grow into incomplete adults who are unable to see beyond the moment or to place things in a wider framework of meaning and value. A spiritual desert has come about as a by-product of the emphasis on high human I.Q. and our consumer-driven culture. The reasons people seek for living their lives are not rational ones, nor are they purely emotional ones, they are in fact spiritual ones.

The importance of the early years for spiritual development

All people, including children, are driven by a specifically human longing to find meaning and value in what they do and experience. Frankl (1985) claims that the search for meaning is one of the primary motivators in children's lives and he suggests that if this deep need for meaning goes unmet, then their lives come to feel shallow and empty. Children have a longing for something towards which they can aspire, for something that takes them beyond themselves and the present moment, for something that gives them and their actions a sense of worth. In other words, children need an overall context for their lives. Spiritual development is inter-linked with every aspect of child development. In particular, it is closely related to children's moral, emotional and social development. To experience spirituality one must be moral and one must also be developed emotionally and socially, accepting and loving of self and others. Spirituality is the very basis from which self-esteem, values, morality and a sense of belonging grow. Spirituality is what gives meaning and direction to life. It involves an awareness of a sacred connection to all creation and also involves a choice to embrace that connection with love. Children's spiritual natures are apparent through their embodied creativity, vivid imagination and open-ended, joyful approach to life (Doe and Walch 1998). Spiritual development is often neglected in young children and if it not developed it will be lost. It is easily damaged and needs sensitive nurturing, but if cared for properly it can be like 'watching a flower blossom'. Without spiritual growth children cannot develop to their full potential and will not fulfil their ambitions and dreams. If they are not helped to develop spiritually it can have a detrimental impact on their lives (Daly 2002).

Spirituality

Ancient societies, from prehistoric times, frequently showed evidence of a concern with spiritual matters and rituals and anthropological studies show evidence of spiritual beliefs and practices in all recorded societies. However, spirituality is to a large extent forgotten in the western world today, and yet developing spiritually meets certain basic needs of humans. People, modern and ancient, have sought a sense of meaning and purpose in their daily lives and personal choices. Over the millennia people have searched for answers to significant questions and people have always looked for and needed a focus for interaction and celebration. Rituals for important life events fulfil the need for a positive feeling of identity and help answer profound questions. Through time, this evolved into a belief in something outside the individual, something great, and for some led to a belief in God and for others, such as humanists, it led to more secular but no less spiritual beliefs (Lindon 1999). Fowler (1981 xiii) says spirituality is;

> so *'fundamental'* that none of us can live well for very long without it, so *'universal'* that when we move beneath the symbols, rituals and ethical patterns that express it, faith is recognisably the same phenomenon in Christians, Marxists, Hindus and Dinka, yet it is so *'infinitely varied'* that each person's faith is unique.

Spirituality is a very vague and broad concept. The word spirit is derived from the Greek word for 'breath' i.e. that which gives life to our lives while being constitutive of that life and this has led to the present definition of spirituality. However few words are as misunderstood in the English language today as is the word 'spirituality'. These tragic misunderstandings have led to neglect of a vital aspect of human life. Spirituality is something vital and non-negotiable which lies at the heart of every child's life. Fowler (1981) contends that spirituality is a human universal. However, how each individual child develops this capacity, how it is activated and grows, depends greatly on how the child is welcomed into the world and what kinds of environment he grows up in. Spirituality is interactive and social, it needs language, rituals, nurturance, a community and its underlying principle and centre is, and must be, love. Spirituality is about being integrated as opposed to falling apart, it is about being in a community versus being lonely, about being in harmony with the earth versus being alienated from it. Regardless of whether or not we let ourselves be consciously shaped by any explicitly religious idea, we act in ways that leave us either unhealthy or healthy, bitter or loving, alienated or in community - what shapes us is our spirituality. Spirituality is what we do, it is the fire that is inside each and every one of us. How we channel it, the disciplines and habits we live by, either lead to a life of integration or disintegration within our bodies, minds and souls, depending on the choices we make.

The 'spiritual' dimension comes from deep within our humanity and finds its expression in aspirations, moral sensibility, creativity, love and friendship. It is also to be found in responses to natural and human beauty, in scientific and artistic endeavours, in appreciation and wonder at the natural world, in intellectual achievement and physical activity. It is the knowledge born from love, from being loved and from recognising that it and our lives are measured in terms of lived love. Spirituality repudiates suffering and persecution and is about selfless love and quests for values and meanings by which to live. It is not a question of what one believes but whether one has lived with compassion and love towards others and if children have a 'right sense of heart' they are on their way to being developed spiritually (Gallagher 1998). Maslow (1970b) in Hemming (1970 p.164) said:

> The spiritual life is part of our biological life. It is the 'highest' part of it – but yet part of it. The spiritual life is part of the human essence. It is a defining characteristic of human nature, without which human nature is not *fully* human. It is part of the real self, of one's identity, of one's inner core, of one's specieshood, of full humanness.

Gilmartin (1996) contends that spirituality is possessed by all people regardless of race, culture, education, intelligence or religion. It is not something acquired but is at the very core of a person's being. He defines spirituality as whatever calls us to transcendence. It is that which motivates us away from being self-focused and self-seeking and is what inspires us to give priority to the welfare of others. It gives a sense of belonging and is an integrating source, and being well integrated implies having principles, values and a philosophy of life that determines how to express and live that life. Most children are taught a theology in early childhood, as parental figures explicitly or implicitly pass on to their children a meaning of life which invariably has some transcendent dimension. Whether this transcendence concerns God or simply one's responsible connectedness to others, teaches the child that life has some particular meaning. This then becomes the basis of a child's spirituality. However, this spirituality must develop and grow and children must be adaptable to a completely new 'genre' of spiritual issues as change occurs, navigating their own life's journey. Often children get entrapped in a concept of God that destroys their potential for in-depth spirituality as their childhood concepts become the basis for their spirituality.

To develop spiritually, children must learn to grow and trust their experiences, which will lead them to a new, hopefully deeper understanding of their beliefs, even if this means rejecting some or all of what they learned in early life. One of the major challenges in life is to become spiritually developed. It takes more strength, courage and ingenuity than either physical or psychological well-being. It is exacerbated by the fact that there are generally reliable guidelines on how to achieve physical and psychological wellness but there is very little guidance on how to develop spiritual wellness. Yet, spiritual wellness and development is necessary for physical and psychological well-being, the three form part of a three-legged stool and like a stool, if one of the legs is broken the stool is useless no matter how strong the other two legs are. Kealy (1994) cites spiritual wellness as knowing the purpose and meaning of life, of being able to identify life's authentic, satisfying, fulfilling human joys and pleasures and accepting responsibility for the freedom of self-determination in life. It is about finding an appropriate source of motivation, which includes spiritual values and/or religious beliefs and is about accepting the need for change in life. It is about how to access the underlying stillness and peace in life, about reaching the higher states of consciousness and is about living in the present and thinking positively and being hopeful. How many early years settings try to develop such wellness in children? If they all did so, would it impact positively on children's experience of education?

Spiritual quotient

At the beginning of the 21st century there is a growing body of scientific data which shows that just as there is an intelligence quotient, there is also a spiritual quotient. Thus, the full picture of human existence can only be completed with a discussion on the spiritual quotient (S.Q.). S.Q. helps humans address and solve problems of meaning and value. It allows us to place our actions and our lives in a wider, richer, more meaning-giving context (Zohar and Marshall 2000). There are three main intelligences: - I.Q. (Intelligence Quotient), E.Q. (Emotional Quotient) and S.Q. (Spiritual Quotient). It is argued that, ideally, these three basic intelligences work together and support one another. Each on its own has separate areas of strength and can function separately but to develop optimally all three must work together. S.Q. is based on the brain's third neural system (the first and second being reason and emotion) and operates from the brain's neurological unifying functions, where synchronous neural oscillations unify data across the whole brain. S.Q. unifies, integrates and has the potential to transform material arising from the other two processes and facilitates a dialogue between emotion and reason, between body and mind and makes us the fully integrated creatures that we can be (Zohar and Marshall 2000).

Spirituality and religion

In the past, spirituality tended to be seen as being synonymous with religion and was the domain of the priest, rabbi and minister. However today, early years practitioners, psychologists, psychiatrists, social workers and counsellors are unable to avoid dealing with this issue; they acknowledge that it has relevance for all humans, especially young children. It is now taken for granted that spirituality is too important to be tied exclusively to religion, yet there is still a tendency to confuse the spiritual with the religious (Dowling 2000). Religions often neglect and ignore what is needed by children and adults to help them develop spiritually. Without losing sight of the significant contributions that religions have made to the world, they have also contributed to wars, human enslavement, gross injustices, victimisation and dehumanising practices. In fact, "too often religions have been destructive of human spirituality" (Gilmartin 1996 p.106). Gallagher (1998) says the passive and spiritually shallow approach to religion which has occurred to date is no longer acceptable and we have to create a different kind of religious community if religion is to be in any way beneficial to children's spiritual development. Part of the present-day unhappiness with religion, despite a simultaneous interest in spirituality, reflects religion's failure to give priority to assessing and caring for the spiritual needs of people, including children.

Spirituality, spiritual development and S.Q. are not the dogma of organised religion and have no necessary connection to religion. However, for some, S.Q. may find a mode of expression through formal religion but being religious does not signify high S.Q. Many humanists and atheists have very high S.Q.s while many actively and vociferously religious people have very low S.Q.s (Zohar and Marshall 2000). Indeed, Allport's studies (1950) some fifty years ago showed that more people had spiritual experiences outside the confines of mainstream religious institutions than they did within them. Personal spiritual experiences are often disassociated from religion and are based instead on love or some profound commitment or insight.

Conventional religion is an externally imposed set of rules and beliefs. It is a top-down approach and is inherited from prophets, priests and holy books and absorbed through tradition and family and one of the dangers of it is in how the expectations and evaluations of others impact on the child. These can be so compellingly internalised that later autonomy of judgement and action can be damaged if children are indoctrinated into the religion of their family and community without developing the broader spiritual dimension (Fowler 1981). In any case, the changes in the world over the past three centuries and especially during the past fifty years or so, have left conventional religions struggling to be meaningful. Thus, spirituality makes religion possible but it does not depend on religion, and the potential for spiritual development is open to every child and is not confined to the development of religious beliefs or conversion to a particular faith.

To limit spiritual development in this way would be to exclude from its scope many children who do not come from overtly religious backgrounds (National Curriculum Council Britain 1993). However, S.Q. can put us in touch with the meaning and essential spirit behind all great religions. A child high in S.Q. can practise any religion but without exclusiveness, bigotry or prejudice. Therefore, enhancing spiritual development is in no way anti-religious and in fact most of us need a religious framework as a guide for our lives, while at the same time having a deep and abiding respect for other traditions and other forms (Zohar and Marshall 2000).

Spiritual development

Young children are deeply spiritual, yet this aspect of child development is almost totally ignored. Dowling (2000 p.96) points out that "there has been almost no study of young children's spiritual development and little guidance on how it should be fostered." Children between three and five years of age are beginning to explore their world in several places at one time and the most influential places are likely to be home, school and television/media. Home is the place where children first learn about themselves and their role in life; they start to learn about relationships and others' roles and begin to ask questions and find answers about the world in which they live. Situations and events that they may have encountered in their young lives include birth and death, love, trust, joy, sadness, hurt, special occasions and religion. All these have a spiritual depth. Rizzuto (1979) states that despite secularisation and religious fragmentation, spirituality is still widely present in our society. Virtually all children reaching school have constructed, with or without religious instruction, an image of God, or at least an image of something greater than themselves. In the past it was suggested that work with young children regarding spirituality was difficult because such children were considered too young to be spiritually aware. What work was done, tended to focus on older children. However, children at four and five are beginning to sort out their experiences of the world and have begun to ask questions about the things they do not understand.

Thus, research on spiritual development needs to begin with the questions children ask as they encounter their world.

Coles (1990) reports on thirty years of work interviewing children age seven upwards about their spirituality. He suggests that for children, spiritual/religious issues do not surface initially as spiritual questions *per se* but arise in the form of questions about the meaning of life, death, the natural world and so on. He claims it is mainly in the context of the family that beliefs and values are formed. However, he concedes that out-of-home settings do have an influential role in aiding young children's spiritual development. He stresses that all issues and questions raised by children need to be explored and explained, as and when they arise, by parents, caregivers and early years practitioners, if children are to be helped to develop spiritually. McCreery (1996) also states that we need to find ways of encouraging such questions and from there to explore issues. She advocates the development of appropriate activities in schools and early years settings to enhance spiritual development by addressing the spiritual in ways that have meaning for young children.

Children are spiritual beings and have naturally what many adults spend years trying to reclaim. Children spend much of their childhoods wondering about nature, about the supernatural, about their friends and about thousands of other things. They start life with an innate sense of awe and wonder about their world, they are naturally open and intuitive and "where there is wonder, there is spirituality" (Doe and Walch 1998 p. xi). The way to maintain it is to recognise and honour children's innate spiritual connection and to ensure that they never lose it by making spiritual development a priority. We try to help children develop optimally and in particular we try to ensure that their cognitive development is optimised. Yet, we miss out on developing the very core of their being - the spiritual. What does spiritual development mean? This question has rarely if ever been asked and there is little published about it in developmental terms. Hull (1996) says the obscurity of what is meant by spiritual development makes it hard to assess and Carr (1995) interprets it as having a close correlation with religious development, but this is only one aspect of spirituality. Spiritual development must be open in the sense that it must give room for critical exploration of the relevant issues by children and should not presuppose significant controversial assumptions. It is not a logical, quantitative process but is rather an evolving, fluid endeavour.

The debate about spiritual development needs to be located within an overall view of educational aims and purposes. There should be a vision of education as a whole, and spiritual development needs to be considered in close relation to the other areas of the work of early years practitioners, such as moral and social development and education for citizenship (McLaughlin 1994; White 1994). Spiritual development relates to that aspect of inner life through which children acquire insights into their personal experiences. It is characterised by reflection, the giving of meaning to experience, valuing a non-material dimension to life and intimations of an enduring reality. Farrer (2000 p.167) claims that spiritual development;

> is a rock upon which character, behaviour, outlook, learning and happiness can be built. It is a means of reaching the inner world which has been so catastrophically neglected by the material lifestyle culture, and it is the route to real fulfillment and understanding.

Spiritual development also entails affiliation and commitment to a large moral ecology beyond individual and individualistic concerns. It embodies a social ethos, a consensus on the common good and on notions of responsibility and loyalty to the community as a whole, as well as a framework of wider beliefs and values. This claim, that spiritual development be seen as part of the process of education of the whole child, raises questions which touch upon some of the central issues relating to the value basis of education and has, and is, being, ignored by many of the powers that be (McLaughlin 1996).

The Office for Standards in Education, Britain (O.F.S.T.E.D.) (1994) suggests that children may show evidence of developing spiritually, if at an appropriate level to their ability and age, they show a comprehension of how people have sought to explain the universe through various myths and stories including religious, historical and scientific interpretations. These explanations should include beliefs they hold personally and children should be able to give some account of these and be able to derive values from them. Also included is some knowledge of the central beliefs, ideas and practices of major world religions and philosophies. Such children should exhibit behaviour and attitudes which stem from such knowledge and understanding and should show awareness of the relationship between belief and action. They should also be capable of responding personally to questions about the purpose of life and to the experience of beauty, pain, suffering and love. Spiritual development is about liberating and nurturing the inner light which lives, however dormant, in every child. It is not just a state of mind but is a way of knowing, a way of being that utterly transforms our understanding and our lives. Helping children develop spiritually entails providing a humanly rich and rounded context of experience and needs to be encountered by the child in a self-evolving way (White 1996).

Scott Peck (1990) claims that spiritual development is a complex, arduous and lifelong task. He says the truth is that life is hard and once people truly know, understand and accept this, then life is no longer as difficult as it could be. Scott Peck cites life as being an endless series of problems which include difficulties and pain, as well as joy. Yet, he proposes that it is the process of meeting and solving problems that gives life its meaning. Problems help children to grow cognitively and spiritually. Facing problems directly and experiencing pain achieves spiritual growth. Delaying gratification, accepting responsibility, being dedicated to the truth and balancing one's life are the tools of spiritual development. Scott Peck (1990 p.18) claims that:

> Delaying gratification is a process of scheduling the pain and pleasure of life in such a way as to enhance the pleasure by meeting and experiencing the pain first and getting it over with. It is the only decent way to live.

Scott Peck contends that the tool or process of delaying gratification can be learned by children quite early in life. However, he stresses that while some children have a well-developed ability to delay gratification some others, including adults, lack the capacity entirely. For children to develop this capacity, it is necessary for them to have self-disciplined role models, to have a sense of self-worth and a degree of trust in the safety of their existence. Adults have a key role in supporting and befriending the young on their spiritual journey (Gallagher 1998). To be dedicated to human spiritual development means being dedicated to the human race and includes personal development as well as caring for others. It is impossible to love another unless you love yourself first and it is not possible to forsake one's own spiritual development in favour of someone else's. Thus, spiritual development is effortful not effortless (Scott Peck 1993).

To develop spiritually, children must constantly revise and extend their understanding to include new knowledge of the larger world and cosmos, and there is no such thing as 'a good hand-me-down spirituality'. To be vital, to be the best of which one is capable, spirituality must be a wholly personal one, developed by questioning and doubting in the experience of one's own reality and experience. Fowler (1981) put forward a six stage theory of growth in faith and spiritual development in his book *Stages of Faith*. These include:

- Stage 1 Undifferentiated faith;
- Stage 2 Mythic-literal faith;
- Stage 3 Synthetic-conventional faith;
- Stage 4 Individative-reflective faith;
- Stage 5 Conjunctive faith;
- Stage 6 Universalising Faith.

However, Fowler warns that though stages and theories are important in that they help measure, grasp and clarify the vital processes of spiritual life, they cannot fully explain the complex processes at work in spiritual development, as they only tell us part of the story. He also concedes that there are correlations between cognitive and moral stages and his stages of spiritual development, admitting that he was deeply influenced by the work of Kohlberg, Piaget and Erikson. He states that spiritual stages are sequential and invariant, with each new stage integrating and carrying forward the operations of all the previous stages. He does not claim that the stages are universal but he does say they are generalisable and cross-cultural.

Scott Peck (1993) refined Fowler's stages down from six to four:

- Stage 1 Chaotic/anti-social;
- Stage 2 Formal/institutional;
- Stage 3 Skeptic/individual;
- Stage 4 Mystical/communal.

Scott Peck claims that no matter what progress is achieved spiritually, remnants of earlier stages are always retained and he contends that children under five years of age are generally at Stage 1. Gallagher (1998) says the whole adventure of spiritual development is more like an oak tree than a ladder. The different stages are not rungs that one leaves behind as one develops, but rather are like the rings of a tree that are still there, adding a different circle progressively. However, despite Scott Peck's and Fowler's stage theories, we do not have a clear picture of the stages of spiritual development, if in fact there are stages at all, and work needs to continue in this area (Rodger 1996). What we do know is that collective spiritual development is low in modern society. We live in a spiritually obtuse culture characterised by materialism, expediency, narrow self-centredness, lack of meaningfulness and commitment. We misuse and abuse our relationships and our environment. We suffer from a lack of symbolic imagination and ignore human qualities and concentrate instead on ever more frenzied doing, getting and spending. We neglect the sacred within ourselves, others and the world and as Maslow (1971) says we 'desacralise'. Yet, these tendencies can be turned around.

Spiritual development can be enhanced and indeed the further evolution of society depends upon it. We are at a very early stage of understanding human spirituality and spiritual development, as they are not aspects of human life and nature which have been studied in depth. Also, there is something vaguely incongruous about trying to measure spirituality. Trying to discern what is true in this area requires sensitivity and can only be done with the greatest of care and with reflective experience. Those who have experience and insight into the area of spiritual development warn against the view that spiritual growth is either automatic or subject to direct influence. Yet, through prioritising spiritual development, we can reconnect children with the deeper sources and meanings within and they can then use these reconnections to serve causes and processes much greater than themselves (Lindon 1999).

Though we do not have a clear scheme of spiritual development, there are a number of generally accepted characteristics of mature human spirituality, and providing children with contexts which support the development of these can foster spiritual growth, insight and understanding. Zohar and Marshall (2000 p.15) set out the indicators of a highly developed spirituality as having:

- the capacity to be flexible;
- a high degree of self-awareness;
- a capacity to face and use suffering;
- an ability to face and transcend pain;
- the quality of being inspired by vision and values;
- a reluctance to cause unnecessary harm;
- a tendency to see the connection between diverse things (being holistic);
- a marked tendency to ask 'why', 'what if' questions and to seek fundamental answers;
- a facility to be what psychologists call 'field-independent', possessing an ability to go against convention when necessary.

Beck (1991) also provides a similar list of what he considers are key spiritual characteristics and contends that spiritual people are characterised by being aware, taking a holistic view, being integrative, expressing a sense of wonder, gratitude, hope, courage, detachment, acceptance, love, gentleness and energy. Evans (1979, 1993) also outlines the characteristics of a mature spiritual being as having basic trust, humility, self-acceptance, responsibility, self-commitment, concern and contemplation. Why would we not want these for our children?

Spiritual development entails taking in the goodness and wonder of the world. It is about people's thoughts and beliefs and is very important for the creativity of the child. It is developed by discovering that special, hidden part of the human and involves a feeling of 'cosmic connectedness'. Spiritual development is about having a belief in something that while not visible or explainable gives a person a sense of peace, well-being, purpose and 'joie de vivre'. It is about having a respect for the unknown and for that which cannot be explained and involves consciously tuning into and nourishing that part of us that acknowledges something mysterious, mystical and powerful beyond everyday things. It is a gradually increasing awareness of elements beyond our control, the ability to believe what we do not entirely understand and the realisation that we are part of the greater scheme of things. It involves the development of the whole person and is different for every child, but yet is a fundamental need of every child. Spiritual development is enhanced by contemplation, reflection and meditation. Being able to detach oneself from the world and having time to reflect, develops a sense of optimism, hope and inner belief to sustain one throughout life. Being spiritually developed provides a life-time resource towards peace and tranquillity in an otherwise crazy materialistic world. Spiritual development is nurtured by helping children to love, respect and appreciate themselves and others in the world. It is about tapping into what is deepest within them and is a life-long process that gives meaning and depth to life. Taking time out, stopping and looking at things, being quiet and thinking, learning to appreciate, all help in spiritual development (Daly 2002).

Bradford (1978) proposed that children possess certain spiritual rights:

- the right to the best of the spiritual heritage of the culture into which he is born;
- the right to express his spiritual belief in private and/or public without discrimination;
- the right to deepen, doubt or alter the spiritual commitment into which he is being nurtured or educated;
- the right to schooling, family life and other institutional support complementary to his spiritual development;
- the right, especially in early life, to such protection from spiritual damage as is reasonable and appropriate.

These rights can be summarised as those of initiation, expression, choice, support and protection and should be available to all children. In a similar vein, Gallagher (1998) argues children have six basic spiritual needs:

- to believe that life has a meaning and purpose;
- to have a sense of community as a place for deepening relationships;
- to be appreciated and loved; to be listened to and heard;
- to experience spirituality as a journey and an adventure of growth;
- to have practical help in developing a mature spirituality.

Do children have these needs and rights fulfilled? Prioritising spiritual development could make such a difference in a child's life. Neglect of this vital area in the past has led to severe negative repercussions for children. There is no reason why it has to continue to be ignored.

Awe, wonder, myths and creativity

Experiencing awe, wonder, myths and creativity can help spiritual development. Farrer (1958) says the stuff of inspiration is living images and it is images which help us to glimpse childhood and spirituality in their full richness, helping to signify and reveal their mystery and mysticism. As Einstein quoted in Knight (1961 p.152) says:

> The fairest thing we can encounter is the mysterious. It is the fundamental emotion which stands at the cradle of true art and true science. He who knows it not and can no longer wonder, no longer feel amazement, is as good as dead, a snuffed out candle.

Lealman (1996) calls for a re-mythologizing of childhood so that we can renew and expand our idea of the child and his holistic development. Myths come out of the perennial mysteries of life and through myths we can identify and name our depths, helping us in our appreciation of the human situation. Myths are not the opposite of truth but are a recognition of mystery; they cluster around images and symbols and give space for the working of the imagination. "Myths of childhood are necessary in order to acknowledge the mystery of the child; they take us beyond the language of information and psychology" (ibid. p.22). Spirituality has its transpersonal dimension in the area of mystical experiences, of wonder, transcendence of self, of cosmic awareness, of glimpses of something more. It is about snapshots of the child's real or higher self, or the self as in Jung or Maslow - the self and its potential for wholeness. Transcendence is one of the most essential qualities of the spiritual and transcendent means something that is beyond the physical world. It takes us further than the limits of our knowledge and experience and puts them in a wider context, giving us a taste of the extraordinary and the infinite. Spiritual development needs this dimension and part of it includes allowing children to experience wonder and awe and involves taking note of the insights of poetry and mythology. This transpersonal perspective can provide a space in which to allow the child to develop spiritually and it offers the possibility of inclusive language, which does not try to impose any particular doctrine (Lindon 1999).

As well as this, the young child possesses a tremendous potential for creating and healing, and these are part of spiritual development (Gilmartin 1996). Yet, children's creative tendencies have been frozen for generations and have been all but killed in the education system. The knowledge base of the arts and humanities is too often used superficially and uninspiringly in classrooms, because early years practitioners and teachers believe they are not well enough prepared or are not good enough at things related to arts, music, history and literature and they make children feel the same. Yet, artistic creativity can be a way of affirming a child's experiences, it is a means of communicating, not a quantity of factual information, but a living dynamic experience. Also, artistic creativity means that the child encounters symbols and these are part of the transpersonal realm. Creativity involves aspects of consciousness (intuition, reverence, awe, perception, acceptance of ambiguity, tentativeness and uncertainty) which formal education and society tend to ignore and neglect. It is not confined to artistic creativity but artistic activity can help to make possible a more open approach to life, an approach that defies cynicism because it is open to fresh ideas and possibilities. Thus, creativity is part of spirituality and part of the whole child.

Programmes such as *Reggio Emilia* in Italy show how young children have the powers to persevere, study and represent the beautiful and orderly world of nature and culture surrounding them. *Reggio* education successfully challenges many false dichotomies: art versus science; individual versus community; child versus adult; enjoyment versus study; nuclear versus extended family. Children who attend *Reggio* schools are encouraged to have a love of learning, an excitement about life, a maturity and self-confidence that will be the foundation for growth. *Reggio* has sought a learning culture characterised by participation, solidarity, reflection, pleasure and wonderment and has allowed the development of a society where children and adults can engage together in projects of social, cultural, spiritual, political and economic significance. In *Reggio* classrooms, education is seen as a communal activity and sharing of culture through joint exploits. The emergent and informal nature of the curriculum makes it particularly open to co-operative work and the informal community like atmosphere is enhanced by the freedom from pressure. Children are free to work and play without frequent interruption and transitions. The whole process guides experiences of joint open-ended discovery and problem solving ability. Through play, self-expression and guided exploration, children gain a deep sense of their history, identity and cultural tradition as well as developing their creative sides (Boyd-Cadwell 1997).

The freedom of children to play and develop creatively changes the world. Yet, intellect dominates education while the soul is ignored. In particular, soul-making subjects like literature, drama, music, the visual and tactile arts are progressively de-souled as the child proceeds through the education system. The arts are seen as not much more than a recreational diversion from real studies and the 'real' subjects are taught without soul. This one-sidedness of education and of conventional teaching is not only narrow but ineffective as well (Neville 1989). It is vital that children notice the beauty, diversity and detail of the natural world around them. It is also important that children find ways to remember and continue to marvel at what they discover through expressing their ideas in many ways such as through language, mime, painting and through playing with leaves, stones, sands, soils, to make small worlds. Children cannot be taught to notice and to participate but through entering into play together and by sharing wonder and enthusiasm in true reciprocal relationships, they develop these abilities (Boyd-Cadwell 1997).

Healing is another aspect of spirituality and is about putting together, about fitting parts into a larger context, achieved from developing a sense of relatedness and participation. It is about having an integrating vision. Spiritual development is that part of us with which we heal ourselves and make ourselves whole. There is an urgent need for healing in our fragmented, consumer-driven and materialistic society and one of the primary experiences of childhood should be relatedness.

Children long for what Eliot (1994 p.19) calls, "a further union, a deeper communion". Unfortunately, our society tends towards exploitation and disintegration, not communion. Such learning experiences do not have a healing effect nor do they encourage a sense of belonging, community, compassion, gentleness, trust or spirituality. To counteract this, spiritual development must be given a part in all curricula. We must begin to deal with real issues, making clear their relevance for life today. Critical, investigative and empathetic skills need to be highly practised. We must aim toward educating the whole child by presenting wholes before going on to study their various parts. Broad overviews and contexts, links with other subjects and integrating various pieces of knowledge and experiences should be what are presented to children

Children must be allowed to participate in their own immediate environment, to be involved in it, touching it and feeling it. Also, they must be made aware of the wider community, nations, world, seas, forests, animals, planets, sun, moon, stars, galaxies, religions, cultural traditions. The healing/whole approach must be integrative, recognising that the whole is greater than the sum of its parts. Children have huge potential for moving on, for changing shape, and they need to be encouraged to have a sense of becoming, and of the world's becoming. They need a focus beyond themselves, "a transcendent instead of an immanent point of reference" (Lealman 1996 p.28). This will not detract from their individual ego but will aid in affirming them as a vital part of a larger whole. One of the greatest insights of the 20th century was the realisation that wholes can be greater than the sum of their parts. The whole can contain a richness, a perspective and dimensionality not possessed by the separate parts. Thus, the whole is not just a larger quantity but also has added quality.

Being spiritually developed means being in touch with a larger, deeper, richer whole. It gives a sense of something beyond, of something more that contains added meaning and value. It can be an awareness of, or an attunement to the mythological, archetypal or religious dimension. It may be a sense of some more profound level of truth or beauty or a belief that our actions are part of some greater process. Thus creating, healing and transcending help to nourish the inner life of the child. However, souls are not nourished nor can they flourish in a setting where everyone is expected to learn the same things and to be pointed towards the same image of excellence, where there is only one way of being a teacher and one way of being a student. Spirituality will flourish where diversity is both a means and an end. Children's souls will also flourish where images are honoured, where creative arts are presented as a means of nourishment and where time to reflect and meditate form part of the curriculum (Neville 1989).

Meditation

Being able to meditate can be part of the process of developing spiritually. Contemplating, meditating, quietening the mind, being able to detach one's self from the world and having the time and the ability to focus the mind develops a sense of inner calm. It involves a state of pure consciousness, during which the child is highly alert and aware but is not letting himself be taken over by past and future thoughts – he is living and being in the present moment, fully experiencing the world. Today, children are uncomfortable with empty or silent times. They become bored and have to fill their time with constant activity. This is compounded by the fact that many early years practitioners overlook a child's need to look inward and do not develop the ability to be still in children. Farrer (2000) claims that the practice of reflection and meditation is at least as rare in educational establishments as it is in the larger world. Not only will practising these help the child's physical and mental health, it will also help him to learn more effectively.

Meditation is a word that is applied to a variety of mental activities, some of which have little in common. In the past, the word had strong religious connotations but today there is substantial non-religious and scientific literature on meditation. Jessel-Kenyon and Shealy (1999) define meditation as the ability to reflect deeply, to engage in contemplation, to consider deeply. They state that scientific evidence has come to light which proves that meditation is good for humans. It is believed that meditation enhances perception and increases the ability to concentrate. It can modify immunity and disease susceptibility and can help fight illness, both physical and mental, when it occurs. It is also seen as helping a person deal better with emotionally loaded and threatening stimuli. It increases energy and alertness, helps people become more tolerant of themselves and others, helps them become more decisive, more creative and to experience a greater sense of well-being. One of the most outstanding and consistent conclusions of meditative research concerns the positive effect of meditation on anxiety. The reduction of anxiety seems to follow almost immediately on learning how to meditate. Not only does meditation reduce present anxiety but it also reduces the susceptibility to becoming anxious (Carrington 1978).

These are strong reasons for adults to meditate themselves, as well as teaching the children in their care how to meditate. Meditation involves a turning from the outer to the inner world. It stills the mind's activity and involves a receptive rather than an assertive engagement with reality. The meditative state is characterised by relaxation of the body and an increase in alpha and theta brain waves (Griffith 1985). If children can successfully shut out external stimuli and shut down their thinking processes at the same time, they will experience a deeply spiritual state of inner peace. Stilling the mind is not easy. However, with regular and disciplined practice, pre-school aged children can learn to focus their minds steadily on where they want to go. If meditation had no other function than this we would still have a strong argument for including it in the curriculum (Neville 1989).

Western culture has a deep suspicion of meditation and this has its source in ignorance and superstition. This is irrational and is specific to western culture. To counter this, many writers on meditation would contend that the kinds of meditative activities which are practicable in the classroom or early years setting should not be called meditation at all. They would reserve the word to refer to the end-state, not the means of getting there and suggest instead calling it 'centring' or 'relaxing' techniques (Hendricks and Wills 1975). There is a variety of centring techniques that are easy for children to incorporate into their daily lives. Focusing on a mantra, resting on the floor in a state of deep quiet, without thoughts or images, listening to a piece of music, guided and spontaneous visualisation, Yoga, T'ai Chi (posture and breathing) are all options that young children could develop. Lindon (1999) says that children as young as four and five have been taught basic meditation techniques and that it has helped them relax and to feel positively calm. Peaceful times with a chance to reflect on and enjoy an experience without rational analysis are part of a rounded approach to education. By legitimising and nurturing all aspects of childhood consciousness, the child can be liberated spiritually. Quiet times and centring techniques have been a valued exercise in the development of children in many cultures but so far have not been seen as valuable for children in the western world.

A spiritual curriculum?

There is no subject on any curriculum which is properly regarded as being devoid of contribution to the spiritual development of children of all ages and there is much that can be done to provide appropriate conditions and stimuli to encourage spiritual growth. Thus, to enable children to optimise their spiritual development, all curricula must develop a human-centred holistic education, which incorporates a shift from a materialistic to an inclusive spiritual notion of what it is to be human and what it is to educate or be educated. It involves a wide broad-based commitment and resource provision for making education part of the process of spiritualising society (Prentice 1996). Only holistic approaches which adopt a position that thinks in terms of the whole child, the whole person, the whole curriculum, the whole school, the whole community and the whole of society are likely to be able to encompass the spiritual development of the young child. The great theorists of the past, Froebel, Rousseau, Pestalozzi and Montessori, advocated it and it is up to contemporary and future education to put it into practice (Best 1996).

Young children are very sensitive to the spiritual world and are very open to being intrigued, engrossed, puzzled and impressed. In particular, the natural world has potential for this - running water, snowflakes, frost and ice, little creatures, (spiders, tadpoles), mirrors, seashells, rainbows, smells - these can all create deep spiritual experiences for children. Early on, spiritual development is affected by what familiar adults, especially parents and early years practitioners, tell and allow children to experience. Children accept the ideas and beliefs of these as right and normal until such time that experience makes them question and wonder and they begin to develop their own sense of spirituality (Lindon 1999). Events which could promote reflection on the spiritual include meditation, nature studies, bringing natural objects into the classroom, silence games, stories (in particular stories which are relevant to children's own life experiences), lighting a candle, blowing bubbles, role play, as well as any situation in which the child may encounter awe, wonder, fear, sadness, danger, failure, reward, success and when children question or problem solve. Also, it is a good idea to allow children to visit different places of worship. They need to be exposed to the great ideas of religious thinkers from around the world and throughout history, as this will encourage them to determine their own ethical thought processes (Dyer 1998). Should not every early years curriculum be a spiritual one?

Research on spiritual development

At present, the issue of children's spirituality and spiritual development is characterised by questions and uncertainties. To date, the relatively small amount of research that has been done to investigate the area of children and spirituality has focused almost exclusively on children's 'God-talk', for example, Taylor (1989) Coles (1990) and Tamminen (1991, 1996). Similarly, the little attention psychologists have given to this area has also focused on children's religious thinking and concepts - Goldman (1964, 1965), Elkind (1971), Fowler (1981), Fowler, Nipkow and Schweitzer (1991) and Reich (1992). By taking this approach, their studies have contributed a disappointingly small amount to our understanding of children's spiritual development. Nye (1996) contends that this narrow focus on the 'religious end' of spirituality may be inappropriate. He claims that evidence for children's early spiritual life should be sought in their perception, awareness and response to those ordinary things and activities that can act as signals of transcendence, what Bradford (1994) calls 'human spirituality'. Thus, a lot more relevant research on this area needs to occur. Educating and developing the spiritual includes coming to an understanding about a kind of reality that is invisible. However, it now seems clear that cognitive development and ability impinge on spiritual development and *vice versa*. Yet, it has been the mistake of many to overlook the spiritual aspect of cognitive development. Psychologists and researchers have tended to focus exclusively on the cognitive domain at the expense of our understanding of the whole child. Contemporary developmental psychologists rarely acknowledge the existence of the spiritual domain in childhood. There are few, if any, contemporary general developmental psychology textbooks which mention spiritual development.

The cognitive developmentalists are probably correct in their assertions about the maturation of children and their growing grasp of complex skills. However, perhaps more important than their results is a question of what they select for observation and measurement. Their work often demonstrates that they have what has been called an 'Acquired Immunity to Mystery Syndrome' (Robinson 1987 p.81). If they looked at and listened to young children as they are and to their silences and questions, perhaps a lot more would be known about truly developing the whole child and in particular about developing the child spiritually. In the past, scientists have been disinclined to discuss spirituality and its role in the lives and development of children. The study of spiritual development has been awkward for academics, because existing science is not equipped to study things that cannot be measured objectively. However, in recent neurobiological, psychological and anthropological studies of human intelligences and in studies of human thinking and linguistic processes, a great deal of scientific evidence for spiritual quotient (S.Q.) is beginning to emerge. To date, scientists have done much of the basic research revealing the neural foundations of S.Q. In 1997, neurologists Ramachandran and Blakeshee discovered the existence of the 'God spot' or 'soul spot' in the human brain. This in-built spiritual centre is located among neural connections in the temporal lobes of the brain. On scans taken with Positron Emission Topography (P.E.T.) these neural areas light up whenever research subjects are exposed to discussions on spiritual and religious topics. These lighting-up experiences vary with culture and people respond to symbols meaningful to their own belief systems (Zohar and Marshall 2000). The 'God spot' or 'soul spot' does not prove the existence of God but does show that the brain has evolved to have a spiritual dimension and thus spiritual development must be a core area of development.

Conclusion

Robinson (1977) claims that a great deal is extinguished in the experience of children, because the adults they come in contact with are spiritually obtuse. The problems and limitations that many people experience come from a loss of connection to their souls and to humanity. Social problems impact heavily on the daily lives of children and emphasising spiritual development can help redress the balance. Spirituality has to do with living life to the full and is about discovering how to become more fully human. It is about self-discovery, discovery of others and of the world. It is not synonymous with religion nor is it opposed to it. It covers a wide range of human experience and can be experienced in awareness, in response and in ways of life and is vital to every child's development. It is important to create and incorporate spiritual habits into the lives of young children, particularly since: "An individual can no more flourish in a spiritually dead environment than could a tree in the midst of an ecological disaster" (Mott-Thornton 1996 p.80). Therefore, it is vital that spiritual development is prioritised, as many children are not living life to the full today.

Neglect of this vital area of child development has led to a "massive denial of spiritual energy, of intellectual enquiry, of aesthetic beauty and public virtue" (Abbs 1994 p.1). The stunting of spiritual development is essentially a state of lacking spontaneity. All levels and forms of being spiritually stunted bring pain and hurt. Ultimately, this loss of spontaneity and response cripples our ability to take responsibility for our lives and actions. Irish medical consultant, Dr Michael

Kearney (1996) calls lack of spiritual development 'soul pain'. He says it arises when a person becomes cut off or is at odds with the deepest part of himself. Just as connectedness with soul may bring wholeness and a sense of significance, soul pain results in an experience of fragmentation, alienation and meaninglessness. Kearney claims that lack of spiritual development is both at the root of and a cause of physical pain and illness. Myss and Shealy (1999) back this contention and state that the medical world is not yet ready to make official the relationship between emotional dysfunction/spiritual deprivation and their natural consequences to the physical body. However, they claim that western medicine is beginning to recognise that more factors have to be involved in the development of disease than just the physical ones.

Children can show a high degree of spirituality. They ask 'why' questions and seek the meaning of their own and others' actions. They struggle to get feelings and events in a larger meaning-giving context if afforded the opportunity. Unfortunately, all too often adults brush children's questions aside or patronise them with answers that they themselves would not accept. This can lead to cynicism, despair or mere conformity in later life, impeding if not killing spiritual development (Zohar and Marshall 2000). However, for children who are encouraged to be spiritual beings, they do experience things which give them deep feelings of well-being, of magic and mystery - experiences which give a glimmer of hope for the future. These children develop value systems of their own which incorporate emotions and feelings such as loyalty, love, integrity, joy, tenderness, kindness and empathy. They experience moments of intensity where beauty and understanding are prominent and many experience religion with all its powerful and mystic messages. Childhood has its moments of wonderment and as the child matures, experiences and value systems change, wither and/or grow (Kirkland 1996). Surely, it should be ensured that all children experience these moments?

If children are to reach their potential they must be allowed to make their spiritual journeys, as knowing and trusting that all life has a purpose and connection gives children meaning in a complex and confusing world. Also, discovering the sacred self allows them to transcend the physical world with all its inherent limitations and enables children to live in a world of everyday miracles (Doe and Walch 1998). Spiritual development is a vital area of child development and is about the formation of informed but personally chosen answers to questions about the nature and meaning of life. Its neglect in the past has led to severe negative repercussions for children and thus in future spiritual development must be a core area of development in all early years settings.

Suggestions/guidelines for enhancing spiritual development

Many things can be done to enhance spiritual development in the early years setting. The following are a list of suggestions which have been selected from various sources including: *The Emotional, Social, Moral and Spiritual Development of the Pre-school Child* (Daly 2002); *Project E.Y.E. An Irish Curriculum for the three to four year old child – Volume One: Spiritual, Emotional and Moral Development, Volume Four: Creative Development* and *Volume Eight: Environmental Awareness and Development Education* (Douglas, Horgan and O'Brien 2000); *Young Children's Personal, Social and Emotional Development* (Dowling 2000); *A Quiet Revolution* (Farrer 2000); *Children as Philosophers* (Haynes 2002); *Understanding World Religions* (Lindon 1999); *The Handbook of Environmental Education* (Palmer and Neal 1994); *Setting the 'What If' Free: Some theoretical perspectives on talking and thinking in an infant classroom - an investigation into one teacher's practice* (Roche 2003); and *Educating the Whole Child: cross-curricular skills, themes and dimensions* (Siraj-Blatchford and Siraj-Blatchford 1995).

- Ensure a happy and peaceful environment is provided in the setting.
- Expose children to stories, art, music, drama, dressing up, poetry and free play on a daily basis.
- Set up a spiritual corner – a small table with a candle, a place for children to place things which have meaning for them at a particular time – a photo of a deceased granny, a picture drawn by a cousin

who lives far away, a feather, a sea shell or stone found during a trip to the beach.

- Show children how to be still and help create a place within and allow time for the mind to soar - dim the lights, rest heads on the table and ask children to pretend to be asleep or ask them lie on the floor with eyes closed. Encourage children to be still by asking them to make their bodies quiet inside and outside. Develop a calm atmosphere in the setting and give children time for reflection, for daydreaming and for just looking. Be still and be with children – stop, observe and listen with children.

- Develop silence games and thinking times. Have quiet times - times for children just to sit and be, to day dream or to think, peacefully absorbed in stroking a soft toy or staring at a flower.

- Try to look at things through the eyes of a child and don't rush children – if a child is focused on looking at a snail moving across a path – give him the time and space to do it.

- Expose children to meditation, imagery guidance and visualisation and create 'mood settings' regularly, such as exposing children to soothing music, lighting a candle, burning some incense or essential oils.

- Introduce children to silent relaxation with eyes closed. Silence provides an opportunity to support the thinking process, reflection and personal expression.

- Show children how to breathe deeply and to their keep spine erect to allow their lungs to expand. With children lying on the floor get them to put one hand on their chest and one hand on the stomach. Encourage them to listen to their breathing and to breathe in slowly through their noses and out through their mouths. Ask them to 'relax' and be 'calm'.

244

- Guide the relaxation through visualisation. Adults do not need specialist training in relaxation techniques, there is a variety of books and tapes available, check your local library or bookshop. Examples of visualisation for young children include 'Go to a place where you feel safe, see your favourite toy/comforter there (teddy bear, blanket). Focus on the object, touching it and holding it' or 'I want you to take your mind to (name part of the body in turn – toes, soles of the feet working up to the head)'. Another way is to ask the children to listen to the sounds they can hear outside the setting – for example a car, then the sounds in the setting, a clock ticking and then in themselves – their breathing and heartbeat. Another approach is to focus on an object (a stone, shells, leaves, fir cone) and then to close eyes and to use the mental reconstruction of it to try and hold the mind in one place. Before commencing, ensure that there is a clear space for every child on the floor, make sure that the room is nice and warm and that every child can get into a comfortable position. Children need more guidance and help in the early stages, with practice it becomes much easier.

- To commence relaxation/visualisation make sure hands and arms are lying loosely. Ask children if their forehead is smooth and invite them to put any worries or frustrations out of their mind and to enjoy this special bit of time for themselves. Children can experience a sense of community, togetherness and connectedness by engaging in such collaborative reflective, meditative exercises.

- Introduce children to yoga. Yoga offers ideas on physical relaxation, breathing and meditation. Use the video 'Yoga for Kids – Colin the Cobra's Forest of Secrets' Currie (2002), read *Yoga – An Illustrated Guide* Kent (2001) and see the article 'Yoga, Yoga,Yoga' in *Volume One of Project E.Y.E.* (Douglas, Horgan and O'Brien 2000).

- Introduce children to T'ai Chi – a Chinese system of meditative exercises characterised by methodically slow circular and stretching movements.

- Play lots of relaxing music – there are a variety of types available with the sound of running water, waves, dolphins, birds, calming melodies and so on.

- Help children develop a healthy respect for life and for living by allowing the child to experience concepts beyond their own environment, encourage problem solving ability and acknowledge the existence of soul, spirit and mind.

- Be prepared to answer as honestly and clearly as you can children's profound questions such as where is God, what is death, why do nice people get hurt, why was I born or when will I die? Reflect on the questions children raise.

- Create opportunities for moments of awe and wonder every day. This could be done by doing something as simple as blowing bubbles, looking at the petals of a flower, taking a walk outside.

- Use natural materials and allow children to be in tune with nature. Have timber furniture and fittings and avoid the use of plastic.

- Awaken the child's sense of spirituality and wonder, explore the differences between fact and fiction, the explainable and the unexplainable – through active experience, by reading, by listening and talking, by whatever means possible.

- Interact with the vital creative forces within the child and allow him the opportunity of experiencing his environment through the senses and through the various intelligences.

- Have a nature table – encourage children to bring in shells, stones, leaves, driftwood, anything they want, use it as a talking point and update it regularly in line with the seasons/weather and so on.

- Discuss the weather and the different seasons. Have a weather chart. Allow children to experience different weather conditions. Let them splash in puddles, to stand in the rain under an umbrella covered with tinfoil, to make a snowman, to throw snowballs.

- Encourage children to observe the changes that occur in nature as the seasons change, ask children what season they like best and why.

- Look at shadows at different times of the day.

- Show children how to note the position of the sun and clouds at different times of the day.

- Discuss plant life and the animal kingdom.

- Plant seeds, plants, flower bulbs and small vegetables.

- Gather flowers and collect summer/autumn fruits.

- Go to the beach and collect shells, stones, sand.

- Let children fly a kite or play with a parachute.

- Provide lots of mirrors around the room for children to look at their reflections, the reflections of others and the reflection of light and sun on them.

- Look at things through a magnifying glass – a sunflower seed, an acorn. Invite children to think hard about the little seed growing. When children open up their eyes, show them pictures of an oak tree or a grown sunflower. Impress on them the power and beauty of nature.

- Play Vivaldi's *Four Seasons* on tape or compact disc – explain to the children that these pieces of music were written to express the moods of each season. Talk about the weather/changes/nature during each of the seasons. During each season's music encourage children to dance, give them a scarf to swing around or ask them to imagine different scenarios – being an old tree sheltering all the little animals in a fierce storm in the autumn, being a little chick breaking out of an egg in the spring time, swimming in the sea on a hot summer's day, throwing snowballs in the winter. The music can be stopped at intervals to ask children how they feel or to give/take suggestions on what to do next.

- Allow children to finger paint and to touch the paint with their feet. Leaves, stones, natural objects can be painted, encourage children to mix paints and to use a variety of materials to paint – sponges, clothes, vegetables, big brushes, small brushes and so on.

- Allow the imagination to speak, encourage children to use art and junk materials at all stages during the session. Encourage them to make collages and inventions with a variety of junk materials (sweet wrappers, pasta shapes, cotton wool, buttons, straws, shoe boxes, ice cream and yogurt cartons, bits of wood, large and small cardboard boxes, everything and anything).

- Ensure children have free access to sand, paint, water and playdough daily. Have lots of equipment for pouring, measuring and mixing the sand and water.

- Ensure children get access to the outdoors everyday regardless of weather, if necessary invest in wellington boots, gloves, scarves etc. Children need to run in the fresh air every day. Whilst outside encourage them to listen to the sounds and to observe nature and what is around them. Give them the opportunity to crawl on the ground and describe what they can see, hear and smell. Let them experience getting dirty.

- Allow children to explore different textures - a tree bark, a rock, slate, fur, feathers, leaves, wood shavings, straw. This will help enhance children's awareness and appreciation of different surface textures and of the different facets of nature and the natural world.

- Allow children to run through leaves in the autumn and let them enjoy raking them up as well as playing with them and seeing the beautiful colours and textures.

- Plant a tree in the outdoor area at the end of each academic year or buy a sapling and give to the child to plant at home.

- Have mini-beast hunting games and ensure children don't hurt or kill small insects or spiders.

- Show children how to look closely at the intricacies of a spider's web, particularly during frosty weather.

- Take a trip to the seaside on a windy day, see and hear the huge waves crashing onto the beach. At the beach go paddling, go crabbing, feel seaweed, dig in the sand, lift rocks to see what is underneath.

- Collect chestnuts – play conkers or sow them and see saplings in the spring, fly sycamore seeds, or again, plant them.

- Have a water feature in the outdoor area, a little fountain or sprinkler, something where you can hear the sound of running water.

- Have a wind chime hanging outside.

- Have a magician visit the setting.

- Ask the local park to cordon off a small area (an acre or two) with a timber fence and allow children to climb trees and to explore freely while being safe and secure.

- Encourage the children to bird watch.

- Try to avoid giving discouraging remarks to children – like 'It is dirty...' or 'What's so interesting about...'. Allow children to relish the newness and delight of the experience.

- Have a potter's wheel in the group and allow children to use it.

- Encourage children to look at paintings and pictorial compositions. Have some prints/pictures in the room of natural scenery, water, sunsets, sunrises, sunflowers, old buildings, churches and so on. Encourage children to really look at and appreciate them. Take children to an art exhibition to look at other paintings. Allow children to host their own exhibition where they can show their own work to others.

- When reading a story, stop from time to time and ask children to close their eyes and to 'see the picture in their mind'.

- Introduce children to a wide variety of music – classical, traditional, modern. Help them to see the beauty in the different types.

- Have a wide variety of musical instruments available in the setting and allow children to make their own musical instruments – drums made out of a biscuit tin, banging spoons together, stones in a jar. Encourage them to make music outdoors.

- Use everyday [changes in weather] or special events [birth, death, separation] to extend understanding. Mark important life events – birthdays, getting a new baby, moving house, losing a pet.

- Tell mythical stories and legends, have books that introduce mystery and wonder into the group.

- Share enjoyment with children and avoid the temptation to reduce all experiences to rational thoughts and explanations, some things are beyond this and it is the mystery and intrigue that makes them special.

- Young children are wired to be intrigued, puzzled and impressed, part of the adult's job is to help this ability to unfold by providing awe-inspiring experiences – letting children put their feet in a stream, finding, watching, touching and holding little creatures and animals – tadpoles, new born puppies, a pet lamb, a small baby. Try to have such moments in every day.

- Have rituals – at lunch-time, before going home, have special ways of doing things and of being together as a group.

- Celebrate - celebrating a range of festivals can help children to become aware of cultures, faiths and traditions other than their own. Involve parents and respect their wishes. Choose which festivals to celebrate. For example, celebrate the key festivals of families whose children attend the setting and celebrate a few that are unfamiliar to anyone in the setting. Establish an individual approach to each festival – capture the special nature of the festival, the underlying meaning and any associated stories.

- As an early years practitioner, consider personal views on spirituality and children's spiritual development. What are your assumptions about its meaning and how could/should the area be addressed in practice?

- Learn about faiths other than your own – from children, parents and colleagues, local people and written material. Stand back from your own beliefs and be willing to find the common human themes in beliefs and practices as well as acknowledging and respecting the differences.

- Introduce children to a variety of faiths and see it as part of their whole development. This will open up possibilities for children and give them a range of experiences relevant to different faiths. Introduce simple ideas, encourage children to explore through doing, support them to answer questions. Do not restrict yourself only to those faiths that are represented in your current group. If the setting makes no effort beyond celebrating one tradition, this tells children that this faith is the only one that matters.

- Take children on visits to different places of worship – church or chapel (Christian), Mandir (Hindu), Synagogue (Jewish) or a Mosque (Muslim). If you can't visit them, provide children with books, photos and videos. Build the visit into other activities/celebrations. Before the visit, talk through what will be expected of children: for example, taking off shoes, covering their heads, whispering.

- Encourage children to use their philosophical imaginations to develop their creative spirit and to make sense of their world, set time aside regularly for thinking time – ask 'what do you think ...?', and 'what if' questions - what do you think beauty is, where does magic come from, what would happen if there were no such things as trees, what if we had no eyes. In the beginning the practitioner can compile a list of questions to be put in the 'thinking box' and the children can pick a question randomly. With practice the children will come up with their own hypotheses and questions.

- Ask children have they wondered about anything during the session and allow time everyday for children, preferably in small groups, to reflect on what they have done.

Children's books which are useful for spiritual development

The Old Boot (ISBN 0711205272) by Chris Baines.
The Hidden Forest (ISBN 0688157602) and *Where the forest meets the sea* (ISBN 0688063632) by Jeannie Baker.
Fairy Collection (ISBN 1865035726) by Shirley Barber.
The Nativity (ISBN 0794505295) by Felicity Brooks.
The Hungry Caterpillar (ISBN 0399213015) and *Papa Please Get the Moon For Me* (ISBN 0887081770) by Eric Carle.
Ruby the Christmas Donkey (ISBN 0763607169) by Mirabel Cecil.
All Kinds of Beliefs (ISBN 0857075056) by Emma Damon.
Dear Tooth Fairy (ISBN 0763621757) by Alan Durant and Vanessa Cabban.
Oliver's Wood (ISBN 1564029328) by Sue Hendra.
My Book of Thanks (ISBN 0763615234) by B.G. Hennessy.
The Friday Nights of Nana (ISBN 076360658) by Amy Hest.
Dear Greenpeace (ISBN 1930332459), *My Friend Whale* (ISBN 0763623105) and *Sally the Limpet* (ISBN 0763617156) by Simon James.
Little Calf (ISBN 0763608998) and *Emma's Lamb* (ISBN 0763604240) by Kim Lewis.
The Circle of Days (ISBN 0763613819) and *In Every Grain of Sand: a child's book of prayers* (ISBN 0763601764) by Reeve Lindbergh.
Let the Lynx Come In (ISBN 1564025314) by Jonathon London.
The Tale of Tobias (ISBN 1564026922) by Jan Mark.
The Book of Beasts (ISBN 076361579X) by Inga Moore.
Who is the World For (ISBN 0763612804) by Tom Pow.

Baby's Book of Nature (ISBN 0751352926) by Roger Priddy.

When a Pet Dies (ISBN 0698116666) by Fred Rogers.

All for the Newborn Baby (ISBN 0763600938) by Phyllis Root.

Elijah's Angel: a story for Chanukah and Christmas (ISBN 0152015582) and *The Dog Who Walked with God* (ISBN 0763604704) by Michael Rosen.

Snow comes to the farm (ISBN 1564024261) by Nathaniel Tripp.

We love them (ISBN 0763603392) and *My great grandpa* (ISBN 0399221557) by Martin Waddell.

The Christmas Miracle of Jonathon Toomey (ISBN 0763619302) by Susan Wojciechowski.

Granddad's Prayers of the Earth (ISBN 076360660X) by Douglas Wood.

CHAPTER SEVEN

Holistic Child Development

Introduction

As detailed in Chapter One, this book utilises Maslow's hierarchy of needs as the conceptual framework with which to consider emotional, social, moral and spiritual development. Looking at this hierarchy allows us to see what children really need in order to reach their potential. Maslow's hierarchy suggests that if the child has his physiological needs satisfied, together with the need for safety from aggressors, he then becomes chiefly concerned with being accepted by his family and social group. Once accepted, he will next concern himself with being esteemed by others, so that he may come to think well of himself. Having at least partially satisfied these needs, he can then move on to cognitive and aesthetic needs and finally to self-actualisation. Self-actualisation means the child becoming what he is capable of and reaching his full potential and when children are self-actualised they have the potential to become better citizens, as well as being more caring and considerate.

Physiological needs

The needs that are usually taken as the starting point for Maslow's motivation theory are the so-called physiological needs or drives. Until fulfilled, these are the most predominant of all needs. This means that for a child who is hungry, getting food is his major motivation. All other needs get pushed into the background. Once the child gets food this is no longer his primary need and the child is dominated by other unsatisfied needs and aims (Maslow 1970a). Many past educators and philosophers also acknowledged this. In particular, the McMillan sisters, in the late 19th and early 20th century, proposed feeding children while at school, as they believed that children could not learn or make friends when they are undernourished, cold or sick. Currently many early years practitioners are aware of this need and many settings now provide food, including breakfast, as some children attend settings without having their physiological needs met at home. Many children today eat meals less regularly, eat less as a family group, snack a lot and frequently eat in front of the television set. Children also have frequent visits to fast food restaurants where the food sold is high in saturated fats, cholesterol, salt and calories. High calorie diets have been linked to increasing obesity in childhood and the risk of subsequent ill health and the heightened risk of developing cancer and heart disease as an adult. On the converse of this, some parents through either religious, health or moral reasons, adopt a strict vegetarian/vegan diet. Some children who experience such diets are presenting with an increase in Vitamin D deficiency and malnutrition in what is commonly called 'muesli malnutrition' (James, Nelson, Ralph and Leather 1997). Making the assumption that children's physiological needs are met before leaving home in the morning is not always valid. Physiological needs also include getting enough physical exercise and getting access to fresh air and the outdoors. Children need to move and run around. Regular exercise needs to be incorporated into the lives of all children, especially young children. Patterns of exercise are set in childhood and today's children are less active than all previous generations. Sedentary children become sedentary adults, with increased risk of heart disease and other health problems (Selwyn 2000). Therefore it is clear that early years settings must ensure that these needs are adequately met. Once physiological needs are met, the child will try to satisfy his next need, that of safety.

Safety needs

Once the physiological needs are relatively well gratified, a new set of needs emerge. The next set of needs on Maslow's hierarchy is safety needs and these include security, stability, dependency, protection, freedom from fear, anxiety and so on. Practically everything looks less important than safety and protection until the child feels safe (Maslow 1970a).

As long ago as the 15th century Luther, in Germany, spoke out against physical punishment and suggested that children could not learn if they feared for their safety (Keatinge 1896). One century after Luther, Comenius, a Czech, again drew attention to the unsystematic and cruel educational experiences to which children were exposed. He stressed that lack of trained and skilled teachers left children feeling insecure and he called these schools 'the slaughterhouses of minds and the terrors of children' (Dupuis 1966). The 17th century produced a most influential English man, John Locke, who also did not look favourably on the schools of his time, disagreeing with their heavy reliance on physical punishment. He advised educators to acknowledge the importance of understanding all the child's needs. He realised the importance of the classroom atmosphere on children's ability to learn and said it was difficult for children to concentrate when they were frightened (Locke cited in Axtell 1968).

The 18th century French writer, Rousseau, stressed that humans needed a good education in order to develop. He again highlighted the negative impact that pushing or hurrying the child could have - making the child fearful and unsure of himself. He repudiated the use of force and corporal punishment in education and he advocated that education be child-centred (Rusk 1918). Many people were influenced by Rousseau. Two such people in Ireland, Richard and Maria Edgeworth, offered advice on how to develop children along practical lines. Like Rousseau, they were against hurrying children and believed they could not learn through forceful means. They advocated that the pace of learning and teaching be adjusted to the age and ability of the individual child, because if the child was presented with tasks that were too difficult, he would become overwhelmed (Curtis and Boultwood 1970). Pestalozzi, in Switzerland, was another disciple of Rousseau's. He also fought against corporal punishment and he advocated learning by doing, urging teachers to introduce simple and concrete things to children before giving them complex or abstract materials. Owen, Welsh capitalist turned utopian socialist, also abhorred corporal punishment, believing it did not enhance children's development (Rusk 1933).

In Germany, Froebel's own childhood experience was one of oppressive fear and as an adult he stressed that all children's lives should be free of it (1887). He emphasised that children needed to live secure lives if they were to develop to their potential, and his lifelong struggle for connection and unity allowed children to live more secure and happy lives. His contention that the child should only experience positive and pleasant things in the early years was also to be admired and ensured that children's safety and security needs were at least partially met. Montessori, from Italy, introduced a philosophy of education based upon her own personal observations of children and her ideology followed on the work of past educators and philosophers. She recognised the importance of not hurrying the child and the need to allow him to develop at his own pace, in order to make him feel secure (1967b). She clearly recognised the negative impact that fear and insecurity could have on the child. In essence, many philosophers and educators of the past, well before Maslow, had at least partially conceived his hierarchy of needs, recognising that if safety needs were not met, then children would not be able to concentrate on or make progress in other areas of their lives.

Current literature reiterates this and shows that more and more children are coming to the end of their emotional and personal resources and suffer from burn out, anxiety, desperation and from a myriad of stress related illnesses (Goleman 1996). Fear and anxiety are taking over their lives and greater output is demanded of them while fewer support mechanisms are there to make them feel safe and secure. Until this situation is redressed, children will not be able to achieve a higher level on Maslow's hierarchy. Being afraid or feeling stressed may mean a child becomes fixated and he may never be able to progress. Severe stress in a child's early years could damage his life-long development (Dowling 2000); Bocchino (1999). On the other hand, a safe child no longer feels endangered, so safety needs are no longer active motivators. To help meet children's safety needs, the early years setting must ensure that children are allowed to become attached to the adults in the setting. Children must be supported to form a secure relationship with at least one key worker, as the attachment relationship impacts on the child's feeling of safety and security. Without such a solid base, the child may become fearful and passive, or angry and aggressive, so attachment is vital (Schickendanz et al. 1990). Also, staff should be responsive to children to ensure that their emotional needs are met and there should be a continuity of experience in routine, location and grouping to make the child feel secure (David 1997). Safety needs can become very urgent if the child feels threatened in any way - if he is stressed, if he is asked to do something which is too difficult, if he is afraid of the adult. Thus, the child can move up Maslow's hierarchy only if he is in a safe, reasonably ordered, predictable and happy environment. A peaceful, smoothly run, stable early years setting can make the children who attend it feel safe and can help ameliorate stressful home situations. Thus, safety needs must be at least partially satisfied before the child can progress to the next rung of the hierarchy, which are the belongingness and love needs (Maslow 1970a).

Belongingness and love needs

If physiological and safety needs are fairly well satisfied, the child's need for love, affection and belongingness will manifest itself. The child will hunger for an affectionate relationship with his main caregiver, family, friends and educational setting. He will strive with great intensity to achieve his goal. He will want to attain such a place more than anything else in the world. He feels sharply the pangs of loneliness, isolation, friendlessness and rejection. Lack of attachment, being without roots, being torn from one's family or community, being a transient or a newcomer rather than a native can have destructive effects on children. They need contact, intimacy and belongingness (Maslow 1970a).

Any good society must satisfy the social needs of children if it is to survive and be healthy. Children are born into a highly complex social world and from birth become active participants in a world of other people. Even young children try to understand the intentions, feelings and actions of others in order to be accepted and to belong to their social world. As far back as Aristotle and maybe even before that, philosophers surmised that humans were social beings (Smith 1984). This was reiterated down through the centuries and was stressed in particular by Froebel. Froebel's vision was to stimulate an appreciation and love for children. He provided a new but small, safe, world for them and there he allowed children to play with one another and to form a community. He stressed the importance of continuity and unity between the home and the school life of the child. Froebel believed that providing a setting similar to the family home, within the school environment, would provide children with opportunities for interacting socially in a non-threatening manner. All the elements of a society of equals were to be experienced there by the child, establishing an atmosphere of love, belongingness and universal good will. The kindergarten was to provide the ideal world for the child, it was to be an institution where future adults could learn the art of co-ordination, co-operation and leadership, as well as allowing them to experience a sense of acceptance and an affiliation to others. Froebel demanded a happy and loving environment for children (Liebschner 1988) and it is now acknowledged that a child's environment plays a distinct role in how his personality traits develop. It impacts on whether he feels accepted and loved or whether he feels isolated and rejected. A nurturing and caring environment can build neural pathways that encourage emotional stability, whereas repeated exposure to stress and inconsistent care and attention can create connections that trigger fear, isolation and apprehension (Bocchino 1999).

Montessori recognised that children are social beings and she said that if children are to adapt to the environment, they must have a sense of belonging. If the child is not given this exposure he will become repressed, underdeveloped and incapable of adaptation because of being deprived of the means necessary to develop socially. Modern society, Montessori claimed, condemned the child to a lonely and unstimulating childhood and this was not good for the child. She said that some of the problems in adult society may be the result of frustrating the strong desire of young children to associate with others (Montessori 1989).

The need to belong and to affiliate is well documented in the attachment relationship. This relationship has been a topic of focus for many years and the attachment relationship is seen to provide a prototype that shapes the remainder of the developing child's life, particularly influencing his capacity for love and his ability to motivate himself (Freud 1933). Bowlby (1953) broke ranks with the Freudian psychoanalytic view and developed the prevailing theory of attachment which guides most development research on the topic today. The attachment relationship is the emotional tie that develops between child and primary caregiver and plays a crucial part in the social and emotional growth of the child. Being without a primary attachment figure in early childhood puts children at risk, as does misattunement in an attachment relationship. Attachment is vital and the quality of the attachment relationship has a profound influence (for better or worse) on the young child's life (Oatley and Jenkins 1996).

Studies such as Parker and Asher (1987) suggest that the first six to seven years of development are critical for the development of social skills, so it is vital that children are helped to develop socially in the early years, both at home and in the early years setting. Being developed socially can lead to happiness and contentedness. Children want to have friends and to be accepted as part of the peer group and this ability to form relationships is important for all aspects of development. Also, the adults in the child's world play a crucial role in providing an environment which is supportive to all children. According to Murray (1999), the increase in the immigration of non-European Union minority ethnic communities has shown up uncomfortable tensions in relation to racism, prejudice, social values, diversity and bullying in Ireland. Irish adults and children are not providing an environment which is equally welcoming and supportive to all and this is blocking the meeting of the belongingness and love needs of some young children. Ireland is not unique in this regard.

Social development is a double-sided process in which children become integrated into the larger social community, while at the same time becoming differentiated as distinctive individuals. If social development is considered a vital component of all activities in which children are engaged, then development in all areas of children's lives can be enhanced. On the reverse, if it is damaged or ignored it can militate against children in all areas of their development, as the relationships we form with others throughout life are the network of our social world and to a large extent measure the success we have in life in that they tend to determine how happy we are (Wood 1981). Without doubt, social development is vital, so early years settings must prioritise it.

Morality also gives us a sense of affiliation and is about learning to live together in a community. A person's definition of being moral has as much, if not more, to do with belonging as it does with defining what is right and wrong. Morality is about living together in love and it takes a long time to develop morally and to learn about being a truly human moral being (Hoffman, in Bornstein and Lamb 1988). Also, the underlying principle and centre of spirituality is and must be love and community. Spirituality is needed by children today, probably more than ever before, as it gives children a sense of not being alone as well as giving them a sense of purpose and direction in life. Spirituality is about being integrated or about falling apart, it is about being in a community or being lonely, about being in harmony with the earth or being alienated from it (Lealman 1996). Hence, spirituality gives a sense of belonging but do we prioritise it everyday?

Social development includes the development of a sense of belonging and affiliation and if these are not prioritised, growth can be inhibited. Early years settings can give children a sense of belonging and can help compensate for social deprivation, isolation and inexperience at home. However, many early years practitioners find it difficult to respond to this need, stressing that they have to compensate for so much already that it is difficult to take on this role on top of everything else (Daly 2002). Unfortunately, many children, on entering an early years setting, will not be socially developed and will not have a sense of being accepted or of being part of a group. If they are not helped to fulfil their social needs in the early years setting how can they progress to any other needs, including the cognitive? Thus, it is vital that social development of all children is put high on the agenda. Once a child feels he is loved and that he belongs, his belongingness and love needs will be at least partially met, so he can move on in his motivational hierarchy to esteem needs.

Esteem needs

All children have a need and a desire for a stable, firmly based belief in themselves as worthwhile individuals. They need self-respect, self-esteem and the esteem of others. Satisfaction of the esteem needs leads to feelings of self-confidence, self-worth, strength and adequacy, allowing children to feel useful and necessary in the world, while neglect of these needs leads to feelings of inferiority, weakness and helplessness (Maslow 1970a).

Many educators and philosophers have recognised the esteem needs of children. Comenius and Froebel, in particular, acknowledged them. Comenius stressed the right of the child to dignity and respect, a view not held by many of his contemporaries. He conceived of the relationship between the teacher and the pupil as being a collaboration requiring respect on the part of both and this was in sharp contrast to the authoritarian model of teaching of his era (Wise 1964). Froebel stressed that young children should only encounter what they are ready for, not what is expected or advocated by society. He believed that childhood was an important period of human growth and development in its own right and that it should not be rushed or belittled. Froebel had an overwhelming love of humanity and he was deeply upset by the arbitrary way in which children were looked upon and cared for. Froebel, like Comenius, Pestalozzi and later, Montessori, was of the opinion that self-activity must be a priority of education and he stressed that experience is the key to development. He saw play as the highest achievement of child development and he emphasised the need to develop a stable and trusting relationship between the teacher and the child, thereby creating a genuine bond and a mutual respect and approval, helping to fulfil children's esteem needs (Bruce et al. 1995).

Montessori was also very much aware of the child's esteem needs. In her classroom, she set up as natural an environment as possible to help children develop. Through her observations, she became convinced that children possess an intense motivation towards their own self-construction and realisation. However, she said that contemporary society was not conducive to recognising the child's needs and that in fact it repressed his potential for self-realisation. Standing (1957) quotes Montessori as calling the young child a forgotten citizen and says she called for an awakening of the social conscience with regard to children's rights. Montessori conceded that children's physical rights had started to be addressed but a corresponding recognition of the child's rights as a developing human personality were not acknowledged. His opportunities to participate, to be competent, to gain approval and to be recognised were sadly lacking. Thus, almost all the great educational thinkers have realised that children's esteem needs must be met if they are to learn well and to develop to their full potential.

Contemporary theorists and psychologists also draw attention to the esteem needs of children. Hartley-Brewer (1998) claims that doing the best for a child comes down to creating in the child self-esteem, self-confidence and self-reliance. Lack of self-esteem is given increasingly as a reason why so many people get themselves into trouble with the law, why so many young people commit suicide and why there is such an increase in mental and stress-related illnesses. Having good self-esteem means that children will have confidence in themselves, will know who they are, will like who they are and will be content to face the world as they are. A confident, trusting child, secure in his own particular abilities, will play, learn, love, give and communicate better. However, developing self-esteem requires both a supportive social milieu and the formation and acceptance of realistic personal goals. If children are to satisfy their esteem needs to be competent and to gain approval, they have to learn to cope with failing as well as experiencing the exhilaration of success. Failing at a task does not mean the child fails as a person. For children to accept this, both adults' and children's attitudes towards winning and achievement must change. The freedom to make mistakes, to cope with frustration and to deal with failure are important aspects of life, and normal emotional development involves a process of coping with the experience of failure. It is an inevitable part of growing up and is the first part of the process of becoming competent (Dyer 1998). Yet what in practice is our reaction to mistakes and failure? Is it one of criticism and judgement or do we praise effort and give the child the confidence to try again? If we are to help him to meet his esteem needs then it must be the former rather than the latter. However, in practice the education system in most of the western world is based on knowing the right answers and achieving the right result. Yet, without prioritising emotional development can our system be called 'education' at all or is what we are trying to do 'miseducation'? We need to be aware that for a child, of all the judgements and beliefs he has, none is more important than the ones he has about himself. His belief in himself, which develops as a result of how he feels he is loved and respected, is the single most telling factor in determining his success and happiness in life (Denham 1998). So maybe we need to reassess the philosophy that underlies our education system and gear it more towards creativity and the possibility and probability of differing answers, rather than just one right or wrong response, if all children's confidence and belief in themselves is to be enhanced. This is vital as it is only when the child's esteem needs are at least partially met that he can progress to cognitive needs. This seems to be forgotten by many policy makers and curriculum planners, who seem to ignore the fact that not prioritising emotional development can fixate a child at a lower level of functioning, inhibiting his growth, which may mean that the child never reaches his full potential, including his cognitive potential.

Cognitive needs

Only when children fulfil needs lower down the hierarchy will they be driven by cognitive needs. Many would have us believe that cognitive needs are children's main motivation. However, in reality it is only when physiological, safety, belongingness and esteem needs are at least partially satisfied that the child will be motivated by cognitive needs. The cognitive needs (perceptual, intellectual, learning) are another basic set of needs. Any danger to them, any deprivation or blocking of their free use, is threatening to the child. Children are curious - searching for knowledge, for truth and for wisdom. Secrecy, censorship, dishonesty and blocking of communication threaten them. The history of mankind supplies us with ample examples where people searched for facts and created explanations in the face of the greatest danger, even to life itself. Studies of psychologically healthy people indicate that they are attracted to the mysterious, to the unknown and unexplained. Children do not have to be taught to be curious. However, they may be taught not to be curious or their curious side may be stultified by not being nurtured and encouraged. The fulfillment of the cognitive need is subjectively satisfying in its own right and the need to gratify it is a pre-requisite for the fullest development of human potential. All human life is a search for meaning and we all have a desire to understand, to systematise, to organise, to analyse, to look for connections and meanings to construct a system of values. However, it is only when needs lower down the hierarchy can be satisfied easily that the child will have the time and energy to devote to intellectual needs and interests (Maslow 1970a).

As far back as Plato, philosophers stressed that early education should be different from the slavish training for mere professional purposes (Lodge 1950). Later, Aristotle emphasised the importance of taking a child's nature and all the influences of his environment into account when educating, as without doing this the child could not learn. Luther further developed this idea, saying that schools would only help children to develop by using their natural curiosity and activity to further their education. His unhappiness with bookish and scholastic learning moved education in the direction of more practical learning (Smith 1984). Comenius also recognised the cognitive needs of the child, believing that everything grew in nature and that children likewise should grow and improve, following nature's laws and through the right education. These ideas were later developed by

Rousseau, Pestalozzi and Froebel. Comenius further stressed that the child needed to know and investigate things for himself. The observations that other people made about things were of little benefit to him. The child had to discover and explore things for himself if his cognitive needs were to be fulfilled (Rusk 1933). Rousseau encouraged the development of curiosity and interest as motivating factors and he advised teachers to act as guides and facilitators. He presented an alternative education, one that envisaged developing the whole child, emphasising nature and the natural way of doing things. He advocated that education be child-centred, informal and developed out of everyday experiences (Wise 1964).

Froebel believed that every child possessed within himself at birth his own full educational potential and that an appropriate educational environment was necessary to help that child reach his potential. He claimed education that aimed only at readying man for the work of the world was not enough. The holistic development of the child should be education's aim. Froebel's most basic principle was a belief in connection and unity and he advocated that there should be a connection between everything in the child's life. He tried to impart to his pupils a thorough knowledge of the inner connections and oneness of all things and he stated that true education was a process, growth taking place day by day, a little at a time, slowly knowing, understanding, exploring and discovering. His theory and practice showed that learning succeeds best when undertaken by a self-active and searching mind. He illustrated that freedom from rote learning can open the door to real understanding and that freedom for children to explore their environment can result in responsible actions and is not in opposition to harmony and order (Bruce et al. 1995).

Montessori also recognised the child's intellectual needs and she advocated that the child should have what he needs at each particular stage, without thinking of the future. Each phase of life was to be lived through fully, so that the child could pass from one juncture to the next, much like Maslow's belief that only when lower down needs were met could the child progress to meeting his higher needs. The aim of all her work was to bring about a new understanding of the potentialities and needs of children. Her revolutionary conception of education as an aid to life is one of the most valuable aspects of the inheritance she left us. She said that, unlike other creatures of the earth, the child must develop his own powers for learning and for reacting to life. She set about developing an educational method to implement her philosophy and attempted to relate theory to practice in a real and meaningful way (Lillard 1972). During the same era, Dewey (1900) claimed that traditional education was a one way channel of communication, with direct and didactic methods which involved rote learning and memorisation. In order to meet children's needs, including the cognitive, Dewey advocated that schools should be special places which concentrated on the best ways of using all children's powers. He pushed for the self-realisation of the child and Roth (1962) says that children all over the world are educated differently today because of him.

Today, most educationalists would agree that discovery, more than instruction, is how children learn best. In particular, the young child learns more by doing than by being told and the mechanisms of the brain are such that indirect, unconscious learning is more powerful and permanent than learning through direct verbal instruction. Indirect teaching methods involve emotion, intentionality, the handling of concrete objects, all of which reinforce learning. Learning through indirect methods often involves conscious or unconscious processes which lead to insight, and insights immediately become part of one's knowing rather than something to be remembered. Verbal instruction (for example answering questions, clarifying, providing labels for the ideas which have arisen) is helpful if it comes after indirect learning. In other words, it is effective in teaching what is already known, but not adequately verbalised (Neville 1989). Unfortunately, education does not always use indirect teaching processes or discovery based learning as the poem *Caring* by Marical Losada (in Zohar and Marshall 2000 p.290) so graphically illustrates. It was inspired by Umberto Maturana's *The Student's Prayer* and is a translated and abridged version of the original. Maturana was a Chilean biologist whose young son became unhappy at school because he felt his teachers were making it impossible for him to learn. They insisted on teaching him what they knew instead of letting him explore and discover things for himself.

> Don't impose on me what you know,
> I want to explore the unknown
> And be the source of my own discoveries.
> Let the known be my liberation, not my slavery.

> The world of your truth can be my limitation
> Your wisdom my negation.
> Don't instruct me: let's walk together.
> Let my richness begin where yours ends.

> Show me so that I can stand
> On your shoulder.
> Reveal yourself so that I can be
> Something different.

> You believe that every human being
> Can love and create
> I understand, then, your fear
> When I ask you to live according to your wisdom.

> You will not know who I am
> by listening to yourself.
> Don't instruct me; let me be
> Your failure is that I be identical to you.

(Losada, in Zohar and Marshall 2000 p.290)

Unfortunately, much of today's early years education and care is tied more and more to instruction and the learning of a predetermined body of knowledge that is underwritten by questions of economy, productivity and achievement. Its value for children and their holistic development is not high on the agenda. From birth, the looming spectre of college and subsequent employment is a defining influence on the way children are educated (O'Donnchadha 2000). The chance for the child to learn what he needs to learn is not easily realised. Also, the evidence from new brain research has added to the demands that children feel, think and behave more competently in a pseudo-academic way than their age and stage would warrant. Technological innovations and discoveries have many positive benefits. However, they are often misused to sell parents and the public, practices and programmes that are not in the best interests of the child. The conception of this type of child competence is resulting in the downward extension of the academic curriculum to optimise 'superkid' potential (Elkind 2001). The pressure for early academic achievement is only one of the many present-day pressures on children but at what price? The cognitive needs of children are underpinned by the need to know, to understand, to discover and to explore at the child's own pace. Only when these are respected and fulfilled will their cognitive needs be met.

Part of the cognitive need is spirituality. Yet, this aspect of development is still equated with the teaching of religion in many countries. This is despite the fact that spirituality tends to give adults and children alike a sense of purpose and direction in life, leading to feelings of happiness, connection and fulfillment. Children, including those of a very young age, constantly try to comprehend how they should think about the gift of life given to them, who gave it to them and for what. Without spirituality, something vital is missing from children's lives. However, the issue of children's spiritual development is rarely mentioned by childcare experts and there is little literature available on the subject in developmental terms. Yet, it is a core area of development and it now seems clear that cognitive development and ability impinge on spiritual development and *vice versa*. It has been the mistake of many to overlook the spiritual aspect of cognitive development, are we going to continue to ignore it?

Also, certain elements are vital in any early years setting if children's cognitive needs are to be met. These elements include the concepts of curriculum, play and quality. Curriculum is the framework that defines how and what children are encouraged to learn and curricula vary and reflect a belief in what is perceived to be important in a particular area or time. Play is the foundation of a child's growth and development and is essential to a child's life. On the other hand, the term 'quality' is used to analyse, describe or understand the essence of a particular thing. It is one of the key terms in current educational debates and researchers are surmising that quality is a subjective, value-based, relative and dynamic concept with the possibility of many perspectives and understandings. They argue that any assessment of quality must be contextualised with diversity being acknowledged and accepted, as quality is no longer seen as one standard of excellence identifiable for all children in all settings. Rather it is seen as a set of core criteria towards which services may progress (Coolahan 1998). Children benefit from good quality early years settings where adults are responsive to them, where the curriculum encourages learning in context, and where ample opportunity is given to play and interact. This is not a romantic view of education, it is a survival one and one which needs to be embraced if children's cognitive needs are to be met and if they are to progress and meet their aesthetic needs.

Aesthetic needs

Maslow says we do not know a lot about these needs, yet he says they are vital needs and the testimony of history, of the humanities and of aestheticians forbids us to ignore them. He stresses that in most humans there is a basic aesthetic need and that this need is found in every culture and in every age, as far back as the caveman (Maslow 1970a). At present, education emphasises left-brain thinking and concentrates on those aspects of knowing and training through memorisation and regurgitation. Current research shows that this kind of approach is only dealing with half of the potential (if indeed half) of the person. The right side of the brain - the creative, intuitive, artistic and feeling side needs to be developed as much as the left side. The bias in favour of left-brain skills and activities is neglecting children's holistic development and yet, it is these intelligences (intuitive, creative and emotional) which provide balance, not only for the individual but for society as a whole (O'Donnchadha 2000). However, the value of aesthetic, creative and affective development is increasingly being recognised and: "There is a growing conviction that an education that is concerned with only one dimension of human experience is no education at all" (Dunn 1988 p.103).

Many philosophers and educators foretold the above belief regarding aesthetic needs many centuries ago. Comenius advocated developing the aesthetic dimensions and right brain development of the child in order to cultivate the full range of his potential (Wise 1964). Rousseau (1782, 1979) advocated educating children according to the laws of nature and he believed exposure to nature and beautiful things were beneficial to the child's development. On the other hand, two of Rousseau's followers, the Edgeworths, have been sharply criticised for downplaying children's aesthetic development by ignoring the study of music, art and poetry (Curtis and Boultwood 1970). While another follower, Pestalozzi, stressed that education was the harmonious development of all the child's power, not just the intellect. His curriculum included music, drama, exposure to nature and play, allowing children to fulfil their creative needs (Boyd 1921). Aesthetic development was also a must for Froebel. He wanted children to live harmoniously with the natural world of beauty that surrounded them and he said their environment should be pure and bright, with fresh air and lots of natural light. He saw play as the highest achievement of child development, being the spontaneous expression of the child's inner being, allowing his creative inner self to have expression (Marenholtz Bulow 1876). Thus, Froebel advocated the holistic development of the child, including the meeting of his aesthetic needs.

Montessori had different views about creativity and play. She de-emphasised play and maintained it was something that only satisfies part of a child's nature. In *The Montessori Method* (1909) she said she abhorred play with toys, seeing them as foolish and degrading. Boyd (1914) says she showed little appreciation of the arts and, in particular, she disliked those arts which require imaginative and creative expression in the early years. For Montessori, creativity is seen to occur after the child reaches the age of seven and prior to this, it is facts not fantasies to which children should be exposed. Boyd (ibid.) goes on to stress the great delight children show in drawing, singing and dancing. He says it shows clearly the relationship that exists between the child's soul and the beauty embodied in the world of culture and art. This seems to indicate that creative arts, though contrary to Montessori's principle of self-education, are not an external imposition that harms the child's development. Instead they are a means of setting free hidden powers which, when developed and used, give a new significance to childhood and help fulfil the child's aesthetic needs. Dewey, on the other hand, emphasised creative development and stressed the widespread benefits of leisure, culture, beauty, joy and creativity for each individual child and for children as a group. In particular, he tried to change the focus of schoolwork, seeing the need for self-activity and play. He systematised the philosophies of his predecessors; in particular those of Comenius, Pestalozzi and Froebel, resulting in a child-centred, integrated, environmentally friendly curriculum which acknowledged the aesthetic needs of every child.

More recently Gilmartin (1996) stated that young children possessed a tremendous potential for creating. However, he goes on to say that children's creative tendencies have been frozen for generations and have been all but killed in the classroom. Yet, artistic creativity can be a way of affirming a child's experiences. It is a means of communicating, not a quantity of actual information but is a living, dynamic experience. Also, artistic creativity means the child encounters symbols and these are part of the transpersonal realm. Creativity involves aspects of consciousness (intuition, reverence, awe, beauty, acceptance of ambiguity and uncertainty) which formal education and society tend to ignore and neglect. Creativity is not confined to artistic creativity but artistic activity can help to make possible a more open approach to life, an approach that defies cynicism because it is open to fresh ideas and possibilities. A broad and balanced curriculum with social and pastoral development should be available if children are to develop aesthetically. As opportunities are seized and skills developed in literature, music, drama, nature and art, children locate their creative dimension. Many believe that creativity can be described as part of spirituality and part of the whole child. Creativity contributes to the child's holistic development and much of what is finest in society is developed through a variety of art forms which contribute to cultural ethos and to a sense of well-being. Arts education is life-enhancing and invaluable in promoting capability and adaptability (Webster 1996). Elkind (2001 p.219) says, "as concerned citizens, we need to assert the value of the arts in the school". He goes on to say that far from being a luxury, time and money spent on the arts enhances learning and development. It reduces stress and gives children an aesthetic perspective to balance their lives. Young children experience moments of intensity where beauty and understanding are prominent and such times help to fulfil children's aesthetic needs. Yet spiritual development is an area that is not high on everyone's agenda. Does this mean that creative development is also not important or that creativity and spiritual development should not be a priority in the early years setting? Many do believe that spiritual development should not be a priority in the early years (Daly 2002). According to Maslow (1970a) the child's aesthetic needs must be met before they can become self-actualised. Are children being allowed to develop this creative side? Yet, until creative needs are at least partially met, the child can never become self-actualised. Only once all other needs lower down the hierarchy are at least partially satisfied can the child aim towards self-actualisation.

Self-actualisation needs

Even when all of the previous needs are satisfied, the child will experience a new discontent and restlessness. As Maslow (1970a p.46) says, "what a man *can* be, he *must* be". Self-actualisation is the tendency for the child to become actualised in what he is potentially, to become everything that he is capable of becoming. Such a child prefers challenge to easy solutions and enjoys psychological well-being and fulfillment. Self-actualisation can be defined as the full use and exploitation of talents, capacities and potentialities, and self-actualised children seem to fulfil themselves and do the best of which they are capable. Unlike the lower down deficit needs which decline once partially met, growth motivation needs (such as the self-actualisation need) become stronger as they are nourished. However, to get to the stage of self-actualisation, children must first have gratified to some degree the needs lower down the hierarchy (the physiological, safety, belonging, esteem, cognitive and aesthetic needs).

The characteristics of the self-actualised child include perceiving reality efficiently and tolerating uncertainty. They accept themselves and others for what they are and are spontaneous in thought and behaviour. They are problem-centred rather than self-centred and have a good sense of humour. They are highly creative and resist enculturation, but are not deliberately unconventional. Such children are concerned for the welfare of humanity and have a deep appreciation of the basic experiences of life. They enjoy satisfying interpersonal relationships with a few rather than many people and they have the ability to look at life objectively (Maslow 1970a).

Maslow's studies established that individuals who possessed the above qualities were among the healthiest one per cent of the population, showing no signs of psychological problems and successfully using their talents and abilities. He also identified behaviours which lead to self-actualisation (1970a). These include:

- the ability to experience life as a child, with absorption and concentration;
- a readiness to attempt the novel rather than keeping to the safe and secure;
- a facility for listening to one's own feelings rather than to tradition or authority or the majority when evaluating experience;
- an honesty that eschews 'game playing';
- a willingness to be unpopular if personal views do not accord with the majority;
- a readiness to assume responsibility;
- the ability to work hard at any task undertaken;
- a readiness to identify personal psychological defences and the courage to abandon them.

Comenius, theologian, philosopher and pedagogue, stressed that only through education could man achieve his full potential and go on to lead a truly harmonious life. His ponderings on child development have set him down as being one of the great educators in the history of the philosophy of education. Comenius saw the aim of education as the fostering of human potential and his proposed curriculum was a liberal one with its cultivation of the full range of human potentialities; spiritual, religious, moral, emotional, aesthetic, cognitive, social and physical (Murphy 1995). His great objective, that every child should be fully educated and that they reach their human potential regardless of nation, class, sex or race is an admirable one and corresponds closely with Maslow's self-actualisation theory.

Many others, including Pestalozzi, advocated educating the whole child - body, mind and spirit. He took up many of Rousseau's ideas, developing and implementing them. His efforts in education were tentative and experimental. Yet, his experiences and beliefs possess a reliability that has endured (Rusk 1918). Froebel, one of the great pioneers of early educational reform, also saw that the child possessed within himself the ability to become everything that he is capable of becoming. Froebel's writings have influenced generations of readers and many contend that Adlerian psychological principles resonate with those of Froebel. Alfred Adler (1870-1937) was an Austrian psychiatrist and psychologist. Adler believed humans were motivated by hopes for the future, not by their past experiences (Adler 1924). He saw humankind in a positive light and he stressed man's drive to fulfil his potential. The mission of Adlerian psychology is to encourage the development of psychologically healthy and co-operative individuals who will pursue the ideals of social equity and democratic living (Stein 1997). Humanistic and transpersonal psychology, as espoused by Maslow, has a similar theme running through it. Many, including Dworetzky (1994), would say that the humanist concept of self-actualisation was derived to a great degree from Adler's ideas and therefore in an indirect way by Froebel.

The aim of Maria Montessori's work was to bring about a new understanding of the potentialities and needs of children. Montessori claimed that education should abandon its traditional preoccupation with the teaching of skills and the transfer of knowledge and should instead aim to aid the basic patterns that direct man from within, so that balanced development can take place. Then and only then can the child reach his full potential. Through her observations,

Montessori became convinced that the child possesses an intense motivation towards self-construction and self-realisation and she believed the full development of himself is the child's unique and ultimate goal in life (Montessori 1909).

Prioritising emotional, social, moral and spiritual development has a significant role to play in helping the child become self-actualised. Children who believe that the world is a positive and miraculous place, wherein they are special and loved, have a huge advantage over children who are doubting and negative (Denham 1998). Emotional development has a huge impact on a child's overall development and it must receive the respect and attention it is due, if children are to reach the level of self-actualisation. Also, humans are social beings from the very start and need contact with others in order to survive. Belongingness, acceptance and affiliation are high on their list of needs. Morality is also about getting along with others and Maslow (1971) highlighted the area of moral development as an important step on the path to the realisation of human potential. He also indicated that if this aspect of development was ignored, it could cause the development of what he called meta-pathologies, which refer to a lack of values, fulfillment and meaninglessness (Maslow ibid.). Children must have their social and esteem needs met before they can progress on the hierarchy of needs. Spirituality is about finding a purpose and meaning in life and is about discovering how to become fully human. It is about self–discovery, discovery of others and of the world. It is not synonymous with religion nor is it opposed to it. It covers a wide range of human experience and is vital to every child's development and as Mott-Thornton (1996 p.80) says: "An individual can no more flourish in a spiritually dead environment than could a tree in the midst of an ecological disaster". Maslow (1971) also recognised the spiritual needs of man and he highlighted his aesthetic needs - the need for beauty, creativity, humility, awe and mysticism. Spirituality and creativity need to be experienced before children can become self-actualised, in order to fulfil personal potential. Self-actualising children despite pain, sorrow and disappointment can enjoy and appreciate the life given to them and though often not orthodox religious believers, they all tend to believe in a meaningful universe and in a life that could be called spiritual. Only holistic approaches which adopt a position which thinks in terms of the whole child, the whole person, the whole curriculum, the whole school, the whole community and the whole of society are likely to help develop children who are self-actualising. It must be ensured that children become the best they can be through challenging their minds, engaging their hearts, using their hands and honouring each other and the world in all its complex beauty and mystery (Boyd-Cadwell 1997). Is this our aim for children? And if it was would the world be a better place for all of us?

CHAPTER EIGHT

A Vision for the Future

Summary of the book

> The hope lies in the unknown, in that second curve, if we can find it. The world is up for reinvention in so many ways. Creativity is born in chaos. What we do, what we belong to, why we do it, when we do it, where we do it - these may all be different and they could be better. Our societies, however, are built on case law. Change comes from small initiatives which work, initiatives which, imitated, become the fashion. We cannot wait for great visions from great people, for they are in short supply at the end of history. It is up to us to light our own small fires in the darkness (Handy 1994 p.271).

Early years practitioners prioritising emotional, social, moral and spiritual development will not solve all our problems. Governments, policymakers, society in general and, in particular, parents must also begin to reassess children's experience of childhood and the world to which we expose them. We all must aim to improve children's experiences and bring them and indeed adults themselves to the level of self-actualisation in order to make the world a better place for all. However, I am lighting my own fire, as Handy (1994) states above by writing this book in the hope that change will come from this small initiative which, when imitated, will become the fashion and that enhancements will reverberate throughout society - after all the world is up for reinvention.

This book is only the beginning and if, as a result of reading it, one practitioner enhances one child's overall development, then it will have been worth writing.

This book highlights the importance of four areas of child development: emotional; social; moral; and spiritual within the context of the holistic development of the young child. I believe that optimal development in these areas can lead to long-term benefits for the child, for his family and for society at large.

Chapter One explained my reasons for writing this book. It detailed my personal experiences as a child and the state of the world we are living in today, to justify the prioritisation of these areas. It went on to put forward the concept of self-actualisation as a concept for developing the whole child.

Chapter Two examined the evolution of our beliefs regarding the emotional, social, moral and spiritual development of the pre-school aged child within the context of holistic development. This examination detailed progression from the time of Plato to the mid 20th century and it emphasised, in particular, the work of three people - John Amos Comenius (1592-1670), Friedrich Froebel (1782-1852) and Maria Montessori (1870-1952). It focused on their work since a review of the literature showed that these three, in particular, stressed the critical importance of aiming for the total development of the child by prioritising all areas of development, including the four areas being emphasised in this book.

Chapter Three addressed the young child's emotional growth and critically analysed the literature regarding this area over the past fifty years or so. It highlighted the finding that emotional development is one of the most fundamental yet elusive aspects of human life and it also pointed out that the present generation of children appear to be more troubled emotionally than the last. The conclusion of this chapter emphasised the need to help children develop emotionally, as emotional literacy and competence is an inoculation for life, which helps enhance overall development as well as preventing and/or minimising the development of emotional problems and psychopathologies (Goleman 1996).

Chapter Four highlighted the widespread feelings of isolation, loneliness, extreme shyness and anxiety which are the reality for many children today. The breakdown of community life and the increase in computerisation, globalisation and the decrease in the support of the extended family and community were cited as possible reasons for children's lack of sociability (Dowling 2000). The chapter went on to stress the importance of the early years and it cited the case of Genie (Pines 1981) to show the crucial importance of early social integration. In conclusion, the fact that humans are social beings from the very start was highlighted and it was pointed out that social development is vital, since one of the main reasons why children must be developed socially is so that society can continue to exist and persist.

Chapter Five is founded on the assumption that morality is based on the ability of humans to live together co-operatively and civilly and that morality is vital for the organisation of society. A number of different views regarding morality similar to those proposed by Harrington (1996) and Fagan (1997) were put forward. The views considered were: morality as emotion; as concern and responsibility for others; as conformity to rules/authority; as conformity to one's own sense of belief; and as self-development. The chapter concluded that it was not possible to pinpoint exactly how children develop morally, but the contention was put that if children were encouraged to combine the above five models of moral development they would optimise their moral development.

Chapter Six put forward the idea that spirituality has to do with love and with finding a meaning and purpose in life as well as being able to experience wonder and awe (Rodger 1996). The chapter contended that religion is not synonymous with spirituality and it stressed the belief that spiritual development is vital for every child. It concluded that a great deal more research is needed to explore all areas of children's spiritual development and it highlighted the fact that neglect of this area in the past has led to severe negative repercussions for children (Abbs 1994). Practical suggestions on how to enhance the young child's emotional, social, moral and spiritual development are presented at the end of each of the respective chapters – Three, Four, Five and Six.

Chapter Seven portrays a picture of what true holistic child development entails. The underlying principle of this chapter is the belief that we owe it to our children to aim for the self-actualisation of each and every child. The chapter specifies a number of areas that need to be prioritised if we want to do the best for our children. The chapter sets down holistic development under the headings used by Maslow in his hierarchy of needs, as I believe this conceptual framework provides an ideal way of outlining for the reader just what is involved in meeting children's needs. Ensuring that children develop holistically is not easy. As the chapter shows theorists for many centuries have been advocating that we do so but thus far we haven't been able to succeed in doing this for the majority of our children.

Chapter Eight: this the final chapter looks back over the book and invites you, the reader, to look anew at the children in your care and at your role in their development.

So what now?

Education must support children in their progress from dependence to independence and must promote the growth of competence, encouraging enquiry, questioning and challenge. It must also promote the growth of citizenship, ecology and peace. To do this, it must be suited to the needs of the child and it must take full cognisance of the social and emotional dimensions of learning. Also, societies must recognise that young children are members of society, not possessions waiting to become adults. They are active co-constructors of their world, their families, their communities and their culture (David 1997). By promoting children's holistic development through meeting their needs, as espoused by Maslow (1970a) self-actualisation can be aimed for. Education today is tied more and more to economic and productivity needs and unfortunately its value for society, for parents, and for children is not acknowledged. These must take a more central position if we are to develop the rights and potential of all children (Moss and Pence 1994). The development of socially competent, self-reliant members of a community of learners must be one of the primary goals of all early years settings and the multiplicity of children's intelligences must be accepted and developed.

Play is also of paramount importance to the early years setting and must be given the recognition it deserves. Play is a natural phenomenon all over the world and is the foundation of a child's growth and development. It is as essential to a child's life as good care, food, sunshine and protection. It strengthens a child's body, improves his mind and helps develop his personality and, "to neglect or ignore the role of play as an educational medium is to deny the child's natural response to the environment and indeed to life itself" (Abbott 1994 p.76). Play is a cauldron in which, at different times and in different contexts, various proportions of cultural, social, cognitive, linguistic, creative, moral, physical, spiritual and emotional ingredients blend. For young children, play is a way of strengthening meaningful learning and co-operation with others and it touches on all dimensions of development and can impact on the sheer joy of living fully (Seefeldt 1992).

However, for play's value to be realised certain conditions must be fulfilled. There must be sensitive, knowing and informed adults involved; play must be carefully organised, structured and planned; and it must be seen as a high status activity, not just something that is done when the real 'work' is over. Children must be given time to develop their play and careful observation of children's activities must occur. The environment plays an important role in children's play. In order for the environment to act as an educator and facilitator of play, it has to be flexible and must undergo frequent modification by the children and adults so that it can remain up to date and responsive to their needs. By creating a pleasant environment and by promoting choices and activities, the environment provides potential for expanding all kinds of learning and play, all of which contribute to a sense of well-being and security in children (Edwards, Gandini and Forman 1998). Play is part of the infrastructure of any civilisation, and any society which neglects its infrastructure is prone to crumbling. Thus, if children are not given the opportunity to play, the whole infrastructure of society is prone to disintegration (Bruce 1994). Therefore, the value of play must be acknowledged in the development of the whole child.

It must also be acknowledged that there is no magic formula for ensuring that our children grow up to be the kind of balanced, happy, caring individuals that we would wish for them. However, allowing them to develop holistically and aiming towards self-actualisation with a corresponding acknowledgement of the needs of others will go some way towards achieving it. However, cognitive development, consumerism and materialism are closely related and are high on many people's agendas and meeting children's needs as espoused in this book will incur a lot of opposition, especially from those who wish to maintain the status quo.

I certainly do not have all the answers, but I do contend that many changes and improvements need to be made if our children are to develop holistically. Part of this involves adapting learning from different countries. As part of this I recommend that early years education and care everywhere be underscored by aspirations similar to those proposed by *Te Whariki,* the national early childhood curriculum in New Zealand. This aspires to allow children to grow up as competent and confident learners and communicators, healthy in mind, body and spirit, secure in their sense of belonging and in the knowledge that they make a valued contribution to society. This philosophy believes that the principles of learning and development in early childhood should be based on empowerment of the child and on a holistic view of the child, family and community. The curriculum has five principles – well-being, belonging, contributing, communicating and exploration. The pedagogy of the curriculum is flexible to meet children's changing needs and offers opportunities for children to be challenged and to consolidate their accomplishments and learning. It enables children to take increasing responsibility for their own learning and care and develops an enhanced sense of self-worth, identity and enjoyment in the child. The critical importance of consistent, warm relationships that connect everything is acknowledged, as is the fact that children learn through their responsive and reciprocal relationships with people, places and things. *Te Whariki* also acknowledges that the wider world of the family and community is an integral part of the curriculum and it is accepted that the well-being of children is deeply interdependent with the well-being of their community and neighbourhood (Smith 1999; New Zealand Ministry of Education 1996). *Te Whariki*, adapted to meet the needs of individual countries and indeed settings, would contribute greatly to children's lives and to their chances of self-actualisation.

I also suggest learning from the increasingly influential model of community approach to providing care and education for young children which is found in the Italian city of Reggio Emilia. This approach to education was guided by Malagussi who dedicated his life to the establishment of an educational community. According to Gardner (1998) the name Malaguzzi deserves to be uttered in the same breath as Froebel, Montessori, Dewey and Piaget. *Reggio* pre-schools exemplify a community-based facility which is democratic at all levels. In *Reggio* classrooms the child is seen as a collaborator. Education has to focus on each child in relation to other children, family, teachers and the community rather than on each child in isolation. There is an emphasis on small groups and the underlying principle is based on the social constructivist model that supports the idea that we form ourselves through our interaction with peers, adults and things in the world around us. *Reggio* municipal pre-schools are in many ways modelled on the lives of extended families and communities. Extended families are characterised by shared responsibility, intimacy, informality and participation while communities are groups who can do together what they cannot accomplish alone and who have a stake in each other's well-being. Although such models will have their own problems, they will endeavour to sort them out because of the symbiotic relationship that is involved (Boyd-Cadwell 1997; Chen et al. 1998).

The *Reggio* approach provides us with new ways to think about: the nature of the child; the role of the teacher; school organisation and management; the design and use of physical environment; and curriculum planning. The approach incorporates parental involvement and makes possible a system of relationships and a forum for discussion. It thinks about children not just as adjuncts to their families or as adults waiting to be made. Instead as Malaguzzi (1993 p.11) says:

> Our image of children no longer associates them as isolated and egocentric, does not see them only engaged in action with objects, does not emphasize only cognitive aspects, does not belittle feelings or what is not logical and does not consider with ambiguity the role of the affective domain. Instead our image of the child is rich in potential, strong, powerful, competent, and most of all, connected to adults and other children.

Such views accept the need to develop the whole child and acknowledge the value in optimally developing the child emotionally, socially, morally and spiritually. However to think that *Reggio* and *Te Whariki* experiences can just be imported wholesale would be to destroy them, but much of their philosophies can be adapted. Programmes and models from overseas can never be transplanted wholesale from one cultural context to another without extensive change and adaptation. Any possible adaptation must begin with a close look at each country's, and indeed individual setting's own situation. Each setting is not just anywhere but is a very particular place and just as no two children are the same, no two early years settings are exactly the same. Importing foreign models wholesale never works and each society must solve its own problems, but this does not mean that cultural diffusion (the exchange and flow of ideas and products) is so hard and delicate that it cannot be expected to occur successfully (Edwards et al. 1998; Chen et al. 1998). Therefore, to attempt the adaptation of approaches such as *Te Whariki* and *Reggio Emilia* is a daunting but worthwhile task.

Lost opportunities

We are all now aware that it is widely accepted that the early years are vital. Yet the National Research Council in the United States (2000) says the growing consensus regarding the importance of the early years stands in stark contrast to the disparate system of care and education that is provided for children. Douglas and Horgan (1998 p.2) claim that; "if we really care about educational standards, educational continuity and the spiritual and psychological well-being of future generations, early childhood services must be a priority target". Are they? Fawcett (2000) contends that almost every aspect of the care and education of small children is consistently undervalued. I have to agree. The only thing that is valued is preparing the child for later academic achievement. As Keniston (1976 p.56) says:

> We measure the success of schools not by the kinds of human beings they promote but by whatever increases in reading scores they chalk up. We have allowed quantitative standards, so central to adult economic systems, to become the principal yardstick for our definition of children's worth.

Thankfully, there are increasing dissatisfactions with such a view of education, with its over-emphasis on academic learning and on end-products. This emphasis on formalised instruction has created undue stress for young children and is undermining their opportunities for holistic development (Hart, Burts and Charlesworth 1997). The excessive importance attached to the end-product of college and work is denying children the process of experiencing and enjoying childhood. However, the United Nation's Convention on the Rights of the Child (1989) has changed the lens through which governments must regard children. Not only must they protect vulnerable children against a range of specified ills, they must also take a holistic approach to guaranteeing all rights for all children. The implication being that governments are called to lead an explicit ethical attitude to children's development ahead of economic and other priorities. As Carroll (2002) says, governments and policy makers are called to make a distinct commitment to enable all children to find meaning and hope. Are governments fulfilling their ethical obligations? Article 27 of the Convention recognises 'the right of every child to a standard of living adequate for the child's physical, mental, spiritual, moral and social development'. While Article 29 says that state parties agree that the education of the child shall be to enhance the development of the child's personality, talents, mental and physical abilities to their fullest potential. It also says that education should be about the preparation of the child for responsible life in a free society, in the spirit of understanding, peace, tolerance, equality of sexes, and friendship among all peoples (ethnic, national and religious groups and persons of indigenous origin) as well as the development of respect for the natural environment. Do the commitments made thus far in implementing the Convention in countries which have ratified it help children actualise their potential in realising their fundamental rights and in fully developing their human capacities? Fawcett (2000) contends that while the convention has been ratified by many countries, in reality the values which underpin it have yet to be felt in the lives of children, and many societies remain ambivalent about the value and treatment of children. Tension remains between the concept of the ideal childhood and the reality of the lived experience. Yet we can begin to make changes which will improve the reality of the lived experience for the children in our care.

Hope for the future

Education can have many benefits beyond that of increasing material living standards. Therefore, education should be seen as development and development education is not so much 'how' or 'what' to teach but 'why'. It starts from a view of what education is, rather than what it is for, and it recognises that children are affected by the *context* in which learning takes place, the *people* in it and the *values* and *beliefs* embedded in it. Thus, the planning of education must be human in character rather than technical and must be an art rather than a science if it is to promote all aspects of the child. If education is to optimise children's overall development, it must be shaped more by the need to create genuinely human interactions and negotiations of meaning rather than by the demands of an intellectual/cognitive content. We are not sure precisely what knowledge and skills the children of today will need in the future. However, we do know that flexibility, the ability to get on with others, self-esteem, self-confidence and the capacity to see that life has a meaning and purpose are attributes that will be needed, no matter what challenges children may face in the future. Therefore, the young child's experience of education should be full of friendship, belonging and challenge as well as emphasising kindness, collaboration and persistence. When educational establishments, including early years settings, provide these, children will develop an emotional bond to the setting and will be motivated to work hard at learning, will care for others, will reflect on their own behaviour and how it affects others. Schools and early years settings must become communities where all children feel known and valued. It is important to minimise competition and to help children develop the feeling that they are all in things together (Hart et al. 1997). At a time when traditional structures of caring have deteriorated, early years settings must become places where adults and children live together, talk and listen to one another and take delight in each other's company. Moral life must be seen in every thought and action, as morality has to do with getting on with others, with seeing another's point of view and of accepting and welcoming diversity. Also, spiritual development must be a named priority in the curriculum, as well as the curriculum being underscored by a spiritual ethos, if we are to aim for the realisation of the full potential of children.

There is a moral obligation on society to nurture the human potential of its youngest citizens. A society which does this, acknowledges that what happens to young children in the here and now will have repercussions in the future. Hayes (1993 p.33) said: "The best way to invest in the future is to show regard for all children. Children are the future and the future depends on the quality of children's early lives". Education should be concerned with the growth of the individual child. Each child's development is like a fingerprint, the basic form is the same, but the detail is like no one else's. The child will grow to his potential if fortunate enough to be placed in a supportive, nourishing, resource-rich environment. Teaching is not about the perfect presentation or performance; it is about listening, facilitating, interpreting, illuminating, synthesising and highlighting (Aronson 1995). You can support, nurture, facilitate.

You the reader

I bared my soul in the first chapter of this book so that I could clarify for the reader the vital importance of emotional, social, moral and spiritual development. I suffered deprivation in these areas in those vital early years. I survived - many other children who encountered deficiencies in these areas were not so lucky, they didn't survive to tell the tale. You can make sure there are more survivors by assisting in the development of the whole child. You may be the only significant adult in a child's life who can provide him with what he needs – encouragement, affection, a listening ear, a role model. You can make changes so that the children in your care have better life experiences. You can start to enhance their holistic development and this will improve their life chances and their childhood memories. Our children are so, so precious and childhood comes but once in a lifetime. The choice is yours. If only somebody had had the insight to do it for me ....

BIBLIOGRAPHY

Abbott, L. (1994). 'Play is ace! Developing Play in Schools and Classrooms' in J. Moles (Ed.), *The Excellence of Play*. Buckingham: Open University Press.

Abbs, P. (1994). *The Educational Imperative*. London: The Falmer Press.

Adler A. (1924) *The Practice and Theory of Individual Psychology*. Translated by P. Radin London: Kagan Paul.

Adorno, T. (1950). *The Authoritarian Personality*. New York: Harper Brothers.

Ahern, B. (2001). Comment made in a speech by An Taoiseach, Mr. Bertie Ahern, at a seminar on 'Social Capital: Lessons for Public Policy Development', held at Dublin Castle on 29 March 2001 quoted in E. Carroll (2002), *The Well-Being of Children*. Dublin: Ashfield Press. Mr Ahern was specifically reflecting on the National Children's Strategy and the concerns regarding spirituality highlighted in that process.

Ainsworth, M., Blehar, M., Waters, E. and Wall, S. (1978). *Patterns of Attachment*. Hillsdale NJ: Erlbaum.

———— (1989). Attachments Beyond Infancy. *American Psychologist*, 44, 709-16.

Allport, G. (1950). *The Individual and His Religion*. New York: Macmillan.

Almy, M. (1975). *The Early Childhood Educator at Work*. U.S.A.: McGraw Hill.

Alston, W.P. (1971). 'Comments on Kohlberg From is to Ought.' In Mischel T. (Ed.), *Cognitive Development and Epistemology*. NY: Academic Press.

Aries, P. (1962). *Centuries of Childhood*. Milan: Credito Italiano.

Aronson, L. (1995). *Big Spirits, Little Bodies*. Virginia Beach, V.A.: A.R.E. Press.

Axtell, J. (1968). *The Educational Writings of John Locke*. Cambridge: Cambridge University Press.

Azmita, M. (1988). 'Peer interaction and problem solving: when are two heads better than one?' *Child Development*, 59, 87-96.

Baier, K. (1958). *The Moral Point of View*. London: Cornell University Press.

Ball, C. (1994). *Start Right: The Importance of Early Learning*. (Report). London: The Royal Society of Arts.

Balter, L. and Tamis-LeMonda, C. (1999*)*. *Child Psychology: A Handbook of Contemporary Issues*. Philadelphia: Psychology Press.

Bandura, A. (1962). 'Social learning through imitation'. In A. Jones, *Nebraska Symposium on Motivation*. Lincoln: University of Nebraska Press.

———— and Walters, R.H. (1969). *Social Learning and Personality Development*. NY: Holt, Rinehart and Winston.

———— (1977). *Social Learning Theory*. Englewood Cliffs: Prentice Hall.

Barnes, E. in Monroe, W.S. (1971). *Comenius and the Beginnings of Educational Reform*. NY: Arno Press Inc.

Barrett, K.C. and Campos, J.J. (1991). 'A Discritical Function Approach to Emotions and Coping.' In E.M. Cummings, A.L. Greene, K.H. Karraker (Eds.), *Lifespan Developmental Psychology: Perspectives on Stress and Coping* (21-41). Hillsdale NJ: Erlbaum.

Bayle, P. (1695). 'Historical Dictionary.' In J. Sadler (1969) (Ed.), *Comenius* London: The Macmillan Company.

Beck, C. (1991). *Better Schools*. London: The Falmer Press.

Beck, J. (1998). *Morality and Citizenship in Education*. London: Cassell.

Beesley, M. (1993). 'Spiritual education in schools.' *Pastoral Care in Education* 11(3), 22-28.

Belsky, J., Steinberg, L. and Walker, A. (1982). 'The Ecology of Daycare' in E. M. Lamb, (Ed.) *Non-traditional Families: Parenting and Child Development*. Hillsdale NJ: Erlbaum.

———— (1997). 'Patterns of attachment making and parenting: An evolutionary interpretation'. *Human Nature,* 8, 361-381.

Bem, S. (1981). 'Gender schema theory: A cognitive approach to sex-typing.' *Psychological Review,* 88(4), July.

Benson, H. (1975). *The Relaxation Response.* New York: William Morrow.

Berger, E. (1996). 'K-12 Character education in Locust Valley.' *The Fourth and Fifth Rs: Respect and Responsibility* 2(2), 1-4.

Berndt, T.J. (1989). 'Obtaining Support from Friends during Childhood and Adolescence.' In D. Belle, (Ed.) *Children's Social Networks and Social Support.* New York: Wiley.

———— and Ladd, G. (1989). *Peer Relationships in Child Development.* NY: Wiley and Sons.

Best, J. (1989). *Cognitive Psychology* (2ⁿᵈ Edition) St. Paul West Publishing Company.

Best, R. (1983). *We've All got Scars: What Boys and Girls Learn in Elementary School.* Bloomington IN: Indiana University Press.

———— (Ed.) (1996). *Education, Spirituality and the Whole Child.* London: Cassell.

Blenkin, G. and Kelly, A.V. (Eds.) (1992). *Assessment in Early Childhood Education.* London: Paul Chapman.

————, Edwards, G. and Kelly, A.V. (1992). *Change and the Curriculum.* London: Paul Chapman.

———— and Kelly, A.V. (1996). *Early Childhood Education: A Developmental Curriculum.* London: Paul Chapman.

Bloom, B. (1981). *All Our Children Learning.* New York: McGraw-Hill.

———— (Ed.) (1956). *Taxonomy of Educational Objectives. 1: Cognitive Domain.* London: Longman.

Blum, L. (1987). 'Particularity and Responsiveness.' In J. Kagan (Ed.), *The Emergence of Morality in Young Children.* Chicago: University of Chicago Press.

Bocchino, R. (1999). *Emotional Literacy: To be a Different Kind of Smart.* London: Sage.

Boldt, S., Devine, B., MacDevitt, D. and Morgan, M. (1998). *Educational Disadvantage and Early School-Leaving.* Dublin: Combat Poverty Agency.

Bornstein, M. and Lamb, M. (Eds.) (1988). *Social, Emotional and Personality Development.* East Sussex: Erlbaum.

Borysenko, J. (1987). *Minding the Body, Mending the Mind.* New York: Bantam.

Bowen, J. (1974). *Theories of Education.* Second edition. Milton: Jacaranda Wiley Ltd.

Bower, G. (1981). Mood and Memory. *American Psychologist,* 36, 129-148.

Bowlby, J. (1953). *Child Care and the Growth of Love.* Harmondsworth: Penguin.

————— (1969). *Attachment and Loss Vol. 1 Attachment.* London: Hogarth Press.

————— (1988). *A Secure Base: Clinical Applications of Attachment Theory.* London: Routledge.

Boyd, W. (1914). *From Locke to Montessori.* London: George G. Harrap and Co.

————— (1921). *The History of Western Education.* NY: The Macmillan Co.

Boyd-Cadwell, L. (1997). *Bringing 'Reggio Emilia' Home.* New York: Teachers College.

Boydston, J. (1977) (Ed.). *1967-1991 The Collected Works of John Dewey.* South Ill: University Press.

Bradburn, E. (1989). *Margaret McMillan Portrait of a Pioneer.* London: Routledge.

Bradford, J. (1978). *The Spiritual Rights of the Child.* London: Church of England Children's Society.

————— (1984). 'Spiritual Rights.' In J.M. Sutcliffe (Ed.) *A Dictionary of Religious Education.* London: SCM Press.

———— (1994). 'The Spiritual Needs and Potential of the Child and Young Person: A Rationale and Discussion'. Paper given at International Colloquium on *Spiritual and Moral Development: From Theory to Practice*. Cambridge: Homerton College.

Bradley, R.H., Whiteside, L., Mundfrom, D.J. and Casey, P.H. (1994) 'Early indicators of resilience and their relation to experiences in the home environments of low birthweight premature children living in poverty' *Child Development* 65 346-360.

Branscombe, N., Castle, K., Dorsey, A., Surbeck, E. and Taylor J. (2000). *Early Childhood Education a Constructivist Perspective* New York: Library of Congress Catalog.

Brazelton, T. (1992). Preface to *Heart Start: The Emotional Foundations of School Readiness*. Arlington VA: National Center for Clinical Infant Programs.

Bredekamp, S. (Ed.) (1987). *Developmentally Appropriate Practice in Early Childhood Programs Serving Children from Birth through Age Eight*. Washington D.C.: NAEYC.

———— and Rosegrant, T. (Eds.) (1992). *Reaching Potentials: Appropriate Curriculum and Assessment for Young Children*, Vol, 1. Washington DC: NAEYC.

———— (1993). Reflections on *Reggio Emilia*. *Young Children,* 49(1), 13-17.

Breen, R. (1990). In J. Mulholland and D. Keogh (Eds.), *Education in Ireland: For What and For Whom*. Dublin: Hibernian Press.

Briggs, D.C. (1975). *Your Child's Self-esteem: The Key to Life*. New York: Doubleday

Brody, R. and Hall, J. (1993). 'Gender and Emotion.' In M. Lewis and J. Haviland (Eds.), *Handbook of Emotions*. New York: Guilford Press.

Bronfenbrenner, U. (1979). *The Ecology of Human Development*. Cambridge MA: Harvard University Press.

Brosterman, N. (1997). *Inventing Kindergarten.* NY: Harry N Abrams.

Brown, B. (1998). *Unlearning Discrimination in the Early Years* Stoke on Trent Trentham Books.

294

Brown, G. and Desforges, C. (1979). *Piaget's Theory: A Psychological Critique.* London: Routledge and Kegan Paul.

Brown, R.W. (1965). *Social Psychology.* London: The Free Press.

Brubacher, J.S. (1962/1969). *Modern Philosophies of Education.* Second edition. NY: McGraw Hill Inc.

Bruce, T. (1994). 'Play, the Universe and Everything!' In J. Moyles *The Excellence of Play.* Buckingham: Open University Press.

————, Findlay, A., Read, J. and Scarborough, M. (1995). *Recurring Themes in Education.* London: Paul Chapman.

———— and Meggitt, C. (1999). *Child Care and Education.* Second Edition. London: Hodder and Stoughton.

Bryant, D. and Clifford, R. (1992). '150 years of kindergarten: How far have we come?' *Early Childhood Research Quarterly*, 147-154.

Bukatto, D. and Daehler, M. (1995). *Child Development: A Thematic Approach.* Second edition. Boston: Houghton Mifflin.

Bukowski, W.M., Hoza, B. and Boivin, M. (1993). 'Popularity, Friendship and Emotional Adjustment during Early Adolescence.' In B. Laursen (Ed.) *New Directions for Child Development: Close Friendships in Adolescence.* San Francisco: Jossey Bass.

————, Newcomb, A. and Hartup, W. (1996). *The Company They Keep: Children's Friendships.* Cambridge Press: Syndicate of the University of Cambridge.

Burgess, T.P. (1993). *A Crisis of Conscience.* Hants: Avebury.

Bush, J. and Phillips, D. (1996). 'International Approaches to Defining Quality.' In S. Kagan S. and N. Cohen (Eds.) *Reinventing Early Care and Education: A Vision for a Quality System.* San Francisco: Jossey-Bass.

Butler, N. (1892). Foreword to *John Amos Comenius in Education.* U.S.: Teachers College

Cadwell, L. and Fyfe, B. (1997). 'Conversations with Children.' In J. Hendrick (Ed.), *First Steps Towards Teaching the 'Reggio' Way.* Upper Saddle River NJ: Prentice-Hall.

Campbell, J. (1995). *Understanding John Dewey: Nature and Co-operative Intelligence.* Chicago: La Salle.

Campos, J.J. (1986). 'Contemporary Issues in the Study of Infant Emotion.' In M. Bornstein and M. Lamb (Eds.) (1988), *Social, Emotional and Personality Development.* East Sussex: Erlbaum.

———, Campos, R. and Barrett, K. (1989). 'Emergent themes in the study of emotional development and emotion regulation'. *Developmental Psychology*, 25, 394-402.

———, Mumme, P., Kermoian, R. and Campos, R. (1994). 'A Functionalist Perspective on the Nature of Emotion.' In N. Fox (Ed.), *The Development of Emotion Regulation: Biological and Behavioural Considerations.* Monographs of the Society for Research.

Cantillon, S., Corrigan, C., Kirby, P. and O'Flynn, J. (2001). *Rich and Poor.* Dublin: Oak Tree Press.

Carr, D. (1995). 'Towards a distinctive conception of spiritual education'. *Oxford Review of Education*, 21(1), 83-98.

Carrington, P. (1978). *Freedom in Meditation.* New York: Anchor.

Carroll, E. (2002). *The Well-Being of Children.* Dublin: Ashfield Press.

Charney, R. (1998). *Teaching Children to Care.* M.A.: Northeast Foundation for Children.

Chazan, B.(1985). *Contemporary Approaches to Moral Education: Analyzing Alternative Theories.* NY: Teachers College.

Chen, J., Krechevsky, M., Viens, J., Isberg, E., Gardner, H. and Feldman, D. (1998). *Building on Children's Strengths: The Experience of Project Spectrum.* New York: Teachers College.

Chipman, M. (1997). 'Valuing Cultural Diversity in the Early Years: Social Imperatives and Pedagogical Insights.' In J. Isenberg and M. Jalongo (Eds.), *Major Trends and Issues in Early Childhood Education.* New York: Teachers College.

Cicchetti, D. and Hesse, P. (1983). 'Affect and Intellect: Piaget's Contributions to the Study of Infant Emotional Development.' In R. Plutchik and H. Kellerman (Eds.), *Emotion: Theory, Research and Experience, Vol.2, Emotion in Early Development.* New York: Academic Press.

Colby, A., Kohlberg, L., Gibbs, J. and Lieberman, M. (1983). 'A longitudinal study of moral judgement', *Monographs of the Society for Research in Child Development* 48(1-2).

Cole, M. and Cole, S. (1989). *The Development of Children*. Oxford: Library of Congress Cataloguing.

Coles, R. (1990). *The Spiritual Life of Children*. London: Harper Collins.

————— (1997). *The Moral Intelligence of Children*. London: Bloomsbury Publishing.

Commission on the Family (1998). *Strengthening Families for Life*. Dublin: Government Publications.

Connolly, A. (1999). In C. Lally 'Irish Toddlers are Suicidal' *Sunday Tribune Newspaper*, June 27th. Dublin.

Coolahan, J. (Ed.) (1998). *Report on the National Forum for Early Childhood Education*. Dublin: The Stationery Office.

Corsaro, W. (1985). *Friendship and The Peer Culture in the Early Years*. Norwood NJ: Ablex Publication Corporation.

Cowan, P.A. (1978). *Piaget with Feeling: Cognitive, Social and Emotional Dimensions*. NY: Holt, Rinehart and Winston.

Cowen, E., Pederson, A., Babigian, H., Izzo, L. and Trost, M. (1973). 'Long-term follow-up of early detected vulnerable children'. *Journal of Consulting and Clinical Psychology*, 41, 438-46.

Crandell, R. (1973). 'The Measurement of Self-esteem and Related Concepts.' In J.P. Robinson and P.R. Shave (Eds.), *Measures of Social Psychological Attitudes*. Ann Arbor Institute for Social Research.

Crossen, S. (1996). *Emerging Morality: How Children Think about Right and Wrong*. http://www.earlychildhoodnews.com/emerging.htm

Cuffano, A. (1995). *Experimenting with the World: John Dewey and the Early Childhood Classroom*. N.Y.: Teachers College.

Cunneen, M.C. (2001). *A Study of Patterns of Gender Socialisation in Early Years Education and Care in Cork City*. Unpublished Ph.D. Thesis Cork: University College Cork.

Currie, B. (2002). *Yoga for Kids, Colin the Cobra's Forest of Secrets* (video) London: Banana Split Production.

Curtis, A. (1986). *A Curriculum for the Pre-school Child* London: NFER-Nelson Publishing.

Curtis, S. and Boultwood, M. (1956/58/70). *A Short History of Educational Ideas.* Cambridge University Tutorial Press: 5th edition 1970.

———— and Boultwood, M. (1966). *An Introductory History of English Education Since 1800.* London: Tutorial Press.

Daly, M. (2002). *The Emotional, Social, Moral and Spiritual Development of the Young Child – Aiming towards Self-Actualisation* Unpublished Ph.D. Thesis Cork: University College Cork.

Dahlberg, G., Moss, P. and Pence, A. (1999). *Beyond Quality in Early Childhood Education and Care: Postmodern Perspectives.* London: Talmer Press.

Damico, A. (1978). *Individuality and Community: The Social and Political Thoughts of John Dewey.* Florida: University Presses of Florida.

Damon, W. (1977). *The Social World of the Child.* San Francisco: Jossey-Bass.

———— (1983). *Social and Personality Development: Infancy through Adolescence.* NY: WW Norton.

———— and Hart, D. (1988). *Self-understanding in Childhood and Adolescence.* NY: Cambridge University Press.

Darwin, C. (1859/1968). *The Origin of the Species.* Harmondsworth Penguin Books.

David, T. (Ed.) (1993). *Educating Our Youngest Children: European Perspectives.* London: Paul Chapman.

———— (1997). *Under 5 - Under Educated?* Buckingham: Open University Press.

———— (1999). 'Early Childhood Education and Care: International Perspectives and Issues.' In *Enhancing Quality in the Early Years: Proceedings of the International Conference on Practice and Policy in Early Childhood Care and Education.* Dublin: Centre for Social and Educational Research (C.S.E.R.).

298

Deacon, T. (1997). *The Symbolic Species.* London: Penguin Press.

Deardon, R.F., Hirst, P.H. and Peters, R.S. (1975). *Education and the Development of Reason.* London: Routledge and Kegan Paul.

Denham, S. (1986). 'Social cognition, social behaviour and emotion in pre-schoolers: contextual validation'. *Child Development*, 57, 194-201.

———— (1998). *Emotional Development in Young Children.* New York: The Guilford Press.

Department of Health (2002) in Britain.
www.wiredforhealth.gov.uk/teaching/ment/fact.html

Derman-Sparks, L. (1989). *The ABC Taskforce Anti-bias Curriculum.* Washington D.C.: National Association for the Education of Young Children.

———— (1998). Foreword in B. Brown *Unlearning Discrimination in the Early Years.* Stoke on Trent: Trentham Books.

Deroche, E. and Williams, M.M.(1998). *Educating Hearts and Minds.* London: Sage.

Dewey, J. (1897). 'My pedagogic creed'. *The School Journal*, LIV(3), Jan. 16, 77-80.

———— (1900). *The School and Society and the Child and the Curriculum.* Expanded edition. Chicago: The University of Chicago Press.

———— (1916). *Democracy and Education.* NY: Macmillan.

———— (1920/1985). *Reconstruction in Philosophy.* NY: Macmillan.

———— (1929/30). *The Quest for Certainty.* London: Allen and Unwin.

———— (1933). *How We Think.* Boston: Heath (First published in 1909).

———— and Watson, G. (1977). 'The Forward View: A Free Teacher in a Free Society.' In W. Kilpatrick (Ed.), *The Teacher and Society.* NY: Appelton-Century.

Dodge, K.A. (1990). 'Nature versus nurture in childhood conduct disorder. It is time to ask a difficult question?' *Developmental Psychology* 26(5), 698-701.

Doe, M. and Walch, M. (1998). *Principles for Spiritual Parenting*. New York: Harper Collins.

Donaldson, M. (1971/1978). *Children's Minds*. London: Fontana.

———— (1989). *Sense and Sensibility*. London: University of Reading.

Donnelly, P. (2001). *Someone to Talk to: A handbook on Childhood Bereavement* Dublin: Barnardos National Children's Resource Centre.

Douglas, F. (1993). *A Study of Pre-school Education in the Republic of Ireland with Particular Reference to those Pre-schools which are Listed by the Irish Pre-school Playgroups Association in Cork City and County*. Ph. D. Thesis Hull, University of Hull.

———— and Horgan, M. (1998). *The Light Beneath the Bushel: A Discussion Paper on Early Years Education*. Cork: University College Cork.

————, Horgan, M. O'Brien, C. (2000). *Project E.Y.E. (Early Years Education) An Irish Curriculum for the Three to Four Year Old Child, Educator's Handbook*, Cork: The Early Years Unit, University College Cork.

————, Horgan, M. O'Brien, C. (2000). *Project E.Y.E. (Early Years Education) An Irish Curriculum for the Three to Four Year Old Child, Volume One: Spiritual, Emotional and Moral Development*, Cork: The Early Years Unit, University College Cork.

————, Horgan, M. O'Brien, C. (2000). *Project E.Y.E. (Early Years Education) An Irish Curriculum for the Three to Four Year Old Child, Volume Four: Creative Development,* Cork: The Early Years Unit, University College Cork.

————, Horgan, M. O'Brien, C. (2000). *Project E.Y.E. (Early Years Education) An Irish Curriculum for the Three to Four Year Old Child, Volume Six: Social Development,* Cork: The Early Years Unit, University College Cork.

————, Horgan, M. O'Brien, C. (2000). *Project E.Y.E. (Early Years Education) An Irish Curriculum for the Three to Four Year Old Child Volume Seven: Cultural Development*, Cork: The Early Years Unit, University College Cork.

————, Horgan, M. O'Brien, C. (2000). *Project E.Y.E. (Early Years Education) An Irish Curriculum for the Three to Four Year Old Child, Volume Eight: Environmental Awareness and Development Education*, Cork: The Early Years Unit, University College Cork.

———— (2002). 'The Moving Spirit: Spirituality and Young Children'. In F. Douglas and M. Horgan, *Lessons for the 21ˢᵗ Century – Research, Reflection, Renewal*: Conference Proceedings, Dublin Institute of Technology, Aungier Street, Dublin, Ireland OMEP

Dowling, M. (2000). *Young Children's Personal, Social and Emotional Development*. London: Paul Chapman.

Downey, M. and Kelly, A.V. (1978). *Moral Education Theory and Practice*. London: Harper and Roe.

Dunn, J., Bretherton, I. and Munn, P. (1987). 'Conversations about feeling states between mothers and their young children.' *Developmental Psychology*, 23, 132-139.

———— (1988). *The Beginnings of Social Understanding*. Oxford: Blackwell.

———— and Brown J. (1991) 'Relationships, Talk About Feelings, and the Development of Affect Regulation in Early Childhood' In J. Garber and K. Dodge (Eds.) *The Development of Emotion Regulation and Dysregulation*, Cambridge: Cambridge University Press

Dupuis, A. (1966). *Philosophy of Education in Historical Perspective*. US: Library of Congress Cataloguing.

Durkheim, E. (1933). *The Division of Labour in Society*. NY: Macmillan.

———— (1953). *The Determination of Moral Facts in Sociology and Philosophy*. Glencoe, Illinois. Free Press.

———— (1956). *Education and Sociology*. Second Edition. Translated by S. Fox, NY: Free Press.

———— (1961). *Moral Education*. NY: Macmillan.

Duska, R. and Whelan, M. (1975). *Moral Development: A Guide to Piaget and Kohlberg*. NY: Library of Congress Cataloguing.

Dweck, C.S. and Leggett, E. (1988). 'A socio-cognitive approach to motivation and achievement'. *Psychological Review*, 95(2), 256-73.

Dworetzky, J. (1994). *Psychology*. MN West Publishing.

Dyer, W.W. (1998). *What Do You Really Want for your Children?* London: Arrow Books.

Edgeworth, M. and Edgeworth, R.T. (1798). *Practical Education*. London: Johnson.

Edwards, C., Gandini, L. and Forman, G. (1998). *The 100 Languages of Children*. C.T.: Ablex Publication Corporation.

Ehrle, J. and Moore, K. (1999). '1997 NSAF Benchmarking Measures of Child and Family Well-being.' In *Report No. 6*. Washington D.C.: Urban Institute.

Einstein, A. in Knight, M. (compiler) (1961). *Humanist Anthology*. London: Pemberton.

Eisenberg, N. and Hand, M. (1979). 'The relationship of pre-schoolers' reasoning about prosocial moral conflicts to prosocial behaviour'. *Child Development*, 50, 228-229.

————— and Neal, C. (1979). 'Children's moral reasoning about their own spontaneous prosocial behaviour'. *Developmental Psychology* 15, 228-229.

————— (Ed.) (1982). *The Development of Prosocial Behaviour*. NY: Academic Press.

————— (1986). *Altruism, Emotion, Cognition and Behaviour*. Hillsdale NJ: Erlbaum.

————— and Strayer, J. (Eds.) (1987). 'History of the Concept of Empathy.' In *Empathy and its Development*. NY: Cambridge University Press.

————— and Fabes, R.A. (1992). 'Emotion, Regulation and the Development of Social Competence.' In M.S. Clark (Ed.) *Review of Personality and Social Psychology, Vol.14, Emotion and Social Behaviour*, 119-150. Newbury Park CA: Sage.

Ekman, P. (1973). *Darwin and Facial Expression: A Century of Research in Review*. New York: Academic Press.

302

———— (1992). 'An argument for basic emotions.' *Cognition and Emotion*, 6, 169-200.

Elkind, D. (1971). 'The Development of Religious Understanding in Children and Adolescents.' In M.P. Stommen (Ed.), *Research on Religious Development*. New York: Hawthorn.

———— (1986). 'Formal education and early childhood education: an essential difference'. *Phi Delta Kappa* 67, 631-636.

———— (1992). *Miseducation: Pre-schoolers at Risk.* New York: Alfred A. Knopf.

———— (2001). *The Hurried Child: Growing Up Too Fast Too Soon.* Third Edition/Revised Third Edition. Cambridge: Perseus Publishing.

Eliot, A. (1994). *The Global Myths: Exploring Primitives, Pagan, Sacred, and Scientific Mythologies*. NY: Truman Tally.

Eliot, L. (1999). *What's Going on in there? How the Brain and Mind Develop in the First Five Years of Life*. London: The Penguin Group.

Elvin, S. (1965). *Education and Contemporary Society*. London/CA: Watts.

Epstein, D. (1995). 'Girls Don't do Bricks: Gender and Sexuality in the Primary Classroom.' In J. and I. Siraj-Blatchford, *Educating the Whole Child*. Buckingham: Open University Press.

Erikson, E. (1963). *Childhood and Society*. London: Imago.

Esser, G. (1990). 'Epidemiology and the course of psychiatric disorders in school-aged children: Results of a longitudinal study'. *Journal of Child Psychology and Psychiatry*, 31, 243-263.

Estes, D., Wellman, H.M. and Wooley, J.D. (1989). 'Children's Understanding of Mental Phenomenon'. In H.W. Reese (Ed.), *Advances in Child Development and Behaviour* San Diego CA: Academic Press.

Evans, D. (1979). *Struggle and Fulfillment*. London: Collins.

———— (1993). *Spirituality and Human Nature*. New York: SUNY.

Eysenck, H.J. (Ed.) (1964). *Experiments in Behaviour Therapy*. Oxford: Pergamon.

Fabes, R.A., Eisenberg, N., Nyman, M. and Michealieu, Q. (1991). 'Young children's appraisal of others' spontaneous emotional reactions.' *Developmental Psychology*, 27, 858-866.

Fagan, S. (1997). *Does Morality Change?* Dublin: Gill and Macmillan.

———— (1988). *Has Sin Changed? A Book of Forgiveness.* Dublin: Gill and Macmillan.

Farrer, A. (1958). *The Glass of Vision.* London: Dacre.

Farrer, F. (2000). *A Quiet Revolution: Encouraging Positive Values in our Children*, London: Random House.

Farrington, D. (1990). 'Childhood Aggression and Adult Violence: Early Precursors and Later Life Outcomes.' In D.J. Pepler and K.H. Rubin (Eds.) *The Development of Childhood Aggression*, Hillsdale NJ: Erlbaum.

Fawcett, M. (2000). 'Historical Views of Childhood' in *Focus on Early Childhood Principles and Realities* edited by M. Boushel, M. Fawcett and J. Selwyn. London: Blackwell Science.

Fein, G. and Rivkin, N. (Eds.) (1986). *The Young Child at Play: Review of Research, Vol. 4.* Washington D.C.: National Association for the Education of Young Children.

Field, R. (1996). *John Dewey [1859-1952].* The Internet Encyclopedia of Philosophy www.utm.edu/research/iep/d/dewey.htm.

Field, T. (1984). 'Separation stress of young children transferring to new school' *Developmental Psychology* 502-508.

Finkelstein, N. and Haskins, R. (1983). 'Kindergarten children prefer same colour peers.' *Child Development*, 54(2), 502-508.

Flavell, J. (1985). *Cognitive Development.* Second edition. Englewood Cliffs NJ: Prentice-Hall.

Fletcher, J. (1966). *Situation Ethics.* London: SCM Press.

Fogel, A. (1980). 'The Role of Emotion in Early Childhood Education.' In *Current Topics in Early Childhood Education*, Vol. III. N.Y.: Ablex Publication Corporation.

Fontana, D. (1984). *The Education of the Young Child*. Oxford: Blackwell.

───── (1995). *Psychology for Teachers*. London: Macmillan Press.

Fowler, J. (1981). *Stages of Faith*. New York: Harper Collins.

─────, Nipkow, K.E. and Schweitzer, F. (1991). *States of Faith and Religious Development: Implications for Church, Education and Society*. New York: Crossroad.

Frankl, V. (1985). *Man's Search for Meaning*. London: Pocket Books.

French, G. (2003). *Supporting Quality: Guidelines for Best Practice in Early Childhood Services*. 2nd Edition Dublin: Barnardos National Children's Resource Centre

Freud, S. (1914). *On Narcissism*. Standard Edition, Vol. XIV, London: Hogarth Press.

───── (1933). *New Introductory Lectures on Psychoanalysis*. Standard Edition Vol, XXII. London: Hogarth Press.

───── (1974). 'The Future of an Illusion'. In *The Collected Works of Sigmund Freud*. London: Hogarth (first published 1928).

Froebel, F. (1899). *Education by Development*. Translated by J. Jarvis. London: Edward Arnold and Co.

───── (1886/1908). *Autobiography of Friedrich Froebel*. Translated by E. Michaelis. London: Moore HK.

───── (1887/1907). *The Education of Man*. Translated by W. Hailmann. NY: Appelton and Co.

───── (1851/1906). *Pedagogics of the Kindergarten*. Translated by J. Jarvis. London: Sidney Appleton.

───── (1912). *Froebel's Chief Writings on Education*. Translated by S. Fletcher and J. Welton. London: Edward Arnold and Co.

Fromberg, D. (1992). 'A Review of Research on Play'. In C. Seefeldt (Ed.), *The Early Childhood Curriculum: A Review of Current Research*. Second edition. New York: Teachers College.

————— (1997). 'The Professional and Social Status of the Early Childhood Educator.' In J. Isenberg and M. Jalongo *Major Trends and Issues in Early Childhood Education*. New York: Teachers College.

Frye, D. and Moore, C. (1993). *Children's Theories of Mind: Mental States and Social Understanding*. Hillsdale NJ: Erlbaum.

Furman, W. and Robbins, P. (1985). 'What's the Point? Issues in the Selection of Treatment Objectives.' In B. Schneider, K. Rubin, and J. Leddingham (Eds.) *Children's Relations: Issues in Assessment and Intervention*. NY: Springer-Verlas.

Gallagher, M.P. (1998). *Will Our Children Believe?* Dublin: Veritas.

Gardner, D. (1969). *Susan Isaacs*. London: Methuen.

Gardner, H. (1983). *Frames of Mind: The Theory of Multiple Intelligences*. New York: Basic Books.

————— (1993). *Multiple Intelligences: The Theory in Practice*. New York: Basic Books.

————— (1998) In, Chen, J. Krechevsky, M. Viens, J., Isberg, E. Gardner, H. Feldman, D. *Building on Children's Strengths: The Experience of Project Spectrum*. New York: Teachers College.

Gardner, J.K. and Gardner, H. (1975). *Studies of Play: An Original Anthology*. New Jersey: Ayer.

Garmezy, N. (1987). *The Invulnerable Child*. New York: Guilford Press.

Garralda, M.E. and Bailey, D. (1986). 'Children with psychiatric disorders in primary care'. *Journal of Child Psychology and Psychiatry and Allied Disciplines* 27 611-624

Gert, B. (1998). *Morality: Its Nature and Justification*. Oxford: Oxford University Press.

Gettman, D. (1987). *Basic Montessori Learning Activities for Under Fives*. Oxford: ABCClio Ltd.

Gilligan, C. (1982). *In A Different Voice*. Cambridge MA: Harvard University Press.

Gilmartin, R. (1996). *Pursuing Wellness: Finding Spirituality*. CT: Twenty Third Publications.

Gnepp, J. (1989). 'Children's Use of Personal Information to Understand Other People's Feelings.' In C. Saarni and P. Harris (Eds.), *Children's Understanding of Emotion*. Cambridge: Press Syndicate of the University of Cambridge.

Goffin, S.C. (1994). *Curriculum Models and Early Childhood Education: Appraising the Relationship*. New York: Merrill and Macmillan.

Goldman, R. (1964). *Religious Thinking from Childhood to Adolescence*. London: Routledge and Kegan Paul.

————— (1965). *Readiness for Religion*. London: Routledge and Kegan Paul.

Goldsmith, H. (1993). 'Genetic influences on personality from infancy.' *Child Development,* 54(2), 331-335.

Goleman, D. (1996). *Emotional Intelligence*. London: Bloomsbury.

————— (1998). *Working with Emotional Intelligence*. London: Bloomsbury.

Goodlad, J. (1984). *What Schools Are For.* Bloomington: Phi Delta Kappa Education Foundation.

Grant, G. (1981). 'The character of education and the education of character.' *Daedalus* 110, 146-150.

Greenberg, P. (1990). 'Why not academic pre-school?' *Young Children* 45(2), 70-80.

Greenfield, P.M. (1984). *Mind and Media: The Effects of Television, Video, Games and Computers*. Cambridge MA: Harvard University Press.

Greenman, J. (1988). *Caring Spaces, Learning Spaces: Children's Environments That Work.* Redmond WA: Exchange Press.

Greenspan, S.I. and Greenspan, N.T. (1985). *First Feelings: Milestones in the Emotional Development of your Baby and Child*. NY: Viking.

Greenspan, S. (1997). In M. Nash, 'Fertile Minds', *Time Magazine* February 10th.

Griffin, E. (1982). *Island of Childhood: Education in the Special World of the Nursery School.* New York: Teachers College.

Griffith, F. (1985). 'Meditation Research: Its Personal and Social Implications.' In J. White (Ed.), *Frontiers of Consciousness.* New York: Julian Press.

Grosskurth, P. (1991). *The Secret Ring: Freud's Inner Circle and the Politics of Psychoanalysis.* Reading MA: Addison-Wesley

Grusec, J. and Mills, R. in J.Worrell (Ed.) (1982). *Psychological Development in the Elementary Years.* NY: Academic Press.

Gunnar M. (1998) 'Quality of care and the buffering of stress physiology: Its potential role in protecting the developing human brain'. *IMPrint*, 21, 4-7

Gunter, B. and McAleer, J. (1997) *Children and Television.* London: Routledge.

Gura, P. (1996). 'What I want for Cinderella: Self-esteem and self-assessment.' *Early Education*, 19, Summer.

Hall, M.A. (1968). 'A conversation with Abraham Maslow.' *Psychology Today* 2(2), 34-37/54-57.

Halstead, J.M. (1994) (Ed.). *Parental Choice and Education: Principles, Policy and Practice.* London: Kogan Page.

Hammés, J.A. (1998). 'Relativism: today's spiritual cancer.' *Position Papers*, 294/295, June/July, 209-212.

Handy, C. (1994). *The Empty Raincoat: Making Sense of the Future.* Berks: Arrow Books.

Hannan, P. (1995). *The Quiet Revolution.* Dublin: The Columbia Press.

Hardy, A. (1979). *The Spiritual Nature of Man.* Oxford: Oxford University Press.

Harlow, H. and Harlow, M. (1962). 'Social deprivation in monkeys.' *Scientific American*, (207), 137-146, November.

Harrington, D. (1996). *What is Morality? The Light Through Different Windows.* London: The Columbia Press.

Hart, C., Burts, D. and Charlesworth, R. (1997). *Integrated Curriculum and Developmentally Appropriate Practice*. Alba NY: State University of NY Press.

————, Burts, D., Darland, M.A., Charlesworth, R., Dewolf, M. and Fleeje, P. (1998). 'Stress behaviours in more and less developmentally appropriate classrooms.' *Journal of Research in Childhood Education*, 12(2), 177-196.

Hartley-Brewer, E. (1998). *Positive Parenting: Raising Children with Self-Esteem*. London: Ebury Press.

Hartup, W. and Moore, S. (1990) 'Early peer relations: developmental significance and prognostic implications'. *Early Childhood Research Quarterly* 5(1): 1-17.

Hartup, W. (1992). 'Friendships and their Developmental Significance.' In, H. McGurk (Ed.), *Child Social Development*. Hove, England: Erlbaum.

———— and Van Lieshout, C. (1995). 'Personality development in social context.' *Annual Review of Psychology*, 46, 655-687.

Haydon, G. (1997). *Teaching About Values: A New Approach*. London: Cassell.

Hayes, N. (1993). *Early Childhood: An Introductory Text*. Dublin: Gill and Macmillan.

————, O'Flaherty, J. with Kernan, M. (1997). *A Window on Early Education in Ireland*. Dublin: Dublin Institute of Technology.

Haynes, J. (2002). *Children as Philosophers Learning Through Enquiry and Dialogue in the Primary Classroom*. London: Routledge Falmer

Hawkes, N. (2000). 'Introduction' in F. Farrer *A Quiet Revolution*. London: Random House

Hazareesingh, S., Simms, K. and Anderson, P. (1989). *Educating the Whole Child*. Building Blocks/Save the Children, London.

Heaslip, P. (1994). 'Making Play Work in the Classroom.' In J. Moyles (Ed.), *The Excellence of Play*. Buckingham: Open University Press.

Helwig, C. (1997). *Making Moral Cognition Respectable (Again): A Retrospective Review of Lawrence Kohlberg.* http://www.apa.org/journals/cnt/mar97/Kohlberg.html

Hemming, J. (1970). *Individual Morality.* London: Panther.

Henderson, R. (1983) in J. Worrell (Ed.). *Psychological Development in the Elementary Years.* NY: Academic Press.

Hendricks, G. and Wills, R. (1975). *The Centring Book.* New York: Prentice Hall.

Hersh, R. and Paolitto, D. (1978). 'Moral Development: Implications for Pedagogy in Readings', in P. Scharf (Ed.) *Readings in Moral Education,* Minneapolis: Winston Press.

Hinman, L. (1985). 'Emotion, Morality and Understanding.' In C. Harding (Ed.) *Moral Dilemmas.* Chicago: Precedent Publishing.

Hislam, J. (1994). 'Sex-differentiated Play Experiences and Children's Choices.' In J. Moyles (Ed.), *The Excellence of Play.* Buckingham: Open University Press.

Hochschild, A.R. (1979). 'Emotion work, feeling rules and social structure.' *American Journal of Sociology,* 85, 551-575.

Hoffman, M. (1970). 'Moral Dilemmas.' In P.H Mussen (Ed.), *Manual of Child Psychology.* NY: Wiley.

————— (1984). 'Empathy, its Limitations and its Role in Comprehensive Moral Theory.' In W. Kurtines and J.L. (Eds.) Gewirtz, *Morality, Moral Behaviour and Moral Development.* NY: John Wiley.

————— (1987). 'The Contribution of Empathy to Justice and Moral Judgement.' In N. Eisenberg and Strayer J. (Eds.), *Empathy and its Development.* NY: Cambridge University Press.

————— (1988) cited in M. Bornstein and M.Lamb, *Developmental Psychology* Hove East Sussex: Erlbaum.

Hoff-Sommers, C. (1985). In L. Solaonzano. 'Rights, wrongs, now schools teach them'. US News and World Report May 13 1985, 51.

Hogan, R. (1973). 'Moral conduct and moral character: A psychological perspective.' *Psychological Bulletin* 22/79.

Hohmann, M. and Weikart, D. (1995/2002). *Educating Young Children.* Ypsilanti Michigan: High/Scope Press.

Hooven, C. and Katz Gottman, J. (1994). 'The Family as a Meta-emotion Culture.' *Cognition and Emotion*, Spring.

Howes, C., Phillips, D.A. and Whitebook, C. (1992). 'Thresholds of quality: Implications for the social development of children in center-based childcare.' *Child Development*, 63, 449-56.

———— and Olenick, M. (1986). 'Family and childcare influences on toddler's compliance.' *Child Development*, 57, 202-216.

Hull, J. (1996). 'The Ambiguity of Spiritual Values'. In, M. Halstead and M. Taylor (Eds.), *Values in Education and Education in Values.* London: Falmer Press.

Humphreys, T. (1993). *A Different Kind of Teacher.* Dublin: Gill and Macmillan.

———— (1996). *Self-Esteem: The Key to Your Child's Education.* Dublin: Gill and Macmillan.

Huston, A.C. (1983). 'Sex Typing.' In P.H. Mussen (Ed.), *Handbook of Child Psychology, Vol. 4: Socialisation, Personality and Social Development.* New York: Wiley.

Hutcheson, P. (1994). 'A Humanist Perspective on Spirituality.' *Humanist in Canada.* Spring.

Hutt, S., Tyler, S., Hutt C. and Christopherson, H. (1989). *Play, Exploration and Learning: A Natural History of the Pre-school.* London: Routledge.

Hyland, A. (2002). *Every Day Matters.* Seminar Report 28th November. Cork: East Cork Area Development.

Hyson, M.C. (1994). *The Emotional Development of Young Children: Building an Emotion-Centred Curriculum.* New York: Teachers College.

Irish Examiner Newspaper (2002). 'One-in-five bullied teens think of suicide.' 2nd May. Cork: Irish Examiner Newspapers.

Irish National Teachers Organisation (I.N.T.O.) (1995). *Early Childhood: Issues and Concerns.* Dublin: I.N.T.O.

Isaacs, S. (1931). *Intellectual Growth in Young Children*. London: Routledge.

————— (1932). *The Children We Teach*. London: University of London Press.

————— (1933). *Social Development in Young Children*. London: Routledge.

————— (1935). *The Psychological Aspects of Child Development*. London: Evans.

————— (1968). *The Nursery Years*. London: Routledge and Kegan Paul.

Isenberg, J. and Jalongo, M. (Eds.) (1997). *Major Trends and Issues in Early Childhood Education - Challenges, Controversies and Insights*. New York: Teachers College.

Izard, C.E. (1971). *The Face of Emotion*. New York: Appelton-Century-Crofts.

—————, Kagan, J. and Zajonc, R. (1984). *Emotions, Cognition and Behaviour*. Cambridge: Cambridge University Press.

James, W., Nelson, M., Ralph, A. and Leather, S. (1997). 'Socioeconomic determinants for health: the contribution of nutrition to inequalities in health'. *British Medical Journal*, 214, 1545-57.

Jacobson, S. and Frye, K. (1991). 'Effect of maternal social support on attachment: experiential evidence.' *Child Development*, 62, 572-582.

Jersild, A.T. (1943). 'Studies of Children's Fears.' In R.G. Barker, J.S. Kounin and H.F. Wright (Eds.), *Child Behaviour and Development*. New York: McGraw Hill.

Jessel-Kenyon, J. and Shealy, C (1999). *The Illustrated Encyclopedia of Well Being*. Hants: Godsfield Press.

Jimenez-Beltraum, D. (2002). Press Release Euro 08/02. World Health Organisation (W.H.O.) Regional Office for Europe and the European Environment. www.who.dk/eprise/main

Jones, R.M. (1972). *Fantasy and Feeling in Education*. Harmondsworth: Penguin Books.

Jung, C.G. (1954). 'On the Nature of the Psyche.' In *The Collected Works of C.J. Jung Vol.8* London: Routledge and Kegan Paul.

Kagan J., Kearsley, R. and Zelano, P. (1978). *Infancy: Its Place in Human Development*. Cambridge MA: Harvard University Press.

————, (1981). *The Second Year: The Emergence of Self-Awareness*. Cambridge MA: Harvard University Press.

————, (1984). *The Nature of the Child*. NY: Basic Books.

Kandel, J. (1946). 'National education in an international world.' *NEA Journal*, April.

Katz, L. (1995). *Talks with Teachers of Young Children*. Norwood NJ: Ablex Publication Corporation.

Kay, W. (1968). *Moral Development*. London: Allen and Unwin.

Kazepides, S.(1997). 'The logic of values clarification.' *The Journal of Educational Thought*, XI, August.

Kealy, S. (1994). *Spirituality for Today*. Cork: Mercier Press.

Kearney, M. (1996). *Mortally Wounded*. Dublin: Mercier Press.

Keatinge, M.W. (1896). *The Great Didactic of John Amos Comenius*. London: Adam and Charles Black.

Kellaghan, T. (1985). 'The Child and the School' in V. Greaney (Ed.), *Children: Needs and Rights*. New York: Irvington.

Kelmer Pringle, M.(1975/1996). *The Needs of Children*. London: Hutchison.

Keniston, K. (1976). 'The 11-year Olds of Today are the Computer Terminals of Tomorrow.' New York Times. February 19th.

Kennedy, D. (1999) cited in J. Haynes (2002), *Children as Philosophers*. London: Routledge.

Kennedy, S. (2002). 'Justice in Irish Society', cited in P. Kirby *The Celtic Tiger in Distress*. Hampshire: Palgrave.

Kent, H. (2001). *Yoga: An Illustrated Guide*. London: Element.

Kerlinger, F. (1973). *Foundations of Behavioural Research* 2nd edition. New York: Holt Rinehart and Winston.

Kesley, M. (1977). *Can Christians Be Educated?* US: Library of Congress Cataloguing.

Kibble, D. (1978). *Moral Education in a Secular School.* Bramcote: Grove Books.

———— (1996). 'Spiritual Development, Spiritual Experience and Spiritual Education.' In R. Best (Ed.), *Education, Spirituality and the Whole Child.* London: Cassell.

Kilpatrick, W.H. (1914). *The Montessori System Examined.* Boston: Houghton Mifflin.

———— (1916). *Froebel's Kindergarten Principles Critically Examined.* NY: The Macmillan Company.

Kilpatrick, W.K. (1992). *Why John Can't Tell Right From Wrong.* New York: Simon and Schuster.

King, M. (1997). *A Better World for Children.* London: Routledge.

Kirby, P. (2002). *The Celtic Tiger in Distress.* Hampshire: Palgrave.

Kirkland, J.P. (1996). 'Helping to Restore Spiritual Values in Abused Children: A Role for Pastoral Carers in Education.' In, R. Best (Ed.), *Education, Spirituality and the Whole Child.* London: Cassell.

Kitson, N. (1994). 'Please Miss Alexander: Will You be the Robber? Fantasy Play: A Case for Adult Intervention. In J. Moyles (Ed.), *The Excellence of Play.* Buckingham: Open University Press.

Kitwood, T. (1990). *Concern for Others: A New Psychology of Conscience and Morality.* London: Routledge.

Klein, M. (1988). *Love, Guilt and Reparation: And Other Works 1921-1945.* London: Virago.

Klinnert, M.D., Campos, J.J., Sorce, J.F., Emde, R.N. and Svejda, M. (1983). 'Emotions as Behaviour Regulators: Social Referencing in Infancy.' In R. Plutchik and H. Kellerman (Eds.), *Emotion: Theory, Research, and Experience, Vol. 2.* New York: Academic Press.

Knight, M. (Compiler) (1961). *Humanist Anthology.* London: Pemberton.

Knitzner, J. (1993). 'Children's mental health policy: Challenging the future.' *Journal of Emotional and Behavioural Disorders 1, 8-16.*

Kohlberg, L. (1963). 'The development of children's orientation towards a moral order.' *Via Humana*, 6(1-2).

————— (1964). 'Development of Moral Character and Moral Ideology.' In, M.L. Hoffman and L.W. Hoffman (Eds.), *Review of Child Development Research, Vol. 1.* NY: Russell Sage Foundation.

————— (1966). 'A Cognitive-Developmental Analysis of Children's Sex Role Concepts and Attitudes.' In E. Maccoby (Ed.), *The Development of Sex Differences.* Stanford: Standford University Press.

————— (1968). 'The child as moral philosopher'. *Psychology Today* (September) 25-30.

————— and Turiel, S. (1981). *Moral Development and Moral Education.* R.S. Peters (Ed.). London: Allen and Unwin.

————— and Fein, G. (1987). *Child Psychology and Childhood Education* New York: Longman.

Kokoschka, O. (Ed.) (1942). *Benes Educand. The Teacher of Nations.* Cambridge: Cambridge University Press.

Koplow, L. (Ed.) (1996). *Unsmiling Faces: How Preschools Can Help.* New York: Teachers College.

Kostelnik, M.J. (1992). 'Myths associated with developmentally appropriate programs.' *Young Children*, 47(4), 17-23.

Kraemer, S. (2000). 'The fragile male.' *British Medical Journal*, 321, 1609-1612 December.

————— (2002). *Every Day Matters.* Seminar Report 28th November 2001. Cork: East Cork Area Development.

Laevers, F. (1999). 'The project experiential education: Well-being and involvement make the difference.' *Early Education*, 27 Spring.

Lally, C. (1999). 'Irish Toddlers are Suicidal' *Sunday Tribune Newspaper*, June 27th. Dublin.

Lally, M. (1991). *The Nursery Teacher in Action*. London: Paul Chapman.

Lamb, M. (1982). 'What Can Research Experts Tell Parents About Effective Socialisation?' In E. Zigler, M. Lamb and I. Child (Eds.), *Socialisation and Personality Development*. Oxford: Oxford University Press.

Landy, S., Peters, R. De V., Arnold, R., Allen, A.B., Brookes, F., and Jewell, S. (1998). 'Evaluation of 'Staying on Track': An identification, tracking, and referral system'. *Infant Mental Health Journal*, 19, 34-58

————— (2002) *Pathways to Competence: Encouraging Healthy Social and Emotional Development in Young Children*. Baltimore: Paul H. Brooks

Langer, E. (1989). *Mindfulness* New York: Addison-Wesley.

————— (1997). *The Power of Mindful Learning*. New York: Addison-Wesley.

Lappe, F. and DuBois, S. (1994). *The Quickening of America*. San Francisco: Jossey-Boss.

Larner, M. and Phillips, S. (1994). 'Defining and Valuing Quality as a Parent.' In P. Moss and A. Pence (Eds.), *Valuing Quality in Early Childhood Services*. London: Paul Chapman.

Lawrence, D. (1996). *Enhancing Self-Esteem in the Classroom*. London: Paul Chapman.

Lawrence, E. (Ed.) (1952). *Friedrich Froebel and English Education*. London: University of London Press.

Lealman, B. (1996). 'The Whole Vision of the Child.' In R. Best (Ed.), *Education, Spirituality and the Whole Child*. London: Cassell.

Le Doux, J. (1998). *The Emotional Brain*. London: Simon and Schuster.

Lerner, E. (1937). *Constant Areas of Moral Judgement in Children*. Manasha Wisconsin: Banta.

Lever, J. (1978). 'Sex differences in the complexity of children's play and games.' *American Sociological Review*, 43(4), 471-483.

316

Lewis, C. (1995). *Educating Hearts and Minds: Reflections on Japanese Pre-schools and Elementary Education.* Cambridge MA: Cambridge University Press.

Lewis, M. (1993). 'Basic Psychological Processes in Emotion.' In M. Lewis M. and J. M. Haviland (Eds.), *Handbook of Emotions.* New York: Guildford Press.

Lickona, T. (1991). *Educating for Character: How Our Schools Can Teach Respect and Responsibility.* NY: Bartan.

———— (1993). 'Character Development in Children.' In A.E. Woolfolk (Ed.), *Readings and Cases in Educational Psychology.* Needham Heights: Allyn and Bacon.

Liebschner, J. (1988). *A Child's Work: Freedom and Play in Froebel's Educational Theory and Practice.* Cambridge: The Lutterwood Press.

Lillard, P. (1972). *Montessori: A Modern Approach.* US: Schocken Books.

Lilley, I. (1967). *Friedrich Froebel: A Selection from his Writings.* London: Syndicates of the Cambridge University Press.

Lindon, J. and Lindon L. (1993). *Caring for the Under-8s.* London: Macmillan Press Ltd.

———— (1999). *Understanding World Religions in Early Years Practice.* London: Hodder and Stoughton.

Locke, J. (1690/1967). *Two Treatises of Government.* Cambridge MA: Cambridge University Press.

———— (1971). *John Locke and Education.* NY: Teachers College.

———— (1968). Cited in J. Axtell. *The Educational Writings of John Locke.* Cambridge MA: Cambridge University Press.

Lodge, R.C. (1950). *Plato's Theory of Education* London: Routledge.

Loizos, C. (1969). 'Play Behaviour in Higher Primates: A review.' In, D. Morris (Ed.), *Primate Ethology.* Chicago: Aldine.

Losada, M. (2000). 'Caring' Translation and Abridgement of Umberto Maturana's 'The Student's Prayer' in D. Zohar and I. Marshall, *Spiritual Intelligence: The Ultimate Intelligence.* London: Bloomsbury.

Lubienski Wentworth, R. (1999). *Montessori for the New Millennium*. N.J.: Erlbaum.

Lytton, H., Watts, D. and Dunn, B. (1986). 'Stability and predictability of cognitive and social characteristics from age two to age nine.' *Genetic, Social and General Psychology Monographs*, 112, 363-398.

Magee, B. (1998). *The Story of Philosophy*. London: Dorling Kindersley

Maccoby, E. (1980). *Social Development, Psychology Growth and the Parent-child Relationship*. New York: Harcourt Brace Jovanovich.

———— and Martin, J.A. (1983). 'Socialisation in the Context of the Family: Parent-child Interaction.' In, P.H. Mussen (Ed.), *Handbook of Child Psychology, Vol. 4: 'Socialisation, Personality and Social Development'*.

MacIntyre, A. (1981). *After Virtue*. London: Duckworth.

Macionis, J.J. (1989). *Sociology* 2nd edition. New Jersey: Prentice-Hall.

MacNamara, V. (1988). *The Truth in Love: Reflections on Christian Morality*. Dublin: Gill and Macmillan.

Macquarrie, J. (1972). *Paths in Spirituality*. London: Harper and Row.

Marcon, R.A. (1999). 'Differential impact of pre-school models on development and early learning of inner-city children: A three-cohort study'. *Developmental Psychology* 35, 358-375.

Malaguzzi, L. (1993). 'For an education based on relationships'. *Young Children* 49(1) 9-12.

Malatesta-Magai, C., Leak, S., Tesman, J., Shepard, B., Culver, C. and Smaggia, B. (1994). 'Profiles of emotional development: Individual differences in facial and vocal expression of emotion during second and third years of life.' *International Journal of Behavioural Development*, 17, 239-269.

Manning, M., Heron, J. and Marshall, T. (1978). 'Styles of Hostility and Social Interactions at Nursery, at School and at Home: An Extended Study of Children.' In L. A. Hersov, M. Berger and D. Shaffer (Eds.). *Aggression and Anti-Social Behaviour in Childhood and Adolescence*, Oxford: Pergamon.

318

Marenholtz Bulow, Baroness Marie B.Von (1887). Reminiscences of Friedrich Froebel. Translated by Mann H. Boston: Lee and Shepard sourced at www./members.tripod.com~froebelweb/Reminiscences of Froebel.

Maslow, A.H. (1948). 'Higher and lower needs'. *Journal of Psychology*, 25, 433-436.

————— (1964). *Religious Values and Peak Experiences*. Columbus: Ohio State University.

————— (1966). *The Psychology of Science: A Reconnaissance*. NY: Harper and Row.

————— (1968). *Toward a Psychology of Being*. Princeton NJ: Van Nostrand.

————— and Chiang, H. (1969). *The Healthy Personality*. NY: Van Nostrand.

————— (1970a). *Motivation and Personality* (Revised Edition). New York: Harper and Row.

————— cited in Hemming, J. (1970b). *Individual Morality*. London: Panther.

————— (1971). *The Farther Reaches of Human Nature*. New York: Viking Press.

————— (1976). *Religions, Values and Peak Experiences*. Baltimore: Penguin.

McCreery, E. (1996). 'Talking to Young Children about Things Spiritual.' In, R. Best (Ed.) *Education, Spirituality and the Whole Child*. London: Cassell.

McKoen, P. (1999). In C. Lally 'Irish Toddlers are Suicidal' *Sunday Tribune Newspaper*, June 27th. Dublin.

McLaughlin, T.H. (1994). 'The Scope of Parents' Educational Rights.' In, J.M. Halstead (Ed.), *Parental Choice and Education. Principles, Policy and Practice*. London: Kogan Page.

————— (1995). 'Liberalism, Education and the Common School.' In, Y. Tamir (Ed.) *Democratic Education in a Multicultural State*. Oxford: Blackwell.

————— (1996). 'Education of the Whole Child?' In, R. Best (Ed), *Education, Spirituality and the Whole Child*. London: Cassell.

McMillan, M. (1900). Cited in W.A. Stewart (1972), *Progressives and Radicals in English Education, 1750-1970*. NJ: Augustus.

——— (1904). Cited in W.A. Stewart (1972), *Progressives and Radicals in English Education, 1750-1970*. NJ: Augustus.

——— (1906). Cited in W.A. Stewart (1972), *Progressives and Radicals in English Education, 1750-1970*. NJ: Augustus.

——— (1907). Cited in W.A. Stewart (1972), *Progressives and Radicals in English Education, 1750-1970*. NJ: Augustus.

McMillan, R. (1930). *The Nursery School*. London: JM Dent.

Meadows, S. (1994). *The Child as Thinker*. London: Routledge.

Mental Health Association of Ireland (M.H.A.I.) (2002). 'What is mental illness?' www.mensana.org

Mental Health Foundation Britain (1999). *Bright Futures: Promoting Children and Young People's Mental Health* Mental Health Foundation, London.

Meyer, J. Burnham, B. Cholvat, B. (Eds.) (1975*). Values Education: Theory, Practice, Problems and Prospects*. Waterloo: Ontario Wilfrid Laurien University Press.

Miller, P. and Garvey, C., (1984). 'Mother-baby Play: Its Origins in Social Support.' In I. Bretherton (Ed.), *Symbolic Play: The Development of Social Understanding*. New York: Academic Press.

Mills C. and Mills D. (1998) 'Dispatches: The Early Years'. London Channel Four Television cited in J. Haynes (2002). *Children as Philosophers Learning Through Enquiry and Dialogue in the Primary Classroom*. London: Routledge Falmer

Mischel, T. (1977). *The Self: Psychological and Philosophical Issues*. Oxford: Blackwell.

Mitchell, P. (1994). *International Colloquium on Spiritual and Moral Development: From Theory to Practice*. Cambridge: Homerton College.

Modgil, S. and Modgil, C. (1986). *Lawrence Kohlberg: Consensus and Controversy*. East Sussex: The Falmer Press.

Molnar, S. (1983). *Human Variation: Races, Types and Ethnic Groups* 2nd edition. Englewood Cliffs NJ: Prentice-Hall.

Monighan-Nourot, P., Scales, B., Van Hoorn, J. with Millie Almy (1987). *Looking at Children's Play. A Bridge Between Theory and Practice.* New York: Teachers College.

———— (1997). 'Playing with Play in Four Dimensions.' In, J. Isenberg M. Jalongo (Eds.), *Major Trends and Issues in Early Childhood Education.* New York: Teachers College.

Monroe, W.S. (1971). *Comenius and the Beginnings of Educational Reform.* NY: Arno Press.

Montemayor, M. (1984) cited in L. Kohlberg, *Review of The Psychology of Moral Development.* NY: Harper and Row.

Montessori, M. (1946). *Education for a New World.* Oxford: Clio Press.

———— (1948). *To Educate the Human Potential.* Oxford: Clio Press.

———— (1961). *What You Should Know About Your Child.* Oxford: Clio Press.

———— (1963a). *Education for a New World.* Wheaton: Theosphical Press.

———— (1963b). *The Secret of Childhood.* Calcutta: Orient Longmans.

———— (1964). *The Montessori Method.* NY: Schocken Books.

———— (1965a). *The Child in the Church.* St. Paul Minn: Catechetical Guild.

———— (1965b). *Spontaneous Activity in Education* (now called) *Scientific Pedagogy as Applied to the Education of Children from Seven to Eleven Years.* NY: Schocken Books.

———— (1967a). *The Discovery of the Child.* NY: Fides Publishers.

———— (1967b). *The Absorbent Mind.* NY: Dell Publishing Co.

———— (1979). *The Child, Society and the World.* Oxford: ABC Clio.

———— (1989). *The Formation of Man.* Oxford: Clio Press.

———— (1992). *Education and Peace*. Oxford: ABC Clio.

Montessori, Mario Junior (1992). *Education for Human Development*: Understanding *Montessori*. Oxford: ABC Clio.

Mooney, B. (2001). In 'Education Matters', *Educational Supplement Irish Times Newspaper*, 12th January Dublin.

Moorish, L. (1967). *Disciplines of Education*. London: Allen and Unwin.

Mosley, J. (1996). *Quality Circle Time*. L.D.A. Wisbech.

Moss, P. and Pence, A. (1994). *Valuing Quality in Early Childhood Services*. London: Paul Chapman.

Mott-Thornton, K. (1996). 'Experience, Critical Realism and the Schooling of Spirituality.' In R. Best (Ed.), *Education, Spirituality and the Whole Child*. London: Cassell.

Moyles, J. (Ed.) (1994). *The Excellence of Play*. Buckingham: Open University Press.

———— (1989). *Just Playing? The Role and Status of Play in Early Childhood Education*. Buckingham: Open University Press.

Murphy, D. (1995). *Comenius: A Critical Reassessment of his Life and Work*. Blackrock, Dublin: Irish Academic Press.

Murphy, M.R. (2001). *Parental Involvement in Early Years Education and Care in the Cork Area*. Unpublished Ph.D. Thesis Cork: University College Cork.

Murray, M. and Keane, C. (1998). *The ABC of Bullying*. Cork: Mercier Press.

Murray, C. (2001). 'Meeting the needs of minority children including Travellers.' *Childlinks*, Spring.

Murray, C. (1999). 'Diversity: A Challenge for Early Years Educators in Ireland.' In *Enhancing Quality in the Early Years: Proceedings of the International Conference on Practice and Policy in Early Childhood Care and Education*. Dublin: C.S.E.R.

Mussen, P. and Eisenberg, N. (1977). *Roots of Caring, Sharing and Helping*. San Francisco: W.H. Freeman.

Munton, A., Mooney, A. and Rowland, L. (1995). 'Deconstructing quality: A conceptual framework for the new paradigm in daycare provision for the under-eights.' *Early Child Development and Care*, 114, 11-23.

Myss, C. and Shealy, C.N. (1999). *The Creation of Health*. London: Bantam Books.

Nabucco, M. (1997). *The Effect of Three Early Childhood Curricula in Portugal on Children's progress in the First Year of Primary School*. Ph.D. Thesis. London: Institute of Education.

Nash, M. (1997). 'Fertile Minds.' *Time Magazine,* February 10th.

National Association for the Education of Young Children (N.A.E.Y.C.) (1991). 'Guidelines for appropriate curriculum content and assessment in programs serving children ages three through eight'. *Young Children* 4(13), 21-38.

National Center for Clinical Infant Programs (1992). *Heart Start: The Emotional Foundations of School Readiness.* Arlington VA: National Center for Clinical Infant Programs.

National Children's Bureau (1998). *Quality in Diversity in Early Learning*. London: National Children's Bureau.

National Curriculum Council (1993). *Spiritual and Moral Development: A Discussion Paper*. York: National Curriculum Council.

National Research Council (2000). *Eager to Learn: Educating our Pre-schoolers*. Washington: National Academy Press.

Nevin, H. (1978). 'Values clarification perspectives on John Dewey with implications for religious education.' *Religious Education*, LXX XIV, 6, Nov/Dec.

Neville, B. (1989). *Educating Psyche*. Victoria, Australia: Harper Collins.

Newby, M. (1996). 'Towards a Secular Concept of Spiritual Maturity' in R. Best (Ed.). *Education, Spirituality and The Whole Child*. London: Cassell.

New Zealand Ministry of Education (1996). *Te Whariki: Early Childhood Curriculum*. Wellington: Learning Media.

Nowicki, S. and Duke, S. (1989/1992). *Helping the Child Who Doesn't Fit In*. Atlanta: Peachtree Publishers.

Nutbrown, C. (1996). *Threads of Thinking*. London: Paul Chapman.

————— (Ed.) (1997). *Respectful Educator – Capable Learners: Children's Rights and Early Education*. Paul Chapman.

Nye, R. (1996). 'Childhood Spirituality and Contemporary Developmental Psychology.' In R. Best (Ed.), *Education, Spirituality and the Whole Child*. London: Cassell.

Oatley, K. and Jenkins, J. (1996). *Understanding Emotions*. Oxford: Blackwell.

O'Donnchadha, R. (2000). *The Confident Child*. Dublin: Gill and Macmillan.

Offend, D.R., Boyle, M.H. and Racine, YA (1989). 'Ontario child and health study: correlates of disorder'. *Journal of the American Academy of Child and Adolescent Psychiatry*, 25, 856-860

Office for Standards in Education in Britain (O.F.S.T.E.D.) (1994). *Spiritual, Moral Social and Cultural Development: An O.F.S.T.E.D. Discussion Paper*. London: H.M.S.O.

Osofsky, J. (2002). Foreword in S. Landy, *Pathways to Competence: Encouraging Healthy Social and Emotional Development in Young Children*. Maryland: Paul H. Brooks.

O'Moore, A.M. (1989). 'Bullying in Britain and Ireland: An Overview.' In E. Rolan and F. Munther (Eds.). *Bullying: An International Perspective*. London: David Fulton.

————— (1997). Self-concept and Bullying Behaviour Among School Children and Adolescents. Abstract, *5th European Congress of Psychology*. Dublin.

—————, Kirkham, C. and Smith, M. (1997). 'Bullying behaviour in Irish schools: A nationwide survey.' *Irish Journal of Psychology*. 18. 141-169.

Organisation Mondiale Education Prescolaire (O.M.E.P.) (1996). 'Integration of Peace Education into Early Childhood Educational Programs'. *International Journal of Early Childhood*, 28(2).

324

Painter, E. (1980). *A History of Education*. London: University Microfilms International.

Palmer, J. and Neal, P. (1994). *The Handbook of Environmental Education*. London: Routledge.

Parker, J. and Asher, S. (1987). 'Peer relations and later personal adjustment: are low accepted children at risk?' *Psychological Bulletin*, 102, 358-389.

———— and Asher, S. (1993). 'Friendship and friendship quality in middle childhood: Links with peer group acceptance and feelings of loneliness and social dissatisfaction.' *Developmental Psychology*, 29, 611-621.

Parten, M. (1932). 'Social participation among pre-school children.' *Journal of Abnormal and Social Psychology*, 27, 243-69.

Pascal, C. and Bertram, T. (1994). 'Evaluating and Improving the Quality of Play.' In J. Moyles (Ed.) *The Excellence of Play*. Buckingham: Open University Press.

———— (1997). *Effective Early Learning*. London: Paul Chapman Publishing.

Perry, D. and Bussey, K. (1984). *Social Development*. Englewood Cliffs: New Jersey: Prentice Hall.

Perry, R. (1997). *Teaching Practice: A Guide for Early Childhood Students*. London: Routledge.

Peters, R.S. (1975). 'Education of the emotions.' In, R.F. Deardon, P.H. Hirst and R. S. Peters *Education and the Development of Reason*. London: Routledge and Kegan Paul.

———— (1977). 'Moral Development a Plea for Pluralism.' In, T. Mischel, *The Self: Psychological and Philosophical Issues*. Oxford: Blackwell.

———— (1981). *Moral Development and Moral Education*. London: Allen and Unwin.

Phillips, D. (1982). 'The behavioural impact of violence in the mass media: A review of the evidence from laboratory and non-laboratory investigations.' *Sociology and Social Research*, 66, 387-388.

———— (1996). 'Reframing the Quality Issue.' In S. Kagan and N. Cohen (Ed.s) *Reinventing Early Care and Education: A Vision for a Quality System.* San Francisco: Jossey-Bass.

Piaget, J. (1929). *The Child's Conception of the World.* NY: Harcourt Bruce Jovanovich.

———— (1932). *The Moral Judgement of the Child.* London: Routledge and Kegan Paul.

———— (1967). *Six Psychological Studies.* New York: Random House

———— and Inhelder, B. (1968). *The Psychology of the Child.* London: Routledge and Kegan Paul.

Pines, M. (1981). 'The civilisation of Genie.' *Psychology Today*, 15, 28-34, September.

Plato (1803). *The Republic.* Translated by Davies J.L. and Vaughan D.J. London: Macmillan.

Plutchik, R. and Kellerman, H. (Eds.) (1983). 'Emotion: Theory, Research and Experience.' *Emotions in Early Development* New York: Academic Press.

Pollard, A. and Filer, A. (1996). *The Social World of Children's Learning.* London: Cassell.

Potts, R., Huston, A. and Wright, J. (1986). 'The effects of television form and violent content on boys' attention and social behaviour.' *Journal of Experimental Child Psychology*, 41, 1-17.

Prentice, R. (1996). 'The Spirit of Education: A Model for the Twenty-first Century.' In R. Best (Ed.), *Education, Spirituality and the Whole Child.* London: Cassell.

Pugh, G., De'Ath, E. and Smith, C. (1994). *Confident Parents Confident Children.* London: National Children's Bureau.

Puka, B. (1983). 'Altruism and Moral Development.' In D.L. Bridgeman (Ed.), *Disciplinary Theories and Strategies.* NY: Academic Press.

Purcell, B. (2001). *For Our Own Good. Childcare Issues in Ireland.* Cork: Collins Press

Radke-Yarrow, M., Zahn-Waxler, C. and Chapman M. (1983). 'Children's Prosocial Dispositions and Behaviour.' In P.H. Mussen (Ed.), *Handbook of Child Psychology, 4, Socialisation: Personality and Social Development.* New York: Wiley.

Raftery, A. (1987). Cited in T. Crooks and D. Stokes (Eds.), *Disadvantage, Learning and Young People: The Implications for Education and Training.* Dublin: Curriculum Development Unit Dublin Trinity College.

Raines, S. (1997). 'Developmental Appropriateness: Curriculum Revisited and Challenged'. In J. Isenberg and M. Jalongo (Eds.), *Major Trends and Issues in Early Childhood Education.* New York: Teachers College.

Ramachandran, V.S. and Blakeshee, S. (1998). *Phantoms in the Brain.* London: Fourth Estate.

Randle D. (1989) *Teaching Green: A Parent's Guide to Education for Life on Earth.* London: Green Print an imprint of Merlin Press.

Ransbury, M. (1982). 'Friedrich Froebel 1872-1982.' *Childhood Education.* USA: University Microfilms International.

Ratcliff, D. (Ed.) (1992). *Handbook of Children's Religious Education.* Birmingham: Religious Education Press.

Raths, L., Harmin, M. and Simon, S. (1978). *Values and Teaching* 2nd edition. Columbus Ohio: Charles E. Merrill.

Readings, B. (1996). *The University in the Ruins.* Cambridge MA: Harvard University Press.

Reich, K.H. (1992). Religious Development Across the Life Span: Conventional and Cognitive Developmental Approaches. In, D. L. Featherman, R. M. Lerner and M. Peerlmutter (Eds.), *Life Span Development and Behaviour,* 11, Hillsdale NJ: Erlbaum.

Reifel, S. and Yeatman, J. (1993). 'From category to context: reconsidering classroom play.' *Early Childhood Research Quarterly* 8(1) 347-367.

Richman, N., Stevenson, J. and Graham, P.J (1982). *Pre-school to School.* London: Academic Press.

Rizzuto, A.M. (1979). *The Birth of the Living God: A Psychoanalytic Study.* Chicago: University of Chicago Press.

Robinson, E. (1977). *The Original Vision*. Oxford: Religious Experience Research Unit.

Robinson, E. (1987). *The Language of Mystery*. London: SCM Press.

Roche, M. (2003) 'Setting the What if Free: Some theoretical perspectives on talking and thinking in an infant classroom - an investigation into one teacher's practice'. In N. Hayes and M. Kernan (Eds.). *Transformations - Theory and Practice in Early Education*, Cork, OMEP

Rodger, A. (1996). 'Human Spirituality: Towards an Educational Rationale.' In R. Best (Ed.), *Education, Spirituality and the Whole Child*. London: Cassell.

Rogers, C. and Kutnick, P. (Eds.) (1990). *The Social Psychology of the Primary School*. London: Routledge.

Rokeach, M. (1975). 'Towards a Philosophy of Values Education' In J. Meyer, B. Burnham and J. Cholvat (Eds.), *Values Education: Theory, Practice, Problems, Prospects*. Waterloo Ontario: Wilfrid Laurien University Press.

Rolheiser, R. (1998). *Seeking Spirituality*. London: Hodder and Stoughton.

Rose, D. (1996). 'Religious Education, Spirituality and the Acceptable Face of Indoctrination.' In R. Best (Ed.), *Education, Spirituality and the Whole Child*. London: Cassell.

Rosenweig, S. (1985) 'Freud and Experimental Psychology: The Emergence of Idiodynamics'. In S. Koch and D.E. Leary (Eds.) *A Century of Psychology as Science*. New York: McGraw-Hill.

Roth, J. (1962). *John Dewey and Self-Realisation*. NJ: Prentice Hall.

Rousseau, J.J. (1762/1979). *Emile: On Education*. London: Penguin Press.

Rubin, Z. (1980). *Children's Friendships*. Cambridge MA: Harvard University Press.

———— (1993). 'The Skills of Friendship.' In M. Donaldson (Ed.), *Early Childhood Development and Education*. Oxford: Blackwell.

Rusk, R. (1918/1969). *The Doctrines of the Great Educators*. London: Macmillan.

———— (1933). *A History of Infant Education*. London: University of London: Macmillan.

Russell, M. (2003). 'The spiritual dimension in addiction', *Eisteach – Quarterly Journal for Counselling and Psychotherapy* 2(1), Dublin.

Ruston, J.P. (1981). 'The Altruistic Personality.' In J.P. Ruston and R.M. Sorretino (Eds.). *Altruism and Helping Behaviour*. Hillsdale NJ: Erlbaum.

———— and Sorretino, R.M. (Eds.) (1981). *Altruism and Helping Behaviour*. Hillsdale NJ: Erlbaum.

Rutter, M, Tizard J. and Yule, M (1976). 'Research report: Isle of Wight studies 1964-1974'. *Psychological Medicine*, 6, 313-332

———— (1981). *Maternal Deprivation Reassessed*. Second edition. Harmondsworth: Penguin.

———— and Rutter, M (1993). *Developing Minds*. Harmondsworth Penguin

———— and the ERA team (1998). 'Developmental catch up and deficit following adoption'. *Journal of Child Psychology and Psychiatry*, 39(4), 465-76.

Ryan, K. (1986). 'The new moral education.' *Phi Delta Kappa*, 68(4), 228-233.

Saarni, C. and Harris, P. (1989). *Children's Understanding of Emotion*. Cambridge: Press Syndicate of the University of Cambridge.

———— (1990). 'Emotional Competence.' In R.A. Thompson (Ed.), *Nebraska Symposium on Motivation, Vol. 36, Socio-emotional Development*. Lincoln: University of Nebraska Press.

————, Mumme, D. and Campos, J.J. (1998). 'Emotional Development: Action, Communication and Understanding.' In W. Damon (Series Ed.) and N. Eisenberg (Vol. Ed.), *Social, emotional and personality development, Vol. 13, Handbook of Child Psychiatry*, 237-309, 5th edition. New York: Wiley.

Sadler, J. (Ed.) (1969). *Comenius*. London: Macmillan.

Sale, R. (1979). *Fairy Tales and After*. Cambridge MA: Harvard University Press.

Sansor, A. Oberklaid, F. Pedlow, R. and Prior M. (1991). 'Risk indicators: Assessment of infancy predictors of pre-school behavioral maladjustment' *Journal of Child Psychology and Psychiatry and Allied Disciplines* 32 609-626

Sapolsky R.M. (1994) *Why Zebras Don't Get Ulcers: A Guide to Stress, Stress Related Disease and Coping.* New York: W.H. Freeman

Sayeed, Z., Guerin, E. and Guerin, F. (2000). *Early Years Play.* London: David Fulton Publishers.

Scally, J. (1997). *Ethics in Crisis.* Dublin: Veritas.

Schlosser, E. (2002). *Fast Food Nation.* New York: Penguin.

Schon, D. (1983). *The Reflective Practitioner.* New York: Basic Books.

————— (1987). *Educating the Reflective Practitioner.* San Francisco: Jossey-Bass.

Schickendanz, J., Schickendanz, D., Hansen, K. and Forsyth, P. (1990). *Understanding Children.* California: Mayfield Publishing Company.

Schweinhart, L.J., Weikart, D.P. and Larner, M.B. (1986). 'Consequences of three pre-school curriculum models through age 15.' *Early Childhood Research Quarterly* 1(1), 15-45.

————— and Weikart, D.P. (1993). *A Summary of Significant Benefits: The High/Scope Perry Pre-school Study Through Age 27.* Ypsilanti Michigan: High/Scope Press.

————— and Weikart, D.P. (1997). 'The High/Scope curriculum comparison study through age 23'. *Early Childhood Research Quarterly*, 12, 117-143.

Scott Peck, M. (1990). *The Road Less Travelled.* London: Arrow Books.

————— (1993). *Further along the Road less Travelled.* N.Y.: Touchstone.

Scraton, P. (Ed.) (1997). *Childhood in Crisis?* London: UCL Press.

Sears, R., Maccoby E. and Levine, M. (1957). *Patterns of Child Rearing.* NY: Harper and Row.

Secondary Examinations Council Religious Education Council (1986). *Religious Studies - A Glossary of Te*rms. London: SEAC/REC.

Seefeldt, C. (1992). *The Early Childhood Curriculum*. Second edition. New York: Teachers College.

Selwyn, J. (2000). 'Technologies and Environments: New Freedoms, New Constraints'. In M. Boushel, M. Fawcett and J. Selwyn (Eds.), *Focus on Early Childhood*. London: Blackwell Science.

Shelton, C.M. (1990). *Morality of the Heart*. NY: The Crossroad Publishing Company.

Shweder, R.A., Turiel, E. and Much, N.C. (1981). 'The Moral Intuitions of the Child.' In J. H. Flavell and L. Ross (Eds.), *Social Cognitive Development: Frontiers and Possible Futures*. Cambridge: Cambridge University Press.

Siegal, M. (1982a). *Fairness in Children: A Social Cognitive Approach to the Study of Moral Development*. London: Academic Press.

———— (1982b). 'Development of Children's Moral Deliberations: Implications for Early Childhood Education.' In N. Nir-Janio, B. Spodek and M. Siegal *Early Children's Education: An Interaction Perspective*. London: Plarum Press.

Simon, S., Howe, L. and Kirschenbaum, H. (1972/1995). *Values Clarification*. NY: Warner Books.

———— and Kohlberg, L. (1972). 'An exchange of opinion between Kohlberg and Simon'. *Learning*, December.

Simpson, E.L. (1974). 'Moral Development Research. A Case Study of Scientific Cultural Bias.' *Human Development*, 17.

Sinetar, M. (1991). *Developing a 21st Century Mind*. New York: Ballantine Books.

Singer, D. and Singer, D. (1980). 'Television Viewing, Family Style and Aggressive Behaviour in pre-school children.' In M. Green (Ed.), *Violence and the Family: Psychiatric, Sociological and Historical Implications*. Boulder Col: Westview Press.

Singer, E. (1996). 'Prisoners of the method: Breaking open the child-centred pedagogy in daycare centres.' *International Journal of Early Years Education* 4(2), 28-40.

Siraj-Blatchford I. and Siraj-Blatchford J. (1995) *Educating the Whole Child.* Buckingham: Open University Press.

——— (1996). *The Early Years: Laying the Foundations for Racial Equality.* Stoke-on-Trent: Trentham Books.

Skinner, B.F. (1953). *Science and Human Behaviour.* New York: Macmillan.

Slavin, R. (1995). *Co-operative Learning: Theory, Research and Practice.* Boston: Allyn and Bacon.

Smilansky, S. and Shefatya, L. (1990). *Facilitating Play: A Medium for Promoting Cognitive, Socio-Emotional and Academic Development in Young Children.* Gaithersburg MD: Psychosocial and Educational Publications.

Smith, A. (1999). 'The Role of an Early Childhood Curriculum: Promoting Diversity Versus Uniformity.' In *Enhancing Quality in the Early Years: Proceedings of the International Conference on Practice and Policy in Early Childhood Care and Education.* Dublin: C.S.E.R.

Smith, G. (1984). *Lives in Education.* Iowa: Educational Studies Press.

Smith, P. (1978). 'A longitudinal study of social participation in pre-school children: solitary and parallel play re-examined.' *Developmental Psychology*, 14, 517-23.

——— and Cowie, H. (1988/1991). *Understanding Children's Development.* Oxford: Blackwell.

Soneson, J.P. (1993). *Pragmatism and Pluralism John Dewey's Significance for Theology.* US: Harvard Theology Review.

Splitter, L. and Sharp, A.M. (1995) *Teaching for Better Thinking.* Melbourne: Australian Council for Educational Research.

Standing, E.M. (1957). *Maria Montessori: Her Life and Works.* London: Hollis and Carter.

Stapleton, L., Lehane, M. and Toner, P. (Eds.) (2000). *Ireland's Environment: A Millennium Report*. Dublin: Environmental Protection Agency.

Starkings, D. (1993). *Religion and the Arts in Education: Dimensions of Spirituality* Sevenoaks London: Faber and Faber.

Staub, E. (1978). *Positive Social Behaviour and Morality Volume 1, Social and Personal Influences*. NY: Academic Press.

Stayton, A., Hogan, B. and Ainsworth, M. (1971). 'Infant obedience and maternal behaviour: The origins of socialisation reconsidered.' *Child Development*, 1057-1069.

Stein, N. and Jewett, J.L. (1986). 'A Conceptual Analysis of the Meaning of Negative Emotions: Implications for a Theory of Development.' In C.E. Izard and P. Read (Eds.), *Measurement of Emotions in Children*. New York: Cambridge University Press.

Stein, N. and Levine L. (1989). 'Making Sense Out of Emotion: The Representation and Use of Goal-structured Knowledge.' In N. Stein, T. Leventhal and T. Trabasso (Eds.), *Psychological and Biological Approaches to Emotion*. Hillsdale: Erlbaum.

————— and Trabasso, T. (1989). 'Children's Understanding of Changing Emotional States.' In P. Harris and C. Saarni (Eds.), *Children's Understanding of Emotion*. Cambridge: Cambridge University Press.

Stein, T. (1997). *Was Adler Influenced by Froebel?*
http://www.ourworld.cympuseerve.com/homepages/hstein/homepage.htm

Steiner, C. with Paul Perry (1997). *Achieving Emotional Literacy*. London: Bloomsbury.

Steiner, R. (1923) 'Margaret McMillan and her work.' *Anthropology*, November.

————— (1926). *The Essentials of Education*. London: Anthroposophical Publishing Company.

Sternberg, R. (1985). *Beyond I.Q. A Triarchic Theory of Human Intelligence*. Cambridge UK: Cambridge University Press.

Steward, W.A. (1972). *Rudolf Steiner Education: The Waldorf Schools*. London: Rudolf Steiner Press.

Stewart, W.A. (1972). *Progressives and Radicals in English Education 1750-1970*. NJ: Augustus M. Kelly.

Spiecker, B. and Straughan, R. (1988). *Philosophical Issues in Moral Education*. Milton Keynes: Open University Educational Enterprises.

Sugarman, B. (1973). *The School of Moral Development*. London: The Trinity Press.

Sullivan, H. (1965). *Personal Psychopathology*. New York: Norton.

Sullivan, K. (2002). *Kids Under Pressure: How to Raise a Stress-free and Happy Child*. London: Paitkus Publishers.

Sylva, K. (1999). 'Early Childhood Education to Ensure a Fair Start for All.' In T. Cox (Ed.) *Combatting Educational Disadvantage*. New York: Falmer Press.

Tamminen, K. (1991). *Religious Development in Childhood and Youth An Empirical Study*. Helsinki: Suomalainen Tiedeakatemia.

———— (1996). 'The Multiplexity of Religious Development of Childhood and Youth' in *Religious Development,* papers presented on the research of Kalevi Tamminen at symposium on Religious Development Research Reports on Religious Education, Institute of Practical Theology, University of Helsinki cited in R. Best (Ed.), *Education, Spirituality and the Whole Child*. London: Cassell.

Tamir, Y. (Ed.) (1995). *Democratic Education in a Multicultural State*. Oxford: Blackwell.

Tangney, J.P., Wagner Barlow, D.H., Marschall, D.E., Sanftner, J., Mohr, R. and Gramzow, R. (1996). 'The relation of shame and guilt to constructive versus destructive responses to anger across the lifespan.' *Journal of Personality and Social Psychology*, 70, 797-809.

Taylor, J. (1989). *Innocent Wisdom Children as Spiritual Guides*. New York: The Pilgrim Press.

Terwogt, M. and Olthof, T. (1989). 'Awareness and Self-Regulation of Emotion in Young Children. In C. Saarni and P. Harris (Eds.), *Children's Understanding of Emotion*. Cambridge: Cambridge University Press.

334

The National Children's Strategy (2000). *Our Children – Their Lives*. Dublin: The Stationery Office.

Thompson, M. (1999). *Ethical Theory*. London: Hodder and Stoughton.

Thompson, R.A. (1994). 'Emotion Regulation: A theme in search of definition.' *Monographs of the Society for Research in Child Development*, 59(2-3).

Thorndike, E.L (1905). *The Elements of Psychology*. New York: Seiler.

Tizard, B. and Hughes, M. (1984). *Young Children's Learning*. London: Fontana.

Tomlinson, P. (1975). 'Political education: Cognitive developmental perspectives for moral education. *Review of Education*, 1(3).

Troy, M. and Sroufe, L. (1987). 'Victimisation among pre-schoolers: role of attachment relationships history.' *Journal of the American Academy of Child and Adolescent Psychiatry*, 26(2), 166-172.

Ulich, R. (1956). *Protecting Education as a Humane Society*. NY: Macmillan.

United Nations (1989). Declaration of the Rights of the Child. UN: Geneva.

————— Population Fund (U.N.F.P.A) (1999). *The State of World Population 1999*. www.nfpa.org/swp/eng/ch01/htmlu

Velez, C.N., Johnson, J and Cohen, P., (1989). 'A longitudinal analysis of selected risk factors from childhood psychopathology.' *Journal of the American Academy of Child and Adolescent Psychiatry* 28, 861-864.

Vygotsky, L. (1962a). *Thought and Language*. Translated by E. Hanfmann. Cambridge: MIT Press.

————— (1962b). 'School Instruction and Mental Development.' In M. Donaldson (1978) *Children's Minds*. London: Fontana.

————— (1978). *Mind in Society*. Cambridge MA: Harvard University Press.

Walker, A. (1969). *Temple of My Familiar*. New York: Harcourt Brace Javanovich

Walsh, D.J. (1991). 'Extending the discussion on developmental appropriateness: A developmental practice.' *Early Education and Development*, 2, 109-119.

Watson, J. (1919/1931). *Behaviourism*. London: Routledge and Kegan Paul.

Webster, D. (1996). 'Spiders and Eternity: Spirituality and the Curriculum.' In R. Best (Ed.), *Education, Spirituality and the Whole Child*. London: Cassell.

Weikart, D. Deloria, D. Lawser, S. and Wiegerink, R. (1970). Longitudinal Results of the Ypsilanti Perry Pre-school Project. *Monographs of the High Scope Educational Research Foundation, No.1.*

Weitzman, L., Eifler, D., Hodaka, E. and Ross, C. (1972). 'Sex-role socialisation in picture books for pre-school children.' *American Journal of Sociology*, 6, 1125-1150.

White, J. (1996). 'Education, Spirituality and the Whole Child: A Humanist Perspective.' In R. Best (Ed.) *Education, Spirituality and the Whole Child*. London: Cassell.

White, P. (1994). 'Citizenship and spiritual and moral development.' *Citizenship*, 3, 7-8.

Whitebread, D. (1996). *Teaching and Learning in the Early Years*. London: Routledge.

Williams, J. and Best, D. (1990) *Measuring Sex Stereotypes: A Multination Study*, Newbury Park CA: Sage.

Wieder, S. and Greenspan, S. (1993). 'The Emotional Basis of Learning.' In B. Spodek (Ed.) *Handbook of Research on the Education of Young Children*. New York: Macmillan.

Wilson, J., Williams, N. and Sugarman, B. (1967). *Introduction to Moral Education*, Harmondsworth Penguin

Winnicott, D.W. (1964). *The Child, the Family and the Outside World*. Harmondsworth: Penguin.

Wise, J. (1964). *The History of Education*. NY: Sheed and Ward.

Wood, M.E. (1981). *The Development of Personality and Behaviour in Children.* London: George G. Harrup.

Woodham, P., Smith, J.P., Slight, O.B., Priestman, H., Hamilton, H.A. and Issacs, N. (1952). *Friedrich Froebel and English Education.* London: Routledge and Kegan Paul.

Woodhead, M. (1996). *In Search of the Rainbow: Pathways to Quality in Large Scale Programmes for Young Disadvantaged Children.* The Hague: Bernard Van Leer Foundation.

Worrell, J. (Ed.) (1982). *Psychological Development in the Elementary Years.* NY: Academic Press.

World Health Organisation (W.H.O.) (1997). www.who.int/whr/1997/exsum.97e.htm

————— (2002a). www.who.dk/healthtopics.html

————— (2002b). 'European Review of Suicide' www.who.int/mental-health/aboutMH.html

Wright, A. (1996). 'The Child in Relationship: Towards a Communal Model of Spirituality.' In R. Best (Ed.), *Education, Spirituality and the Whole Child.* London: Cassell.

www.aaabooksearch.com – website for finding and reviewing books

Wynne, E. (1986). 'Character Development: Renewing an old commitment.' *Principal*, 65(3), 31.

Youngblade, L. and Belsky, J. (1990). 'Social and Emotional Consequences of Child Maltreatment.' In R. Hammerman and M. Hersen (Eds.), *Children at Risk: An Evaluation of Factors Contributing to Child Abuse and Neglect.* New York: Plenum Press.

Zahn-Waxler, C. and Kochanska, G. (1990). 'The Origins of Guilt.' In R.A. Thompson (Ed.), *Nebraska Symposium on Motivation, Volume 36, Socio-emotional Development.* Lincoln: University of Nebraska.

—————, Kochanska, G., Krupnick, J. and McKnew, D. (1990). 'Patterns of guilt in children of depressed and well mothers.' *Developmental Psychology*, 26, 51-49.

Zeitlin, S. and Williamson, G. (1994). *Coping in Young Children*. Maryland: Paul H. Brookes.

Zillman, D., Bryant, J. and Huston, A. (1994). *Media, Children and The Family*. NJ: Erlbaum.

Zohar, D. and Marshall, I. (2000). *Spiritual Intelligence: The Ultimate Intelligence*. London: Bloomsbury.

INDEX

A

Abbott · 281
Abbs · 240, 279
Academic · 8, 9, 10, 11, 12, 23, 77, 92, 133, 160, 248, 285
Academic Achievement · 12, 268, 285
Achievement · 4, 9, 23, 33, 63, 113, 219, 261, 263, 267, 270
Adler · 14, 274
Adult Example · 25, 33
Aesthetic Needs · 16, 17, 253, 264, 269, 270, 271, 272, 273, 275
Aggression · 22, 87, 99, 108, 120, 140, 149, 157, 206
Ainsworth · 107
Allport · 222
Alston · 188
Altruism · 15, 155, 186
Anschauung · 52
Anxiety · 84, 85, 86, 87, 88, 89, 94, 107, 109, 114, 133, 155, 255, 256, 278
Aries · 57
Aristotle · 38, 41, 43, 59, 258, 264
Aronson · 113, 216, 287
Attachment · 81, 104, 106, 107, 110, 118, 134, 139, 140, 152, 156, 257, 259
Attachments · 23, 106, 140, 152, 153, 185
Attunement · 107
Authority · 183, 187, 190, 192, 200, 212, 273
Autonomy · 11, 74, 95, 103, 108, 187, 189, 222
Awe · 17, 20, 27, 34, 224, 231, 232, 238, 245, 249, 271, 275, 279
Axtell · 48, 255

B

Bandura · 190
Bandura and Walters · 144, 191
Barrett and Campos · 101

Basic needs · 20
Beck · 176, 199, 229
Belongingness and love · 17
Belongingness and love needs · 16, 257
Belsky, Steinberg and Walker · 107
Bem · 142
Berger · 199
Best · 13, 142, 143, 237
Blum · 99
Bocchino · 61, 97, 98, 101, 117, 257, 258
Boldt, Devine, MacDevitt and Morgan · 9, 10
Bornstein and Lamb · 176, 260
Borysenko · 85
Bower · 92
Bowlby · 106, 107, 259
Boyd · 43, 49, 50, 52, 66, 72, 75, 76, 78, 270, 276
Boyd-Cadwell · 233, 276, 283
Bradburn · 65
Bradford · 230, 239
Bradley, Whiteside, Mundform and Casey · 89
Brain · 84, 85, 90, 91, 93, 97, 101, 221, 236, 239, 266, 267, 269, 270
Branscombe, Castle, Dorsey, Surbeck Taylor 7, 32, 38, 41, 53, 65, 197
Brazelton · 84
Bredekamp · 12
Breen · 9
Briggs · 110
Brody and Hall · 104
Bronfenbrenner · 135, 136
Brown · 180, 213
Brubacher · 62
Bruce · 281
Bruce and Meggitt · 63, 65
Bruce, Findlay, Read and Scarborough · 58, 62, 63, 262, 265
Bukatto and Daehler 1995 · 94
Bukowski, Newcomb and Hartup · 151, 155
Bully · 140, 150
Bullying · 33, 148, 149, 150, 165, 197, 204, 259

C

Campbell · 87
Campos, Campos and Barrett · 96
Carr · 224
Carrington · 236
Carroll · 285
Character · 40, 41, 46, 51, 52, 54, 64, 71, 73, 74, 77, 78, 178, 179, 180, 182, 195, 198, 199, 200
Character Development · 52, 78, 177, 179
Character Education · 26, 178, 179
Charney · 154, 200
Chazan · 194
Chen, Krechevsky, Viens, Isberg, Gardner and Feldman · 11, 12, 189, 284
Child Development · 17, 27, 34, 81, 135, 140, 147, 199, 217, 223, 240, 242, 261, 270, 273, 278
Child-centred · 35, 48, 50, 63, 66, 80, 255, 265, 271
Childhood · 21, 32, 37, 45, 48, 49, 50, 54, 55, 57, 59, 65, 71, 82, 85, 87, 88, 91, 92, 95, 100, 105, 107, 109, 117, 136, 149, 241, 254, 256, 259, 261, 271, 277, 282, 285, 288
Citizenship · 40, 197, 225, 280
Cognitive · 3, 13, 17, 22, 23, 24, 25, 26, 27, 33, 38, 46, 59, 66, 73, 84, 92, 93, 94, 104, 108, 110, 116, 134, 139, 141, 144, 145, 151, 154, 157, 184, 187, 189, 191, 224, 227, 239, 253, 261, 263, 264, 266, 268, 273, 274, 281, 284, 286
Cognitive Development · 22, 26, 92, 140, 187, 190, 191, 224, 239, 282
Cognitive Needs · 16, 263, 265, 268, 269
Cole and Cole · 136, 144, 149, 154
Coles · 26, 176, 182, 199, 224, 238
Comenius · 35, 38, 43, 44, 45, 46, 47, 57, 59, 66, 76, 80, 255, 261, 264, 270, 271, 273, 278
Community · 7, 17, 18, 30, 40, 53, 54, 66, 68, 78, 79, 88, 97, 122, 133, 136, 137, 138, 141, 154, 157, 158, 165, 169, 173, 183, 185, 189, 198, 199, 200, 201, 205, 209, 211, 212, 215, 216, 218, 222, 225, 230, 234, 237, 244, 257, 258, 260, 276, 278, 280, 282
Competition · 56, 113, 163
Confidence · 23, 40, 88, 89, 106, 110, 112, 114, 117, 118, 120, 148, 198, 208, 261, 262
Confident · 23, 106, 110, 112, 115, 122, 139, 262, 282
Connolly · 20
Conscience · 25, 46, 53, 70, 108, 175, 176, 185, 188, 192, 262
Consumerism · 6, 211
Contemplation · 229, 230, 235
Coolahan · 269
Corporal Punishment · 40, 42, 43, 50, 52, 54, 255
Courage · 18, 19, 115, 178, 184, 193, 208, 220, 229, 273
Cowan · 95

Creativity · 8, 19, 58, 108, 217, 219, 229, 231, 232, 263, 270, 271, 275, 277
Crooks and Stokes · 9
Crossen · 190
Culture · 79, 102, 142, 146, 147, 151, 167, 168, 170, 177, 180, 216, 219, 225, 228, 230, 232, 236, 240, 269, 270, 280
Cultures · 147, 168, 169, 177, 188, 237, 249
Curricula · 12, 28, 151, 170, 182, 234, 237, 268
Curriculum · 9, 10, 11, 27, 28, 29, 34, 40, 44, 46, 47, 49, 52, 54, 55, 64, 65, 76, 80, 117, 159, 179, 182, 194, 201, 209, 211, 212, 235, 236, 237, 238, 263, 268, 269, 270, 271, 274, 276, 282, 287
Curtis · 159, 171, 201
Curtis and Boultwood · 40, 51, 55, 256, 270

D

Dahlberg, Moss and Pence · 5
Dalai Lama · 215
Daly · 4, 21, 23, 24, 26, 27, 159, 201, 217, 230, 242, 261, 272
Damon · 137, 139
David · 257, 280
Denham · 85, 116, 263, 275
Depression · 3, 22, 23, 83, 85, 87, 88, 89, 105, 109, 112, 148, 155
Deprivation · 35, 135, 241, 260, 264, 287
Derman-Sparks · 147
Deroche and Williams · 174, 194
Desperation · 83, 84, 256
Development Education · 209, 286
Dewey · 31, 46, 49, 50, 75, 76, 77, 78, 79, 266, 271
Discipline · 91, 115, 149, 186, 202
Discovery · 5, 46, 73, 78, 134, 195, 240, 266, 275
Discrimination · 146, 147, 230
Diversity · 22, 141, 146, 148, 158, 199, 233, 235, 259, 269, 287
Dodge · 139
Doe and Walch · 217, 224, 242
Donaldson · 86
Donnelly · 117
Douglas · 14, 156, 159
Douglas and Horgan · 284
Douglas, Horgan and O'Brien ·117, 201, 242
Dowling · 112, 117, 137, 159, 201, 221, 223, 242, 257, 279
Downey and Kelly · 92, 180, 191
Dramatic Play · 45, 81
Dunn · 138, 139, 152, 200, 269
Dunn and Brown · 103
Dunn, Bretherton and Munn · 104
Dupuis · 43, 45, 255
Durkheim · 176, 185, 186
Duska and Whelan · 25, 185, 187
Dworetzky · 13, 22, 94, 274
Dyer · 84, 113, 238, 263

E

Early Years Education and Care · 146, 267
Ecological Approach · 135
Ecology · 76, 136, 225, 280
Edgeworth · 255
Edgeworths · 51, 270
Education · 2, 3, 4, 7, 8, 9, 10, 12, 16, 17, 18, 26, 32, 35, 37, 38, 39, 40, 41, 42, 43, 44, 45, 46, 47, 48, 49, 50, 51, 52, 53, 54, 55, 56, 57, 58, 59, 62, 64, 65, 66, 67, 69, 70, 71, 72, 73, 74, 75, 76, 77, 79, 81, 82, 84, 90, 92, 94, 97, 98, 100, 136, 145, 146, 147, 154, 169, 174, 176, 178, 182, 186, 193, 194, 195, 197, 200, 207, 209, 210, 212, 219, 220, 225, 232, 233, 237, 255, 256, 261, 263, 264, 265, 266, 267, 269, 270, 271, 273, 274, 280, 282, 284, 285, 286, 287
Educators · 34, 37, 39, 46, 47, 49, 50, 55, 58, 59, 66, 78, 81, 82, 178, 179, 189, 254, 255, 256, 261, 270, 273
Edwards, Gandini and Forman · 158, 281, 284
Einstein · 231
Eisenberg · 181, 189
Eisenberg and Fabes · 101, 111
Eisenberg and Neal · 181
Ekman · 96
Eliot · 91, 97, 100, 106, 135, 234
Elkind · 12, 59, 133, 145, 238, 268, 272
Emile · 48, 49, 50, 51, 57, 66
Emotion · 13, 84, 92, 94, 95, 96, 97, 102, 103, 115, 123, 183, 185, 200, 221, 231
Emotion regulation · 102, 103
Emotional · 1, 2, 3, 4, 5, 8, 12, 15, 17, 18, 19, 21, 22, 23, 28, 32, 34, 35, 83, 84, 85, 86, 87, 88, 89, 90, 91, 92, 93, 94, 95, 96, 97, 98, 100, 101, 102, 103, 104, 105, 106, 107, 108, 109, 110, 111, 113, 114, 115, 116, 117, 120, 121, 122, 123, 128, 129, 140, 141, 147, 153, 154, 155, 216, 217, 241, 253, 256, 258, 259, 263, 269, 274, 275, 277, 278, 279, 280, 281, 287
Emotional Competence · 8
Emotional Competency · 97, 98
Emotional Development · 4, 22, 23, 32, 35, 38, 45, 49, 52, 58, 59, 61, 65, 78, 84, 86, 87, 88, 89, 90, 91, 92, 93, 94, 95, 97, 103, 104, 106, 107, 108, 110, 111, 113, 114, 115, 116, 117, 122, 128, 129, 140, 141, 201, 242, 263, 278
Emotional Intelligence (E.I.) · 98, 108
Emotional Literacy · 98, 278
Emotional Problems · 90, 117, 278
Emotional Quotient (E.Q.) · 98, 221
Emotional well-being · 12
Emotionality · 14, 41, 90, 111
Emotions · 22, 23, 32, 41, 50, 58, 72, 73, 83, 84, 85, 86, 88, 89, 90, 91, 92, 93, 94, 95, 96, 97, 98, 99, 100, 101, 102, 103, 104, 109, 116, 117, 123, 124, 130, 157, 184, 185, 241
Empathy · 18, 73, 99, 116, 241

Environment · 5, 6, 7, 8, 17, 39, 40, 41, 55, 58, 59, 60, 61, 62, 63, 65, 67, 68, 70, 71, 72, 73, 74, 76, 78, 88, 90, 91, 102, 103, 107, 108, 115, 117, 121, 135, 136, 142, 144, 145, 158, 163, 169, 174, 179, 180, 198, 200, 207, 210, 211, 212, 218, 228, 234, 240, 242, 245, 257, 258, 259, 262, 264, 265, 270, 275, 281, 286, 287
Environmental Education · 201
Environments · 10, 89, 109, 167
Erikson · 14, 67, 94, 227
Esteem Needs · 16, 261, 262, 264, 275
Evans · 229
Externalising Disorders · 87
Eysenck · 190

F

Facilitator · 193, 281
Facilitators · 51, 63
Fagan · 5, 175, 183, 195, 279
Failure · 9, 89, 109, 112, 113, 114, 115, 194, 222, 238, 263, 267
Fairness · 25, 116, 176, 197, 207, 213
Family · 1, 7, 17, 18, 42, 49, 52, 60, 78, 81, 88, 91, 101, 107, 108, 111, 117, 118, 119, 134, 136, 137, 138, 139, 145, 147, 152, 157, 165, 176, 179, 200, 202, 205, 222, 224, 230, 253, 254, 257, 258, 278, 279, 282
Farrer · 175, 178, 215, 225, 231, 235, 242
Farrington · 149
Fawcett · 10, 83, 197, 284, 286
Feelings · 20, 27, 32, 39, 58, 63, 65, 75, 81, 82, 83, 84, 88, 89, 92, 93, 94, 96, 97, 98, 99, 100, 104, 108, 111, 113, 115, 116, 117, 120, 121, 122, 123, 124, 128, 130, 182, 184, 185, 190, 191, 196, 241, 258, 261, 268, 273, 278, 284
Fein and Rivkin · 152
Field · 152
Finkelstein and Haskins · 141
Fogel · 109
Fontana · 3, 16, 18, 189, 192
Fowler, Nipkow and Schweitzer · 238
Fragmentation · 193, 215, 223, 241
Frankl · 217
Freedom · 39, 46, 47, 60, 62, 68, 73, 74, 81, 113, 120, 178, 180, 186, 196, 207, 220, 233, 255, 263, 265
French · 117
Freud · 14, 67, 73, 80, 94, 95, 143, 144, 192, 193, 259
Friends · 1, 17, 24, 146, 152, 153, 154, 155, 158, 160, 161, 162, 165, 171, 202, 224, 254, 257, 259
Friendship · 24, 151, 152, 153, 196, 212, 219, 285, 286
Froebel · 35, 38, 43, 44, 45, 46, 49, 55, 56, 57, 58, 59, 60, 61, 62, 63, 66, 67, 69, 72, 75, 76,

80, 82, 237, 256, 258, 261, 265, 270, 271, 274, 278
Fulfillment · 16, 20, 21, 25, 225, 264, 268, 272, 275
Furman and Robbins · 155

G

Gallagher · 219, 222, 227, 228, 230
Gardner · 82, 97, 177
Garmezy · 89
Garralda and Bailey · 87
Gender · 106, 110, 141, 142, 145, 147, 157, 168
Gender Roles · 142, 145
Gender Stereotyping · 33
Genie · 134, 279
Gert · 174, 177
Gettman · 68, 201
Gilligan · 189
Gilmartin · 219, 222, 232, 271
God · 2, 57, 58, 62, 177, 218, 220, 223, 238, 239, 245, 252
God spot · 239
Goldman · 238
Goldsmith · 90
Goleman · 22, 41, 83, 85, 90, 92, 117, 256, 278
Goodlad · 179
Greenfield · 157, 158
Greenman · 61
Greenspan · 56
Greenspan and Greenspan · 95
Griffith · 236
Grosskurth · 14
Growth Needs · 15, 20
Grusec and Mills · 182, 183
Guilt · 95, 99, 100, 148
Gunnar · 134
Gunter and McAleer · 158
Gura · 111

H

Hammés · 5, 26
Handy · 277
Hannan · 173
Harlow and Harlow · 135
Harrington · 183, 195, 279
Hart, Burts and Charlesworth · 285, 287
Hartley-Brewer · 23, 109, 110, 159, 262
Hartup and Moore · 155
Hawkes · 175
Hayes · 287
Hayes, O'Flaherty and Kernan · 156
Haynes · 8, 196, 197, 242
Hazareesingh, Simms and Anderson · 11
Helwig · 190
Hemming · 219
Hendricks and Wills · 236

Hersh and Paolitto · 194
Heuristic · 35, 46, 80
Hierarchy of Needs · 12, 15, 16, 34, 256, 275, 280
Hoffman · 176, 260
Hoff-Somers · 184
Hohmann and Weikart · 117, 153, 159
Holism · 174
Holistic · 4, 7, 8, 13, 15, 19, 29, 32, 34, 47, 73, 82, 229, 231, 237, 265, 267, 269, 270, 271, 276, 278, 279, 280, 285, 288
Holistic Child Development · 13, 34, 253, 279
Holistic Development · 19, 29, 32, 47, 73, 82, 86, 231, 265, 267, 269, 270, 271, 278, 280, 285, 288
Hooven, Katz and Gottman · 108
Howes and Olenick · 156
Hull · 224
Humanistic · 13, 14, 15, 274
Humphreys · 64, 86, 109, 110
Hyland · 10
Hyson · 96, 117

I

Idealism · 56
Independence · 9, 68, 72, 73, 109, 115, 118, 186, 280
Inoculation · 117, 278
Institutional Racism · 146
Instruction · 8, 11, 12, 25, 26, 45, 53, 189, 190, 223, 266, 267, 285
Instrumentalism · 80
Intelligence · 8, 10, 41, 77, 85, 88, 92, 176, 182
Intelligence Quotient (I.Q.) · 8,11, 92, 97, 179, 216, 221
Internalising Disorders · 87
Ireland · 18, 20, 23, 24, 26, 27, 51, 83, 87, 88, 146, 148, 156, 255, 259
Irish Examiner Newspaper · 149
Isaacs · 35, 39, 80, 81, 82
Isenberg and Jalongo · 136
Italy · 67, 232, 256

J

Jacobson and Frye · 152
James, Nelson, Ralph and Leather · 254
Jessel-Kenyon and Shealy · 235
Jimenez-Beltraum · 7
Jones · 192
Jung · 14, 231
Justice · 8, 178, 186, 188, 197, 198, 207, 208, 209

K

Kagan · 91, 184
Kay · 187, 199
Kealy · 220
Kearney · 241
Keatinge · 255
Kellaghan · 9
Kelmer Pringle · 108
Keniston · 285
Kennedy · 18, 196, 197
Kent · 244
Kilpatrick · 62, 72, 189
Kindergarten · 45, 57, 60, 152, 258
King · 181
Kirby · 5, 18
Kirkland · 241
Kitwood · 25, 175, 179, 182, 189
Klein · 80
Knight · 231
Knitnzer · 90
Kohlberg · 144, 184, 187, 188, 189, 192, 194, 227
Kokoschka · 47
Koplow · 103
Kraemer · 104, 105

L

Lally · 20, 30, 64, 195
Landy · 87, 106, 107, 112, 115, 149, 153
Langer · 97
Lappe and Dubois · 86
Lawrence · 110, 112
Le Doux · 97
Lealman · 231, 234, 260
Lewis · 99, 109, 114, 116, 131
Liebschner · 56, 57, 60, 63, 258
Lillard · 67, 74, 75, 76
Lilley · 58, 61
Lindon · 27, 201, 218, 229, 232, 237, 238
Literacy · 10, 13, 98, 174
Locke · 11, 38, 47, 49, 51, 55, 66, 76, 255
Lodge · 41, 264
Losada · 266, 267
Love · 18, 21, 23, 27, 46, 47, 52, 56, 61, 67, 70, 74, 94, 95, 96, 106, 108, 109, 111, 116, 117, 174, 176, 179, 183, 184, 185, 199, 207, 215, 217, 218, 219, 222, 223, 226, 227, 229, 230, 241, 252, 257, 258, 259, 260, 261, 262, 267, 279
Lubienski Wentworth · 47, 69, 75
Luther · 38, 42, 43, 255, 264
Lytton · 152

M

Maccoby · 145
Maccoby and Martin · 92
Macionis · 134, 157
MacNamara · 177
Magee · 197
Malaguzzi · 283
Malatesta-Magai, Leak, Tesman, Shephard, Culver and Smaggia · 104
Manning, Heron and Marshall · 149
Marenholtz Bulow · 56, 61, 63
Maslow · 12, 13, 14, 15, 16, 17, 19, 20, 21, 27, 34, 64, 219, 228, 231, 253, 255, 256, 257, 261, 264, 265, 269, 272, 273, 274, 275, 280
Materialism · 24, 228, 282
Mature · 18, 19, 85, 105, 109, 141, 229, 230
Maturity · 18, 90, 97, 195, 199
McCreery · 224
McKoen · 83
McLaughlin · 225
McMillan · 63, 254
Media · 145, 157, 175, 202, 223
Meditate · 235, 236
Meditating · 235
Meditation · 230, 235, 236, 238, 243, 244
Mental Health · 23, 32, 83, 85, 87, 155
Mental Health Association · 87
Mental Illness · 88
Miller · 152, 164
Miller and Garver · 152
Mills and Mills · 8
Misattunement · 107, 259
Mischel · 144
Miseducation · 12, 263
Mistakes · 33, 113, 114
Montessori · 35, 39, 45, 46, 49, 59, 61, 62, 63, 66, 67, 68, 69, 70, 71, 72, 73, 74, 75, 237, 256, 258, 261, 262, 265, 270, 274, 278
Montessori Junior · 73
Mooney · 88
Moorish · 76, 81
Moral · 1, 2, 3, 4, 5, 8, 12, 15, 17, 18, 19, 21, 25, 28, 32, 34, 35, 37, 38, 40, 41, 42, 44, 46, 47, 49, 52, 53, 59, 61, 74, 76, 77, 81, 82, 92, 99, 104, 110, 116, 141, 154, 173, 174, 175, 176, 177, 178, 179, 180, 181, 182, 184, 185, 186, 187, 188, 189, 190, 191, 192, 193, 194, 195, 198, 199, 200, 201, 202, 203, 205, 208, 212, 213, 217, 219, 225, 227, 253, 254, 260, 274, 275, 277, 278, 279, 281, 285, 287
Moral Development · 22, 25, 33, 39, 40, 41, 42, 49, 74, 77, 117, 140, 174, 175, 176, 177, 178, 179, 182, 185, 186, 187, 188, 189, 190, 191, 192, 193, 194, 198, 199, 200, 201, 202, 213, 242, 275, 279
Moral Judgement · 187
Moral Knowledge · 176, 180
Moral Realism · 188
Moral Relativism · 180, 188

Morality · 24, 33, 40. 54, 71, 74, 173, 174, 176, 177, 178, 180, 182, 183, 184, 185, 186, 187, 188, 189, 190, 191, 192, 193, 194, 195, 200, 201, 202, 260, 279, 275, 287
Mosley · 196
Moss and Pence · 280
Motivation · 20, 64, 68, 114, 181, 220, 253, 262, 264, 272, 275
Mott-Thornton · 240, 275
Moyles · 117
Murphy · 43, 46, 47, 274
Murray · 146, 147, 148, 149, 150, 259
Murray and Keane · 148, 149, 150
Mussen · 181
Myss and Shealy · 241

N

Nash · 56
National Curriculum Council · 223
National Research Council · 64, 284
Nature versus Nurture · 90
Neglect · 5, 11, 14, 28, 45, 85, 88, 91, 120, 125, 159, 218, 221, 228, 232, 242, 261, 271, 279, 281
Neville · 173, 233, 235, 236, 266
New Zealand · 282
Nutbrown · 11, 116
Nye · 238

O

O'Donnchadha · 92, 114, 133, 267, 269
O'Moore · 150
O'Moore, Kirkham and Smith · 150
Oatley and Jenkins · 87, 88, 90, 102, 107, 259
Obedience · 40, 62, 187, 188, 190, 191
Offend, Boyle and Racine · 87
Orbus Pictus · 44
Osofsky · 106, 109
Owen · 38, 54, 256

P

Painter · 42
Palmer and Neal · 201, 242
Pansophism · 43
Parents · 1, 2, 4, 12, 13, 30, 42, 45, 50, 51, 57, 63, 64, 71, 81, 88, 100, 104, 108, 109, 112, 118, 119, 121, 125, 130, 140, 147, 150, 152, 153, 155, 156, 158, 159, 161, 166, 167, 170, 192, 199, 202, 210, 212, 224, 238, 249, 250, 254, 268, 277, 280
Parker and Asher · 137, 155, 259
Parten · 151
Peak Experiences · 20

Pedagogy · 39, 46, 65, 282
Peers · 55, 86, 93, 147, 149, 151, 152, 153, 156, 202
Perry · 29, 31
Perry and Bussey · 143
Pestalozzi · 38, 44, 45, 50, 51, 52, 53, 54, 58, 59, 66, 76, 78, 80, 237, 256, 261, 265, 270, 271, 274
Peters · 192
Phillips · 157
Physiological Needs · 15, 16, 19, 64, 253, 254, 255
Piaget · 43, 44, 52, 67, 81, 95, 144, 187, 188, 189, 192, 227
Pines · 134, 279
Plato · 34, 38, 39, 40, 41, 49, 66, 76, 82, 264
Play · 38, 39, 40, 42, 45, 48, 52, 54, 55, 59, 60, 61, 63, 64, 72, 75, 79, 81, 82, 92, 94, 107, 118, 120, 121, 125, 128, 134, 136, 137, 142, 143, 145, 151, 153, 155, 156, 157, 158, 160, 161, 162, 163, 164, 165, 166, 167, 170, 195, 198, 203, 204, 205, 207, 208, 233, 238, 242, 246, 248, 258, 259, 261, 262, 269, 270, 275, 281
Plutchik and Kellerman · 95
Potts, Huston and Wright · 157
Prejudice · 146, 148, 223, 259
Prentice · 237
Pretend Play · 152
Problem Solve · 238
Problem Solving · 101, 106, 113, 162, 206, 245
Project E.Y.E. · 159, 201, 242, 244
Project work · 161, 205
Pro-social · 33, 93, 181, 184, 189
Psychopathologies · 87, 89, 103, 117, 278
Psychopathology · 88, 90, 104
Punishment · 25, 47, 115, 139, 175, 187, 189, 191, 197, 255, 256
Purcell · 11, 84

Q

Quality · 9, 32, 61, 117, 135, 139, 152, 154, 155, 156, 176, 177, 180, 199, 215, 229, 234, 268, 287

R

Race · 71, 141, 153, 168, 219, 227, 274
Racism · 24, 33, 146, 148, 259
Radke-Yarrow, Zahn-Waxler and Chapman · 98, 99, 139
Raftery · 9
Ramachandran and Blakeshee · 239
Randle · 215
Ratcliff · 79
Readings · 10
Reflective Practitioner · 28, 31

Reggio Emilia · 68, 232, 283, 284
Reich · 238
Religion · 33, 43, 45, 46, 61, 134, 168, 177, 197, 215, 219, 221, 222, 223, 240, 241, 268, 275, 279
Religions · 221, 242
Religious · 19, 21, 26, 34, 43, 46, 49, 53, 70, 79, 80, 146, 147, 169, 193, 199, 218, 220, 221, 222, 223, 224, 226, 234, 235, 238, 240, 254, 274, 275, 285
Respect · 5, 7, 17, 18, 25, 26, 27, 30, 40, 44, 50, 52, 61, 62, 68, 71, 73, 74, 76, 111, 115, 136, 146, 153, 161, 163, 166, 175, 176, 178, 184, 185, 186, 188, 189, 198, 201, 204, 207, 208, 211, 212, 213, 223, 229, 245, 249, 261, 275
Responsibility · 7, 11, 26, 30, 46, 80, 86, 108, 113, 122, 123, 138, 156, 161, 175, 178, 181, 183, 185, 186, 192, 198, 200, 201, 206, 207, 209, 211, 220, 225, 226, 229, 240, 273
Reward · 33, 108, 187, 188, 190, 191, 238
Rights · 46, 50, 115, 166, 174, 183, 188, 197, 198, 208, 209, 230, 262, 280, 285
Rituals · 160, 217, 218, 249
Rizzuto · 223
Robinson · 239, 240
Roche · 202, 242
Rodger · 228
Rogers · 15
Rogers and Kutnick · 108
Role Models · 227
Rolheiser · 216
Rosenzweig · 14
Rote Learning · 47, 52, 55, 62, 77, 265, 266
Roth · 266
Rousseau · 38, 44, 48, 49, 50, 51, 52, 54, 56, 57, 59, 66, 76, 78, 237, 255, 265, 270, 274
Rubin · 153, 156
Rules · 25, 98, 100, 108, 125, 134, 137, 138, 152, 169, 173, 175, 177, 181, 183, 186, 187, 190, 192, 200, 202, 203, 206, 207, 212, 222, 279
Rusk · 255, 265, 274
Russell · 216
Rutter · 87, 105, 106
Rutter and ERA · 134
Rutter and Rutter · 105
Rutter, Tizard and Yule · 87
Ryan · 178

S

Saarni · 100, 104
Safety · 253, 254, 255, 256, 257, 264, 273
Safety Needs · 16, 257
Sapolsky · 109
Scaffold · 151, 161, 204
Scharf · 193
Schickendanz, Schickendanz, Hansen and Forsyth · 108, 116, 140, 257
Schlosser · 6

Schon · 31
Schweinhart and Weikart · 11, 86, 133
Scott Peck · 226, 228
Sears, Maccoby and Levine · 190
Secularisation · 223
Seefeldt · 281
Self-activity · 58, 59, 60, 73, 79, 261, 271
Self-actualisation · 4, 13, 15, 16, 17, 18, 19, 21, 22, 34, 253, 272, 277, 278, 280, 282, 283
Self-actualisation Needs · 16, 272
Self-awareness · 30, 98, 99, 184, 229
Self-concept · 110, 112
Self-confidence · 2, 3, 9, 73, 112, 115, 286
Self-development · 183, 193, 194, 279
Self-esteem · 2, 3, 11, 13, 15, 23, 24, 73, 88, 106, 108, 109, 110, 111, 112, 114, 117, 120, 130, 148, 150, 152, 155, 217, 261, 262, 286
Self-image · 110, 111
Self-realisation · 68, 79, 262, 266, 275
Self-reliance · 23, 73, 198, 209, 262
Self-reliant · 280
Self-worth · 11, 84, 111, 227, 261, 282
Selwyn · 254
Sense of Mastery · 11, 102
Shame · 7, 95, 99, 100, 148
Shelton · 177, 184, 185, 194
Siegal · 25, 189, 191
Simon, Howe and Kirschenbaum · 194
Singer and Singer · 157
Siraj-Blatchford · 86, 201
Skinner · 13
Slavin · 97
Smith · 40, 41, 42, 52, 53, 54, 57, 77, 80, 141, 152, 258, 264, 283
Smith and Cowie · 106, 110
Social · 1, 2, 3, 4, 8, 11, 12, 15, 17, 18, 19, 21, 22, 23, 26, 28, 32, 34, 35, 37, 38, 40, 41, 43, 45, 46, 47, 51, 52, 53, 54, 58, 61, 62, 64, 65, 71, 72, 76, 77, 78, 79, 81, 82, 86, 88, 91, 92, 93, 95, 98, 99, 100, 104, 105, 107, 110, 111, 114, 116, 120, 121, 133, 134, 135, 136, 137, 138, 139, 140, 141, 143, 144, 145, 146, 148, 149, 151, 152, 153, 154, 155, 156, 157, 158, 159, 160, 161, 162, 163, 165, 174, 176, 180, 181, 183, 184, 185, 186, 187, 189, 191, 199, 200, 209, 211, 217, 218, 221, 225, 228, 253, 258, 259, 260, 262, 271, 274, 275, 277, 278, 279, 280, 281, 285, 287
Social Competence · 2, 133, 134, 152, 153
Social Development · 2, 17, 22, 24, 33, 48, 51, 52, 58, 65, 71, 72, 79, 81, 133, 134, 135, 136, 137, 138, 140, 148, 149, 152, 154, 155, 156, 158, 159, 217, 225, 260, 278, 279
Social Isolation · 134
Social Rules · 98, 138
Social Skills · 33, 137, 149, 153
Social Structure · 133
Socialisation · 104, 108, 136, 137, 138, 139, 140, 142, 143, 144, 145, 155, 157, 178, 189, 191
Society · 7, 18, 19, 22, 25, 35, 39, 48, 49, 50, 52, 54, 55, 57, 60, 65, 70, 71, 73, 76, 77, 78, 80,

86, 89, 102, 108, 115, 133, 135, 136, 137, 138, 142, 145, 146, 148, 158, 165, 173, 174, 175, 176, 178, 179, 180, 182, 185, 186, 189, 193, 197, 198, 200, 212, 216, 223, 228, 232, 233, 237, 258, 259, 261, 262, 269, 271, 276, 277, 278, 279, 280, 281, 282, 284, 285, 287

Spiritual · 1, 2, 3, 4, 8, 12, 15, 17, 18, 19, 21, 27, 28, 32, 34, 35, 37, 38, 42, 46, 51, 53, 56, 58, 60, 61, 67, 69, 70, 76, 79, 82, 92, 93, 116, 141, 215, 216, 217, 219, 220, 221, 222, 223, 224, 225, 226, 227, 228, 229, 230, 231, 232, 234, 236, 237, 238, 239, 240, 241, 242, 250, 253, 268, 272, 274, 275, 277, 278, 279, 281, 284, 285, 287

Spiritual Development · 1, 3, 4, 8, 12, 15, 17, 22, 27, 32, 34, 37, 38, 42, 61, 69, 70, 82, 93, 159, 201, 216, 217, 222, 223, 224, 225, 226, 227, 228, 229, 230, 231, 232, 233, 234, 237, 238, 239, 240, 241, 242, 250, 253, 268, 272, 275, 278, 279

Spiritual Quotient (S.Q.) · 221, 222, 223, 239

Spirituality · 2, 15, 26, 27, 34, 46, 58, 61, 70, 140, 215, 216, 217, 218, 219, 221, 222, 223, 224, 227, 228, 229, 230, 231, 232, 233, 235, 238, 239, 240, 241, 245, 250, 260, 268, 271, 279

Standing · 66, 67, 76, 262

Stapleton, Lehane and Toner · 7

Stayton, Hogan and Ainsworth · 182

Stein · 274

Steiner · 39, 65, 98

Stress · 7, 17, 23, 45, 61, 84, 85, 86, 95, 101, 102, 105, 107, 108, 120, 126, 127, 133, 144, 152, 161, 207, 210, 256, 258, 262, 270, 272, 279, 285

Structured Play · 60

Success · 9, 24, 44, 64, 66, 81, 84, 92, 93, 97, 104, 113, 114, 116, 153, 260, 263

Suicide · 3, 12, 20, 23, 105, 148, 216, 262

Sullivan · 102

T

Tabula Rasa · 11, 38, 48, 55

Tamminen · 238

Tangney, Wagner Barlow, Marschall, Sanftner, Mohr and Gramzow · 99

Taylor · 238

Te Whariki · 282, 284

Television · 157, 160, 167, 175, 211, 254

Temperament · 65, 88, 90, 91, 94, 116, 139

The Edgeworths · 38, 51

The National Association for the Education of Young Children (N.A.E.Y.C.) · 12

The National Children's Strategy · 83

Thompson · 103, 177, 180

Thorndike · 13

Tizard and Hughes · 152

Transcendence · 219, 231, 239

Transpersonal Psychology · 15

Troy and Sroute · 140

U

Ulich · 47

United Nation's Convention on the Rights of the Child · 285

Unity · 11, 20, 47, 56, 58, 67, 186, 207, 215, 256, 258, 265

V

Values Clarification (V.C.) · 193, 194

Vygotsky · 140, 141, 191

W

Walker · 19

Watson · 13, 96

Webster · 272

Well-being · 3, 8, 22, 27, 34, 49, 83, 85, 89, 95, 103, 110, 120, 128, 154, 155, 220, 229, 236, 241, 271, 272, 281, 282, 284

White · 225, 226

Whitebread · 111, 114

Wilderspin · 54

Williams · 143, 171

Wilson, Williams and Sugarman · 201

Wise · 48, 51, 80, 261, 270

Wonder · 219, 224, 229, 231, 233, 238, 245, 249, 279

Wood · 173, 260

World Health Organisation (W.H.O.) · 6, 7, 21

Worrell · 182, 183

Wynne · 179

Z

Zahn-Waxler and Kochanska · 99

Zillman, Bryant and Huston · 182

Zohar and Marshall · 221, 222, 223, 229, 240, 241, 266, 267

Zone of Proximal Development (Z.P.D.) · 141

MELLEN STUDIES IN EDUCATION

1. C. J. Schott, **Improving The Training and Evaluation of Teachers at the Secondary School Level: Educating the Educators in Pursuit of Excellence**
2. Manfred Prokop, **Learning Strategies For Second Language Users: An Analytical Appraisal with Case Studies**
3. Charles P. Nemeth, **A Status Report on Contemporary Criminal Justice Education: A Definition of the Discipline and an Assessment of Its Curricula, Faculty and Program Characteristics**
4. Stephen H. Barnes (ed.), **Points of View on American Higher Education: A Selection of Essays from** *The Chronicle of Higher Education* (Volume 1) **Professors and Scholarship**
5. Stephen H. Barnes (ed.), **Points of View on American Higher Education: A Selection of Essays from** *The Chronicle of Higher Education* (Volume 2) **Institutions and Issues**
6. Stephen H. Barnes (ed.), **Points of View on American Higher Education: A Selection of Essays from** *The Chronicle of Higher Education* (Volume 3) **Students and Standards**
7. Michael V. Belok and Thomas Metos, **The University President in Arizona 1945-1980: An Oral History**
8. Henry R. Weinstock and Charles J. Fazzaro, **Democratic Ideals and the Valuing of Knowledge In American Education: Two Contradictory Tendencies**
9. Arthur R. Crowell, Jr., **A Handbook For the Special Education Administrator: Organization and Procedures for Special Education**
10. J.J. Chambliss, **The Influence of Plato and Aristotle on John Dewey's Philosophy**
11. Alan H. Levy, **Elite Education and the Private School: Excellence and Arrogance at Phillips Exeter Academy**
12. James J. Van Patten (ed.), **Problems and Issues in College Teaching and Higher Education Leadership**
13. Célestin Freinet, **The Wisdom of Matthew: An Essay in Contemporary French Educational Theory**, John Sivell (trans.)
14. Francis R. Phillips, **Bishop Beck and English Education, 1949-1959**
15. Gerhard Falk, **The Life of the Academic Professional in America: An Inventory of Tasks, Tensions & Achievements**
16. Phillip Santa Maria, **The Question of Elementary Education in the Third Russian State Duma, 1907-1912**
17. James J. Van Patten (ed.), **The Socio-Cultural Foundations of Education and the Evolution of Education Policies in the U.S.**
18. Peter P. DeBoer, **Origins of Teacher Education at Calvin Colege, 1900-1930: And Gladly Teach**
19. Célestin Freinet, **Education Through Work: A Model for Child-Centered Learning**, John Sivell (trans.)
20. John Sivell (ed.), **Freinet Pedagogy: Theory and Practice**
21. John Klapper, **Foreign-Language Learning Through Immersion**
22. Maurice Whitehead, **The Academies of the Reverend Bartholomew Booth in Georgian England and Revolutionary America**
23. Margaret D. Tannenbaum, **Concepts and Issues in School Choice**
24. Rose M. Duhon-Sells and Emma T. Pitts, **An Interdisciplinary Approach to Multicultural Teaching and Learning**
25. Robert E. Ward, **An Encyclopedia of Irish Schools, 1500-1800**

26. David A. Brodie, **A Reference Manual for Human Performance Measurement in the Field of Physical Education and Sports Sciences**

27. Xiufeng Liu, **Mathematics and Science Curriculum Change in the People's Republic of China**

28. Judith Evans Longacre, **The History of Wilson College 1868 to 1970**

29. Thomas E. Jordan, **The First Decade of Life, Volume I: Birth to Age Five**

30. Thomas E. Jordan, **The First Decade of Life, Volume II: The Child From Five to Ten Years**

31. Mary I. Fuller and Anthony J. Rosie (eds.), **Teacher Education and School Partnerships**

32. James J. Van Patten (ed.), **Watersheds in Higher Education**

33. K. (Moti) Gokulsing and Cornel DaCosta (eds.), **Usable Knowledges as the Goal of University Education: Innovations in the Academic Enterprise Culture**

34. Georges Duquette (ed.), **Classroom Methods and Strategies for Teaching at the Secondary Level**

35. Linda A. Jackson and Michael Murray, **What Students Really Think of Professors: An Analysis of Classroom Evaluation Forms at an American University**

36. Donald H. Parkerson and Jo Ann Parkerson, **The Emergence of the Common School in the U.S. Countryside**

37. Neil R. Fenske, **A History of American Public High Schools, 1890-1990: Through the Eyes of Principals**

38. Gwendolyn M. Duhon Boudreaux (ed.), **An Interdisciplinary Approach to Issues and Practices in Teacher Education**

39. John Roach, **A Regional Study of Yorkshire Schools 1500-1820**

40. V.J. Thacker, **Using Co-operative Inquiry to Raise Awareness of the Leadership and Organizational Culture in an English Primary School**

41. Elizabeth Monk-Turner, **Community College Education and Its Impact on Socioeconomic Status Attainment**

42. George A. Churukian and Corey R. Lock (eds.), **International Narratives on Becoming a Teacher Educator: Pathways to a Profession**

43. Cecilia G. Manrique and Gabriel G. Manrique, **The Multicultural or Immigrant Faculty in American Society**

44. James J. Van Patten (ed.), **Challenges and Opportunities for Education in the 21st Century**

45. Barry W. Birnbaum, **Connecting Special Education and Technology for the 21st Century**

46. J. David Knottnerus and Frédérique Van de Poel-Knottnerus, **The Social Worlds of Male and Female Children in the Nineteenth Century French Educational System: Youth, Rituals, and Elites**

47. Sandra Frey Stegman, **Student Teaching in the Choral Classroom: An Investigation of Secondary Choral Music Student Teachers' Perceptions of Instructional Successes and Problems as They Reflect on Their Music Teaching**

48. Gwendolyn M. Duhon and Tony Manson (eds.), **Preparation, Collaboration, and Emphasis on the Family in School Counseling for the New Millennium**

49. Katherina Danko-McGhee, **The Aesthetic Preferences of Young Children**

50. Jane Davis-Seaver, **Critical Thinking in Young Children**

51. Gwendolyn M. Duhon and Tony J. Manson (eds.), **Implications for Teacher Education – Cross-Ethnic and Cross-Racial Dynamics of Instruction**

52. Samuel Mitchell, **Partnerships in Creative Activities Among Schools, Artists and Professional Organizations Promoting Arts Education**

53. Loretta Niebur, **Incorporating Assessment and the National Standards for Music Education into Everyday Teaching**
54. Tony Del Valle, **Written Literacy Features of Three Puerto Rican Family Networks in Chicago: An Ethnographic Study**
55. Christine J. Villani and Colin C. Ward, **Violence and Non-Violence in the Schools: A Manual for Administration**
56. Michael Dallaire, **Contemplation in Liberation – A Method for Spiritual Education in the Schools**
57. Gwendolyn M. Duhon, **Problems and Solutions in Urban Schools**
58. Paul Grosch, **Recognition of the Spirit and Its Development as Legitimate Concerns of Education**
59. D. Antonio Cantu, **An Investigation of the Relationship Between Social Studies Teachers' Beliefs and Practice**
60. Loretta Walton Jaggers, Nanthalia W. McJamerson and Gwendolyn M. Duhon (eds.), **Developing Literacy Skills Across the Curriculum: Practical, Approaches, Creative Models, Strategies, and Resources**
61. Haim Gordon and Rivca Gordon, **Sartre's Philosophy and the Challenge of Education**
62. Robert D. Buchanan and Ruth Ann Roberts, **Performance-Based Evaluation for Certificated and Non-Certificated School Personnel: Standards, Criteria, Indicators, Models**
63. C. David Warner III, **Opinions of Administrators, Faculty, and Students Regarding Academic Freedom and Student Artistic Expression**
64. Robert D. Heslep, **A Philosophical Guide for Decision Making by Educators: Developing a Set of Foundational Principles**
65. Noel P. Hurley, **How You Speak Determines How You Learn: Resource Allocation and Student Achievement**
66. Barry W. Birnbaum, **Foundations and Practices in the Use of Distance Education**
67. Franklin H. Silverman and Robert Moulton, **The Impact of a Unique Cooperative American University USAID Funded Speech-Language Pathologist, Audiologist, and Deaf Educator B.S. Degree Program in the Gaza Strip**
68. Tony J. Manson (ed.), **Teacher Education Preparation for Diversity**
69. Scott D. Robinson, **Autobiostories Promoting Emotional Insights into the Teaching and Learning of Secondary Science**
70. Francis Oakley, **The Leadership Challenge of a College Presidency: Meaning, Occasion, and Voice**
71. Melvin D. Williams, **The Ethnography of an Anthropology Department, 1959-1979: An Academic Village**
72. Kevin McGuinness, **The Concept of Academic Freedom**
73. Alastair Sharp, **Reading Comprehension and Text Organization**
74. Nicholas Beattie, **The Freinet Movements of France, Italy, and Germany, 1920-2000: Versions of Educational Progressivism**
75. Anne P. Chapman, **Language Practices in School Mathematics: A Social Semiotic Approach**
76. Wendy Robinson, **Pupil Teachers and Their Professional Training in Pupil-Teacher Centres in England and Wales, 1870-1914**
77. Barbara A. Sposet, **The Affective and Cognitive Development of Culture Learning During the Early and Middle Childhood Curriculum**
78. John P. Anchan and Shiva S. Halli, **Exploring the Role of the Internet in Global Education**
79. James J. Van Patten and Timothy J. Bergen, **A Case Study Approach to a Multi-Cultural Mosaic in Education**

80. Jeffrey L. Hoogeveen, **The Role of Students in the History of Composition**
81. Rose M. Duhon-Sells and Leslie Agard-Jones (eds.), **Educators Leading the Challenge to Alleviate School Violence**
82. Rose Marie Duhon-Sells, Halloway C. Sells, Alice Duhon-Ross, Gwendolyn Duhon, Glendolyn Duhon-JeanLouis (eds.) **International Perspectives on Methods of Improving Education Focusing on the Quality of Diversity**
83. Ruth Rees, **A New Era in Educational Leadership–One Principal, Two Schools: Twinning**
84. Daniel J. Mahoney, **An Organizational, Social-Psychological, and Ethical Analysis of School Administrators' Use of Deception**
85. Judith Longacre, **The Trial and Renewal of Wilson College**
86. Michael Delucchi, **Student Satisfaction with Higher Education During the 1970s—A Decade of Social Change**
87. Samuel Mitchell, **The Value of Educational Partnerships Worldwide with the Arts, Science, Business, and Community Organizations**
88. Susan Davis Lenski and Wendy L. Black (eds.), **Transforming Teacher Education Through Partnerships**
89. Ana Maria Klein, **Learning How Children Process Mathematical Problems**
90. Laura Shea Doolan, **The History of the International Learning Styles Network and Its Impact on Educational Innovation**
91. Gail Singleton Taylor (ed.), **The Impact of High-Stakes Testing on the Academic Futures of Non-Mainstream Students**
92. G.R. Evans, **Inside the University of Cambridge in the Modern World**
93. Agnes D. Walkinshaw, **Integrating Drama with Primary and Junior Education: The Ongoing Debate**
94. Joe Marshall Hardin and Ray Wallace (eds.), **Teaching, Research, and Service in the Twenty-First Century English Department: A Delicate Balance**
95. Samuel Mitchell, Patricia Klinck, and John Burger (eds.), **Worldwide Partnerships for Schools with Voluntary Organizations, Foundations, Universities, Companies, and Community Councils**
96. Emerson D. Case, **Making the Transition from an Intensive English Program to Mainstream University Courses–An Ethnographic Study**
97. Roberta A. McKay and Susan E. Gibson, **Social Studies for the 21st Century–A Review of Current Literature and Research**
98. Edith Sue Kohner Burford, **Investigating the Reasons University Students in the South Central United States Have to Retake First-Year English Composition**
99. Christina Isabelli-García, **A Case Study of the Factors in the Development of Spanish Linguistic Accuracy and Oral Communication Skills: Motivation and Extended Interaction in the Study Abroad Context**
100. Rose Duhon-Sells (ed.), **Best Practices for Teaching Students in Urban Schools**
101. Wendy P. Hope, **The Impact of Teachers' Perceptions and Pedagogical Practices on the Educational Experiences of Immigrant Students from the Commonwealth Caribbean**
102. Mary Catherine Daly, **Developing the Whole Child–The Importance of the Emotional, Social, Moral, and Spiritual in Early Years Education and Care**